CROQUIS P

WRITER KWANGHYUN SEO
ARTIST JINHO KO

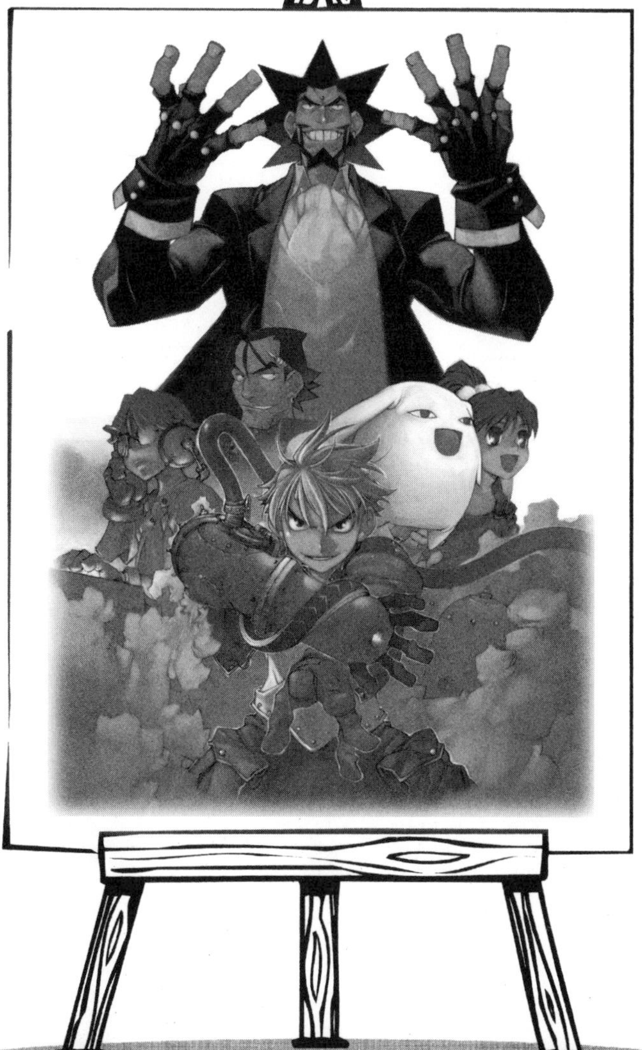

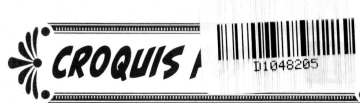

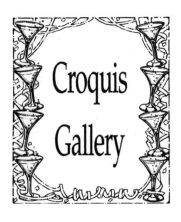

Croquis Gallery

A WORD FROM THE CREATORS

OUT OF ALL THE COMIC
BOOKS I'VE WRITTEN,
CROQUIS POP IS THE
MOST FUN TO WORK ON.
I HOPE THE READERS
LOVE IT AS MUCH AS
I DO!

--KWANGHYUN SEO

HELLO! WOW. IT'S BEEN A WHILE SINCE I'VE SOLD...I MEAN, PUBLISHED A BOOK. ^^;;

POP CULTURE IS IN CONSTANT FLUX, AND RIGHT NOW IS NOT THE BEST OF TIMES FOR THE COMIC BOOK INDUSTRY, LET ALONE COMIC BOOK ARTISTS! BUT WE CAN'T GIVE UP! COMIC ARTISTS HAVEN'T HAD A CHANCE TO SHINE YET! IF EVEN A FEW FANS SHOW THE LEAST BIT OF INTEREST, IT REALLY INSPIRES AN ARTIST TO DO HIS BEST WORK. I HOPE FANS OF *CROQUIS POP* LOVE AND ADORE THIS COMIC!

HMM... *CROQUIS POP* IS A FANTASY STORY SET AROUND THE COMIC BOOK SCENE IN KOREA. GIVE IT A CHANCE, EVEN IF IT ISN'T YOUR STYLE! EVEN IF IT LOOKS BORING! OH, I'M NOT BEGGING YOU...NEVER! JUST DON'T THROW THE BOOK AWAY...PLEASE!

--JINHO KO

ART GALLERY

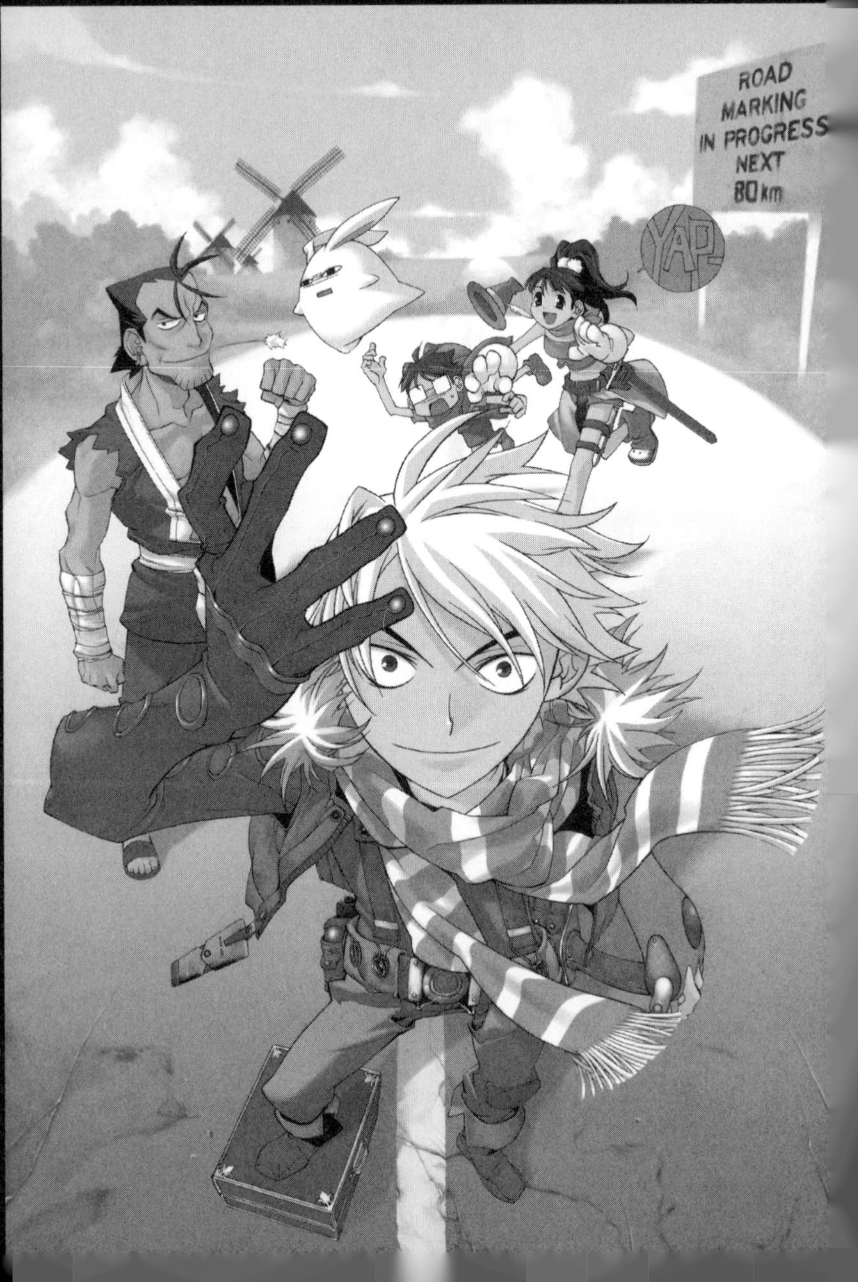
ROAD
MARKING
IN PROGRESS
NEXT
80 km
YAP!

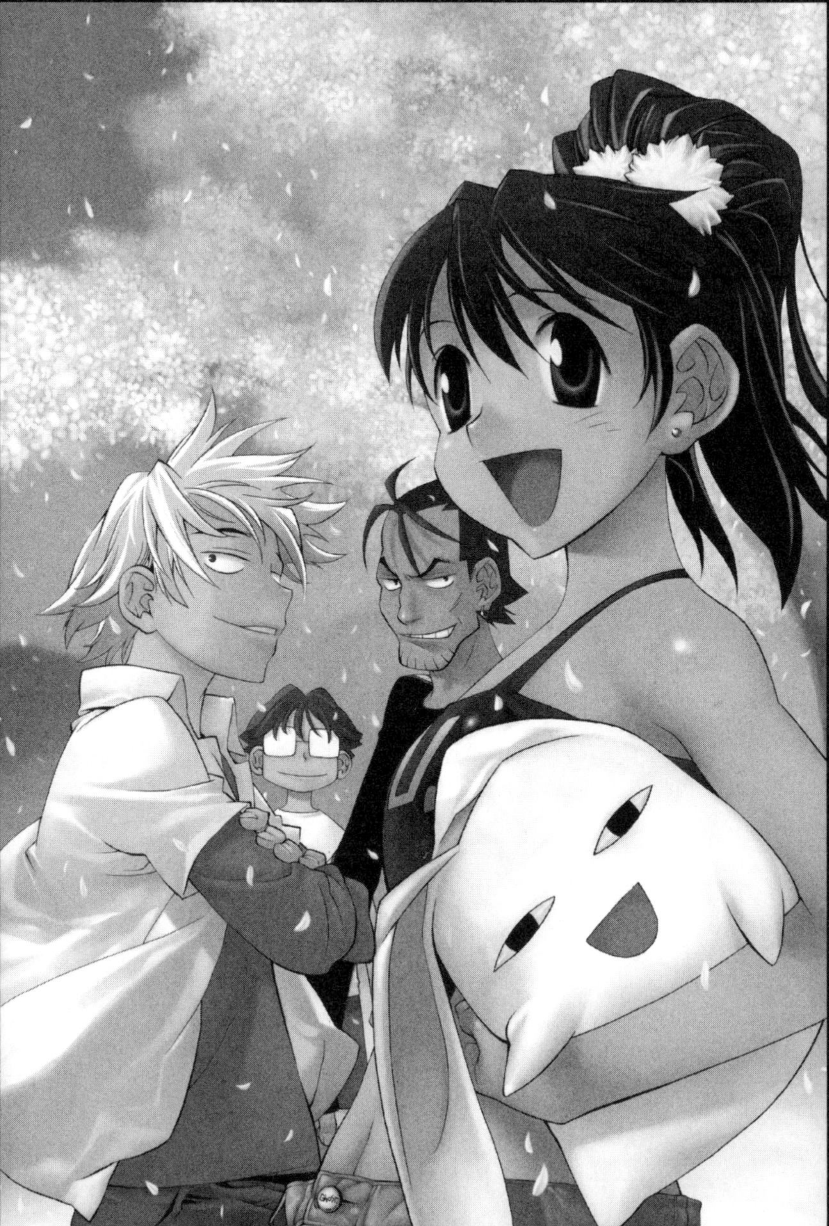

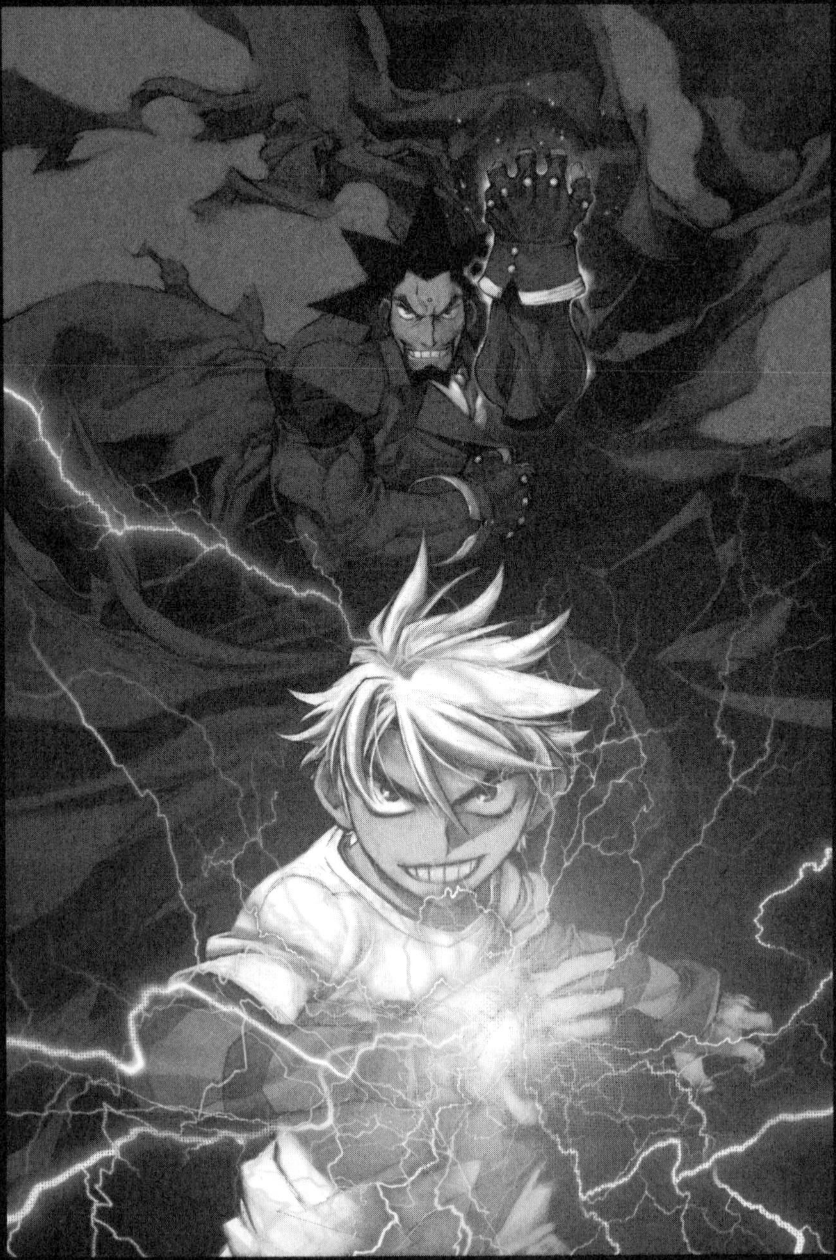

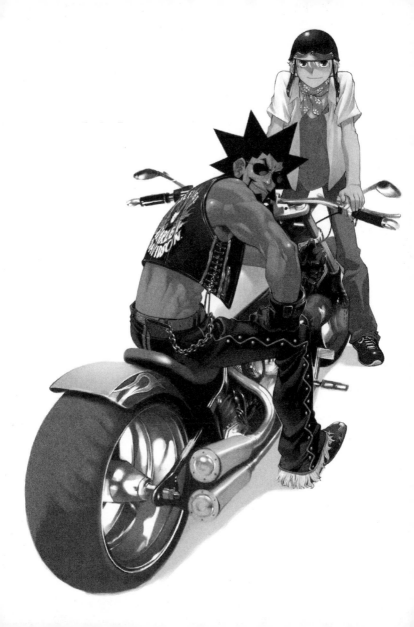

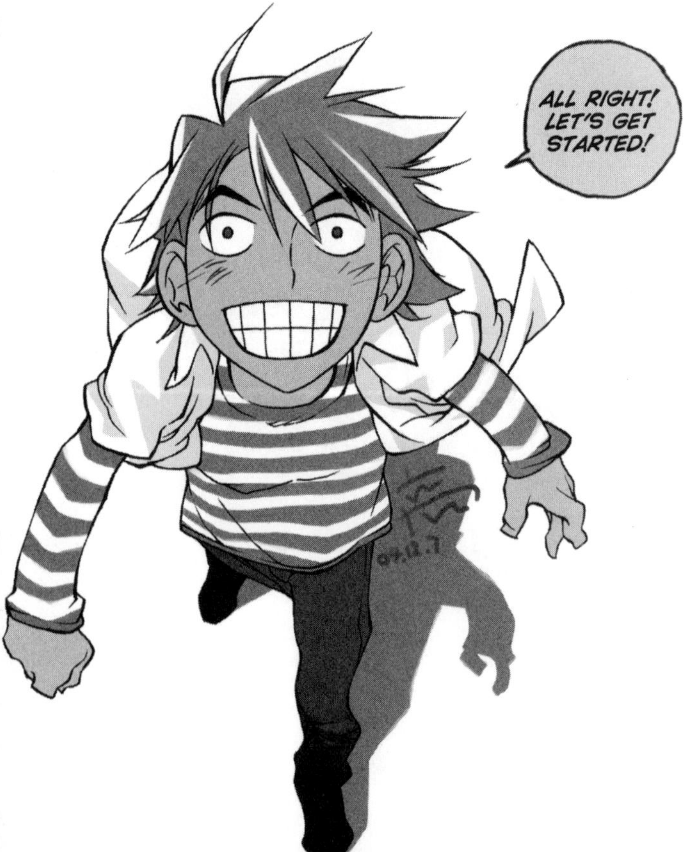
ALL RIGHT! LET'S GET STARTED!
04.12.7

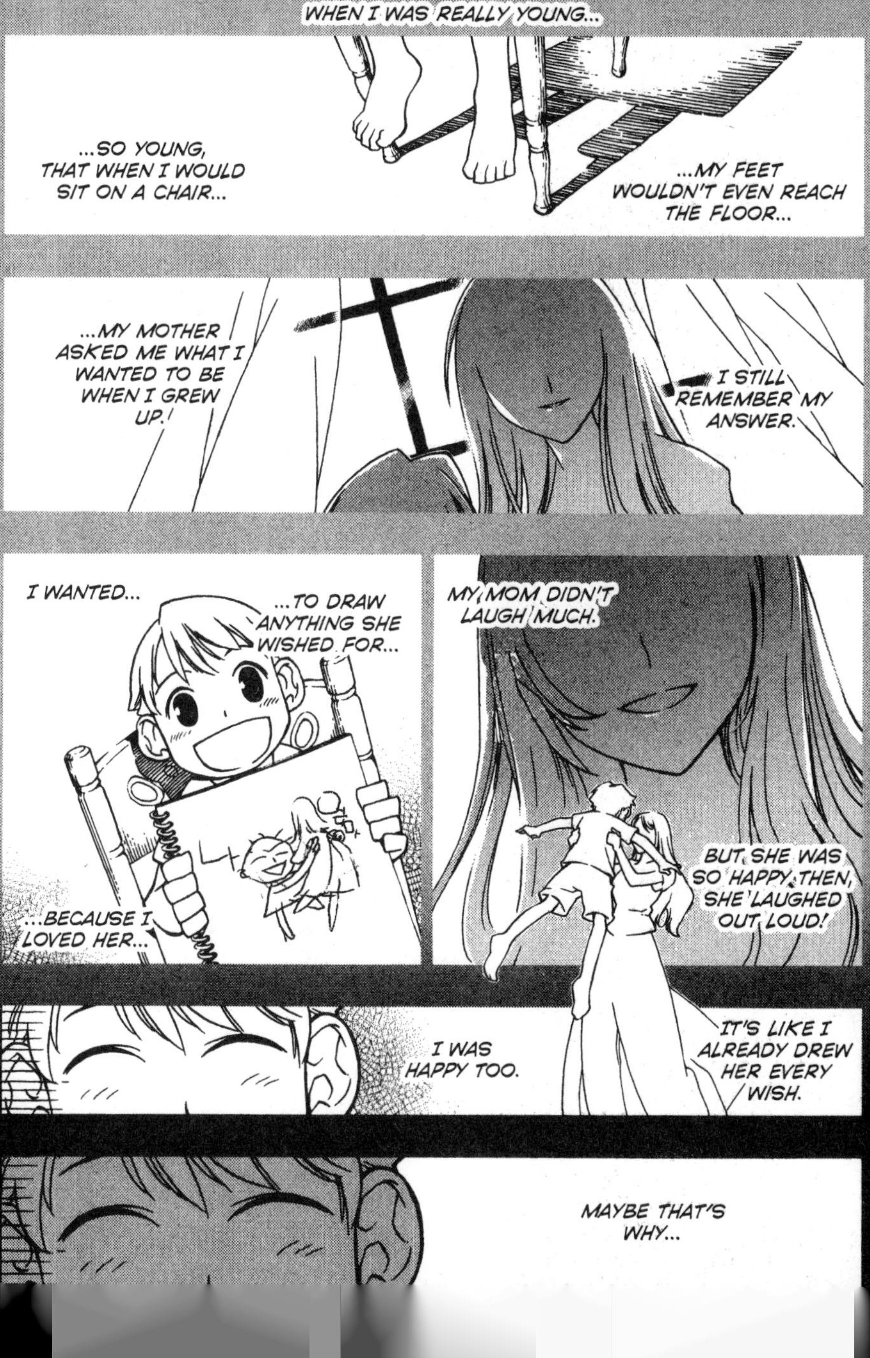
WHEN I WAS REALLY YOUNG...
...SO YOUNG, THAT WHEN I WOULD SIT ON A CHAIR...
...MY FEET WOULDN'T EVEN REACH THE FLOOR...
...MY MOTHER ASKED ME WHAT I WANTED TO BE WHEN I GREW UP.
I STILL REMEMBER MY ANSWER.
I WANTED...
...TO DRAW ANYTHING SHE WISHED FOR...
...BECAUSE I LOVED HER...
MY MOM DIDN'T LAUGH MUCH.
BUT SHE WAS SO HAPPY THEN, SHE LAUGHED OUT LOUD!
IT'S LIKE I ALREADY DREW HER EVERY WISH.
I WAS HAPPY TOO.
MAYBE THAT'S WHY...

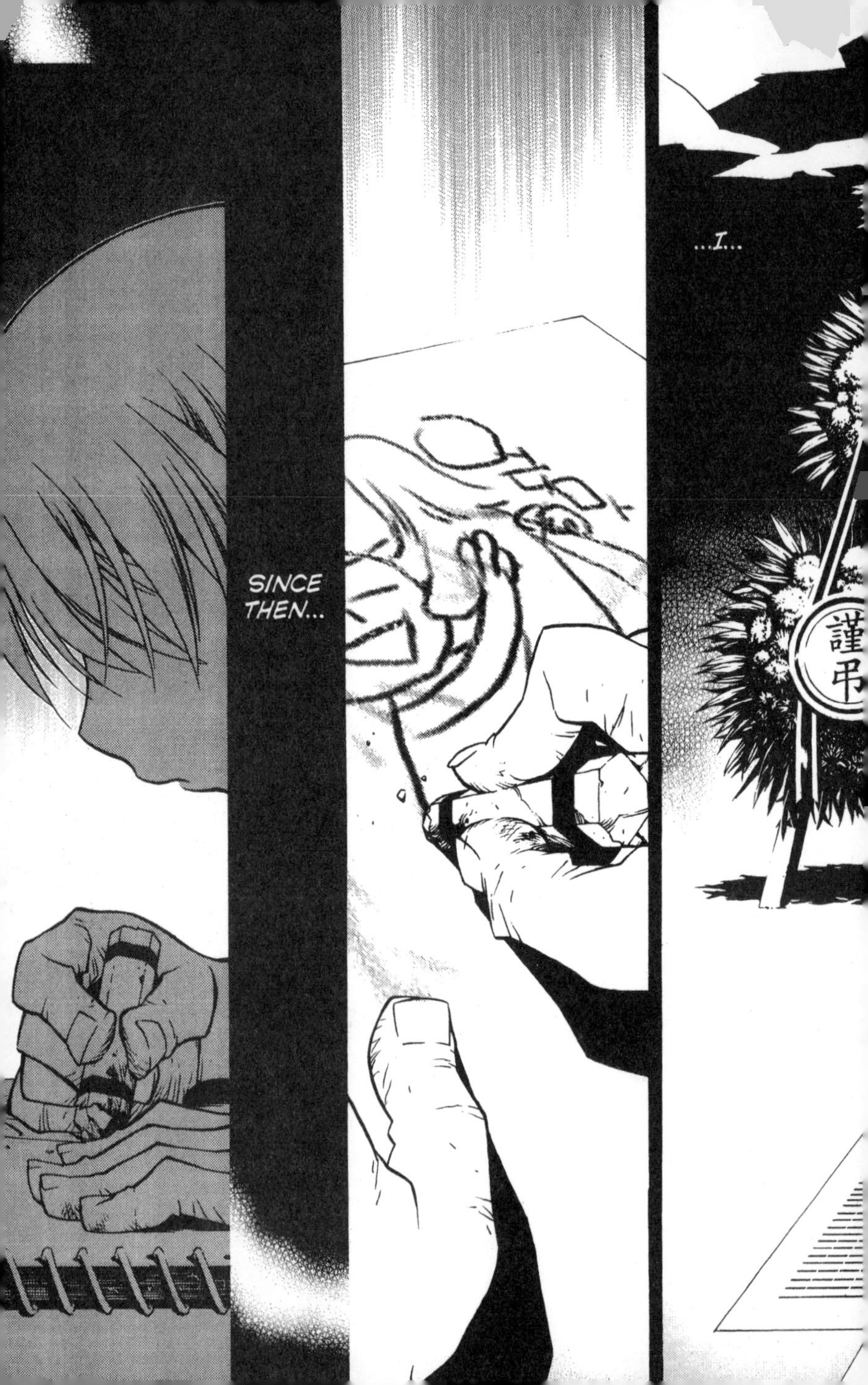
...I...
謹弔
SINCE THEN...

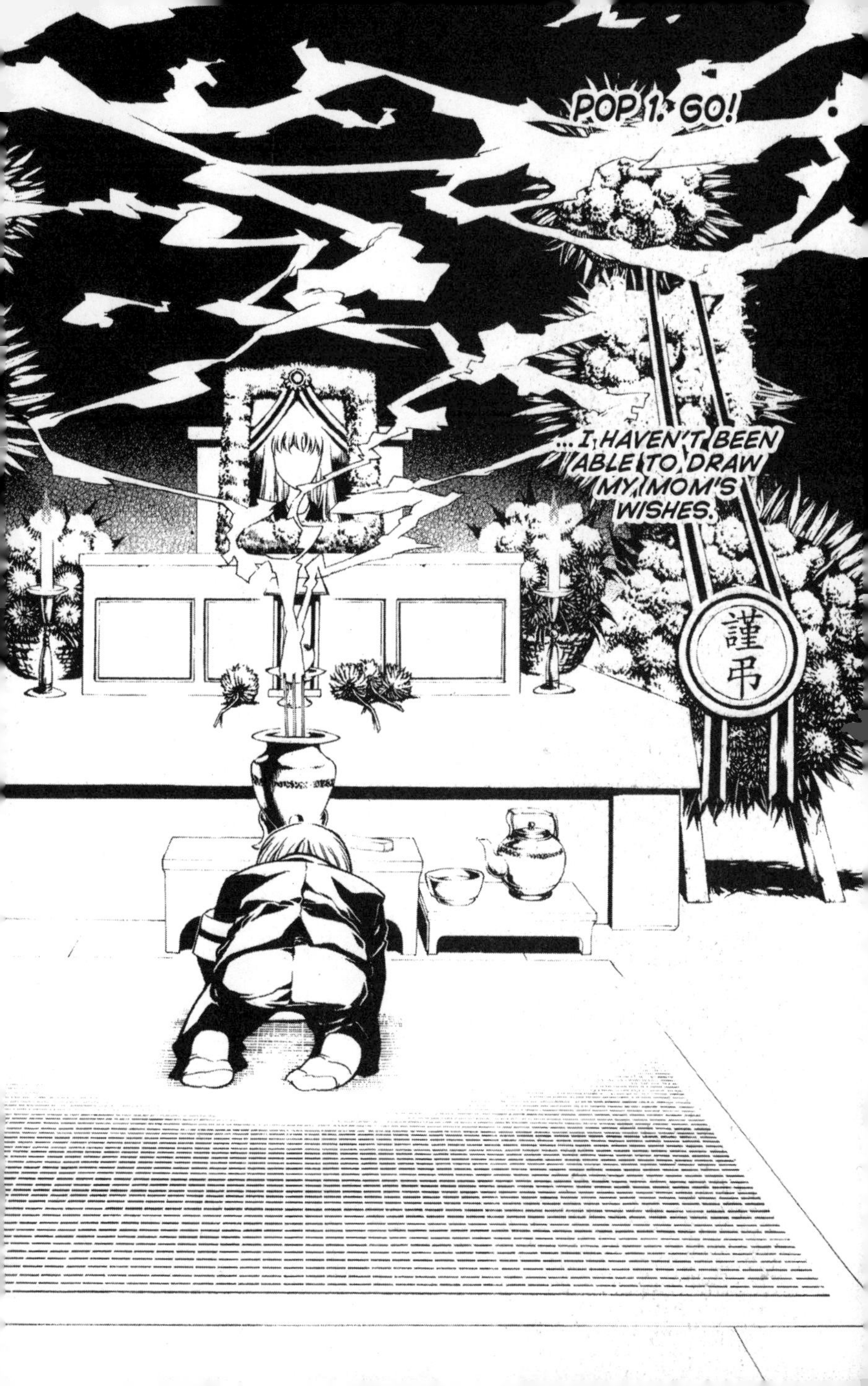
POP 1: GO!
...I HAVEN'T BEEN ABLE TO DRAW MY MOM'S WISHES.
謹弔

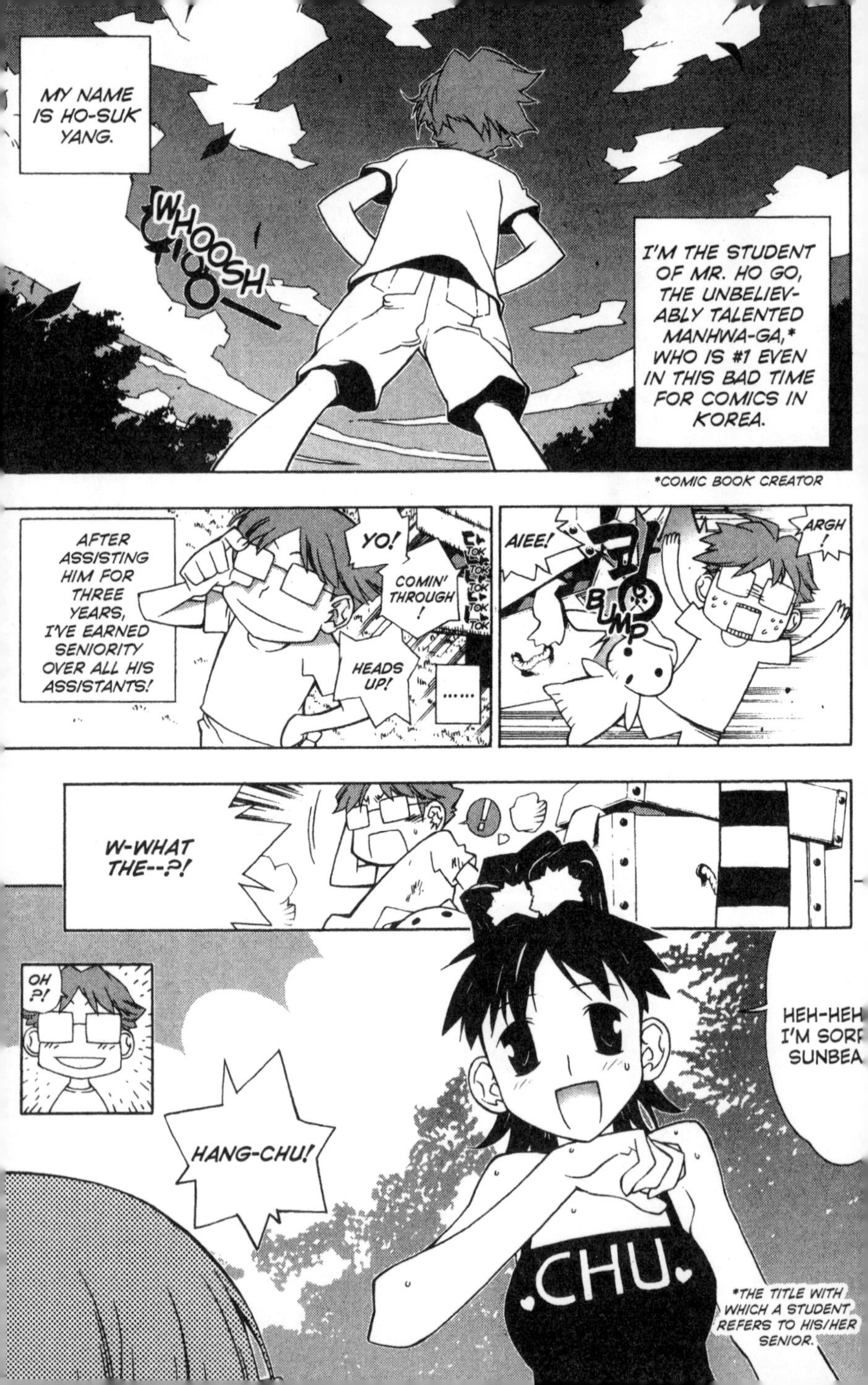
MY NAME IS HO-SUK YANG.
WHOOSH
I'M THE STUDENT OF MR. HO GO, THE UNBELIEVABLY TALENTED MANHWA-GA,* WHO IS #1 EVEN IN THIS BAD TIME FOR COMICS IN KOREA.
*COMIC BOOK CREATOR
AFTER ASSISTING HIM FOR THREE YEARS, I'VE EARNED SENIORITY OVER ALL HIS ASSISTANTS!
YO!
COMIN' THROUGH!
TOK TOK TOK TOK TOK
HEADS UP!
......
AIEE!
ARGH!
BUMP
W-WHAT THE--?!
!
OH ?!
HANG-CHU!
HEH-HEH I'M SORR SUNBEA
.CHU.
*THE TITLE WITH WHICH A STUDENT REFERS TO HIS/HER SENIOR.

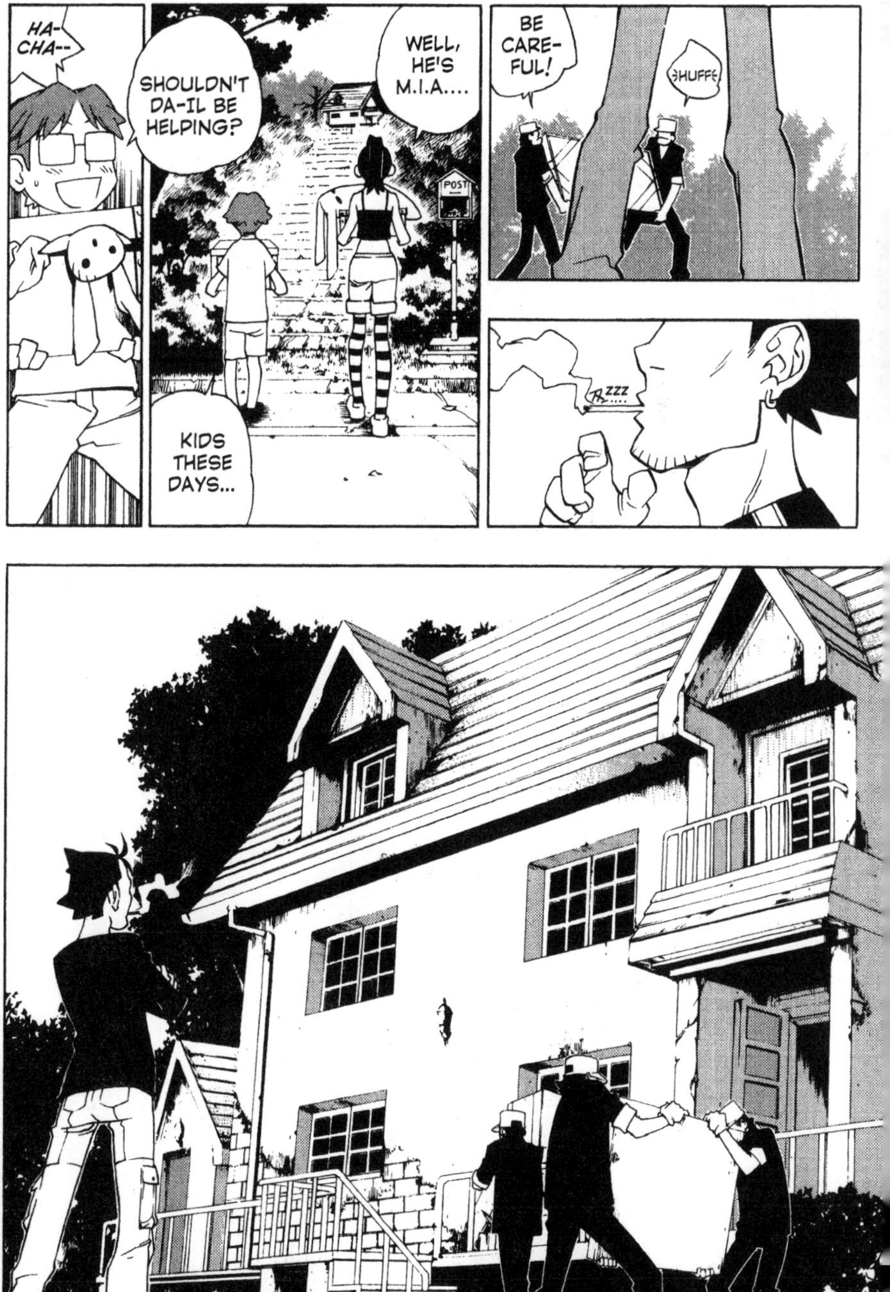
HA-CHA--
SHOULDN'T DA-IL BE HELPING?
WELL, HE'S M.I.A....
KIDS THESE DAYS...
POST
BE CARE-FUL!
HUFF
ZZZ

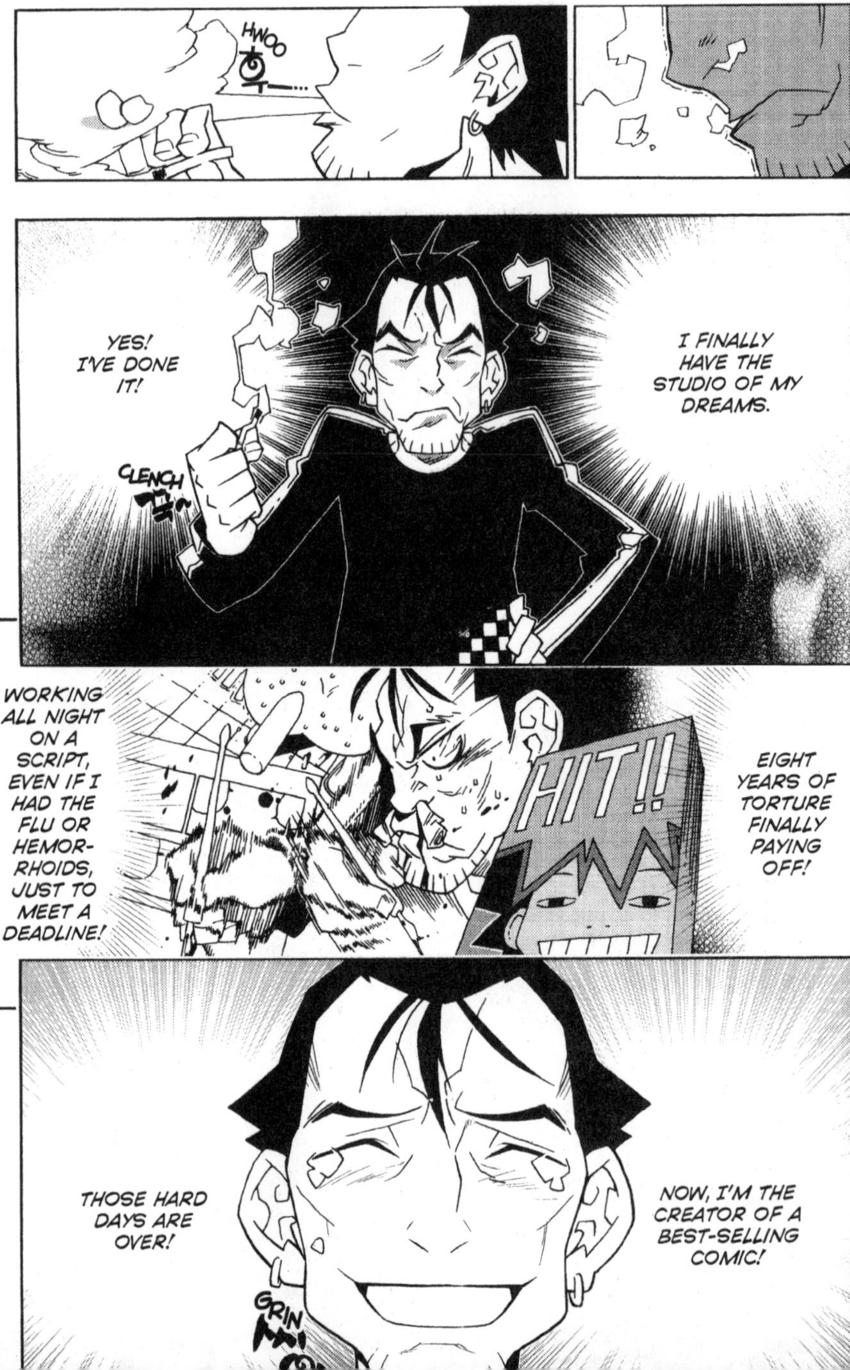

HWOO
YES! I'VE DONE IT!
I FINALLY HAVE THE STUDIO OF MY DREAMS.
CLENCH
WORKING ALL NIGHT ON A SCRIPT, EVEN IF I HAD THE FLU OR HEMOR-RHOIDS, JUST TO MEET A DEADLINE!
HIT!!
EIGHT YEARS OF TORTURE FINALLY PAYING OFF!
THOSE HARD DAYS ARE OVER!
NOW, I'M THE CREATOR OF A BEST-SELLING COMIC!
GRIN

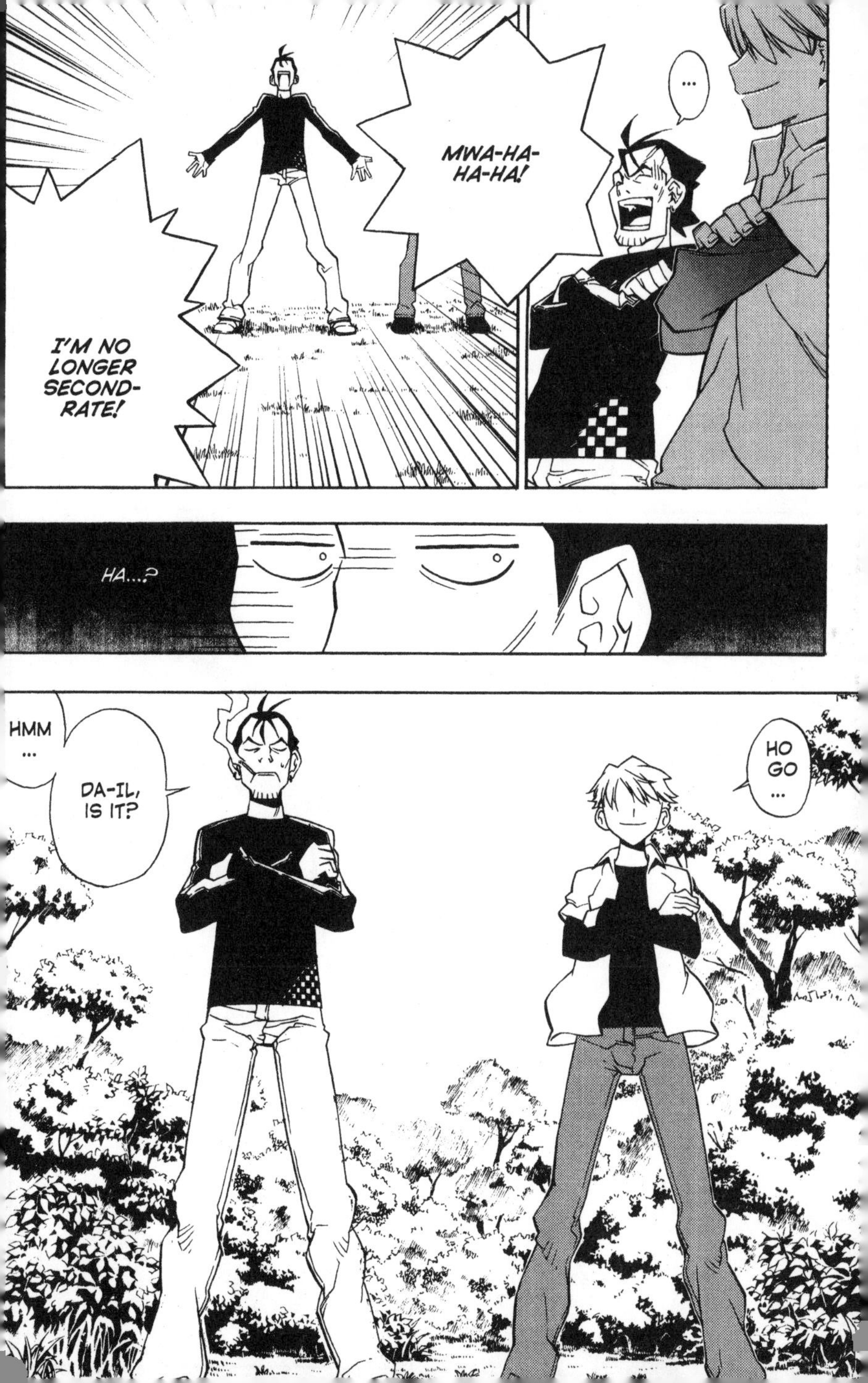
...
MWA-HA-HA-HA!
I'M NO LONGER SECOND-RATE!
HA...?
HO GO ...
HMM ...
DA-IL, IS IT?

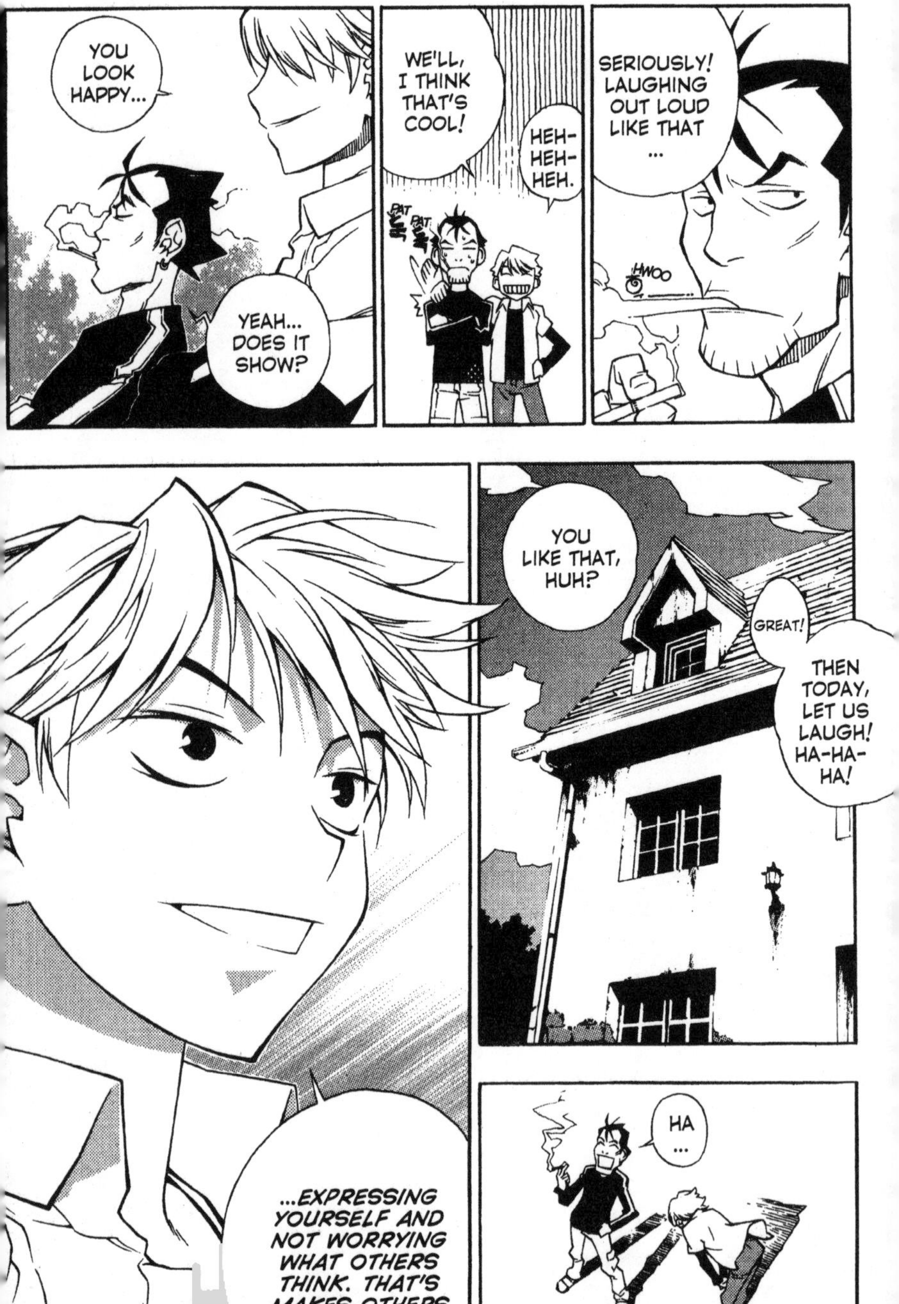
YOU LOOK HAPPY...
YEAH... DOES IT SHOW?
WE'LL, I THINK THAT'S COOL!
HEH-HEH-HEH.
PAT PAT
SERIOUSLY! LAUGHING OUT LOUD LIKE THAT ...
HWOO
...EXPRESSING YOURSELF AND NOT WORRYING WHAT OTHERS THINK. THAT'S MAKES OTHERS LAUGH AS WELL.
YOU LIKE THAT, HUH?
GREAT!
THEN TODAY, LET US LAUGH! HA-HA-HA!
HA ...

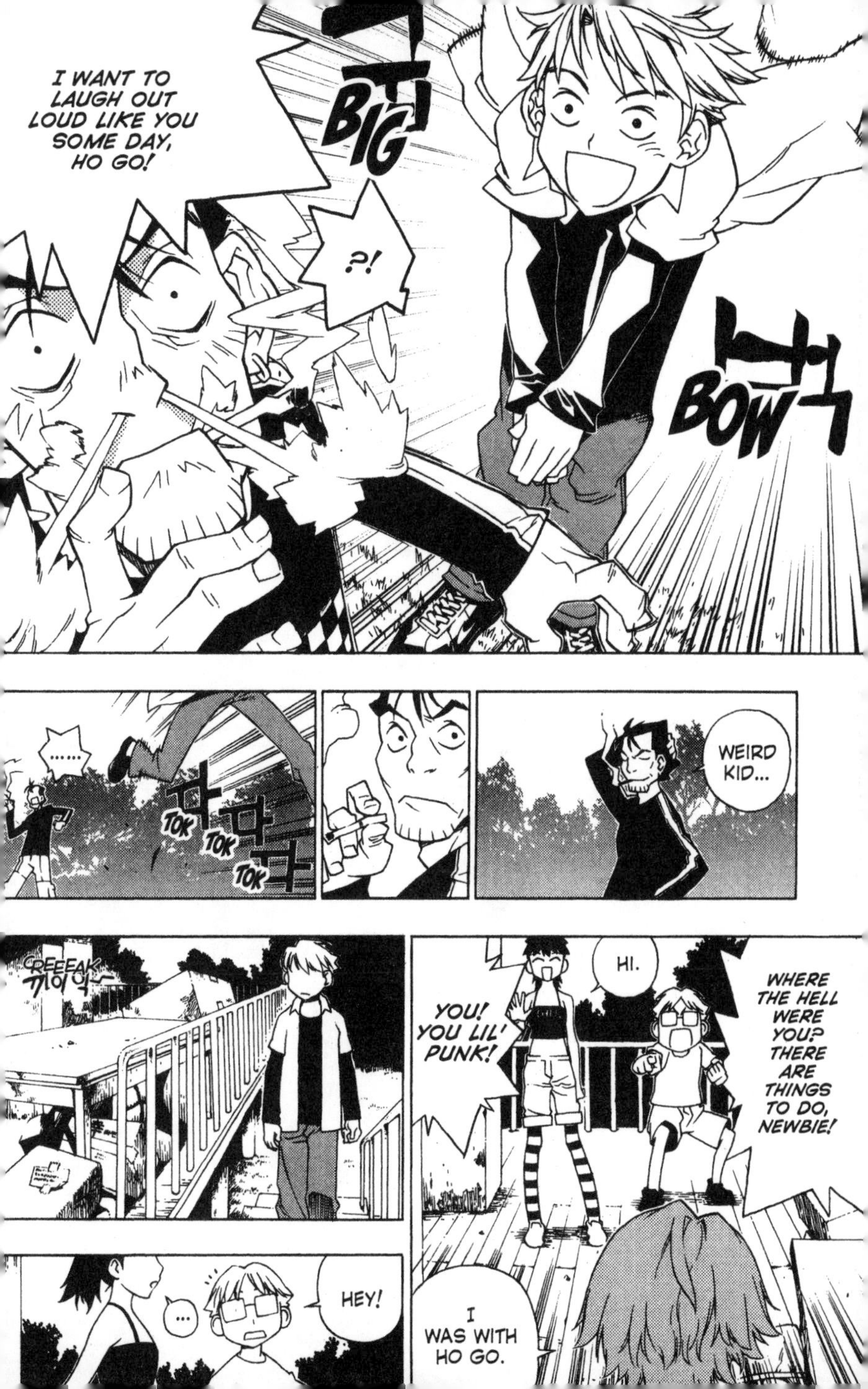
I WANT TO LAUGH OUT LOUD LIKE YOU SOME DAY, HO GO!
BIG
?!
BOW
......
TOK
TOK
TOK
WEIRD KID...
CREEEAK
끼이익
YOU! YOU LIL' PUNK!
HI.
WHERE THE HELL WERE YOU? THERE ARE THINGS TO DO, NEWBIE!
...
HEY!
I WAS WITH HO GO.

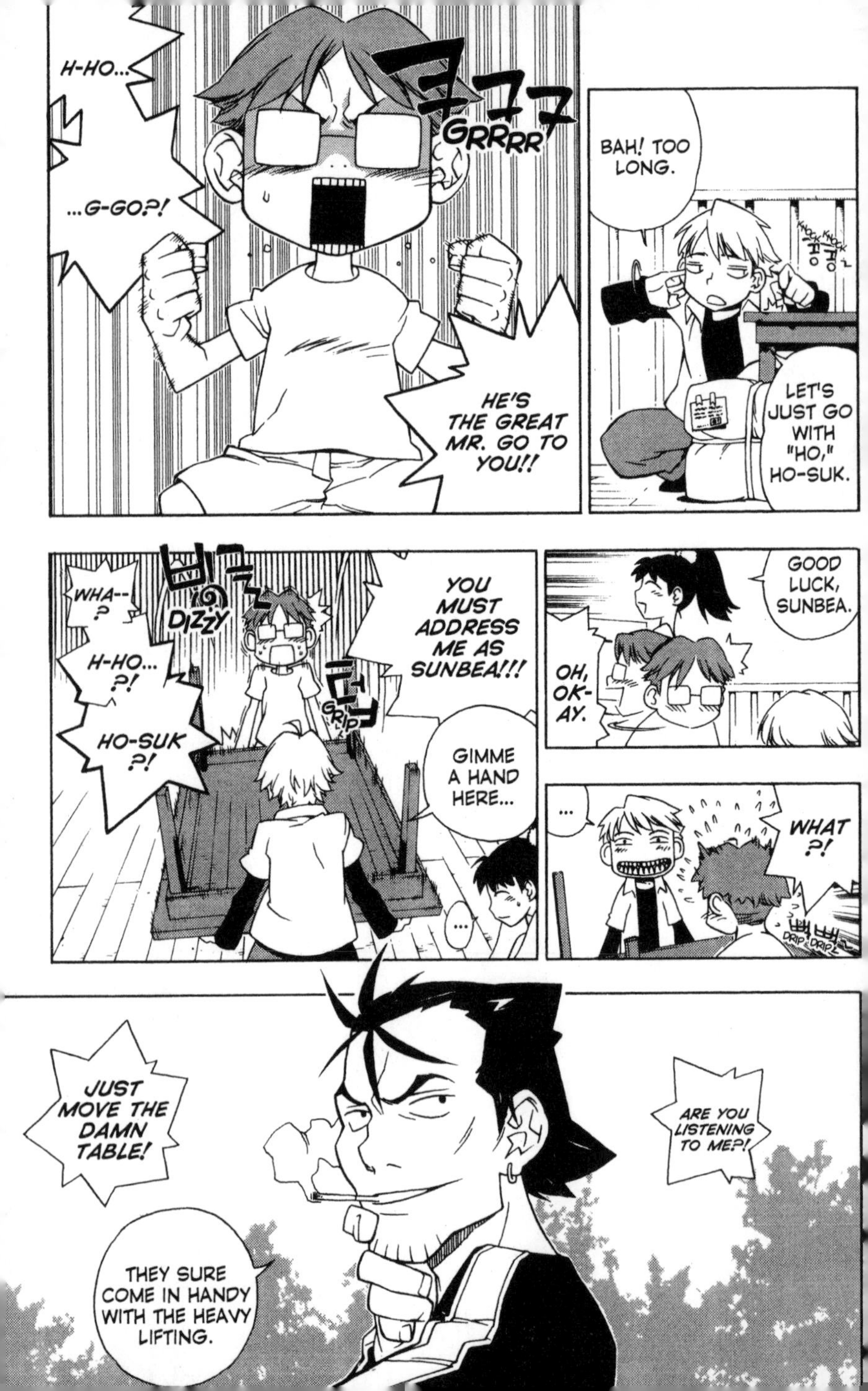
H-HO...
...G-GO?!
GRRRR
HE'S THE GREAT MR. GO TO YOU!!
BAH! TOO LONG.
KNOCK KNOCK
LET'S JUST GO WITH "HO," HO-SUK.
WHA--?
H-HO...?!
HO-SUK?!
DIZZY
YOU MUST ADDRESS ME AS SUNBEA!!!
GRIP
GIMME A HAND HERE...
...
GOOD LUCK, SUNBEA.
OH, OK-AY.
...
WHAT?!
DRIP DRIP
JUST MOVE THE DAMN TABLE!
ARE YOU LISTENING TO ME?!
THEY SURE COME IN HANDY WITH THE HEAVY LIFTING.

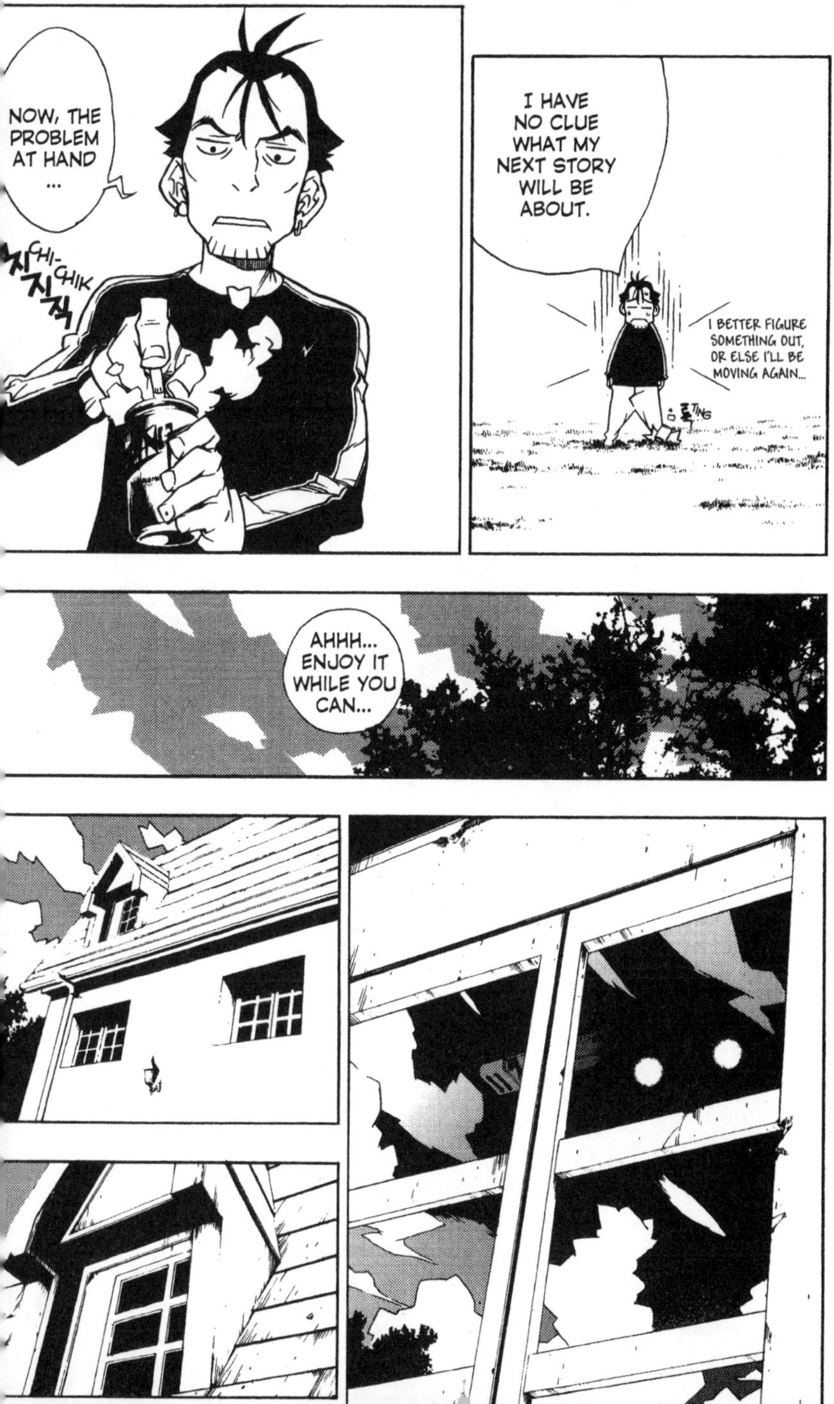
NOW, THE PROBLEM AT HAND ...
CHI-CHIK
I HAVE NO CLUE WHAT MY NEXT STORY WILL BE ABOUT.
I BETTER FIGURE SOMETHING OUT, OR ELSE I'LL BE MOVING AGAIN...
TING
AHHH... ENJOY IT WHILE YOU CAN...

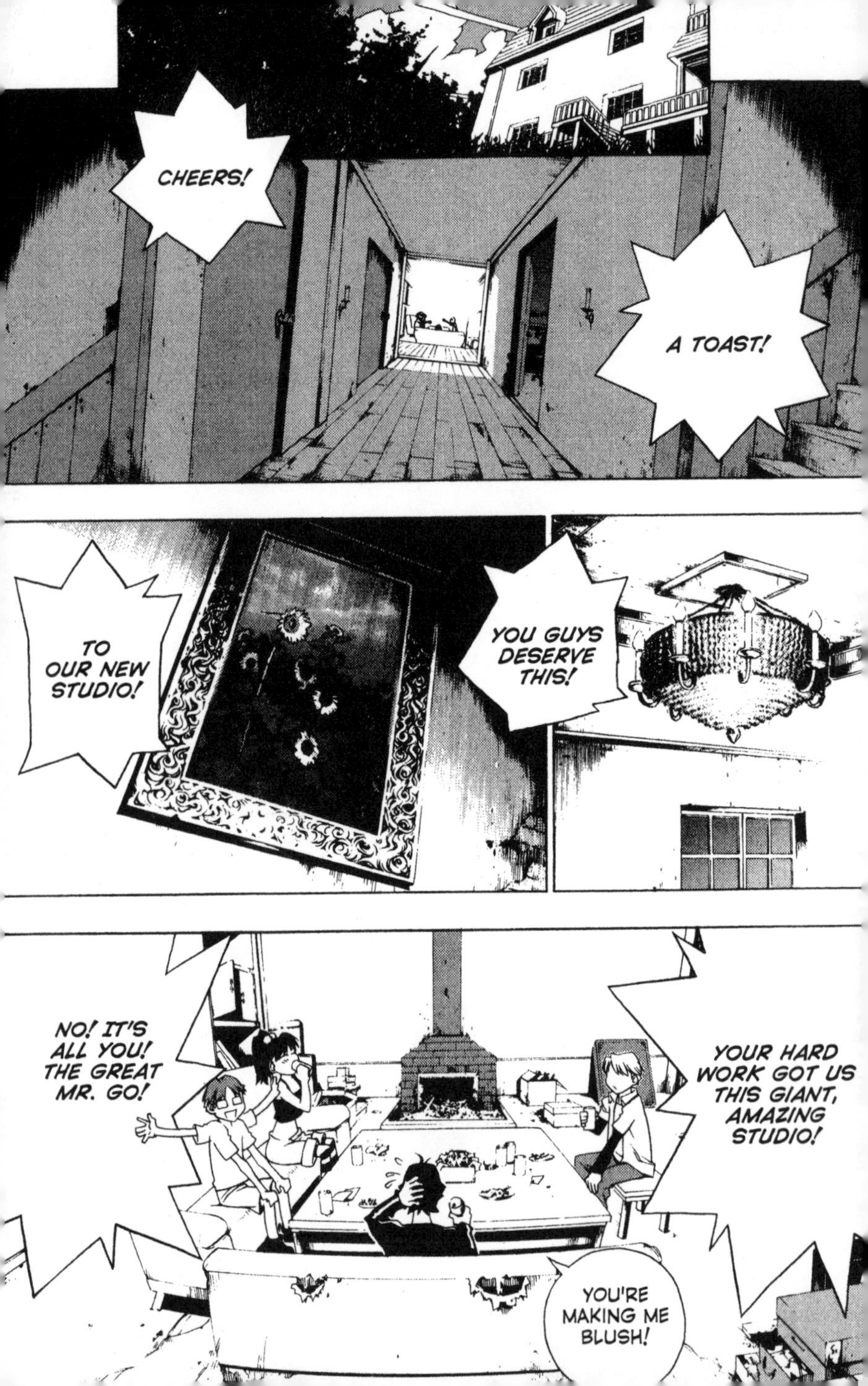
A TOAST!
CHEERS!
YOU GUYS DESERVE THIS!
TO OUR NEW STUDIO!
YOUR HARD WORK GOT US THIS GIANT, AMAZING STUDIO!
NO! IT'S ALL YOU! THE GREAT MR. GO!
YOU'RE MAKING ME BLUSH!

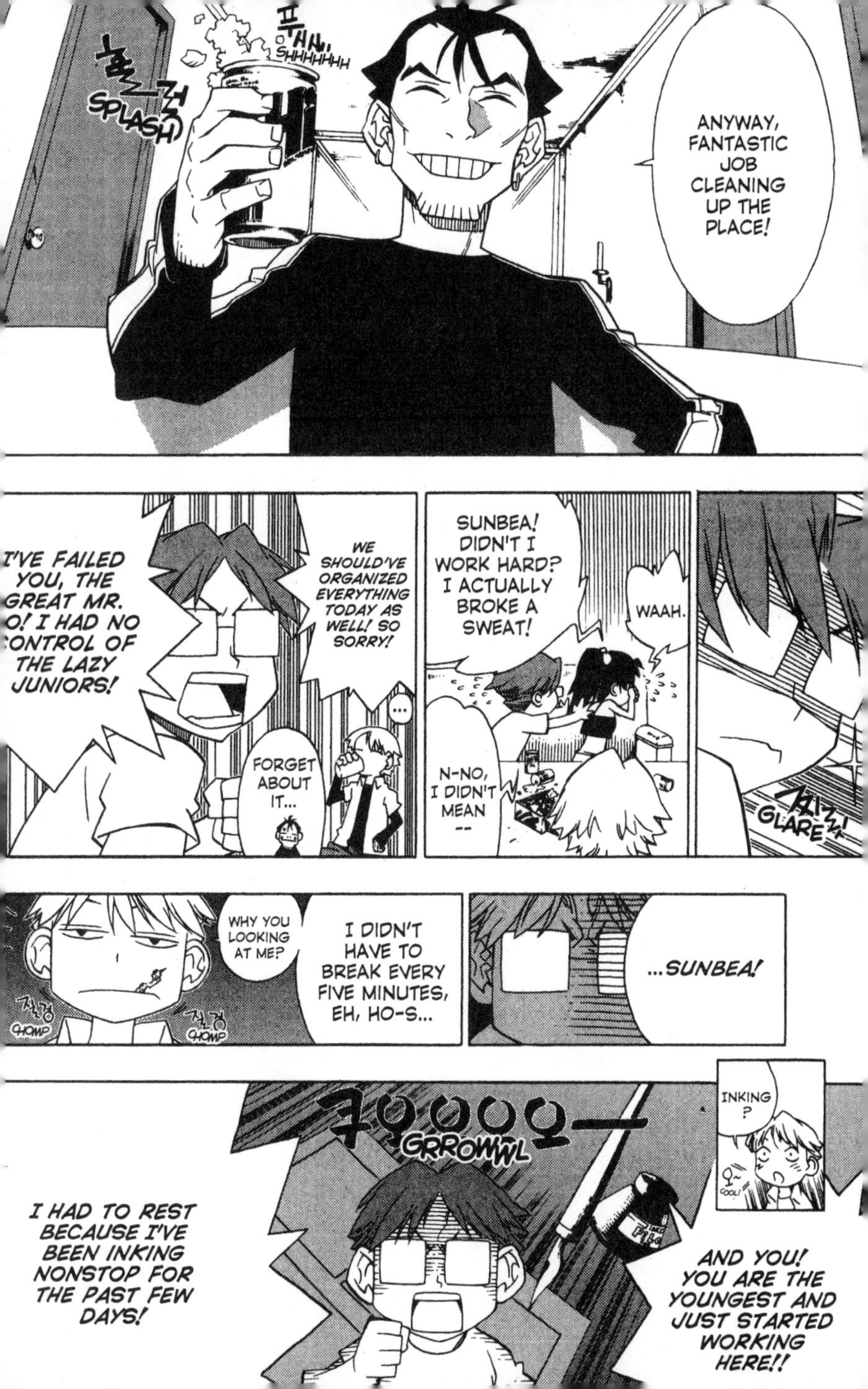

SPLASH
SHHHHHHH
ANYWAY, FANTASTIC JOB CLEANING UP THE PLACE!
I'VE FAILED YOU, THE GREAT MR. O! I HAD NO CONTROL OF THE LAZY JUNIORS!
WE SHOULD'VE ORGANIZED EVERYTHING TODAY AS WELL! SO SORRY!
...
FORGET ABOUT IT...
SUNBEA! DIDN'T I WORK HARD? I ACTUALLY BROKE A SWEAT!
WAAH.
N-NO, I DIDN'T MEAN --
GLARE
WHY YOU LOOKING AT ME?
CHOMP
CHOMP
I DIDN'T HAVE TO BREAK EVERY FIVE MINUTES, EH, HO-S...
...SUNBEA!
GRROWWL
I HAD TO REST BECAUSE I'VE BEEN INKING NONSTOP FOR THE PAST FEW DAYS!
INKING?
COOL!
AND YOU! YOU ARE THE YOUNGEST AND JUST STARTED WORKING HERE!!

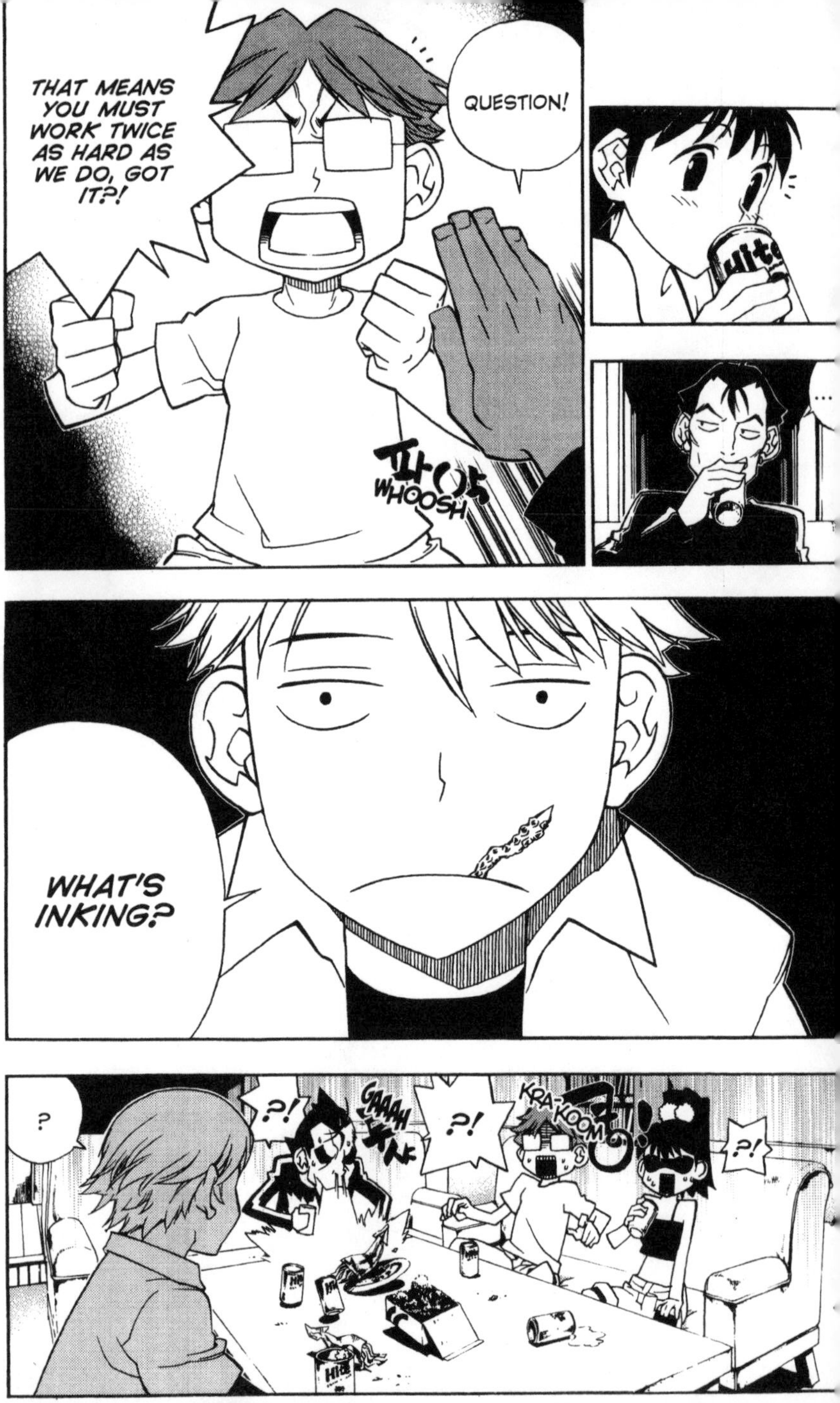
THAT MEANS YOU MUST WORK TWICE AS HARD AS WE DO, GOT IT?!
QUESTION!
WHOOSH
...
WHAT'S INKING?
?!
KRA-KOOM
?!
GAAAH
?!
?

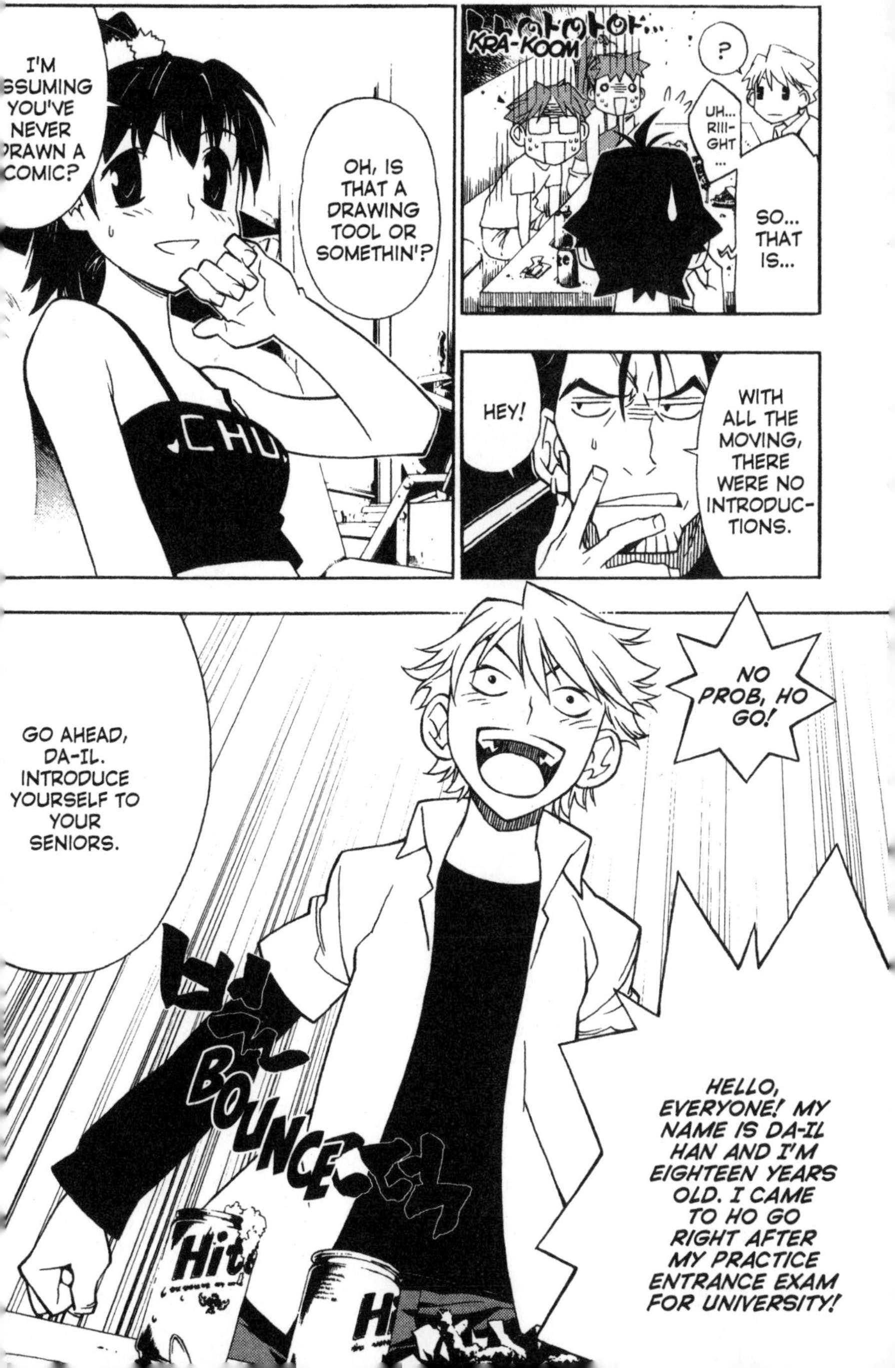
I'M SSUMING YOU'VE NEVER RAWN A COMIC?
OH, IS THAT A DRAWING TOOL OR SOMETHIN'?
KRA-KOOM
?
UH... RIIII-GHT ...
SO... THAT IS...
HEY!
WITH ALL THE MOVING, THERE WERE NO INTRODUCTIONS.
GO AHEAD, DA-IL. INTRODUCE YOURSELF TO YOUR SENIORS.
NO PROB, HO GO!
BOUNCE
HELLO, EVERYONE! MY NAME IS DA-IL HAN AND I'M EIGHTEEN YEARS OLD. I CAME TO HO GO RIGHT AFTER MY PRACTICE ENTRANCE EXAM FOR UNIVERSITY!
Hite

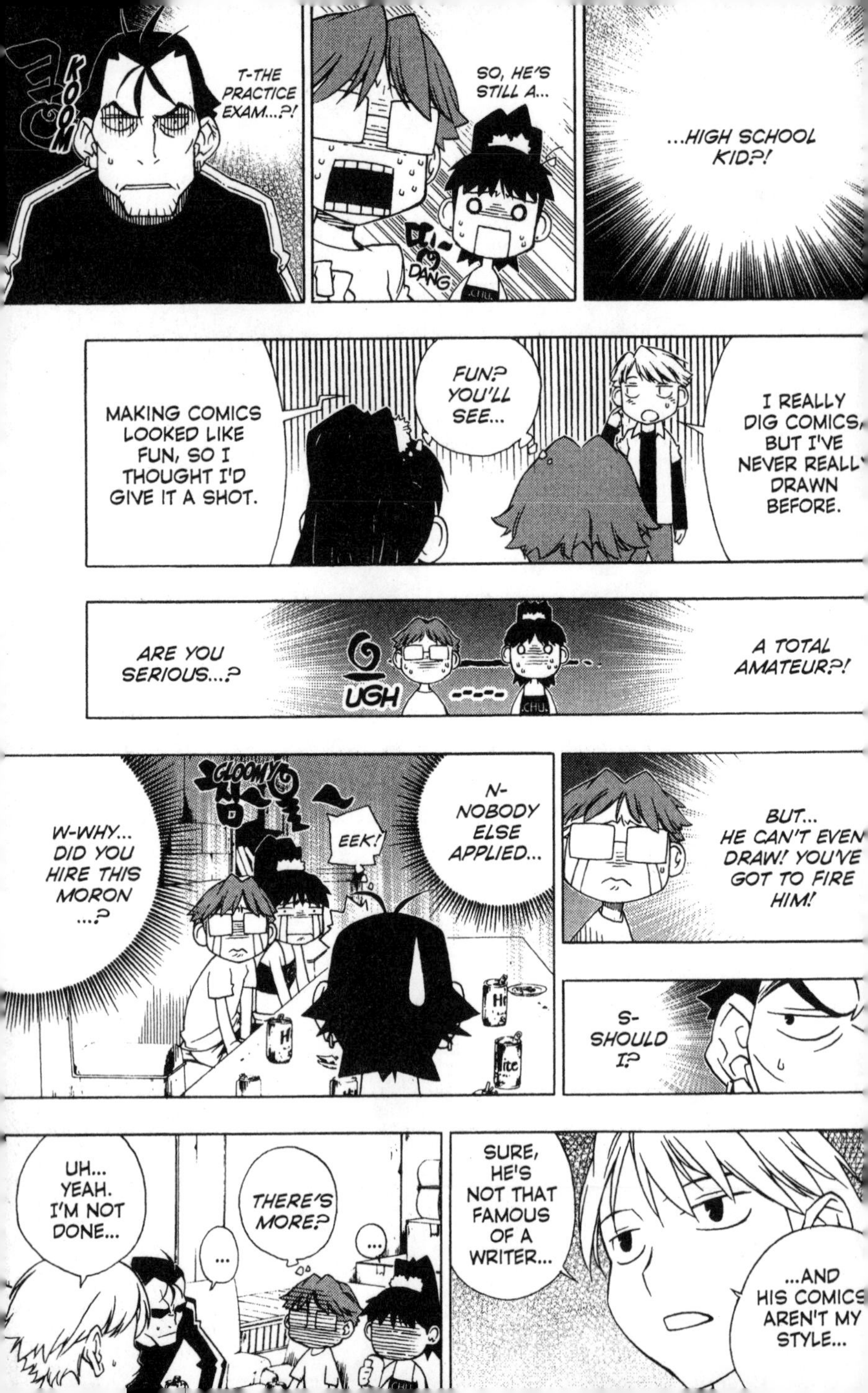
KOOM
T-THE PRACTICE EXAM...?!
SO, HE'S STILL A...
DANG
...HIGH SCHOOL KID?!
MAKING COMICS LOOKED LIKE FUN, SO I THOUGHT I'D GIVE IT A SHOT.
FUN? YOU'LL SEE...
I REALLY DIG COMICS, BUT I'VE NEVER REALLY DRAWN BEFORE.
ARE YOU SERIOUS...?
UGH
A TOTAL AMATEUR?!
W-WHY... DID YOU HIRE THIS MORON ...?
GLOOMY
EEK!
N-NOBODY ELSE APPLIED...
BUT... HE CAN'T EVEN DRAW! YOU'VE GOT TO FIRE HIM!
S-SHOULD I?
UH... YEAH. I'M NOT DONE...
...
THERE'S MORE?
...
SURE, HE'S NOT THAT FAMOUS OF A WRITER...
...AND HIS COMICS AREN'T MY STYLE...

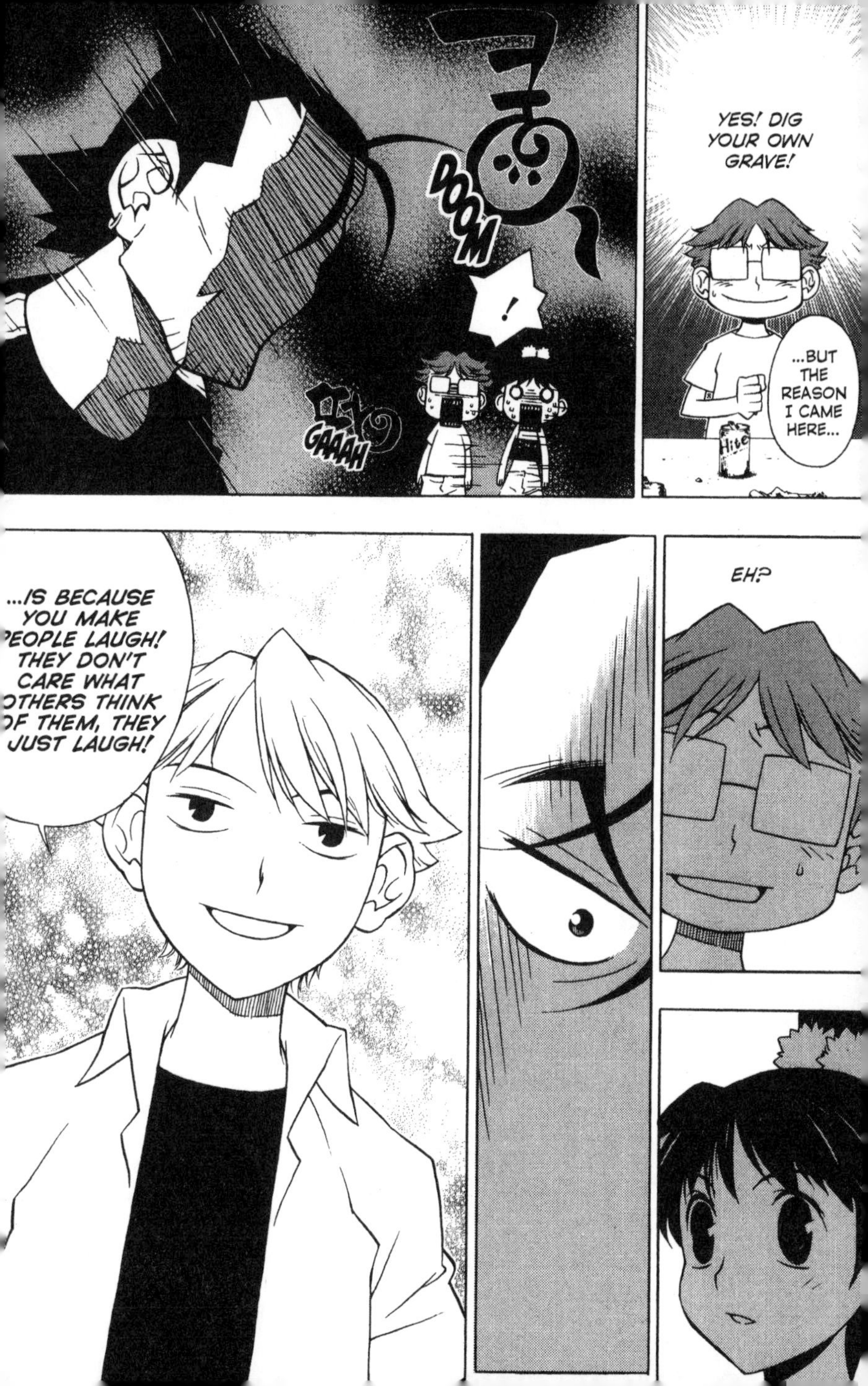
YES! DIG YOUR OWN GRAVE!
...BUT THE REASON I CAME HERE...
DOOM
!
GAAAH
EH?
...IS BECAUSE YOU MAKE PEOPLE LAUGH! THEY DON'T CARE WHAT OTHERS THINK OF THEM, THEY JUST LAUGH!

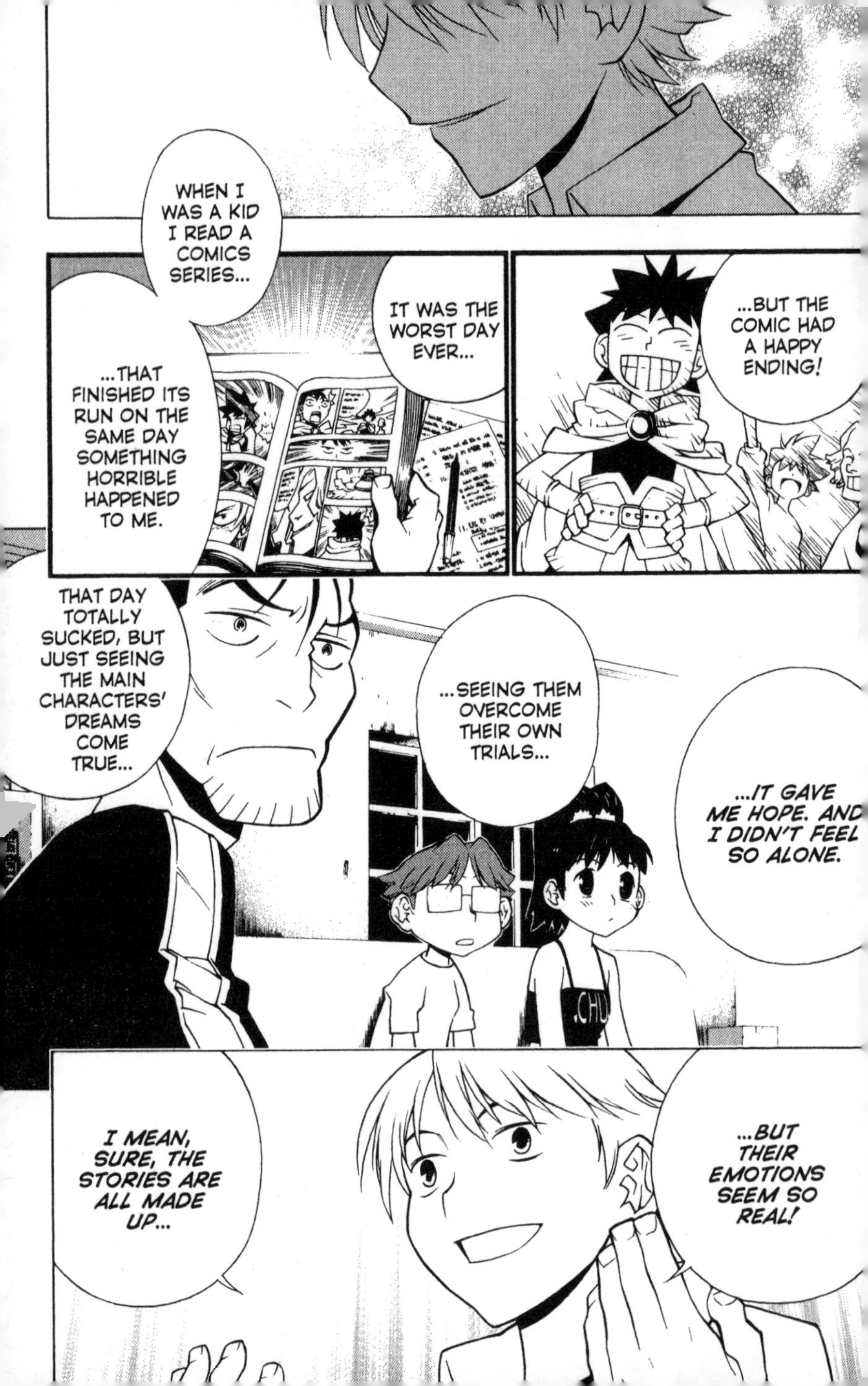

WHEN I WAS A KID I READ A COMICS SERIES...
...THAT FINISHED ITS RUN ON THE SAME DAY SOMETHING HORRIBLE HAPPENED TO ME.
IT WAS THE WORST DAY EVER...
...BUT THE COMIC HAD A HAPPY ENDING!
THAT DAY TOTALLY SUCKED, BUT JUST SEEING THE MAIN CHARACTERS' DREAMS COME TRUE...
...SEEING THEM OVERCOME THEIR OWN TRIALS...
...IT GAVE ME HOPE. AND I DIDN'T FEEL SO ALONE.
I MEAN, SURE, THE STORIES ARE ALL MADE UP...
...BUT THEIR EMOTIONS SEEM SO REAL!

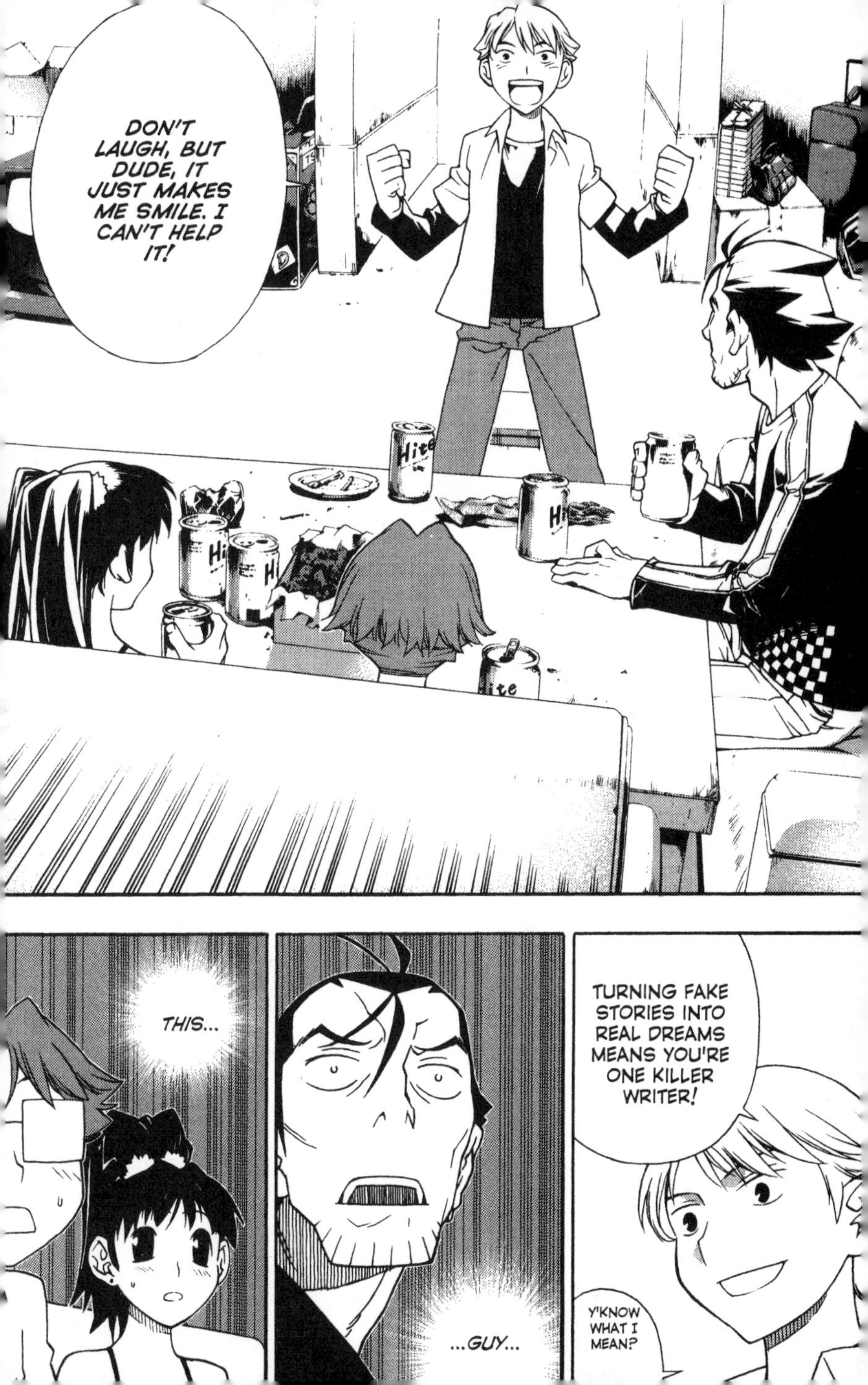
DON'T LAUGH, BUT DUDE, IT JUST MAKES ME SMILE. I CAN'T HELP IT!
TURNING FAKE STORIES INTO REAL DREAMS MEANS YOU'RE ONE KILLER WRITER!
Y'KNOW WHAT I MEAN?
THIS...
...GUY...

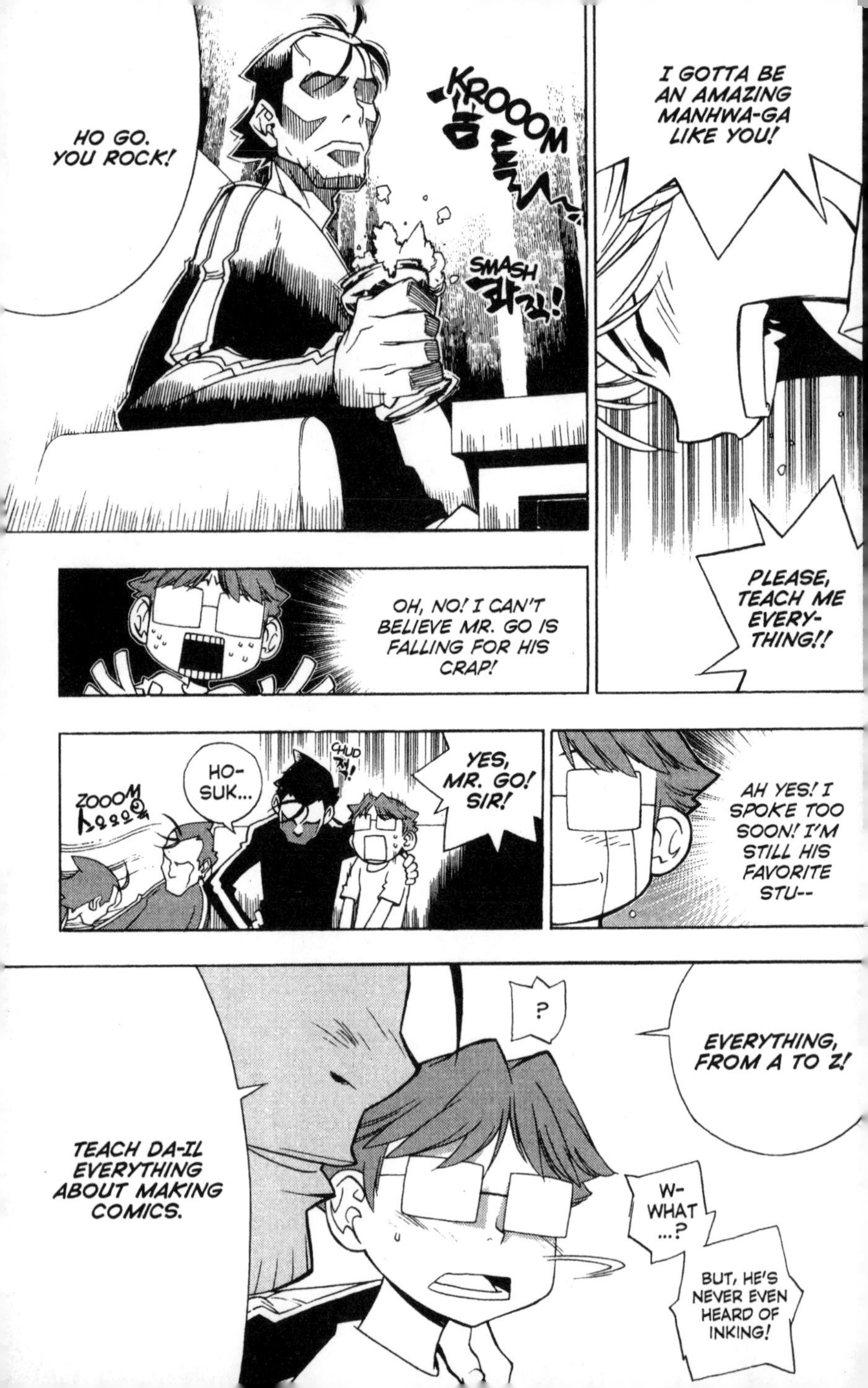
HO GO. YOU ROCK!
KROOOM
SMASH
I GOTTA BE AN AMAZING MANHWA-GA LIKE YOU!
PLEASE, TEACH ME EVERYTHING!!
OH, NO! I CAN'T BELIEVE MR. GO IS FALLING FOR HIS CRAP!
ZOOOM
HO-SUK...
CHUD
YES, MR. GO! SIR!
AH YES! I SPOKE TOO SOON! I'M STILL HIS FAVORITE STU--
EVERYTHING, FROM A TO Z!
?
TEACH DA-IL EVERYTHING ABOUT MAKING COMICS.
W-WHAT ...?
BUT, HE'S NEVER EVEN HEARD OF INKING!

SO, I'M IN?

OF COURSE!

I'LL MOLD YOU INTO A MASTER LIKE ME!

THANK YOU! I'LL DO MY BEST!

THUMBS UP

N-NO! THIS CAN'T BE HAPPENING! I'M THE FAVORITE--!

RRRRING

THIS IS IT!

RRRRING

RRRRING

LEMME DISTRACT HIM...

HELLO? YOU'VE REACHED THE STUDIO OF THE GREAT MANHWA-GA MR. HO GO!

CHANG

WAIT! I'M NOT HERE...

TWINKLE

IT'S THE EDITOR, MR. GO!

I SAID I'M NOT HERE.

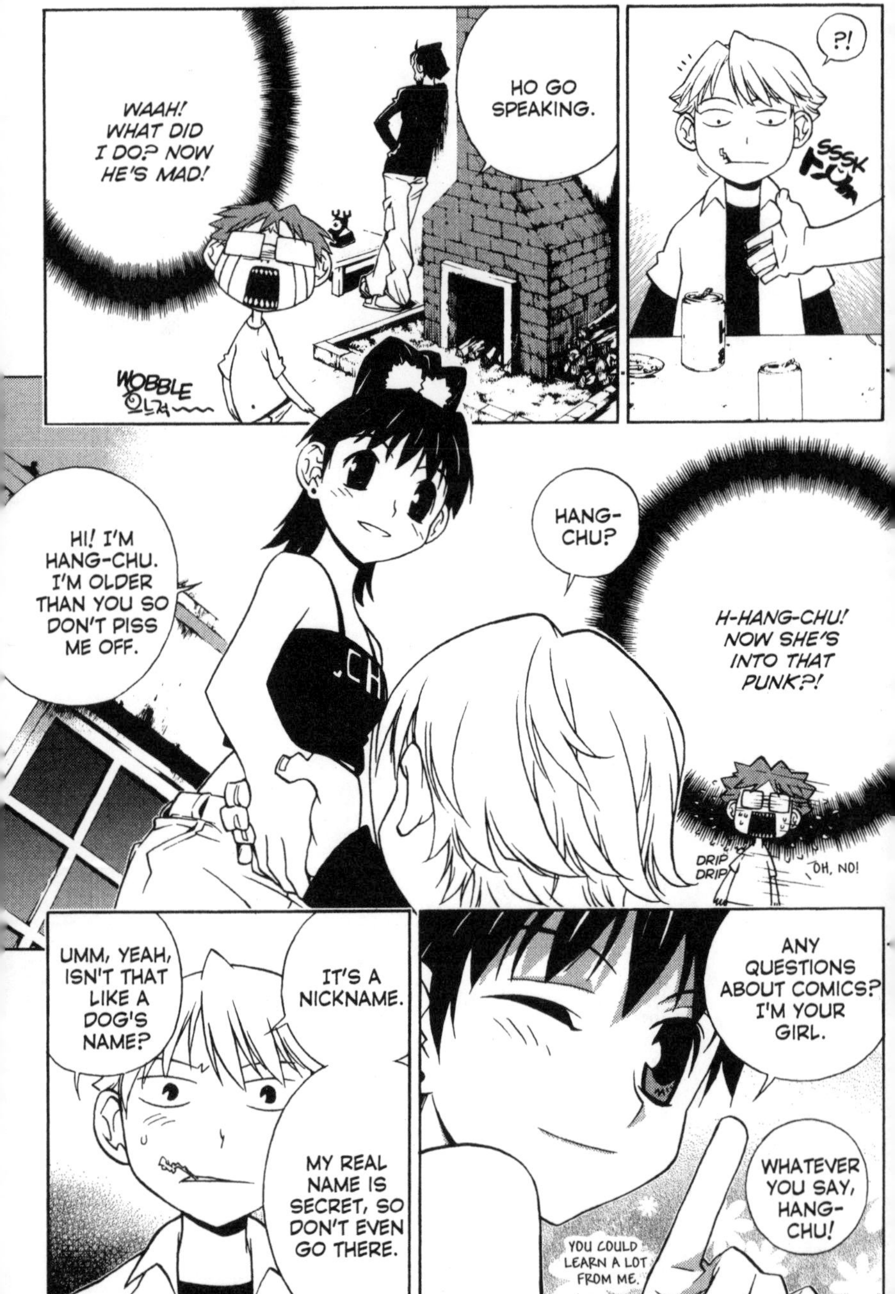
?!
SSSK
HO GO SPEAKING.
WAAH! WHAT DID I DO? NOW HE'S MAD!
WOBBLE
HANG-CHU?
HI! I'M HANG-CHU. I'M OLDER THAN YOU SO DON'T PISS ME OFF.
H-HANG-CHU! NOW SHE'S INTO THAT PUNK?!
DRIP DRIP
OH, NO!
ANY QUESTIONS ABOUT COMICS? I'M YOUR GIRL.
IT'S A NICKNAME.
UMM, YEAH, ISN'T THAT LIKE A DOG'S NAME?
WHATEVER YOU SAY, HANG-CHU!
YOU COULD LEARN A LOT FROM ME.
MY REAL NAME IS SECRET, SO DON'T EVEN GO THERE.

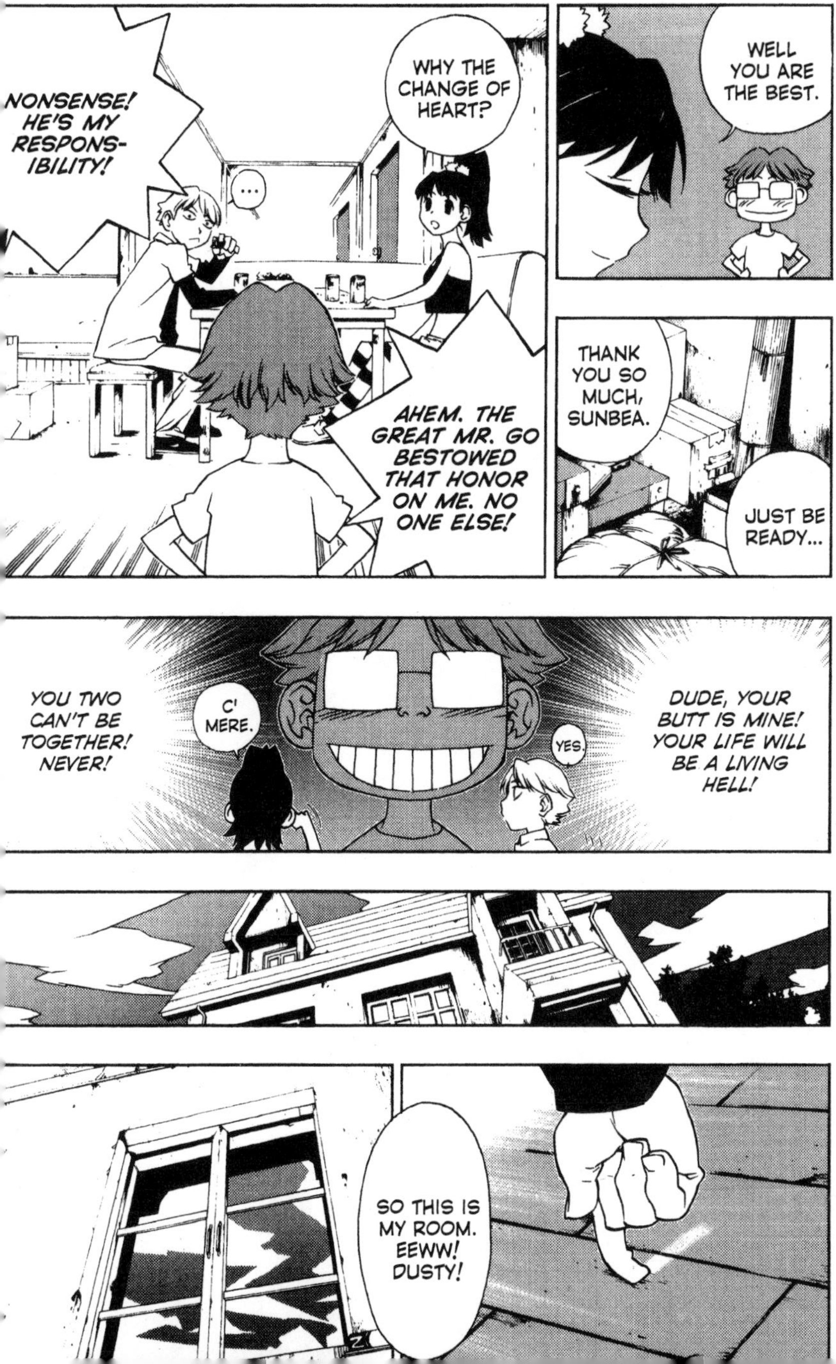
WHY THE CHANGE OF HEART?
...
NONSENSE! HE'S MY RESPONS-IBILITY!
AHEM. THE GREAT MR. GO BESTOWED THAT HONOR ON ME. NO ONE ELSE!
WELL YOU ARE THE BEST.
THANK YOU SO MUCH, SUNBEA.
JUST BE READY...
YOU TWO CAN'T BE TOGETHER! NEVER!
C' MERE.
YES.
DUDE, YOUR BUTT IS MINE! YOUR LIFE WILL BE A LIVING HELL!
SO THIS IS MY ROOM. EEWW! DUSTY!

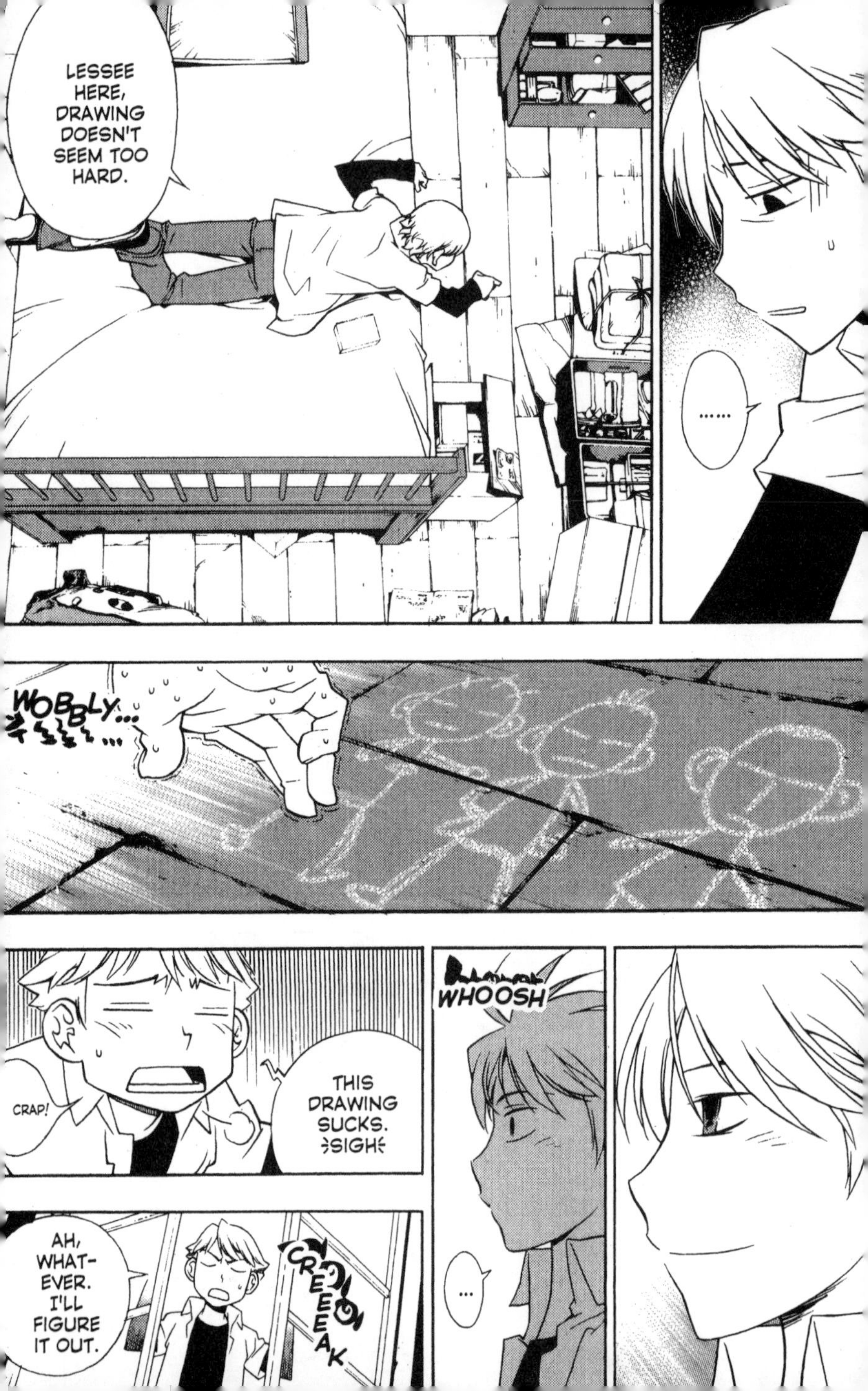

......
LESSEE HERE, DRAWING DOESN'T SEEM TOO HARD.
WOBBLY...
WHOOSH
...
THIS DRAWING SUCKS. SIGH
CRAP!
AH, WHAT-EVER. I'LL FIGURE IT OUT.
CREEEEAK

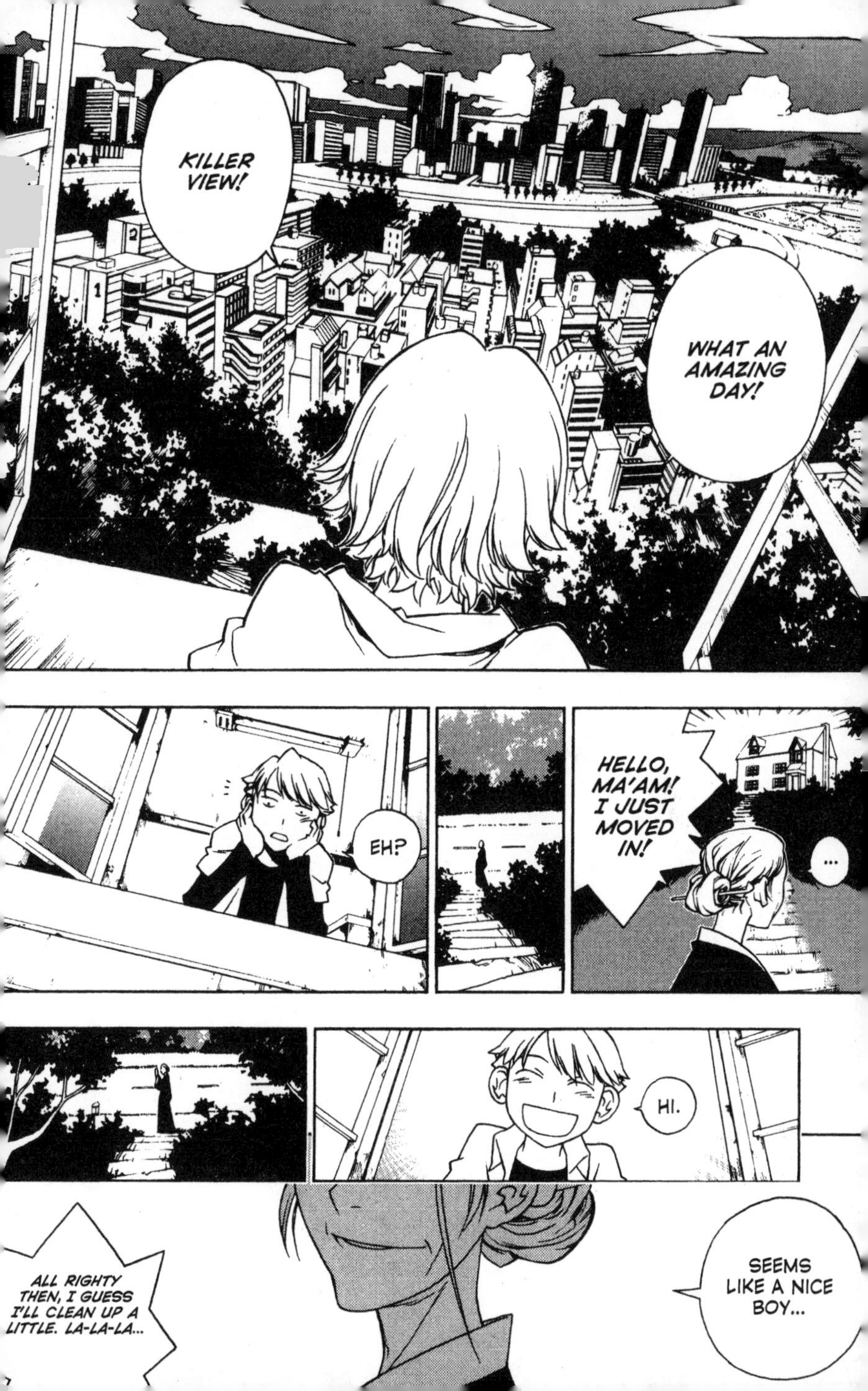
KILLER VIEW!
WHAT AN AMAZING DAY!
EH?
HELLO, MA'AM! I JUST MOVED IN!
...
HI.
ALL RIGHTY THEN, I GUESS I'LL CLEAN UP A LITTLE. LA-LA-LA...
SEEMS LIKE A NICE BOY...

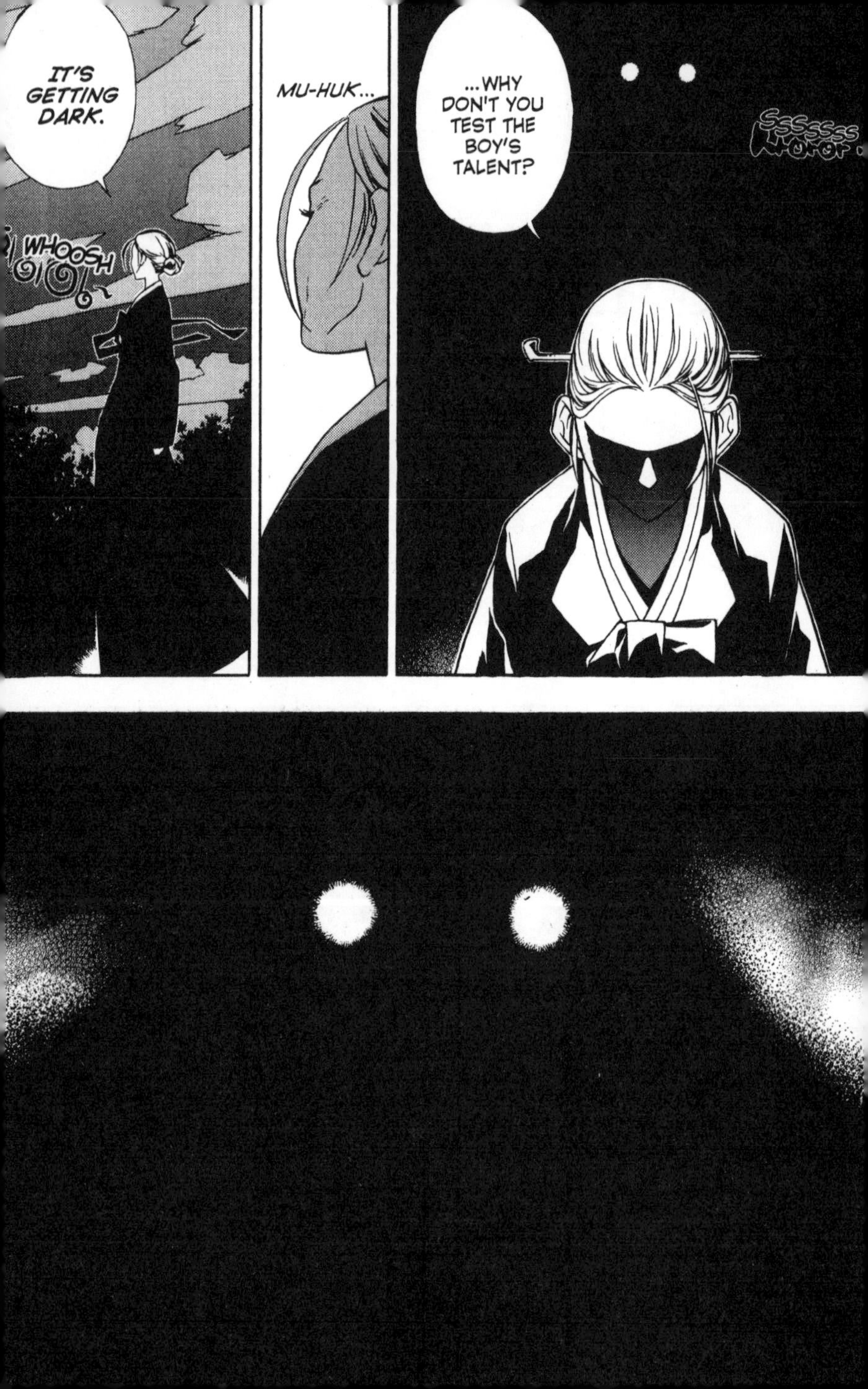

IT'S GETTING DARK.
WHOOSH
MU-HUK...
...WHY DON'T YOU TEST THE BOY'S TALENT?
SSSSSSS

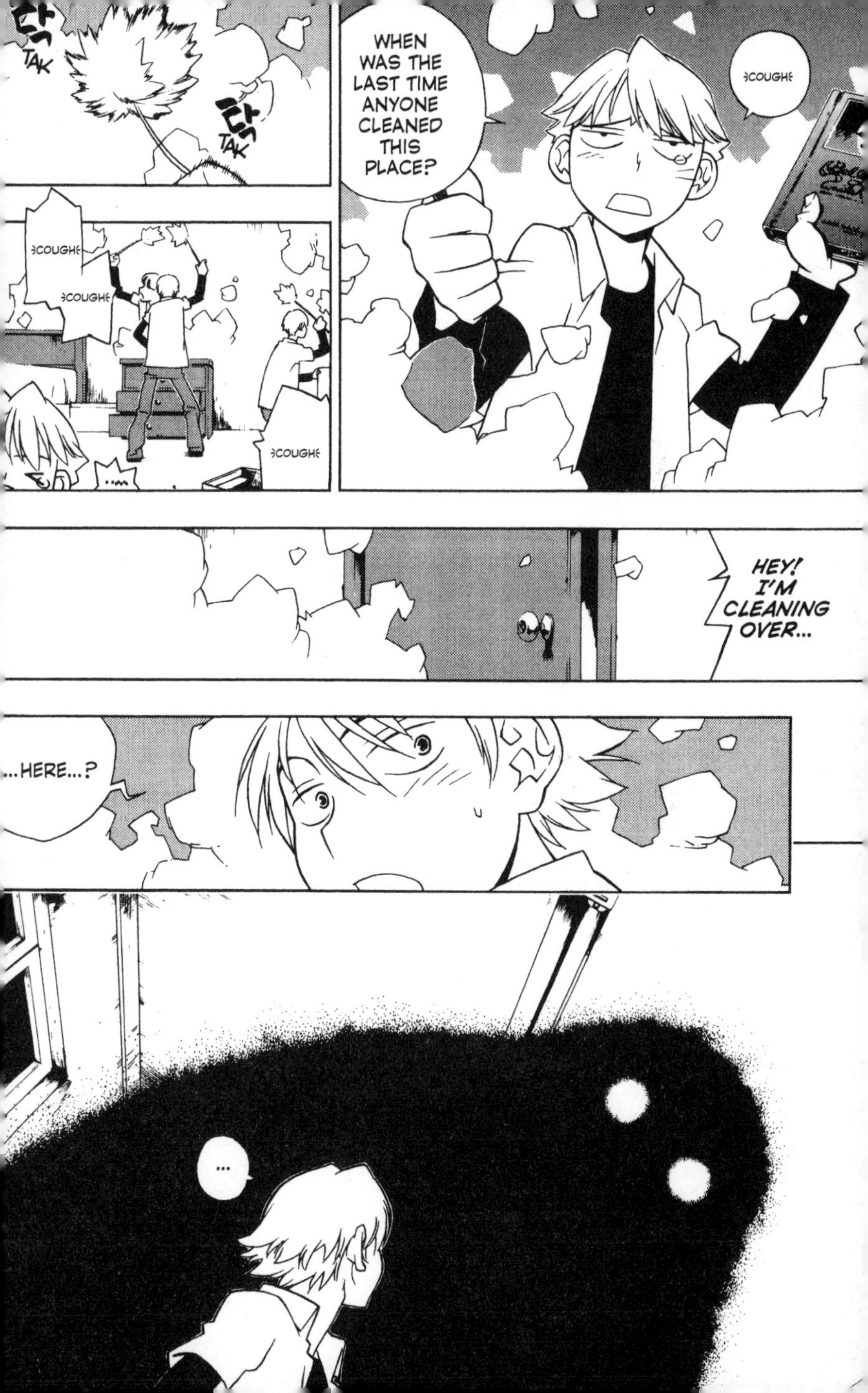

WHEN WAS THE LAST TIME ANYONE CLEANED THIS PLACE?
COUGH
TAK
TAK
COUGH
COUGH
COUGH
...
HEY! I'M CLEANING OVER...
...HERE...?
...

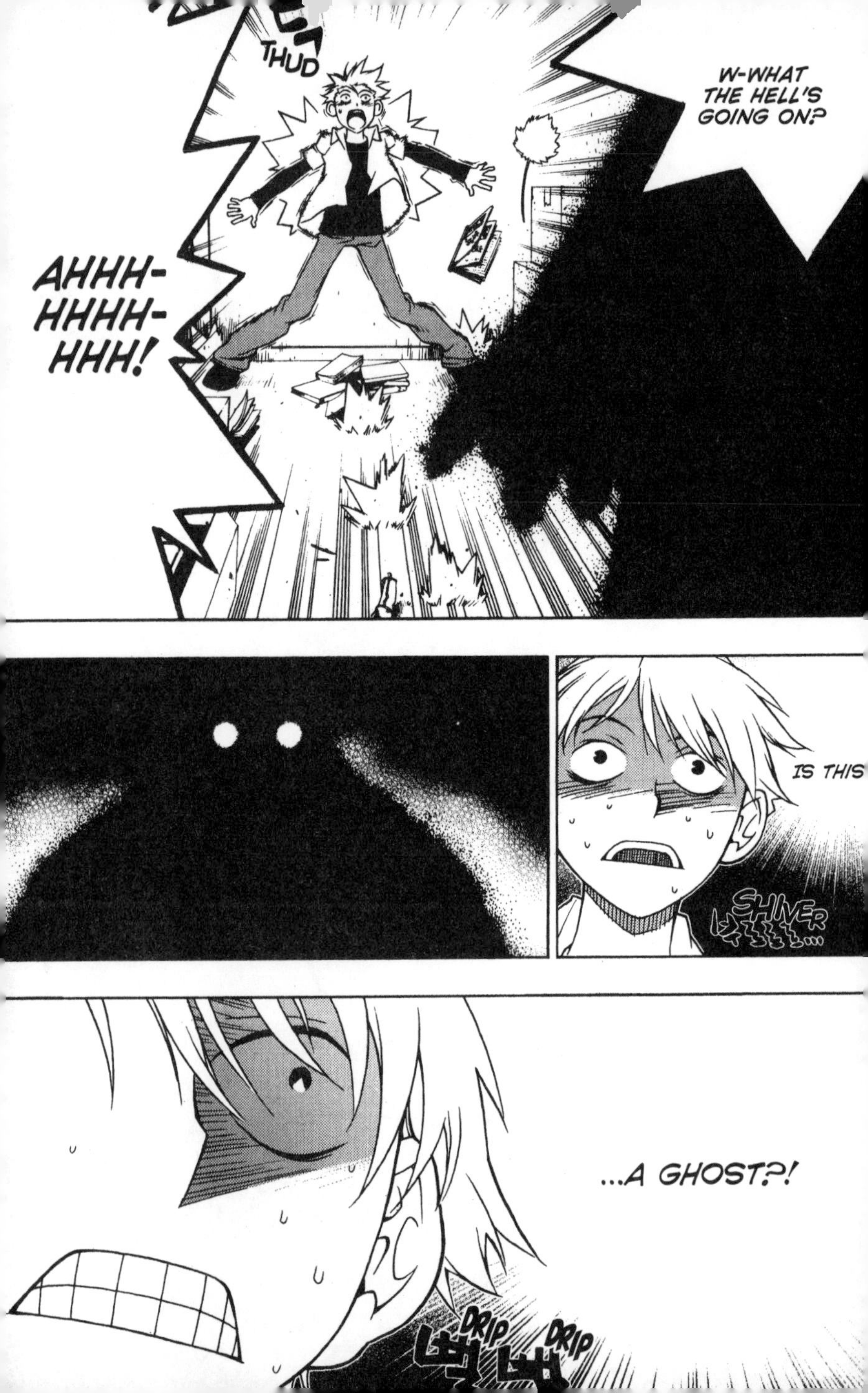
W-WHAT THE HELL'S GOING ON?
THUD
AHHH-HHHH-HHH!
IS THIS
SHIVER
...A GHOST?!
DRIP
DRIP

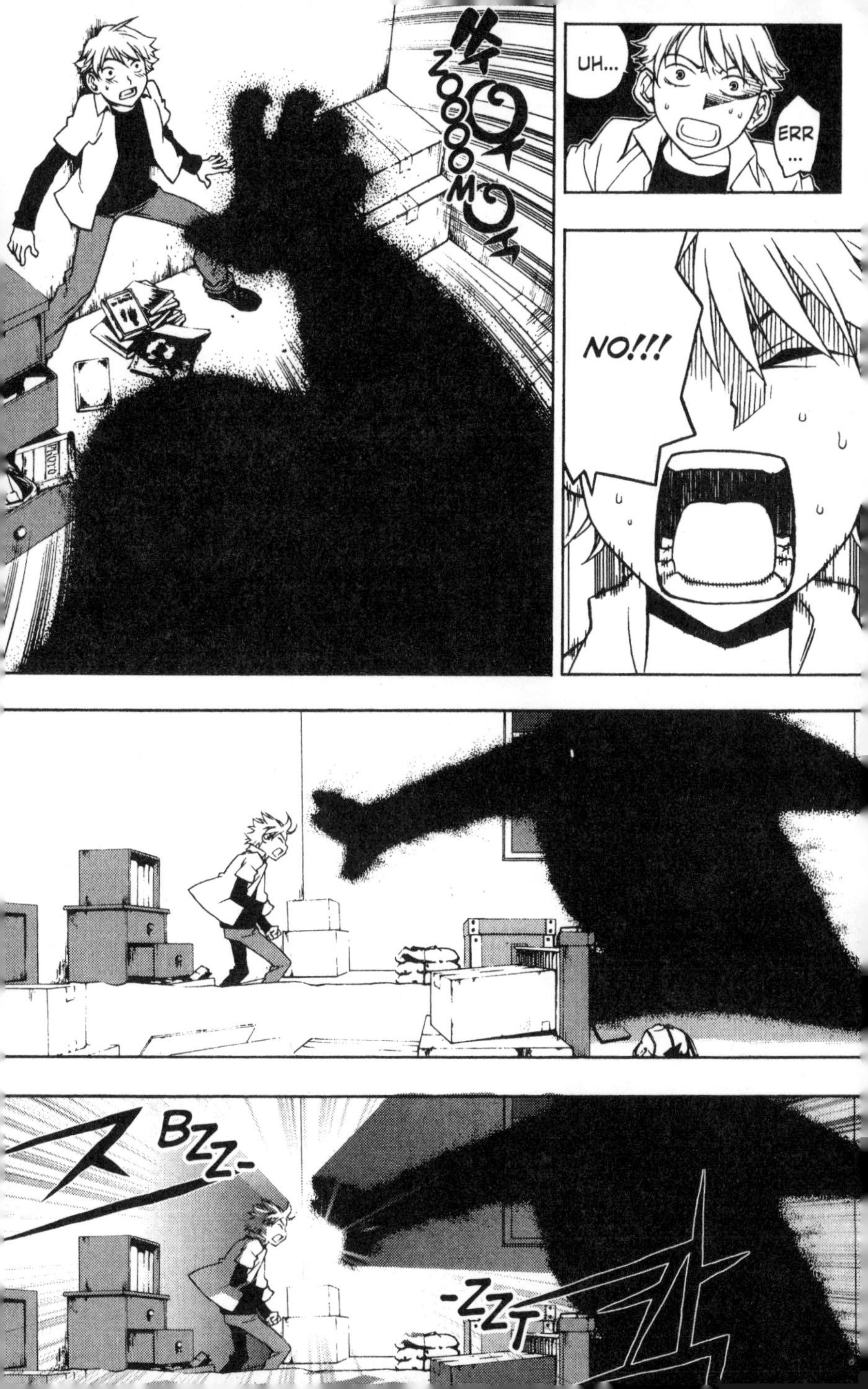
UH...
ERR ...
NO!!!
ZOOOOOM
BZZ-
-ZZT

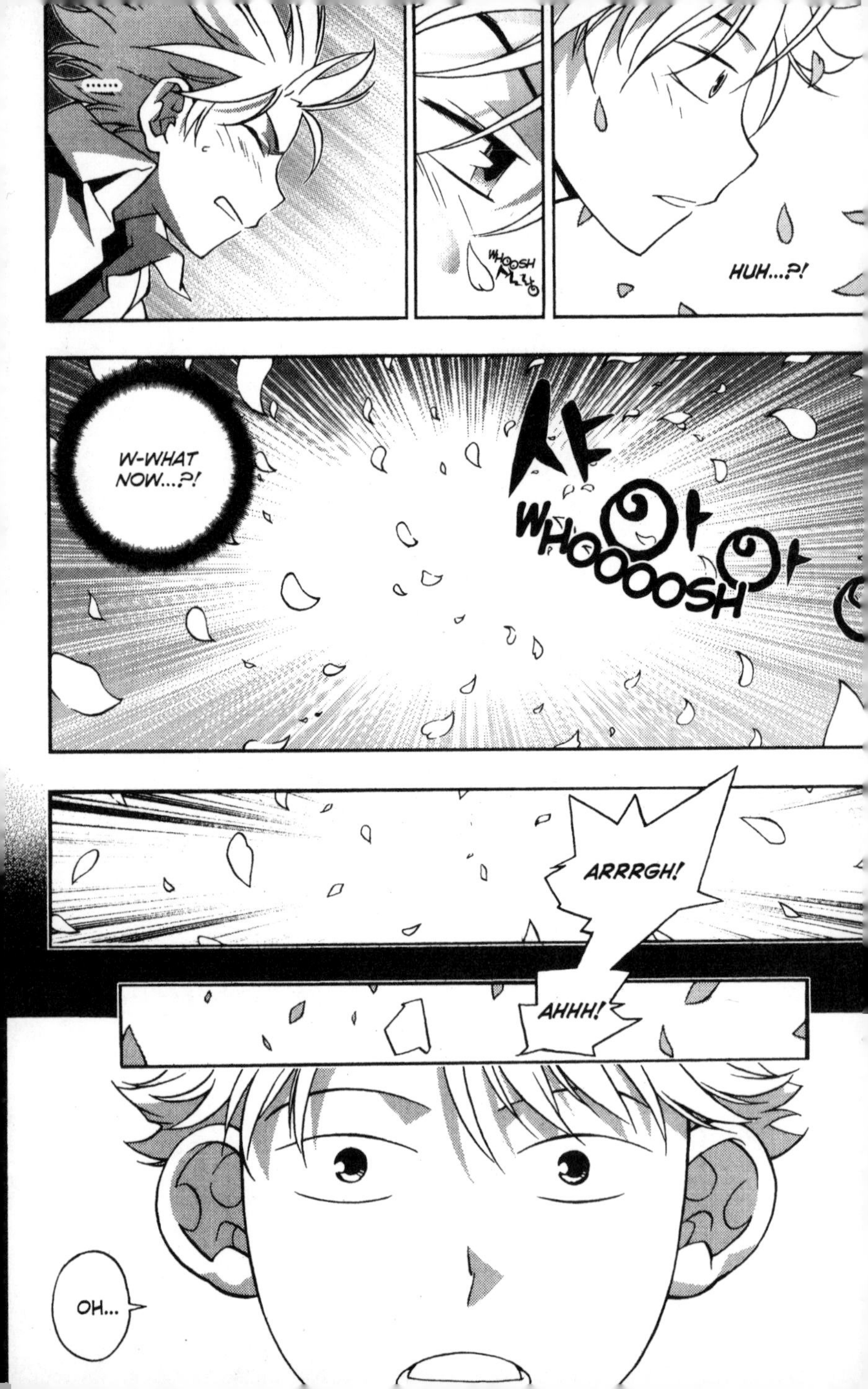
HUH...?!
WHOOSH
......
WHOOOOOSH
W-WHAT NOW...?!
ARRRGH!
AHHH!
OH...

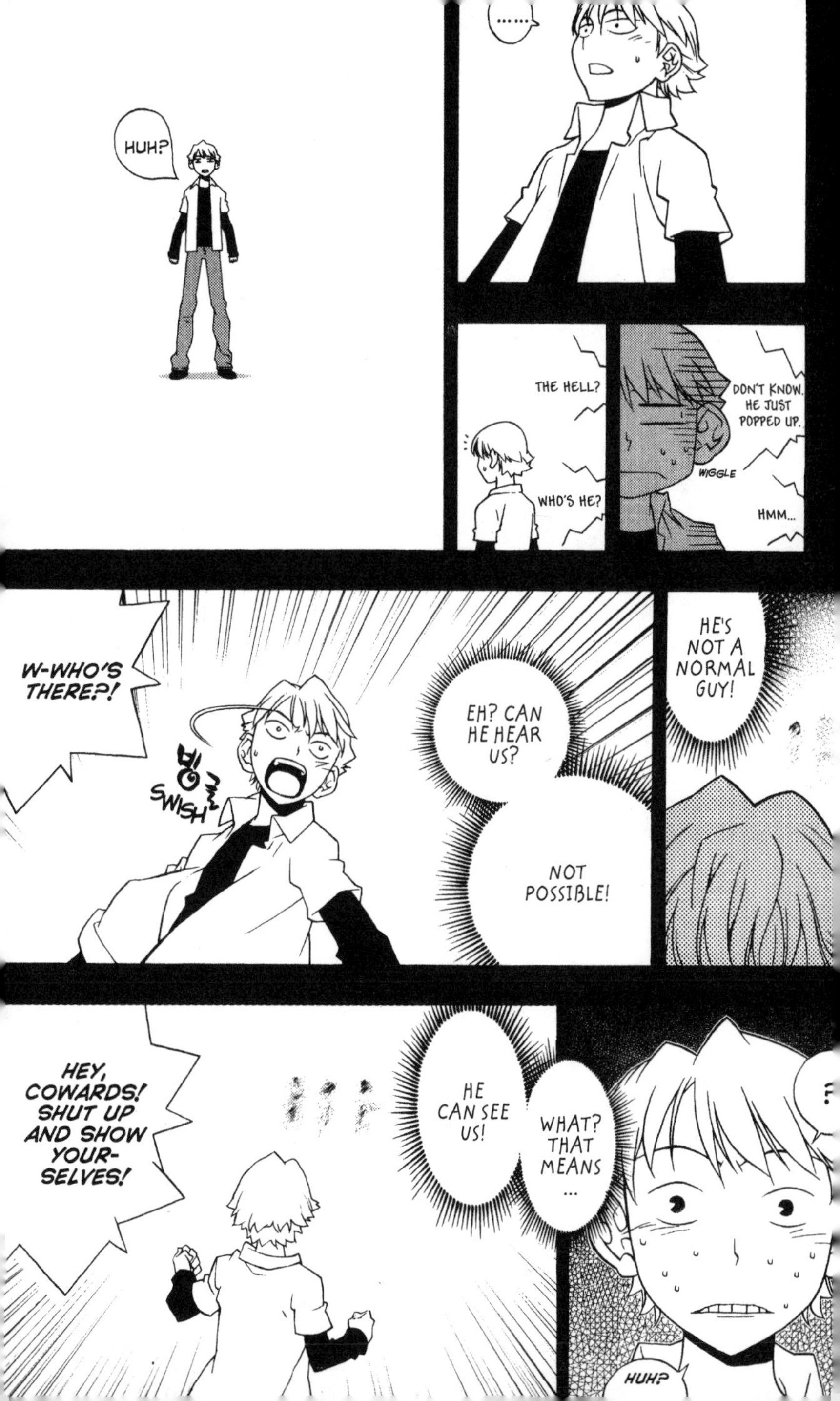
......
HUH?
DON'T KNOW. HE JUST POPPED UP.
WIGGLE
HMM...
THE HELL?
WHO'S HE?
HE'S NOT A NORMAL GUY!
EH? CAN HE HEAR US?
NOT POSSIBLE!
W-WHO'S THERE?!
SWISH
HUH?
HE CAN SEE US!
WHAT? THAT MEANS ...
HEY, COWARDS! SHUT UP AND SHOW YOUR-SELVES!

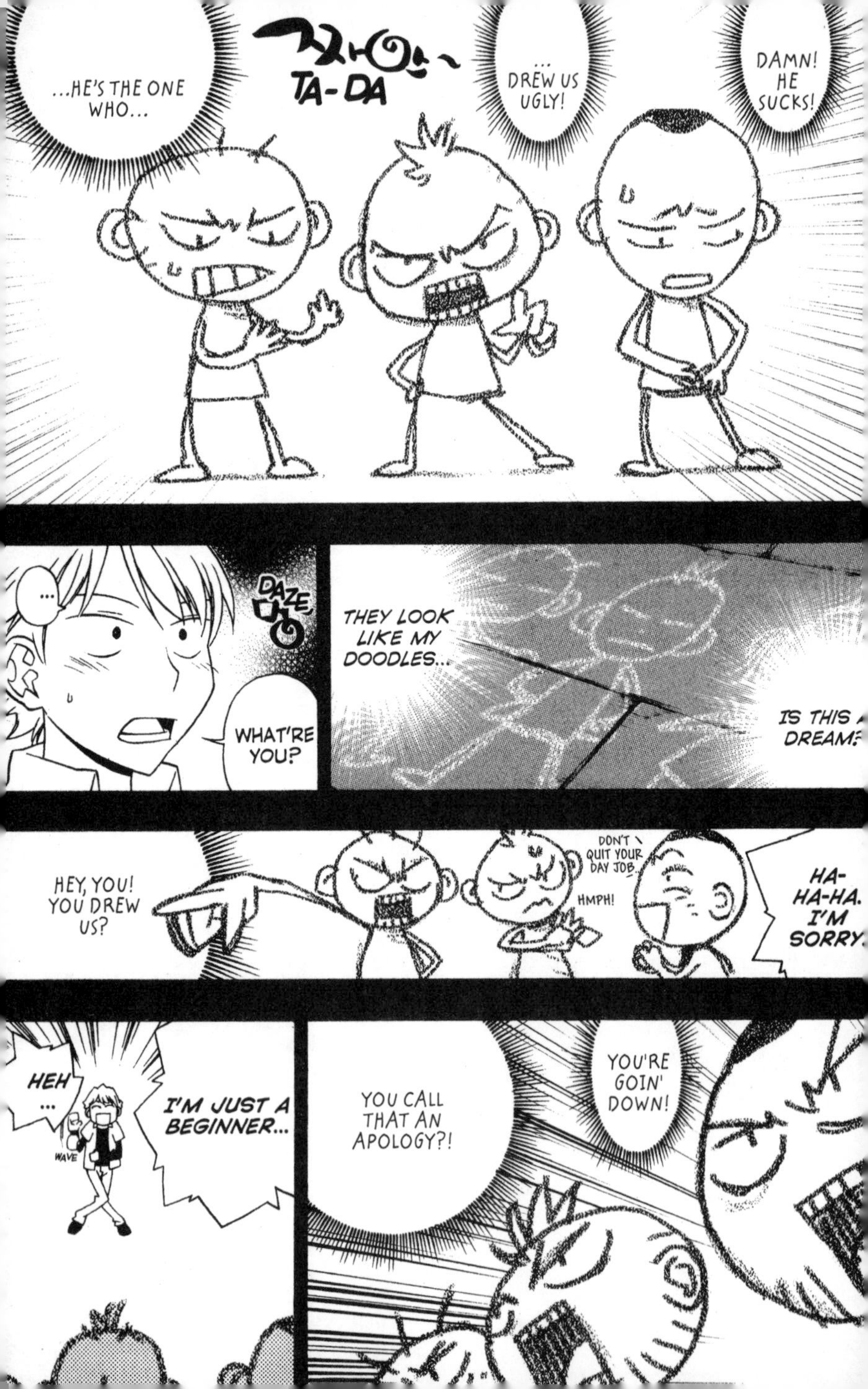
...HE'S THE ONE WHO...
TA-DA
... DREW US UGLY!
DAMN! HE SUCKS!
...
DAZE
WHAT'RE YOU?
THEY LOOK LIKE MY DOODLES...
IS THIS A DREAM?
HEY, YOU! YOU DREW US?
HMPH!
DON'T QUIT YOUR DAY JOB.
HA-HA-HA. I'M SORRY.
HEH ...
WAVE
I'M JUST A BEGINNER...
YOU CALL THAT AN APOLOGY?!
YOU'RE GOIN' DOWN!

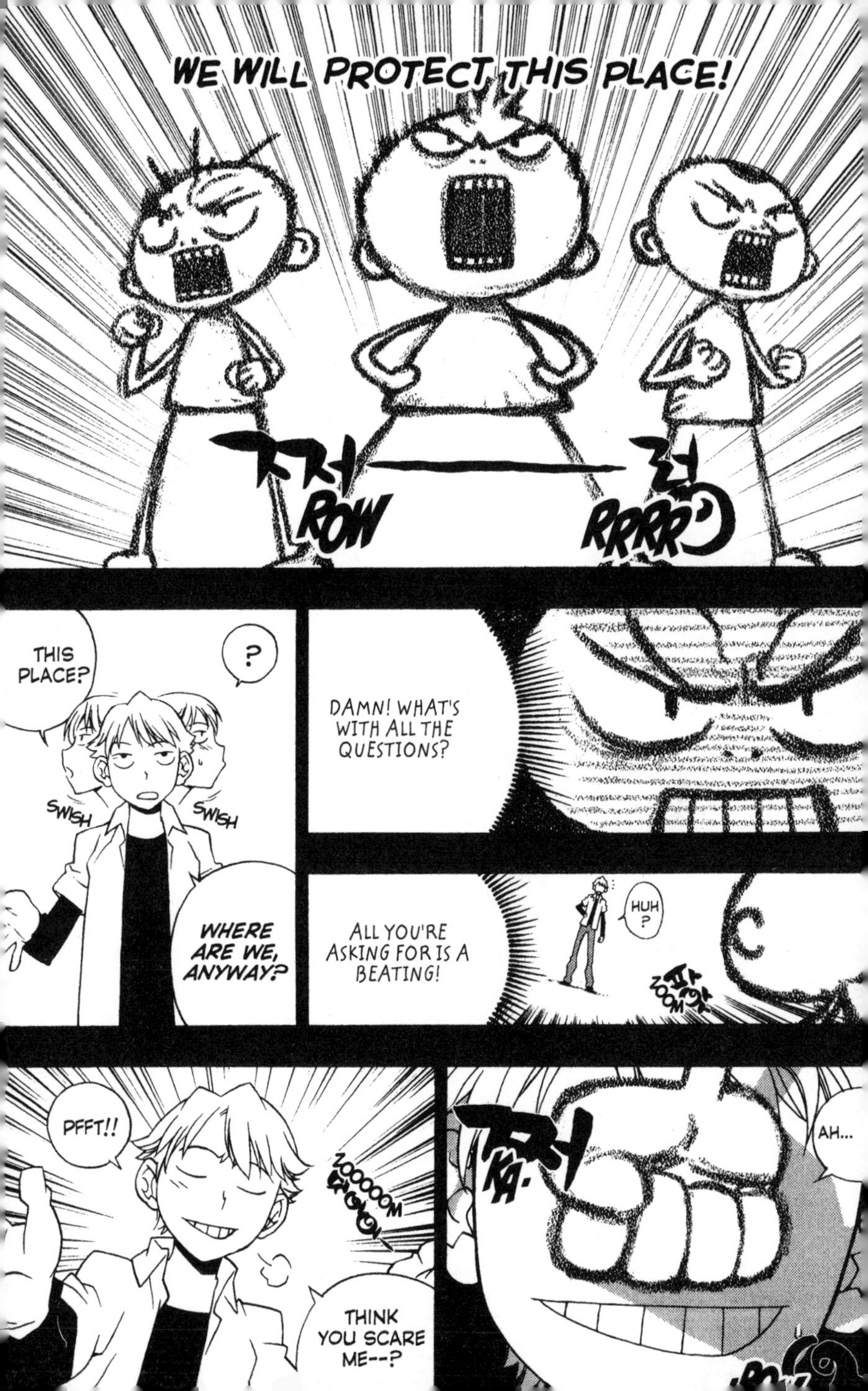

WE WILL PROTECT THIS PLACE!
ROW
RRRR
THIS PLACE?
?
SWISH
SWISH
WHERE ARE WE, ANYWAY?
DAMN! WHAT'S WITH ALL THE QUESTIONS?
HUH?
ALL YOU'RE ASKING FOR IS A BEATING!
ZOOM
PFFT!!
THINK YOU SCARE ME--?
KA
AH...

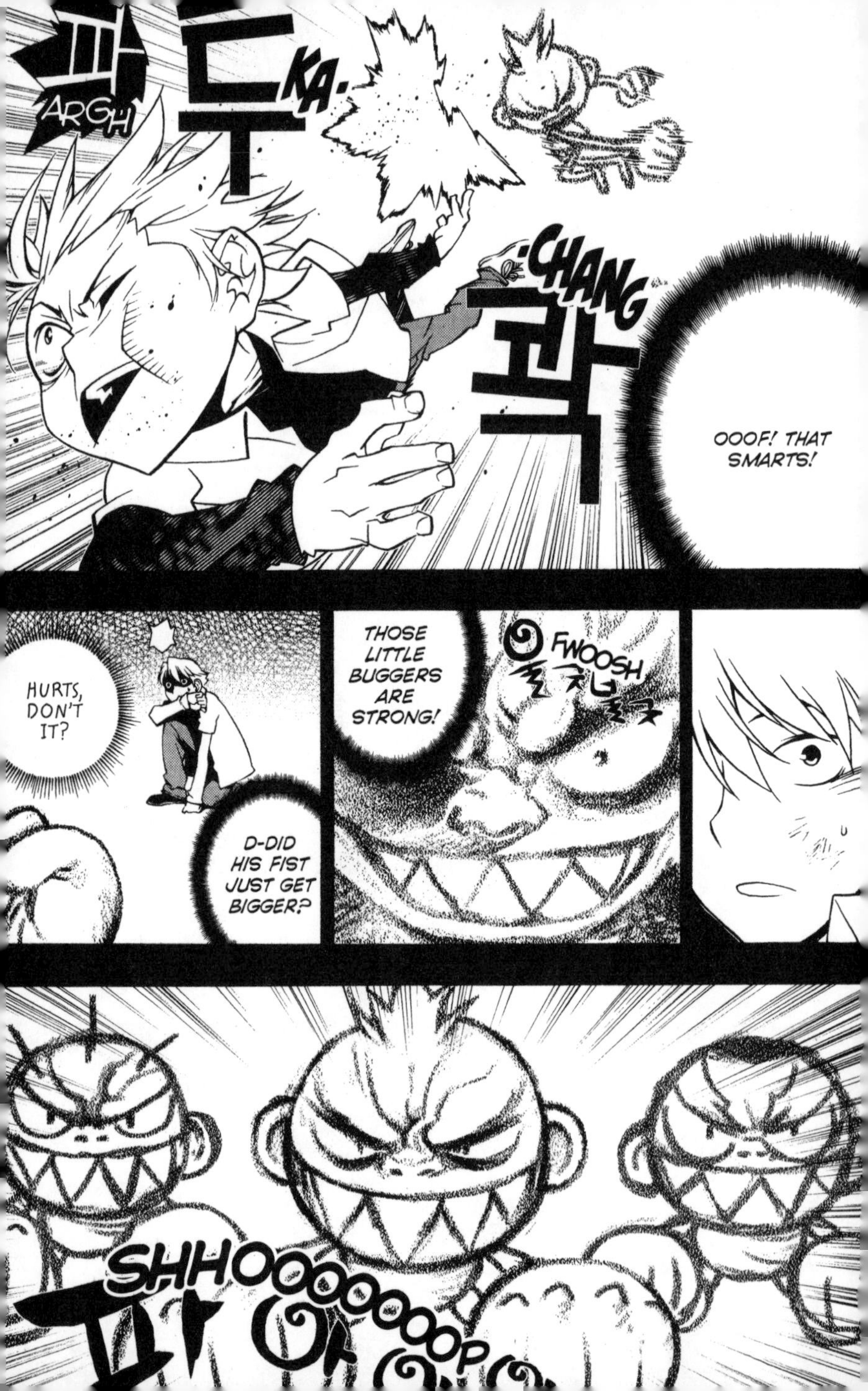

ARGH
KA-
CHANG
OOOF! THAT SMARTS!
HURTS, DON'T IT?
D-DID HIS FIST JUST GET BIGGER?
THOSE LITTLE BUGGERS ARE STRONG!
FWOOSH
SHHOOOOOOOOOP

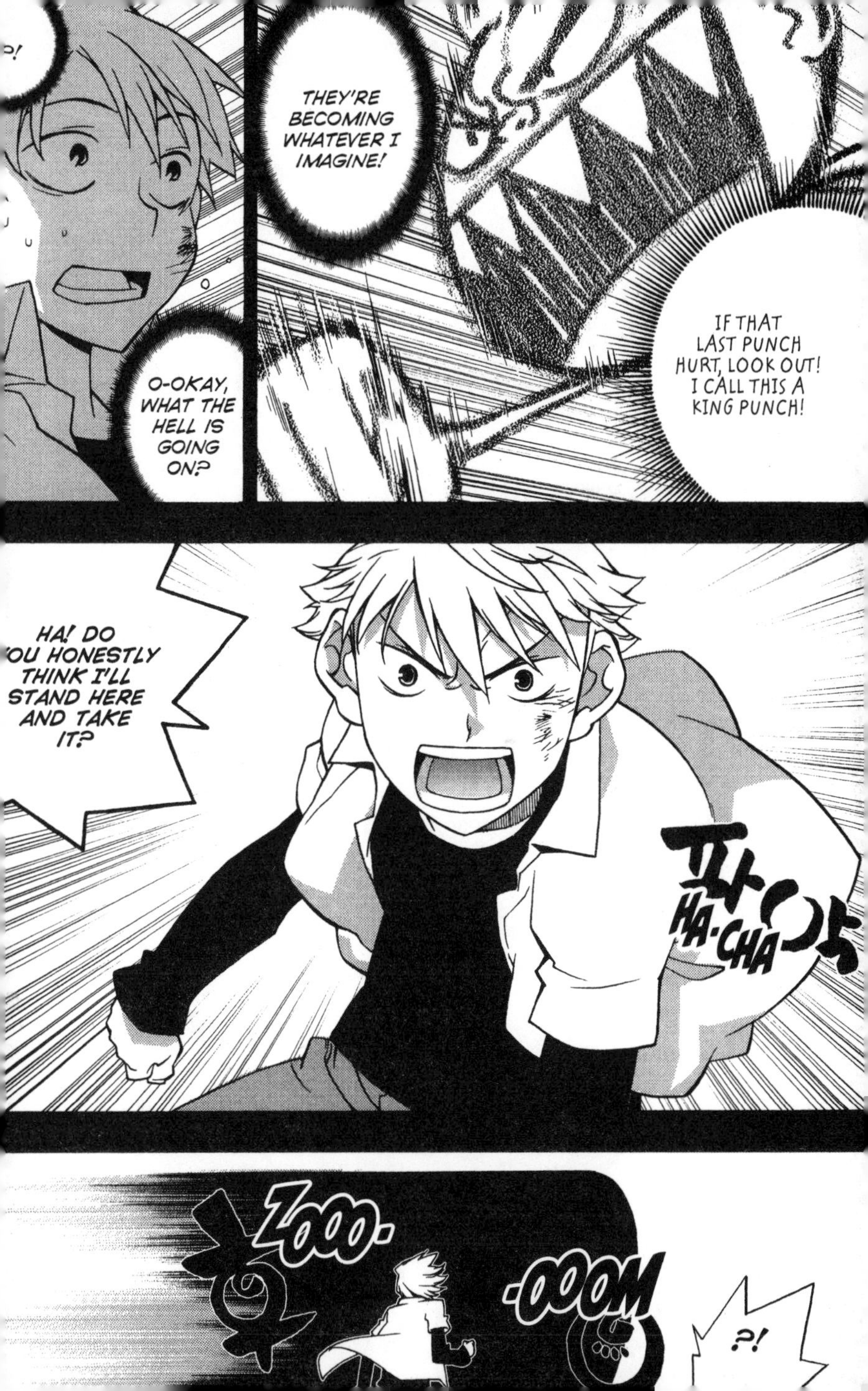
THEY'RE BECOMING WHATEVER I IMAGINE!
IF THAT LAST PUNCH HURT, LOOK OUT! I CALL THIS A KING PUNCH!
?!
O-OKAY, WHAT THE HELL IS GOING ON?
HA-CHA
HA! DO OU HONESTLY THINK I'LL STAND HERE AND TAKE IT?
ZOOO-
-OOOM
?!

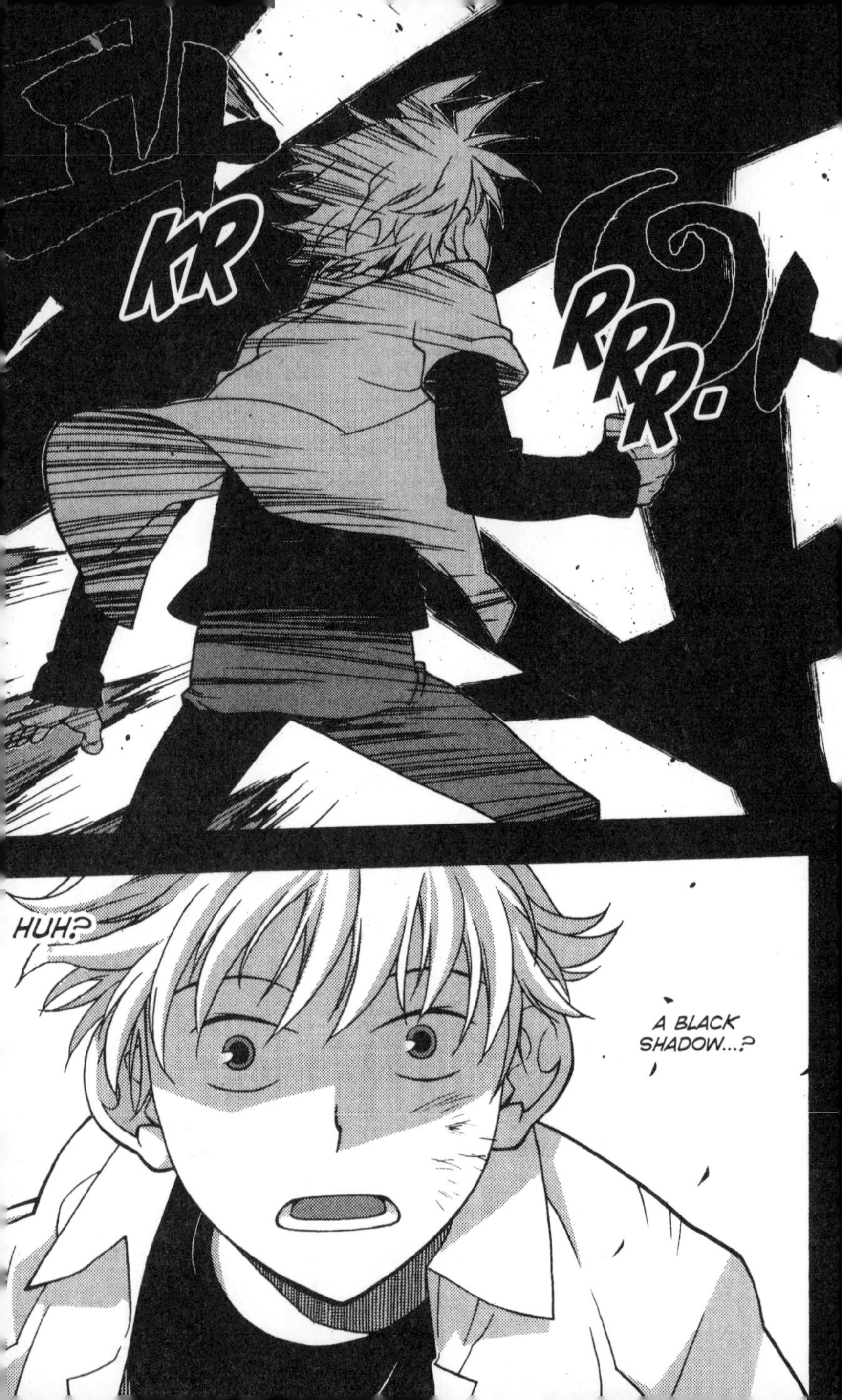

KR
RRR.
HUH?
A BLACK SHADOW...?

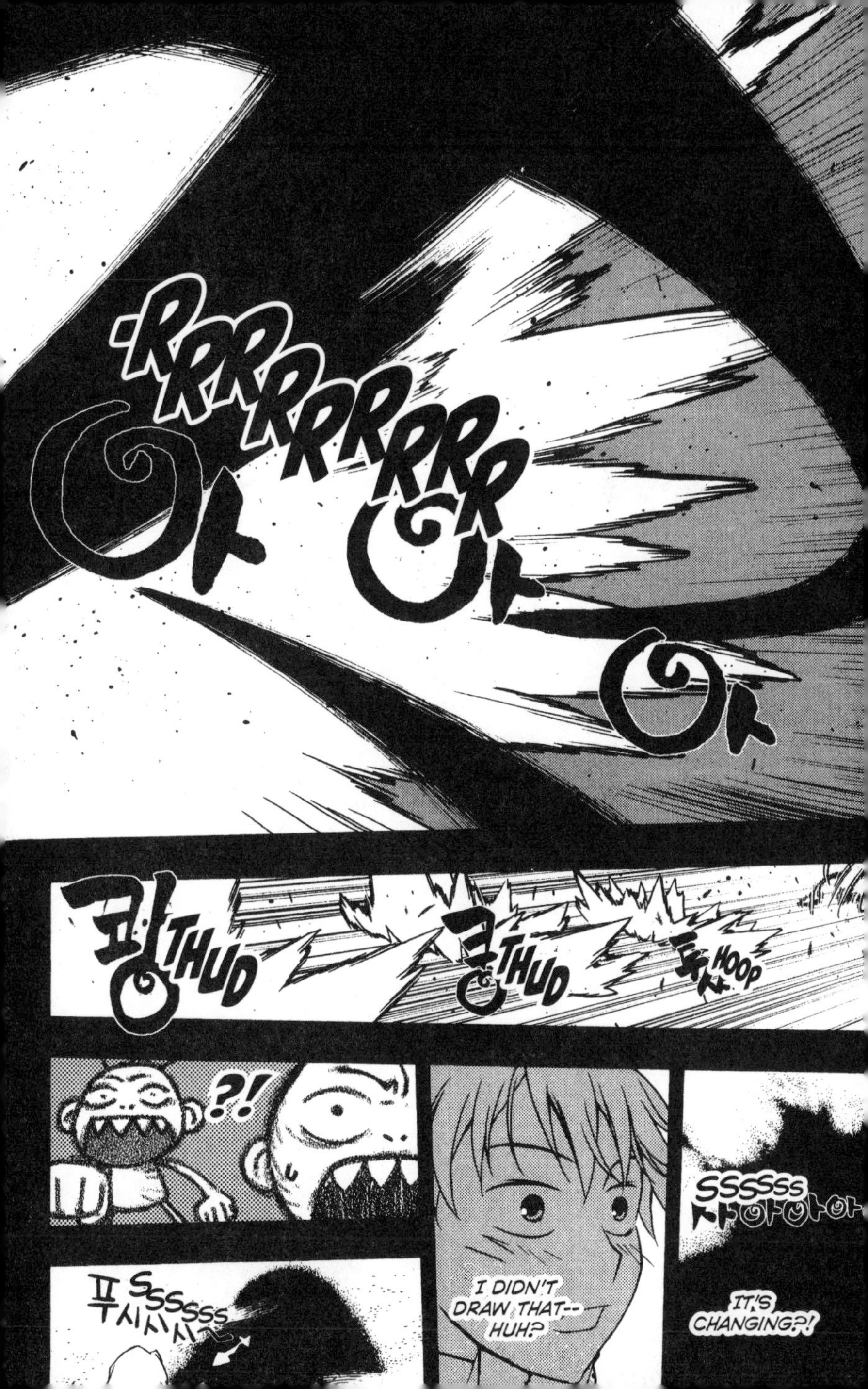

RRRRRRRRRR
아아아
쾅 THUD
쿵 THUD
HOOP
?!
I DIDN'T DRAW THAT-- HUH?
SSSSSS
사아아아
IT'S CHANGING?!
푸시시시
SSSSSSS

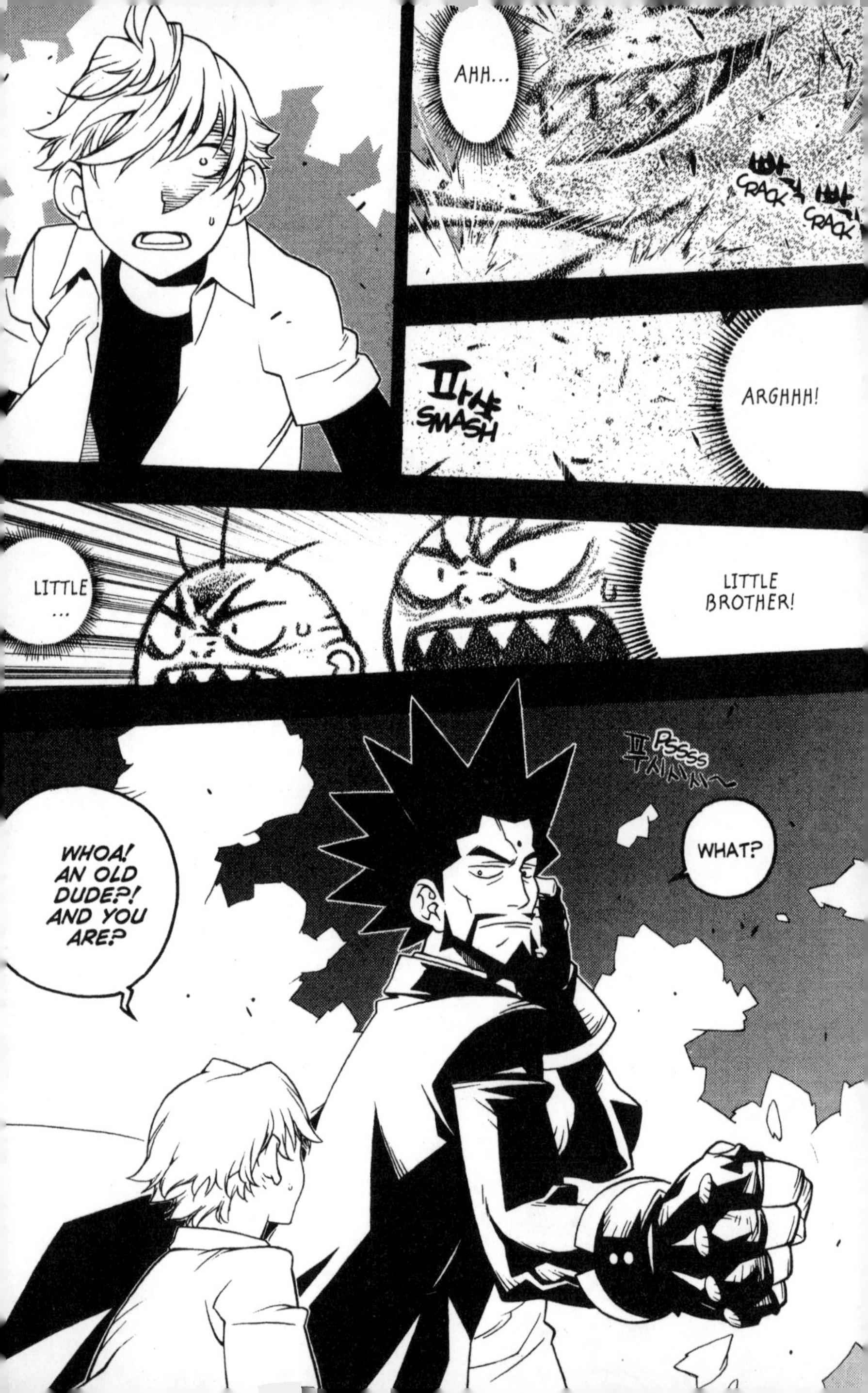
AHH...
CRACK
CRACK
SMASH
ARGHHH!
LITTLE ...
LITTLE BROTHER!
PSSSS
WHOA! AN OLD DUDE?! AND YOU ARE?
WHAT?

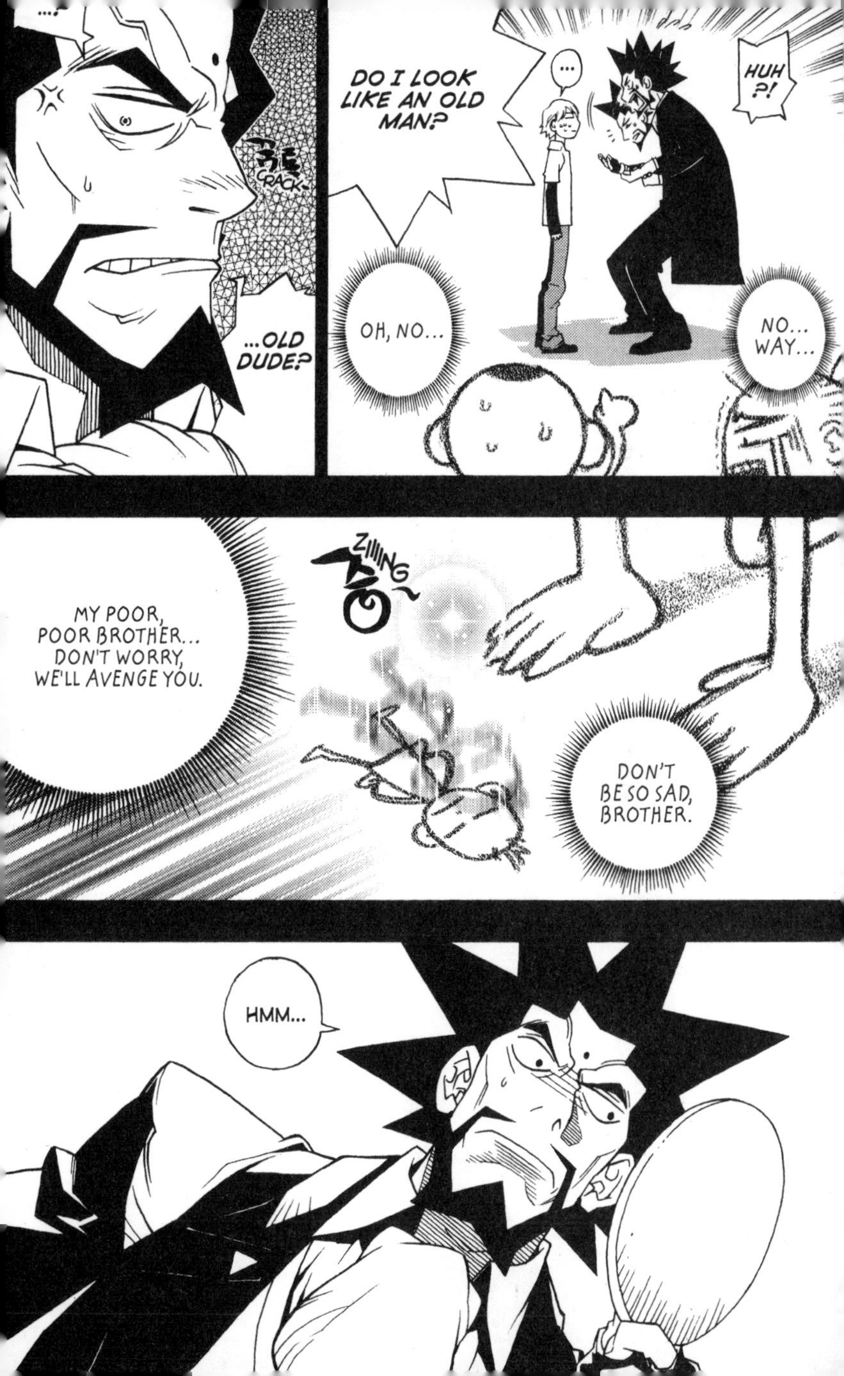
HUH ?!
...
DO I LOOK LIKE AN OLD MAN?
NO... WAY...
OH, NO...
...
CRACK
...OLD DUDE?
ZIIING
DON'T BE SO SAD, BROTHER.
MY POOR, POOR BROTHER... DON'T WORRY, WE'LL AVENGE YOU.
HMM...

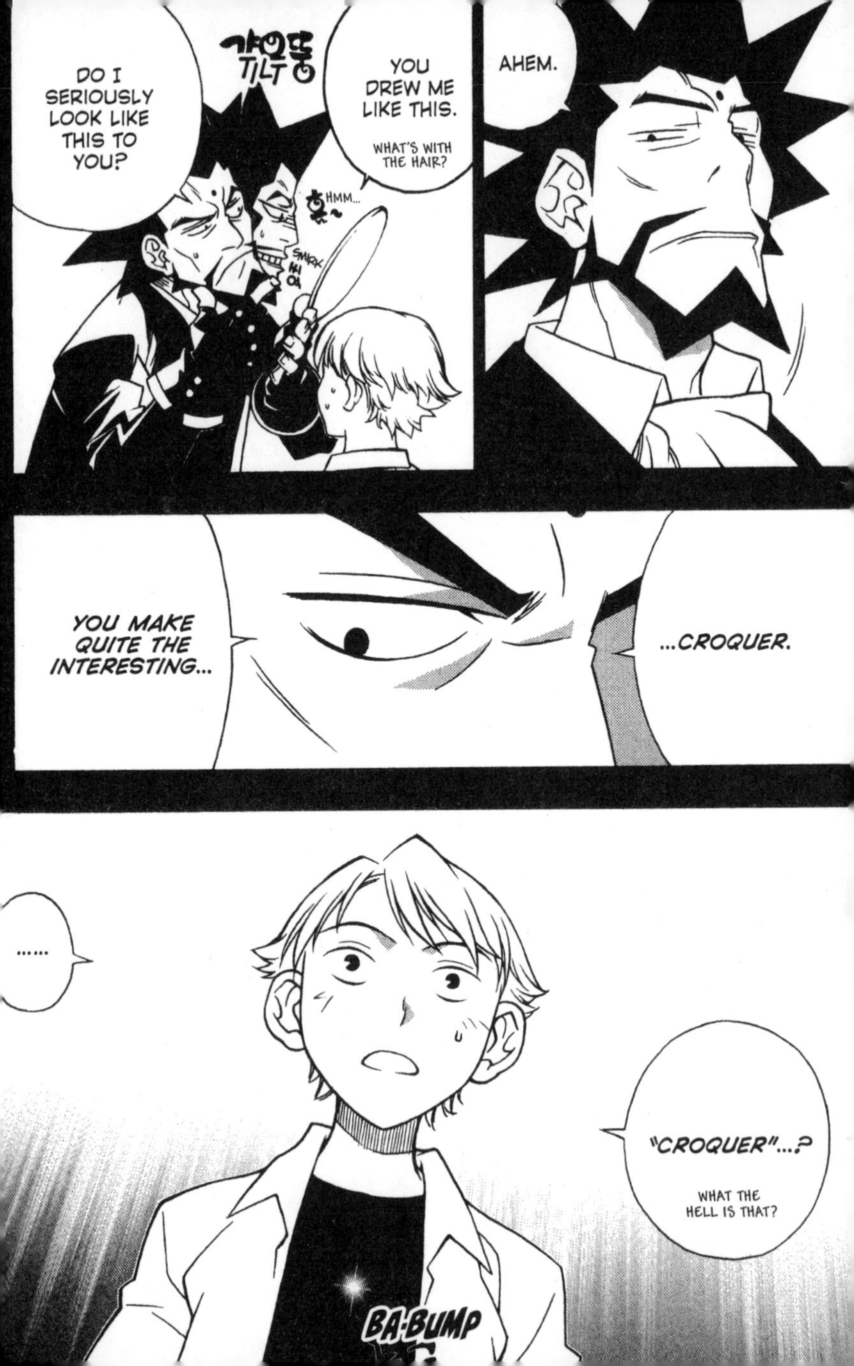
DO I SERIOUSLY LOOK LIKE THIS TO YOU?
TILT
YOU DREW ME LIKE THIS.
WHAT'S WITH THE HAIR?
HMM...
SMIRK
AHEM.
YOU MAKE QUITE THE INTERESTING...
...CROQUER.
......
"CROQUER"...?
WHAT THE HELL IS THAT?
BA-BUMP

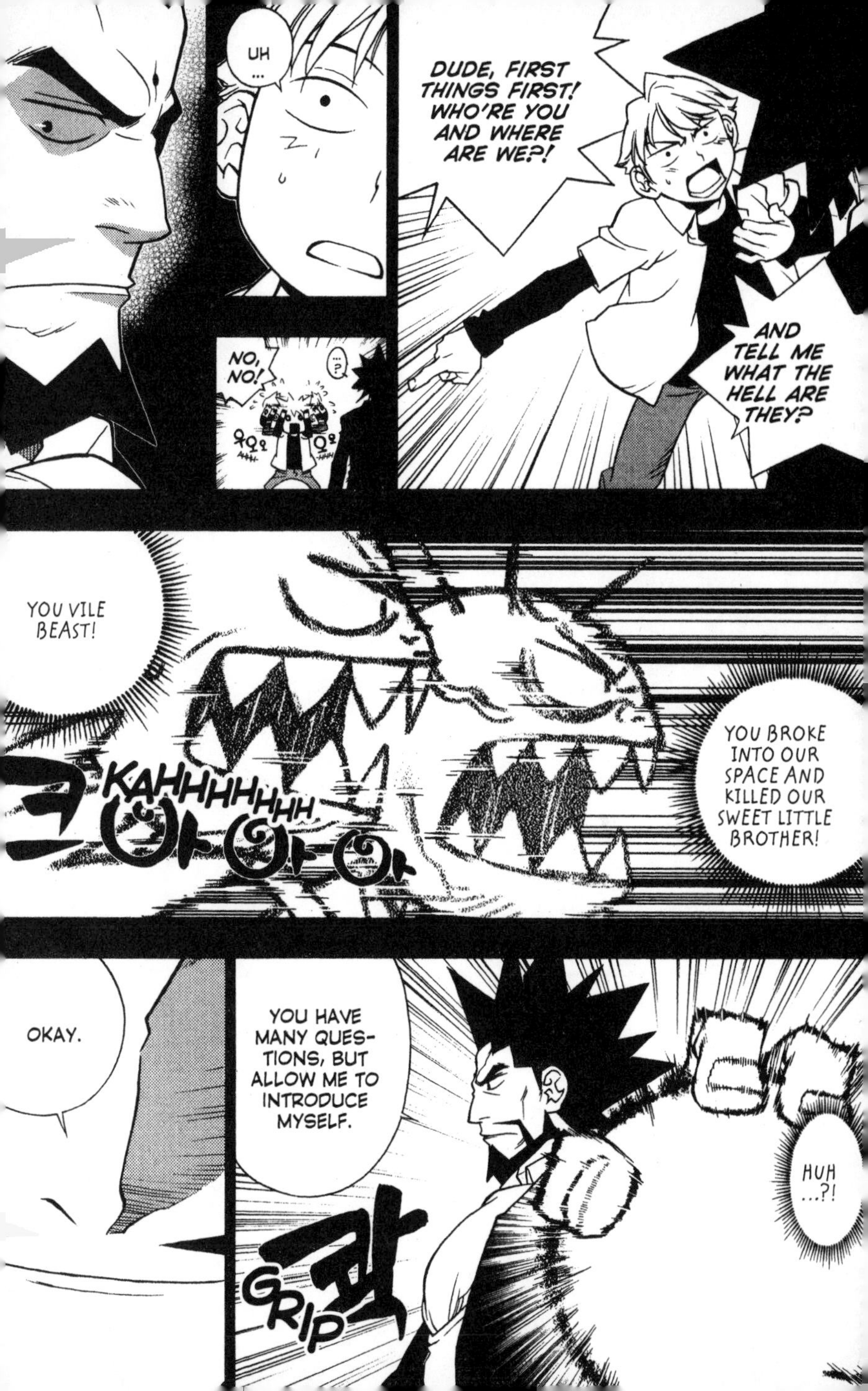
UH ...
DUDE, FIRST THINGS FIRST! WHO'RE YOU AND WHERE ARE WE?!
AND TELL ME WHAT THE HELL ARE THEY?
NO, NO!
...?
YOU BROKE INTO OUR SPACE AND KILLED OUR SWEET LITTLE BROTHER!
YOU VILE BEAST!
KAHHHHHHHH
HUH ...?!
YOU HAVE MANY QUES-TIONS, BUT ALLOW ME TO INTRODUCE MYSELF.
OKAY.
GRIP

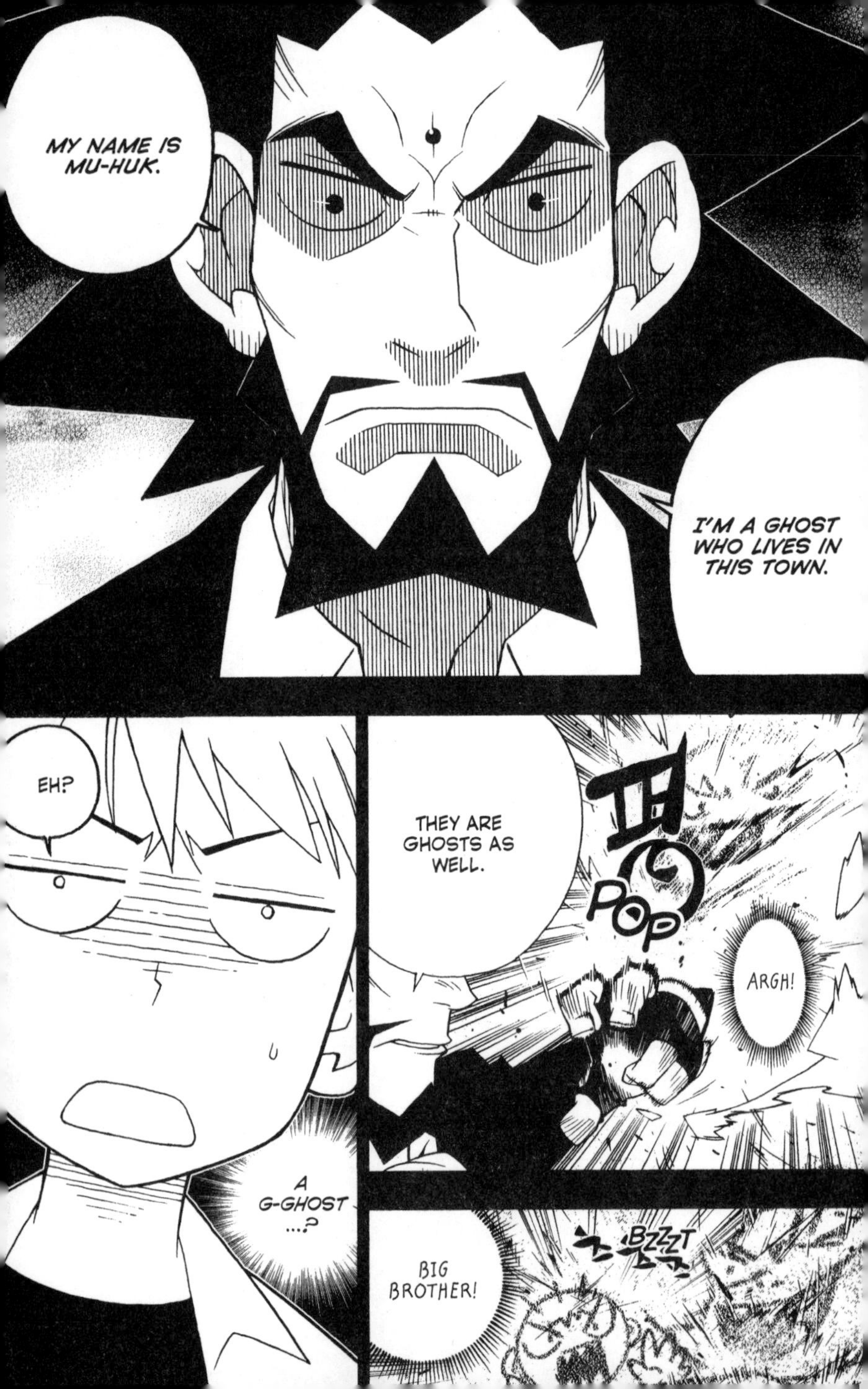
MY NAME IS MU-HUK.
I'M A GHOST WHO LIVES IN THIS TOWN.
EH?
A G-GHOST ...?
THEY ARE GHOSTS AS WELL.
POP
ARGH!
BIG BROTHER!
BZZZT

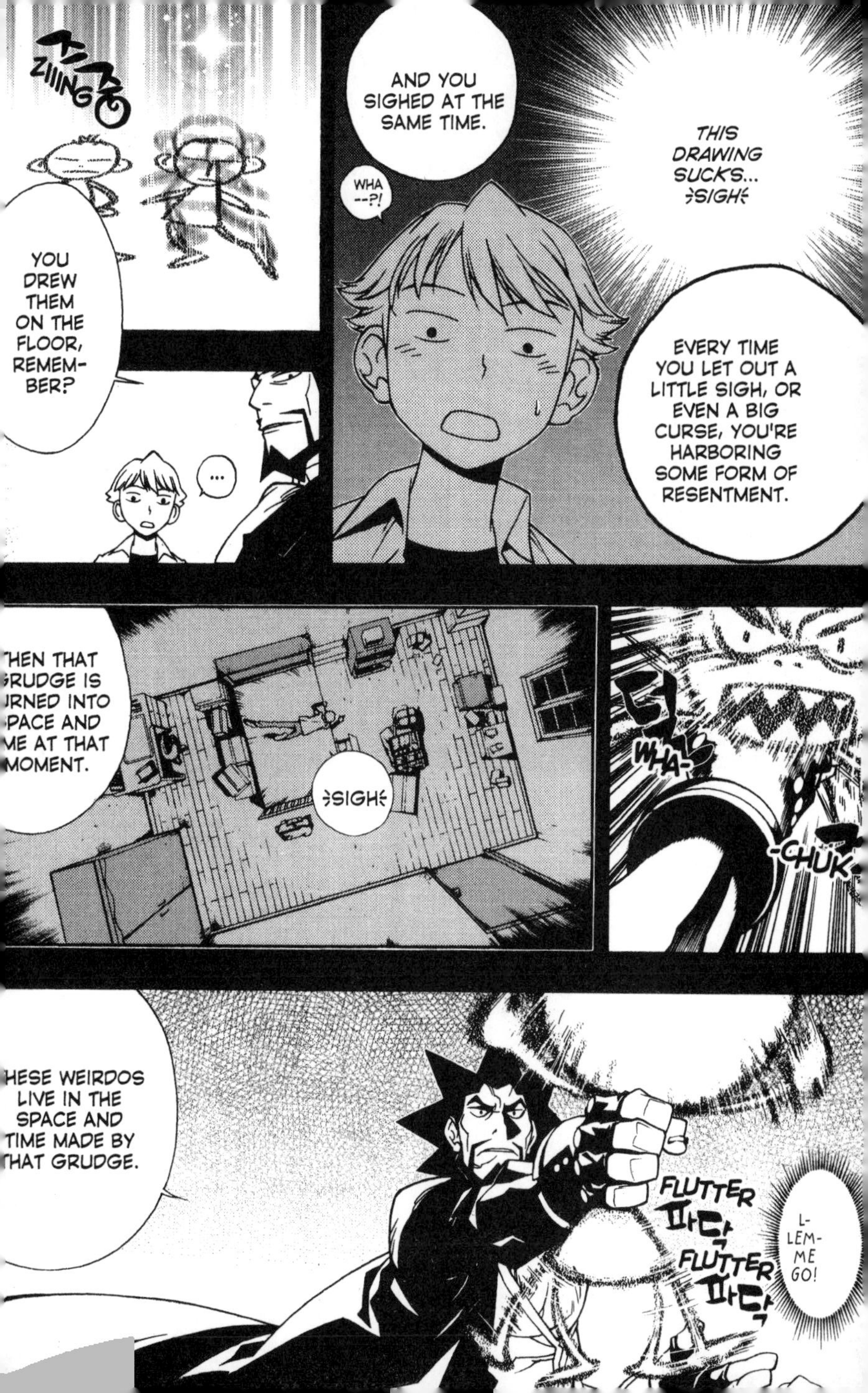
ZIIING
YOU DREW THEM ON THE FLOOR, REMEMBER?
...
AND YOU SIGHED AT THE SAME TIME.
WHA--?!
THIS DRAWING SUCKS... SIGH
EVERY TIME YOU LET OUT A LITTLE SIGH, OR EVEN A BIG CURSE, YOU'RE HARBORING SOME FORM OF RESENTMENT.
HEN THAT RUDGE IS RNED INTO PACE AND ME AT THAT MOMENT.
SIGH
WHA-
-CHUK-
HESE WEIRDOS LIVE IN THE SPACE AND TIME MADE BY HAT GRUDGE.
FLUTTER 파닥
FLUTTER 파닥
L-LEMME GO!

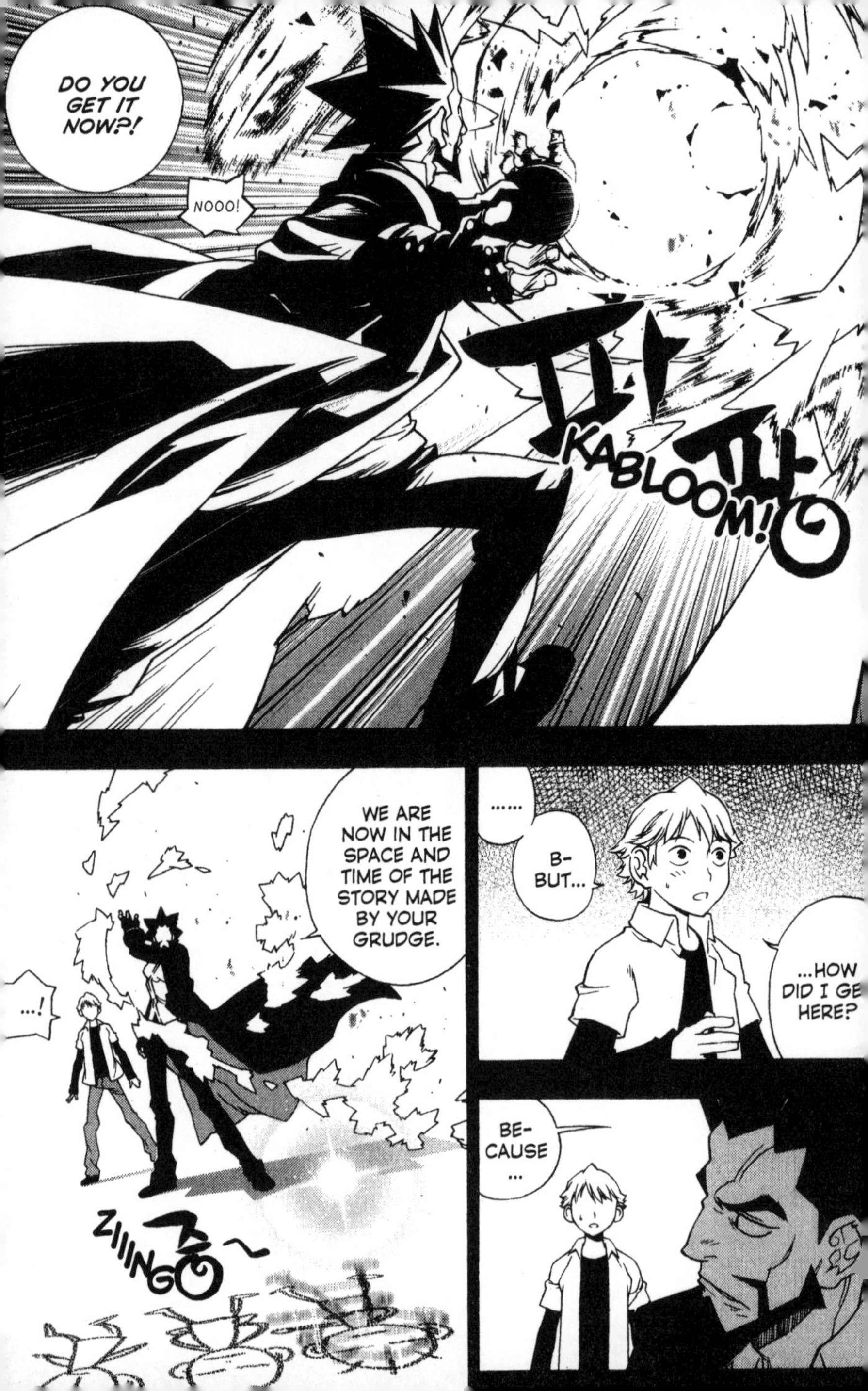

DO YOU GET IT NOW?!
NOOO!
KABLOOM!
......
B-BUT...
...HOW DID I GE HERE?
BE-CAUSE ...
WE ARE NOW IN THE SPACE AND TIME OF THE STORY MADE BY YOUR GRUDGE.
...!
ZIIING

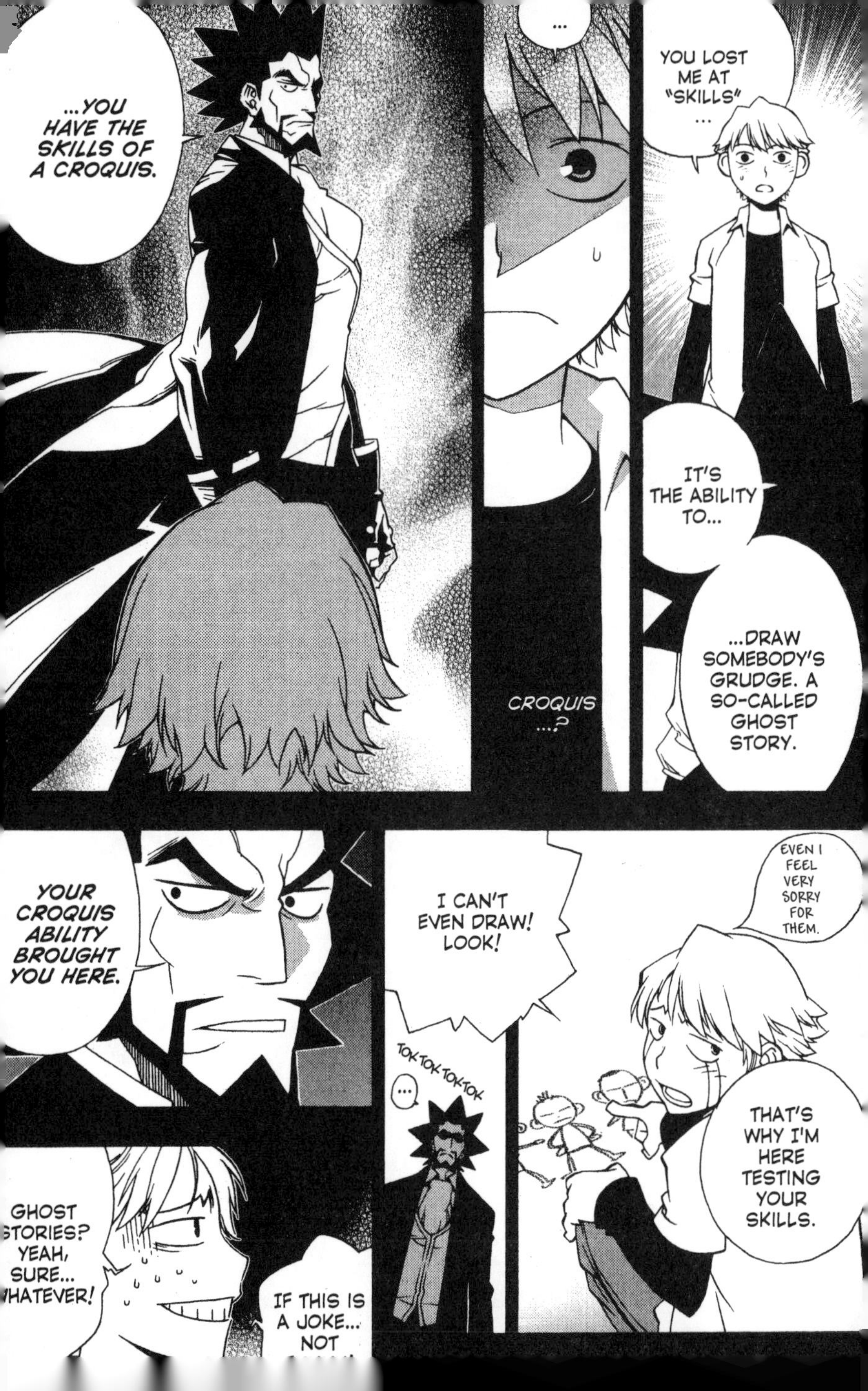
...YOU HAVE THE SKILLS OF A CROQUIS.
...
YOU LOST ME AT "SKILLS"...
IT'S THE ABILITY TO...
CROQUIS ...?
...DRAW SOMEBODY'S GRUDGE. A SO-CALLED GHOST STORY.
YOUR CROQUIS ABILITY BROUGHT YOU HERE.
GHOST STORIES? YEAH, SURE... WHATEVER!
IF THIS IS A JOKE... NOT
I CAN'T EVEN DRAW! LOOK!
TOK TOK TOK TOK
...
EVEN I FEEL VERY SORRY FOR THEM.
THAT'S WHY I'M HERE TESTING YOUR SKILLS.

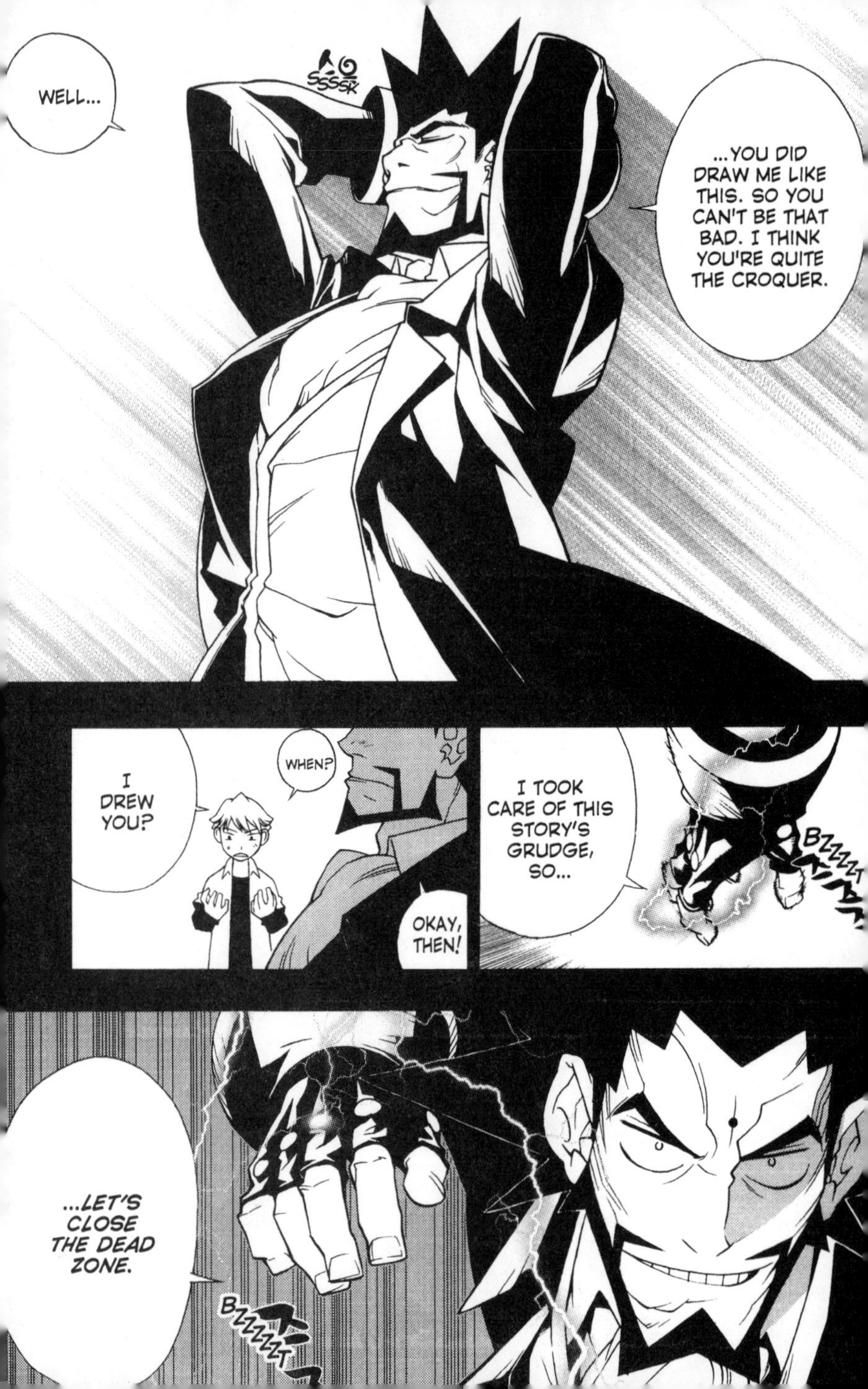

WELL...
SSSSK
...YOU DID DRAW ME LIKE THIS. SO YOU CAN'T BE THAT BAD. I THINK YOU'RE QUITE THE CROQUER.
I DREW YOU?
WHEN?
OKAY, THEN!
I TOOK CARE OF THIS STORY'S GRUDGE, SO...
BZZZZZT
...LET'S CLOSE THE DEAD ZONE.
BZZZZZZT

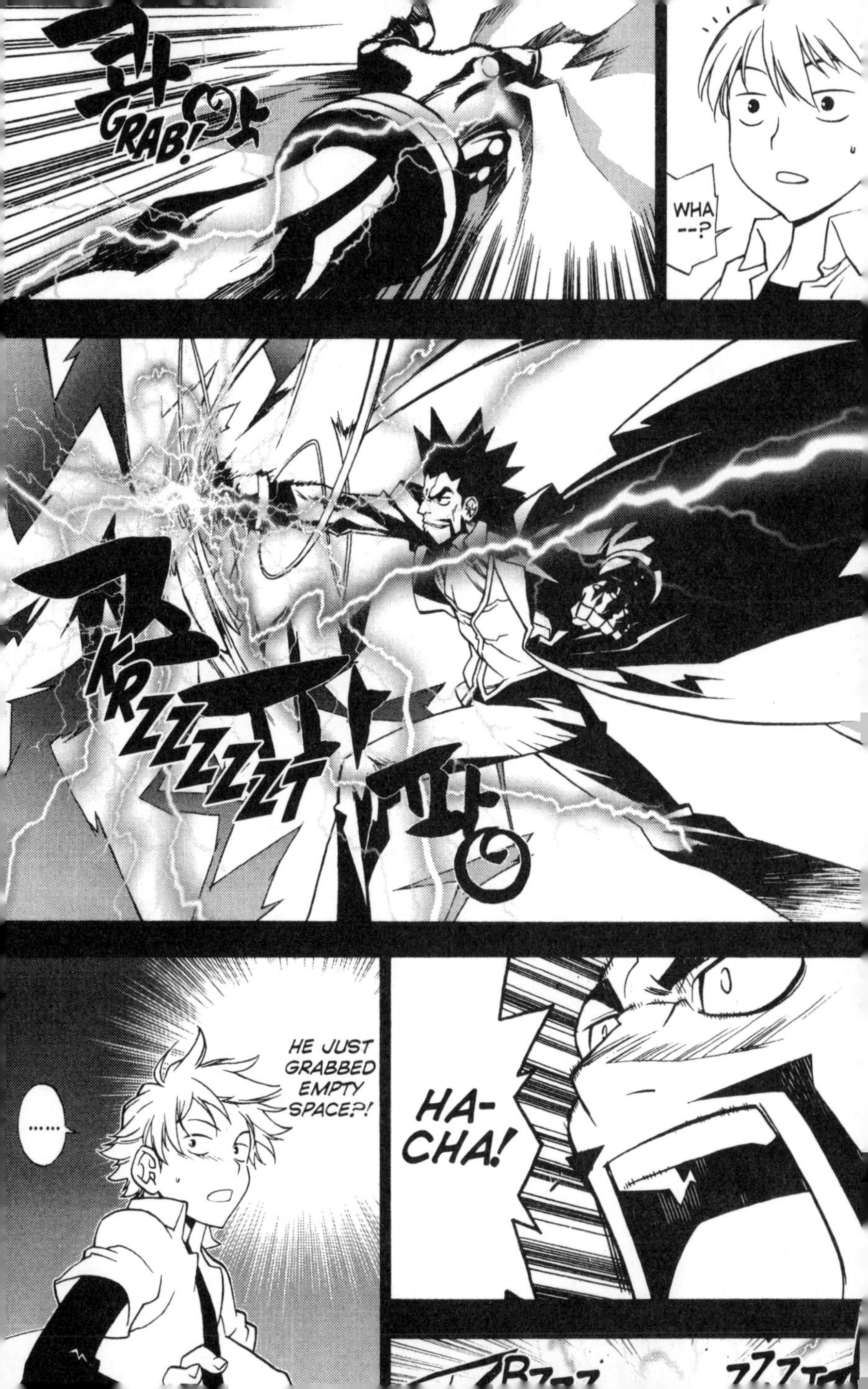
GRAB!
WHA --?
KRZZZZZZT
....
HE JUST GRABBED EMPTY SPACE?!
HA-CHA!

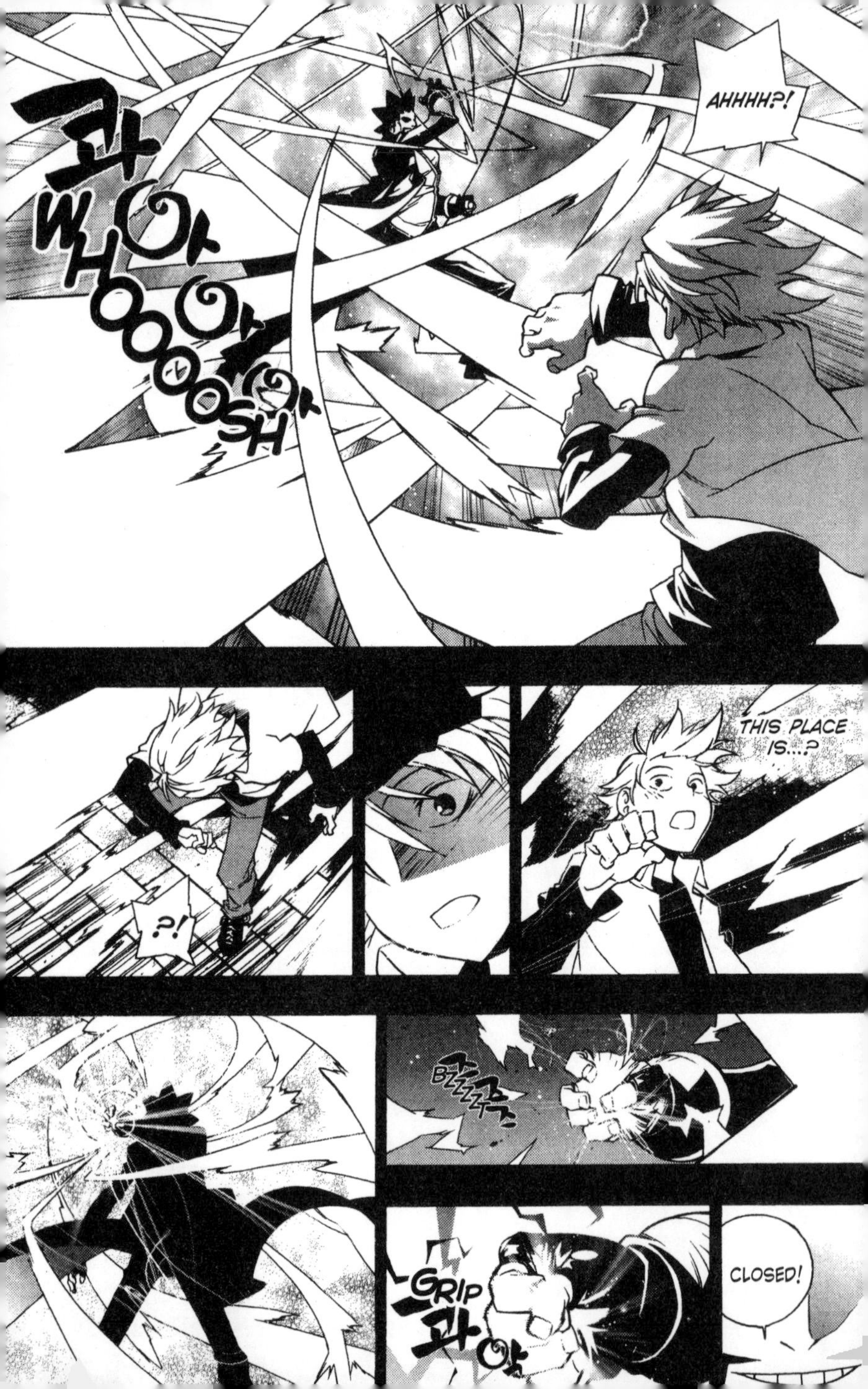

과
WHOOOOOSH
AHHHH?!
?!
THIS PLACE IS...?
BZZZZZT
GRIP
과
CLOSED!

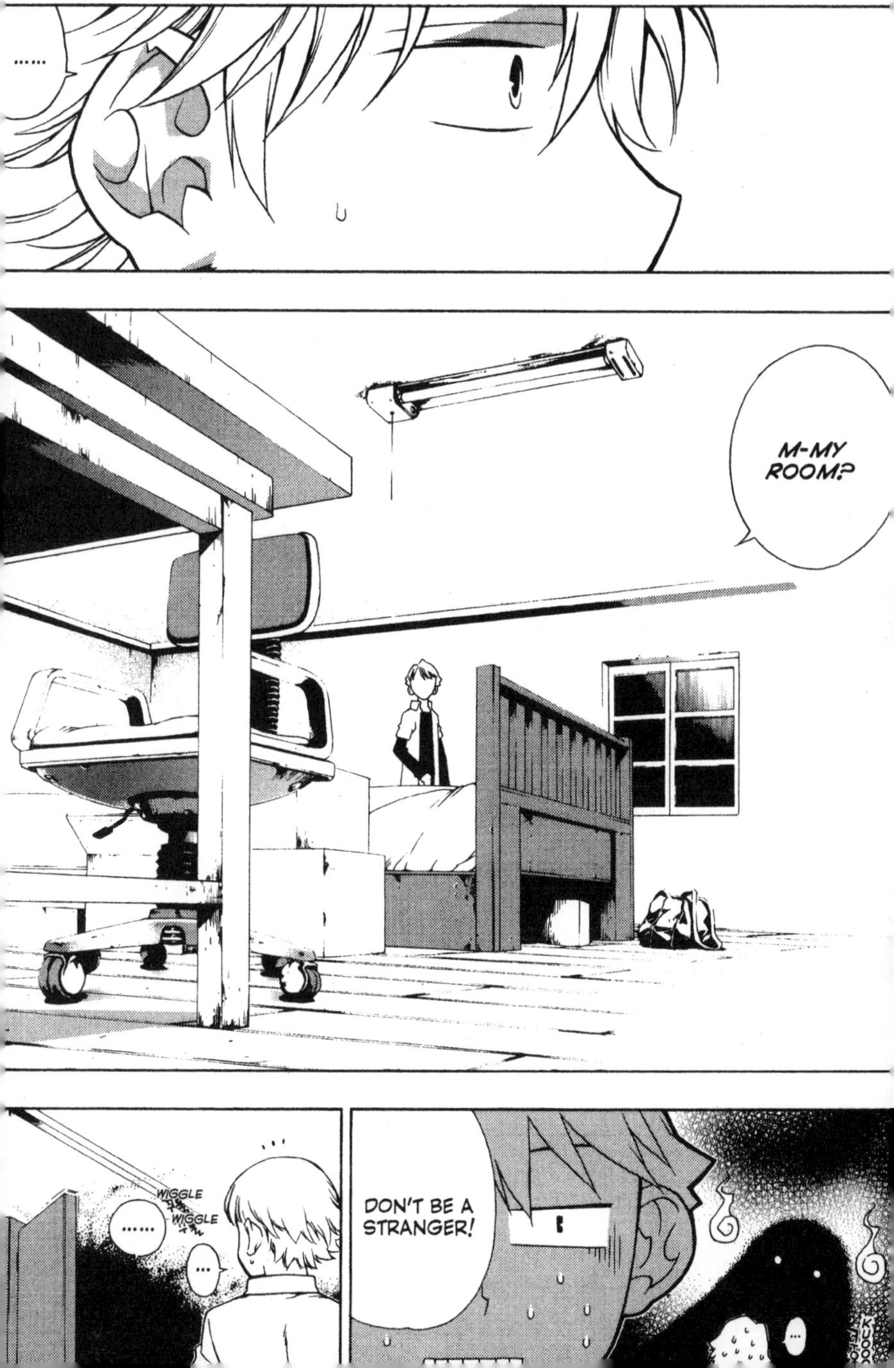

......
M-MY ROOM?
DON'T BE A STRANGER!
...
...
WIGGLE WIGGLE
......
...

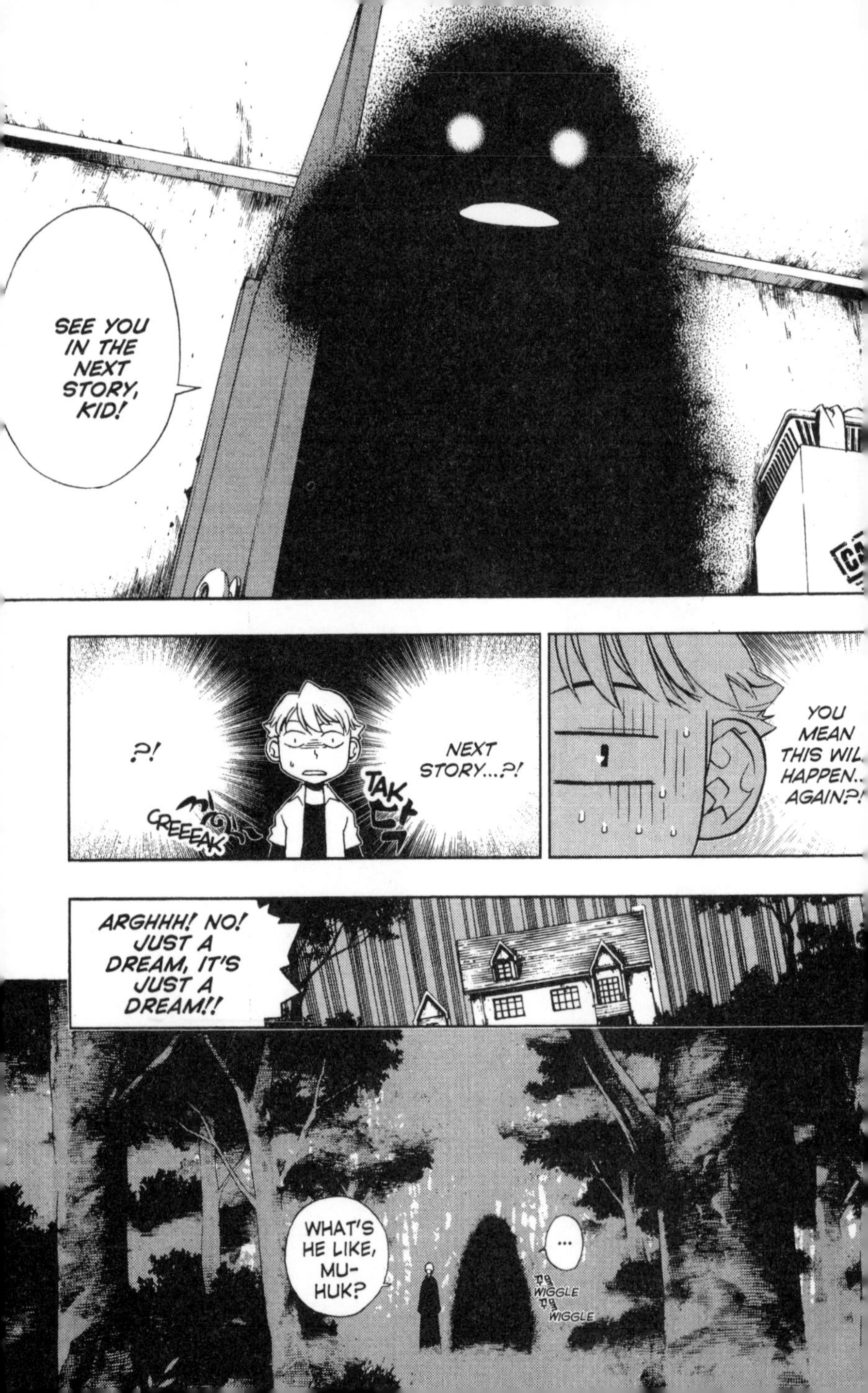
SEE YOU IN THE NEXT STORY, KID!
?!
CREEEAK
TAK
NEXT STORY...?!
YOU MEAN THIS WIL HAPPEN.. AGAIN?!
ARGHHH! NO! JUST A DREAM, IT'S JUST A DREAM!!
WHAT'S HE LIKE, MU-HUK?
...
WIGGLE
WIGGLE

CROQUIS POP

크로키팝

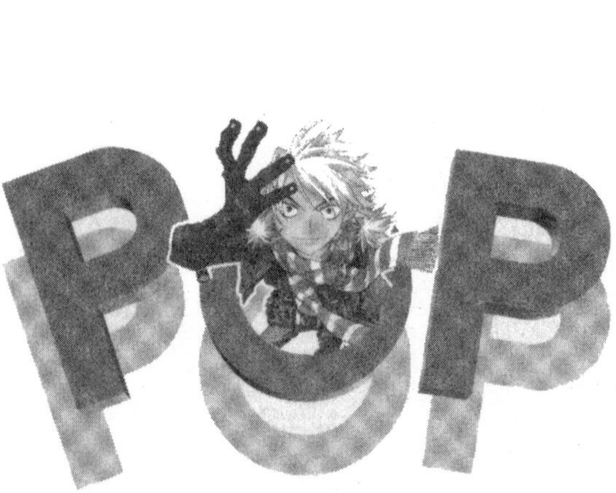
POP

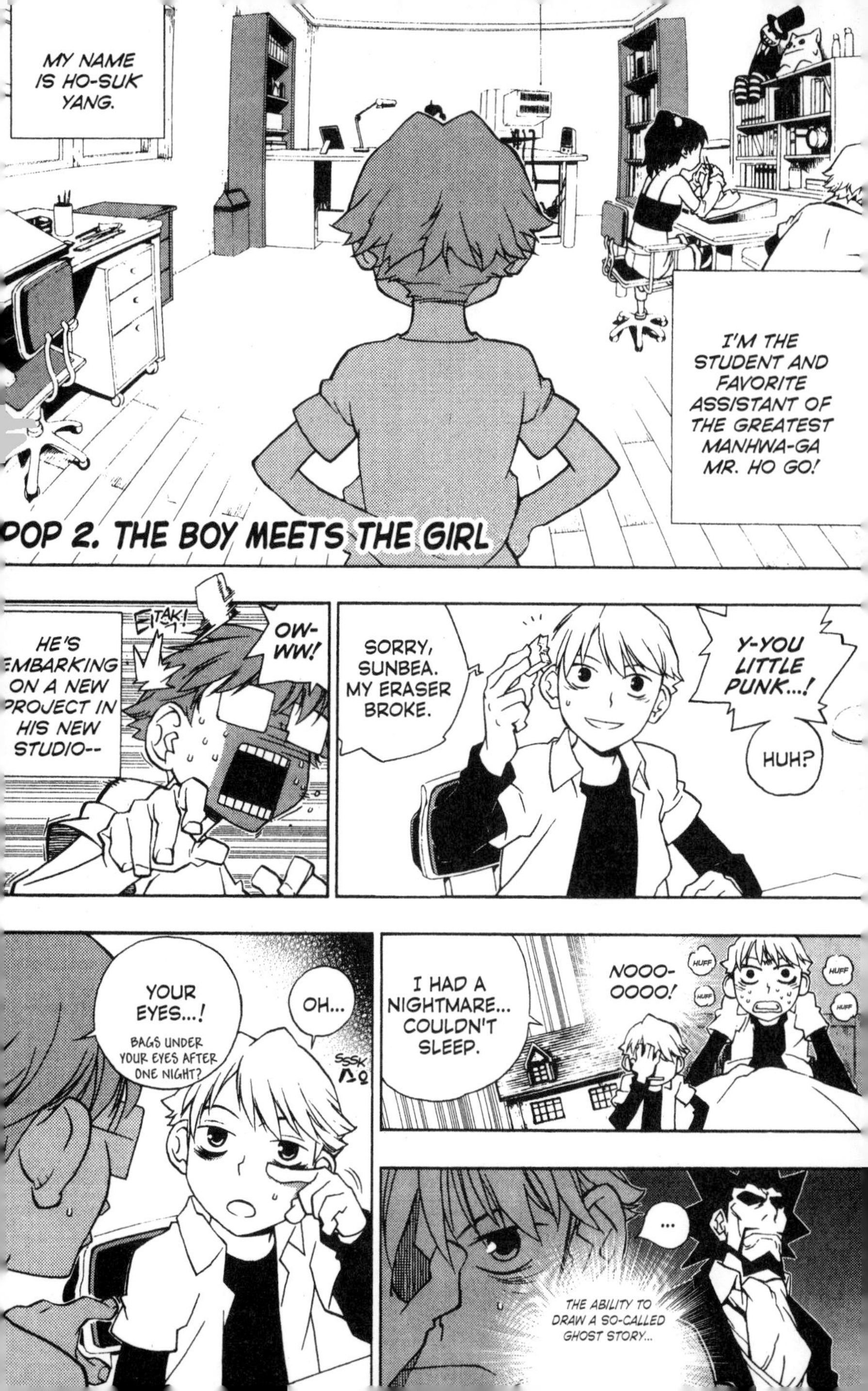
MY NAME IS HO-SUK YANG.
I'M THE STUDENT AND FAVORITE ASSISTANT OF THE GREATEST MANHWA-GA MR. HO GO!
POP 2. THE BOY MEETS THE GIRL
HE'S EMBARKING ON A NEW PROJECT IN HIS NEW STUDIO--
TAK!
OW-WW!
SORRY, SUNBEA. MY ERASER BROKE.
Y-YOU LITTLE PUNK...!
HUH?
YOUR EYES...!
BAGS UNDER YOUR EYES AFTER ONE NIGHT?
OH...
SSSK
I HAD A NIGHTMARE... COULDN'T SLEEP.
NOOO-OOOO!
HUFF
HUFF
HUFF
HUFF
...
THE ABILITY TO DRAW A SO-CALLED GHOST STORY...

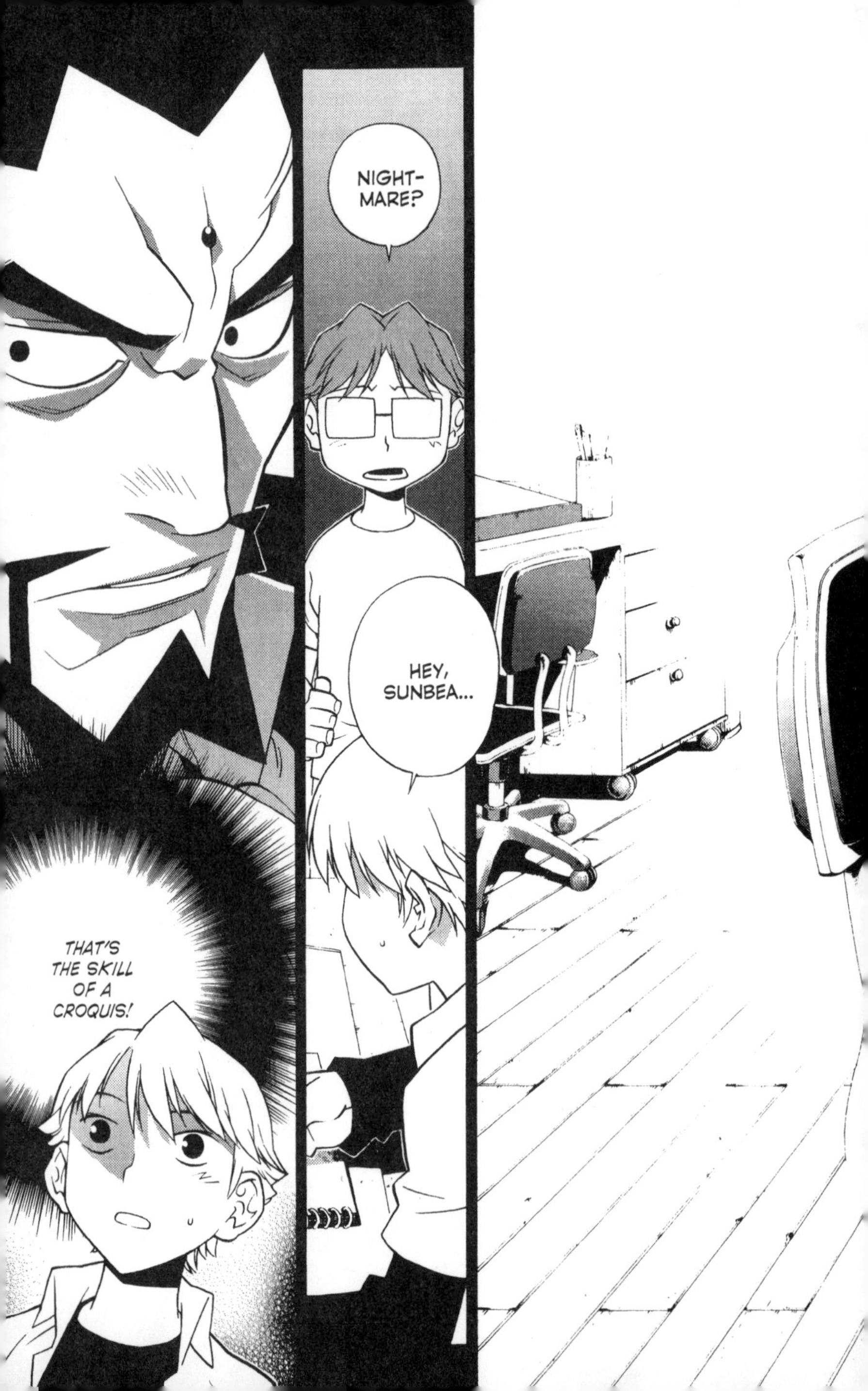
NIGHT-MARE?
HEY, SUNBEA...
THAT'S THE SKILL OF A CROQUIS!

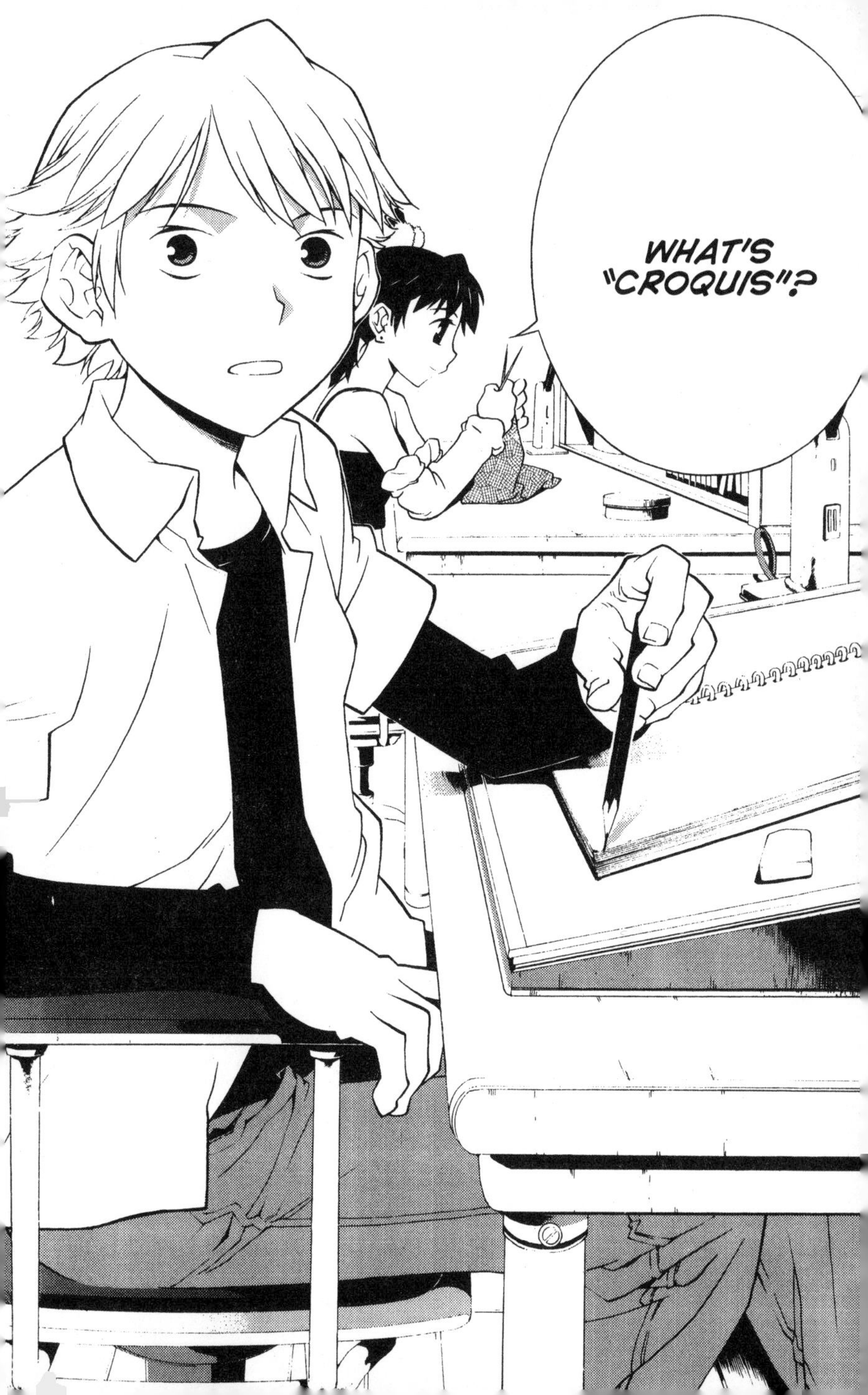
WHAT'S "CROQUIS"?

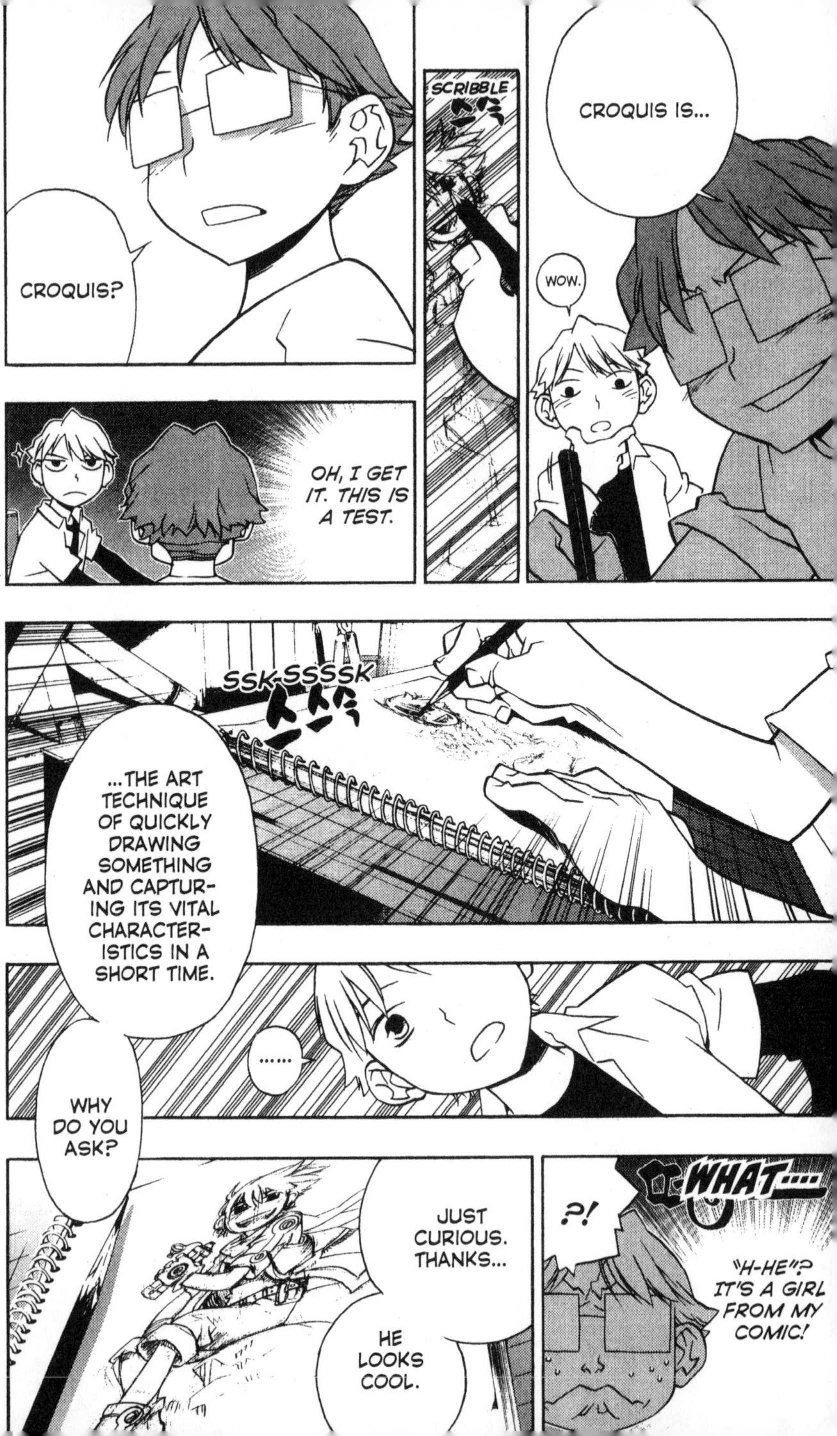
CROQUIS?
OH, I GET IT. THIS IS A TEST.
SCRIBBLE
CROQUIS IS...
WOW.
SSK-SSSSK
...THE ART TECHNIQUE OF QUICKLY DRAWING SOMETHING AND CAPTURING ITS VITAL CHARACTERISTICS IN A SHORT TIME.
......
WHY DO YOU ASK?
JUST CURIOUS. THANKS...
HE LOOKS COOL.
WHAT....
?!
"H-HE"? IT'S A GIRL FROM MY COMIC!

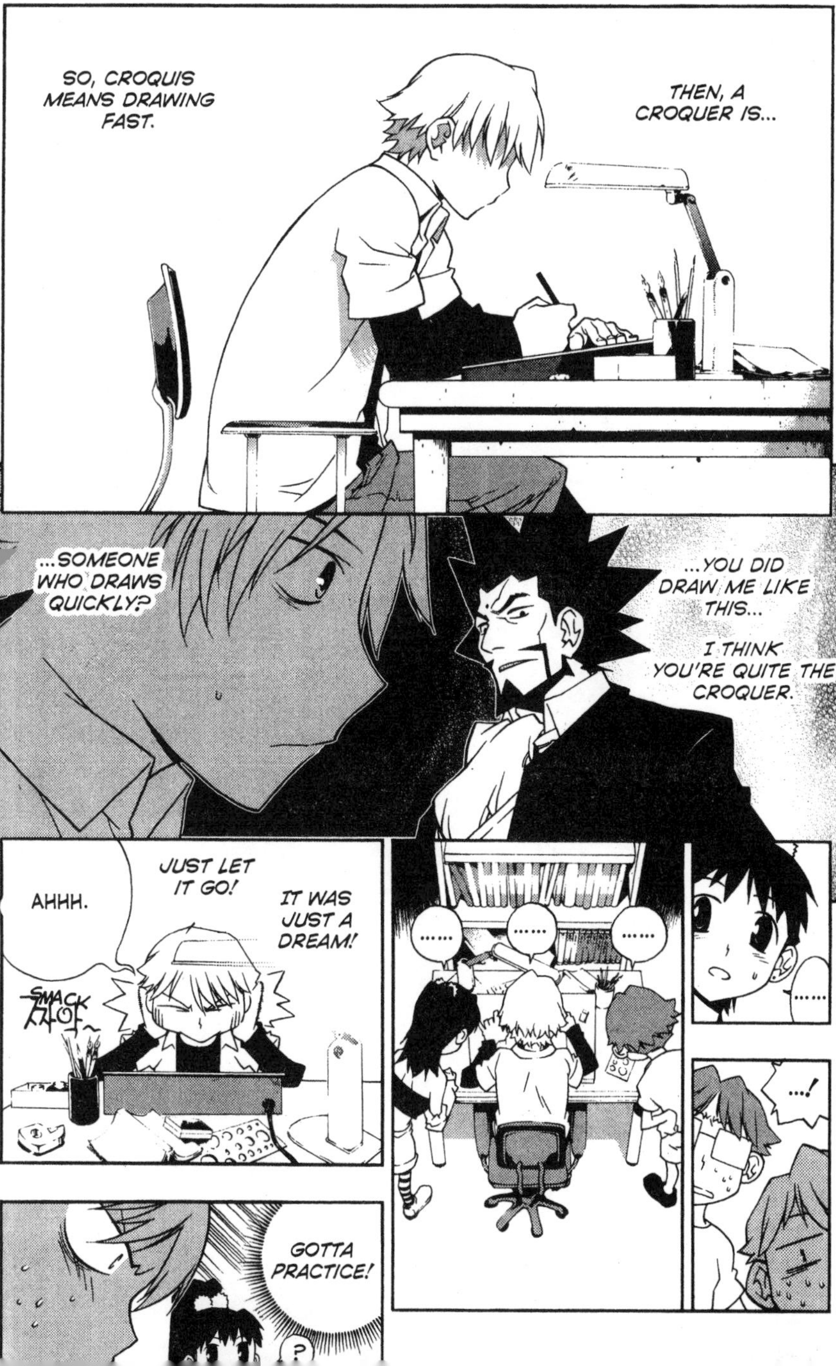

SO, CROQUIS MEANS DRAWING FAST.
THEN, A CROQUER IS...
...SOMEONE WHO DRAWS QUICKLY?
...YOU DID DRAW ME LIKE THIS...
I THINK YOU'RE QUITE THE CROQUER.
AHHH.
JUST LET IT GO!
IT WAS JUST A DREAM!
SMACK
......
......
......
......
...!
GOTTA PRACTICE!
?

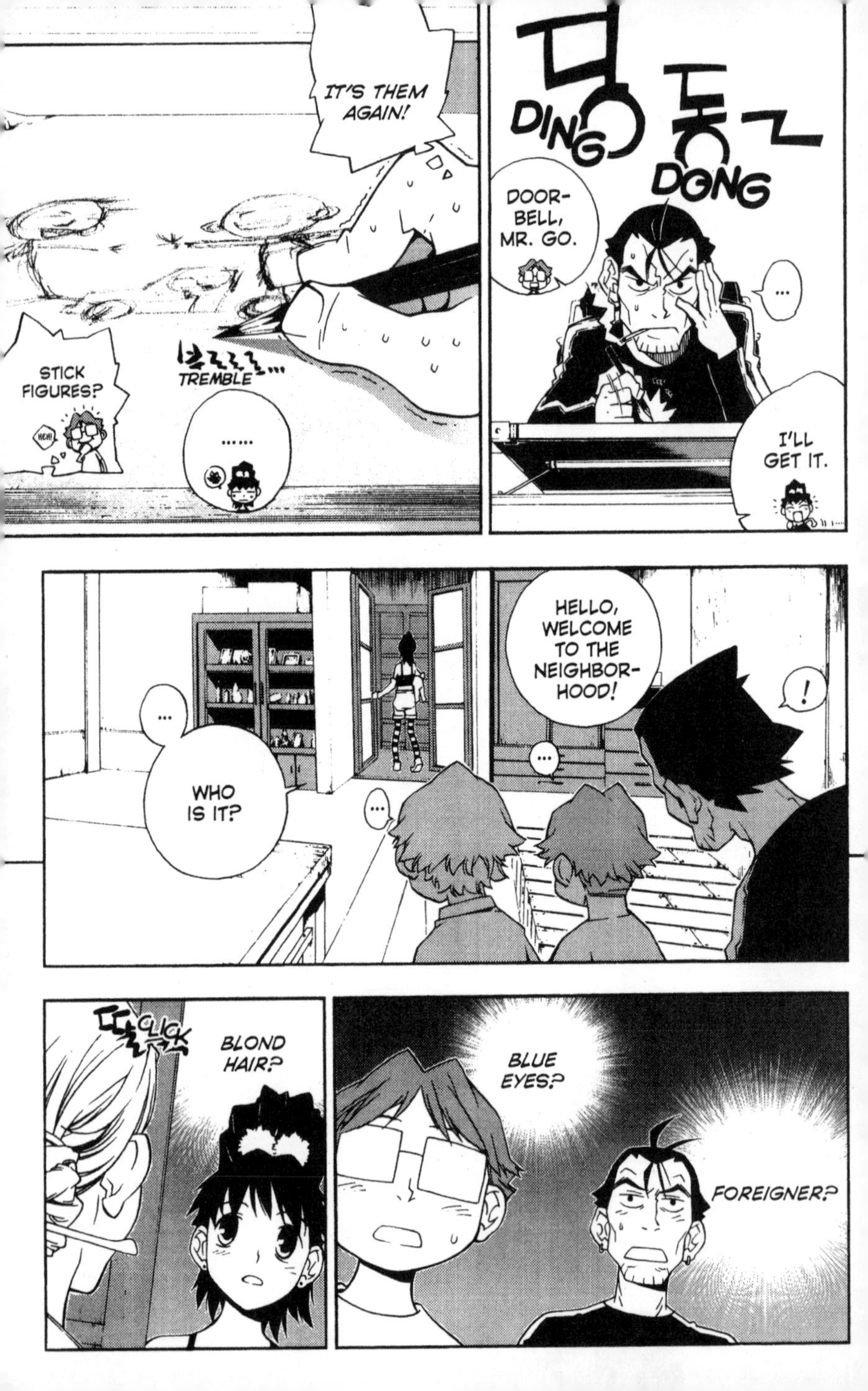

IT'S THEM AGAIN!
STICK FIGURES?
HEH!
TREMBLE
......
DING DONG
DOOR-BELL, MR. GO.
...
I'LL GET IT.
HELLO, WELCOME TO THE NEIGHBOR-HOOD!
...
WHO IS IT?
...
...
!
CLICK
BLOND HAIR?
BLUE EYES?
FOREIGNER?

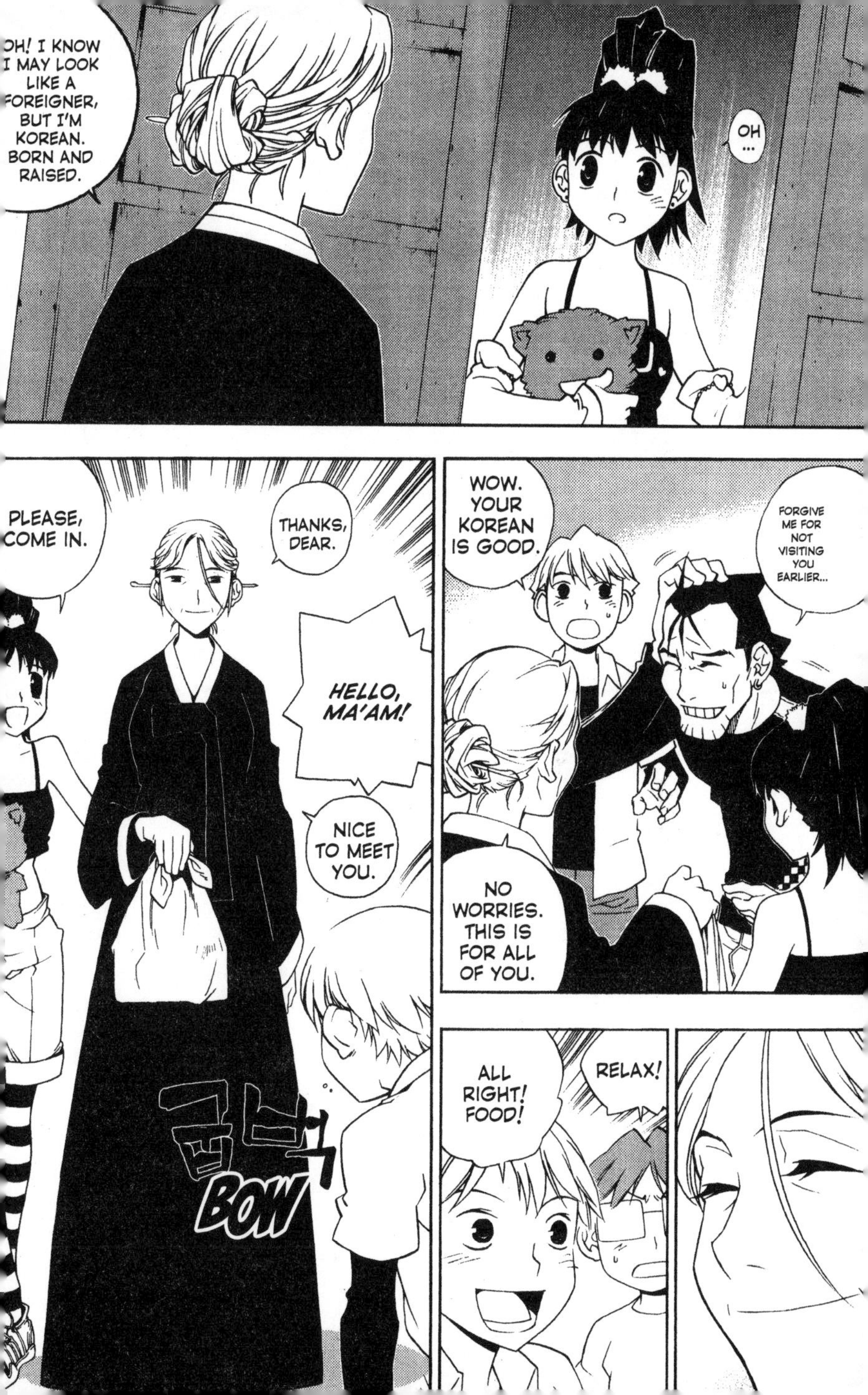
OH! I KNOW I MAY LOOK LIKE A FOREIGNER, BUT I'M KOREAN. BORN AND RAISED.
OH ...
PLEASE, COME IN.
THANKS, DEAR.
HELLO, MA'AM!
NICE TO MEET YOU.
BOW
WOW. YOUR KOREAN IS GOOD.
FORGIVE ME FOR NOT VISITING YOU EARLIER...
NO WORRIES. THIS IS FOR ALL OF YOU.
ALL RIGHT! FOOD!
RELAX!

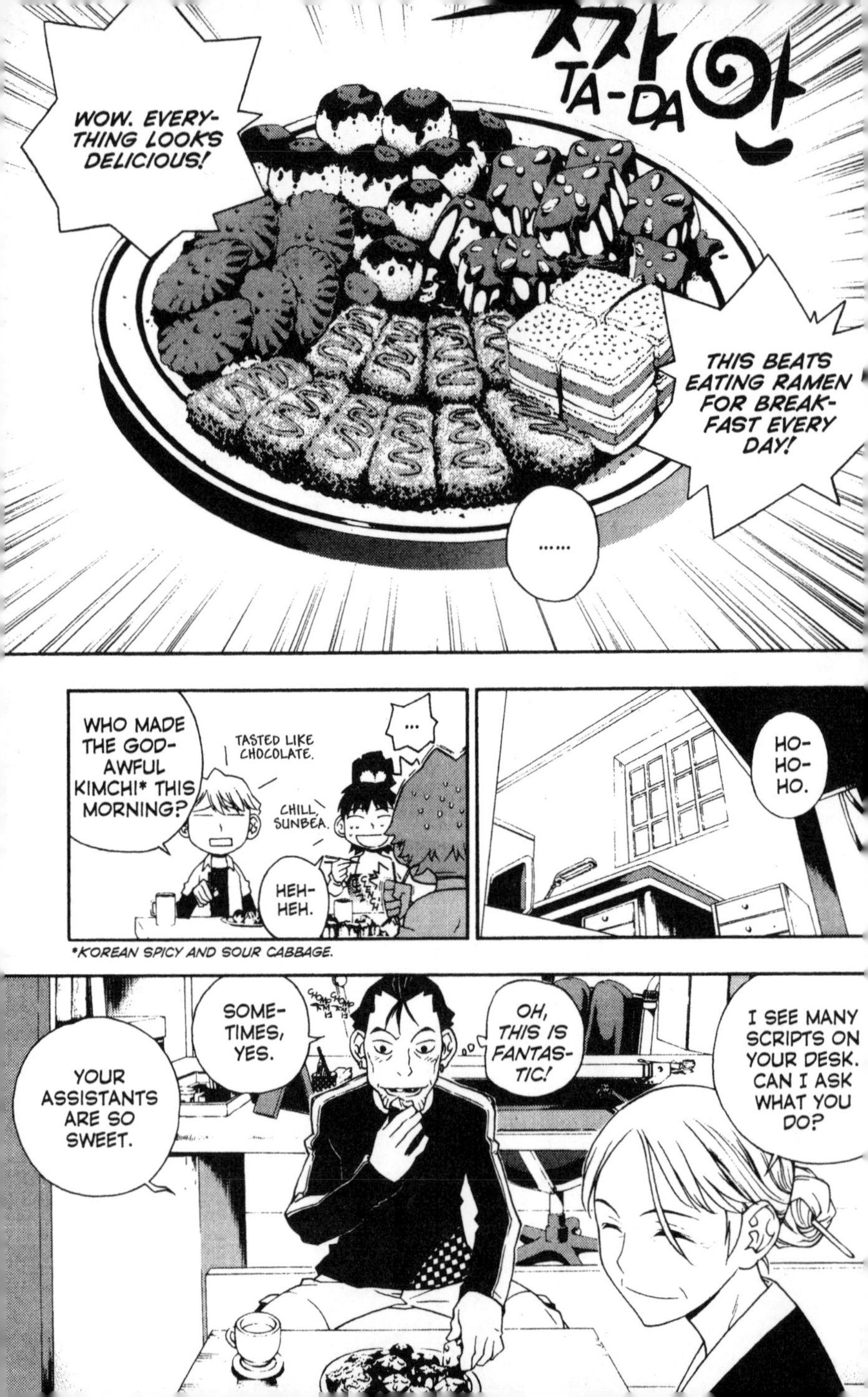
TA-DA
WOW. EVERY-THING LOOKS DELICIOUS!
THIS BEATS EATING RAMEN FOR BREAK-FAST EVERY DAY!
......
WHO MADE THE GOD-AWFUL KIMCHI* THIS MORNING?
TASTED LIKE CHOCOLATE.
...
CHILL, SUNBEA.
HEH-HEH.
HO-HO-HO.
*KOREAN SPICY AND SOUR CABBAGE.
YOUR ASSISTANTS ARE SO SWEET.
SOME-TIMES, YES.
OH, THIS IS FANTAS-TIC!
I SEE MANY SCRIPTS ON YOUR DESK. CAN I ASK WHAT YOU DO?

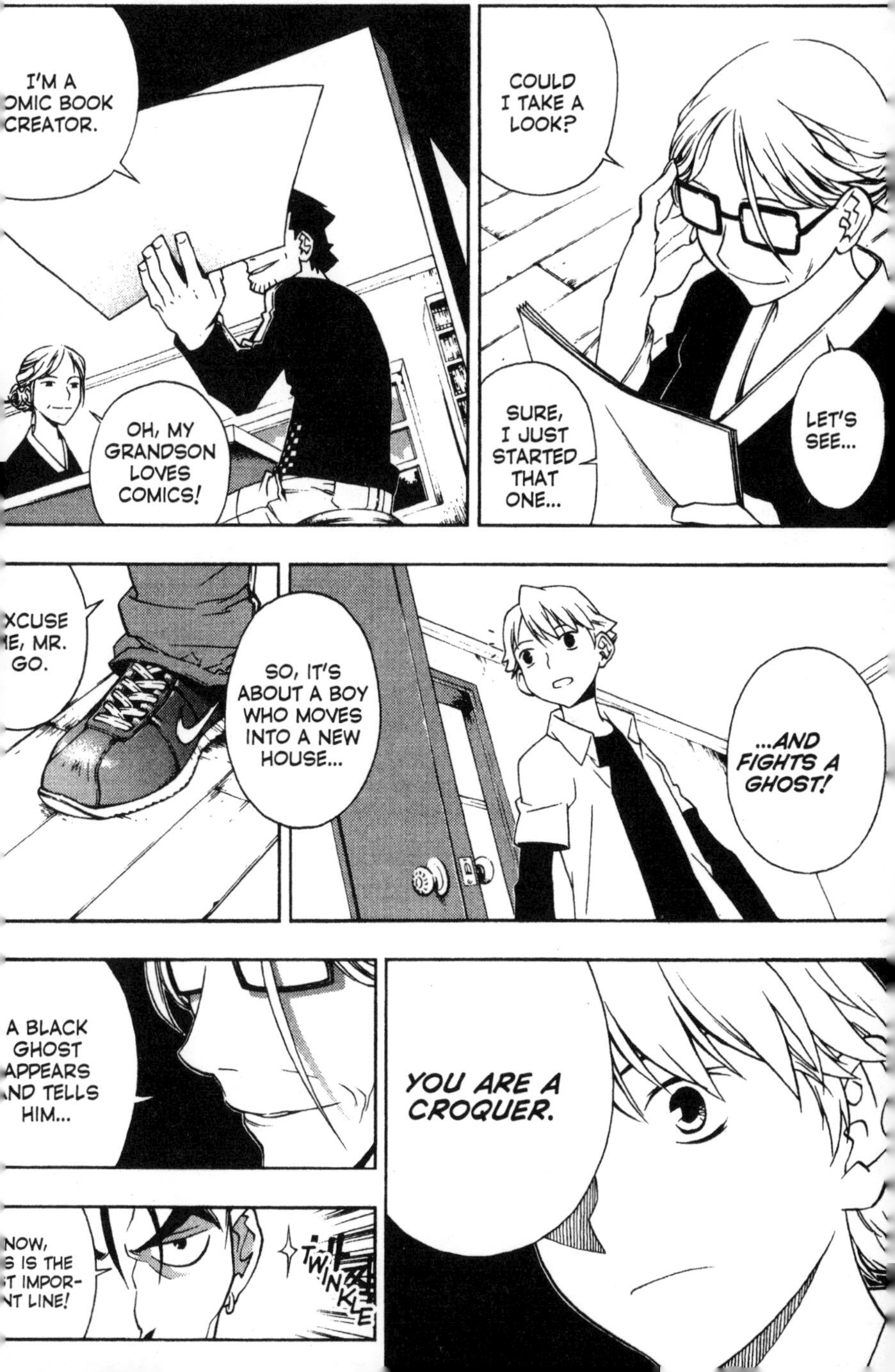

I'M A
OMIC BOOK
CREATOR.
OH, MY GRANDSON LOVES COMICS!
COULD I TAKE A LOOK?
SURE, I JUST STARTED THAT ONE...
LET'S SEE...
XCUSE
IE, MR.
GO.
SO, IT'S ABOUT A BOY WHO MOVES INTO A NEW HOUSE...
...AND FIGHTS A GHOST!
A BLACK
GHOST
APPEARS
ND TELLS
HIM...
NOW,
S IS THE
T IMPOR-
NT LINE!
TWINKLE
YOU ARE A CROQUER.

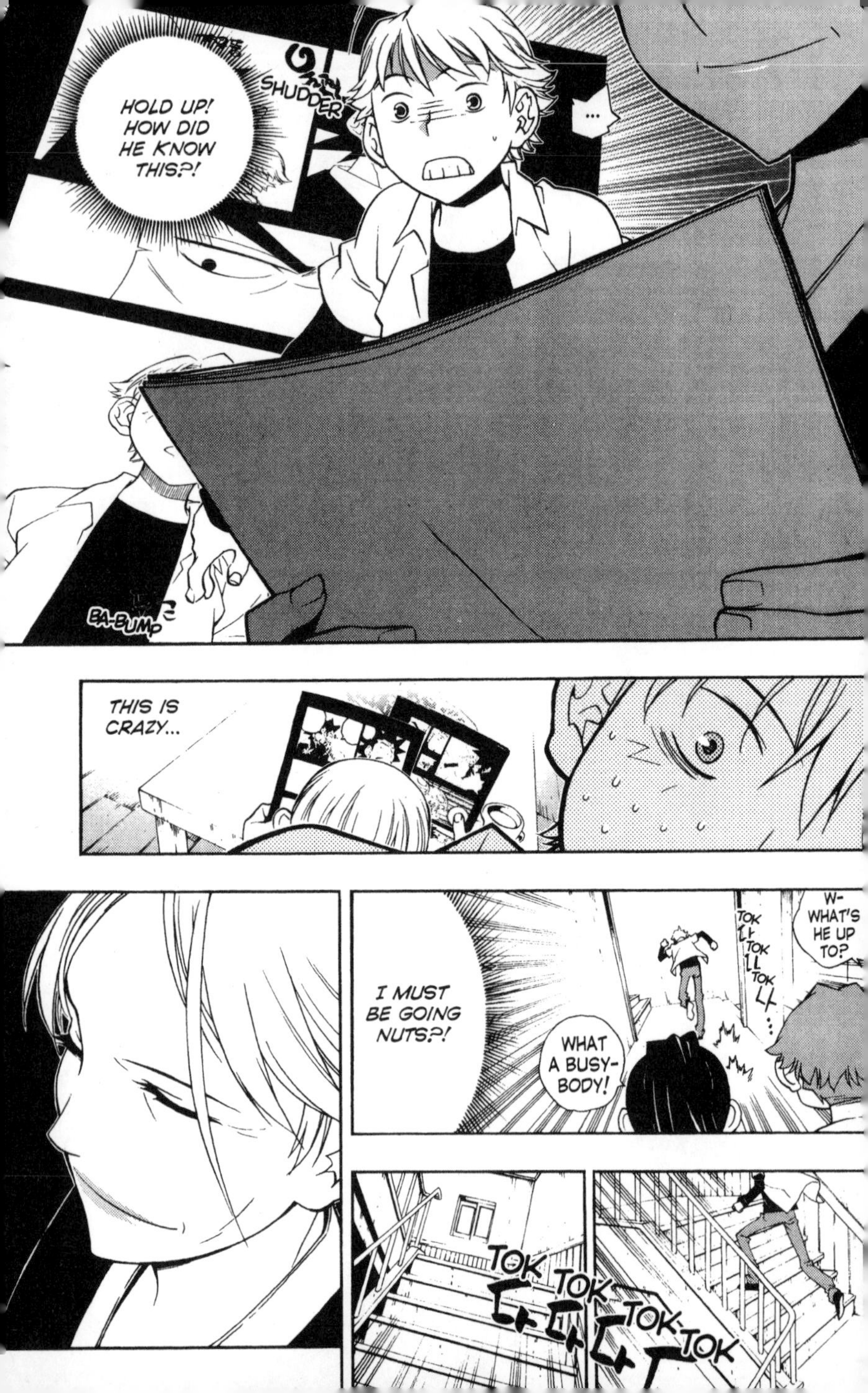
HOLD UP! HOW DID HE KNOW THIS?!
SHUDDER
...
BA-BUMP
THIS IS CRAZY...
I MUST BE GOING NUTS?!
W-WHAT'S HE UP TO?
TOK TOK TOK
...
WHAT A BUSY-BODY!
TOK TOK TOK-TOK

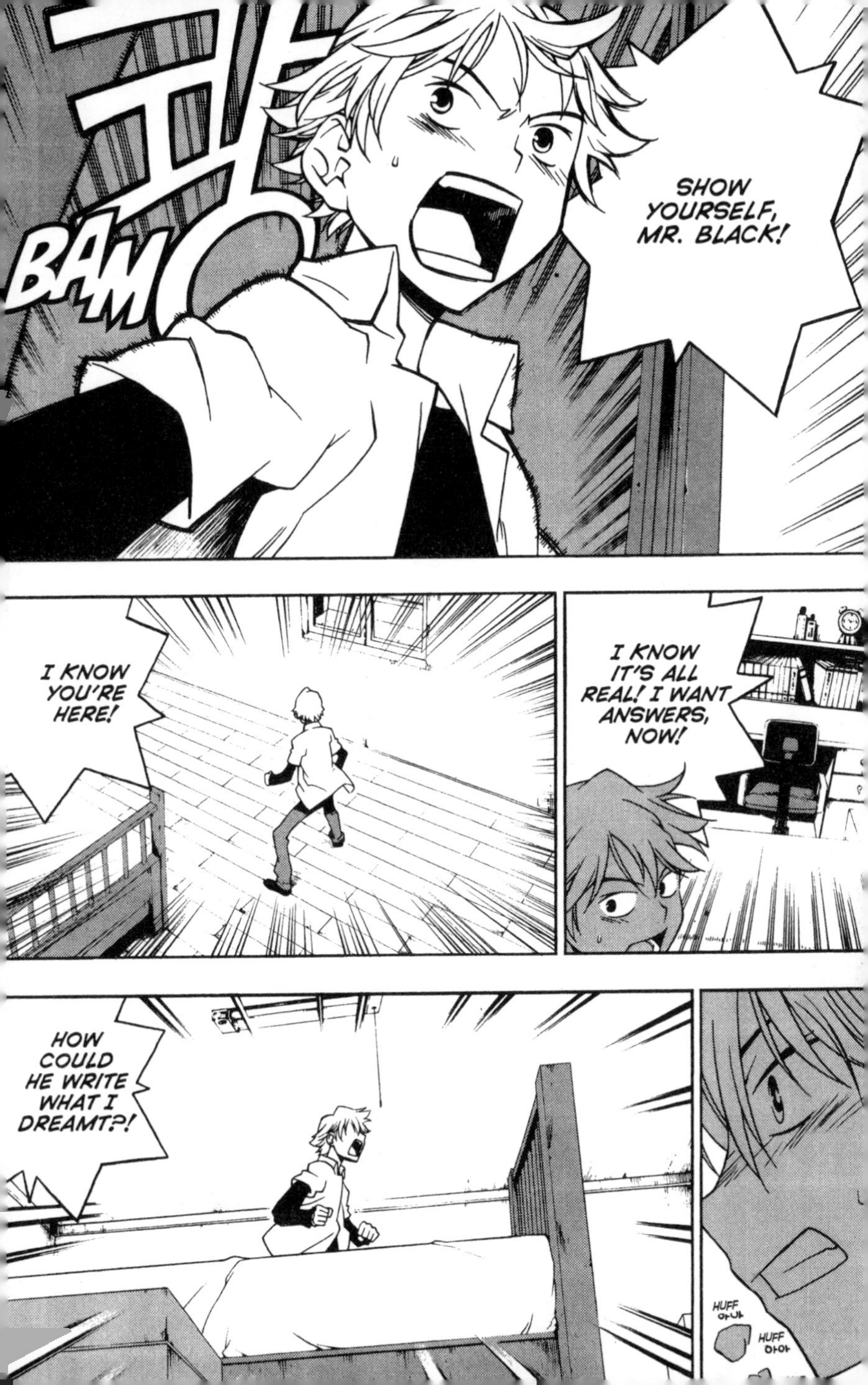
BAM
SHOW YOURSELF, MR. BLACK!
I KNOW YOU'RE HERE!
I KNOW IT'S ALL REAL! I WANT ANSWERS, NOW!
HOW COULD HE WRITE WHAT I DREAMT?!
HUFF
HUFF

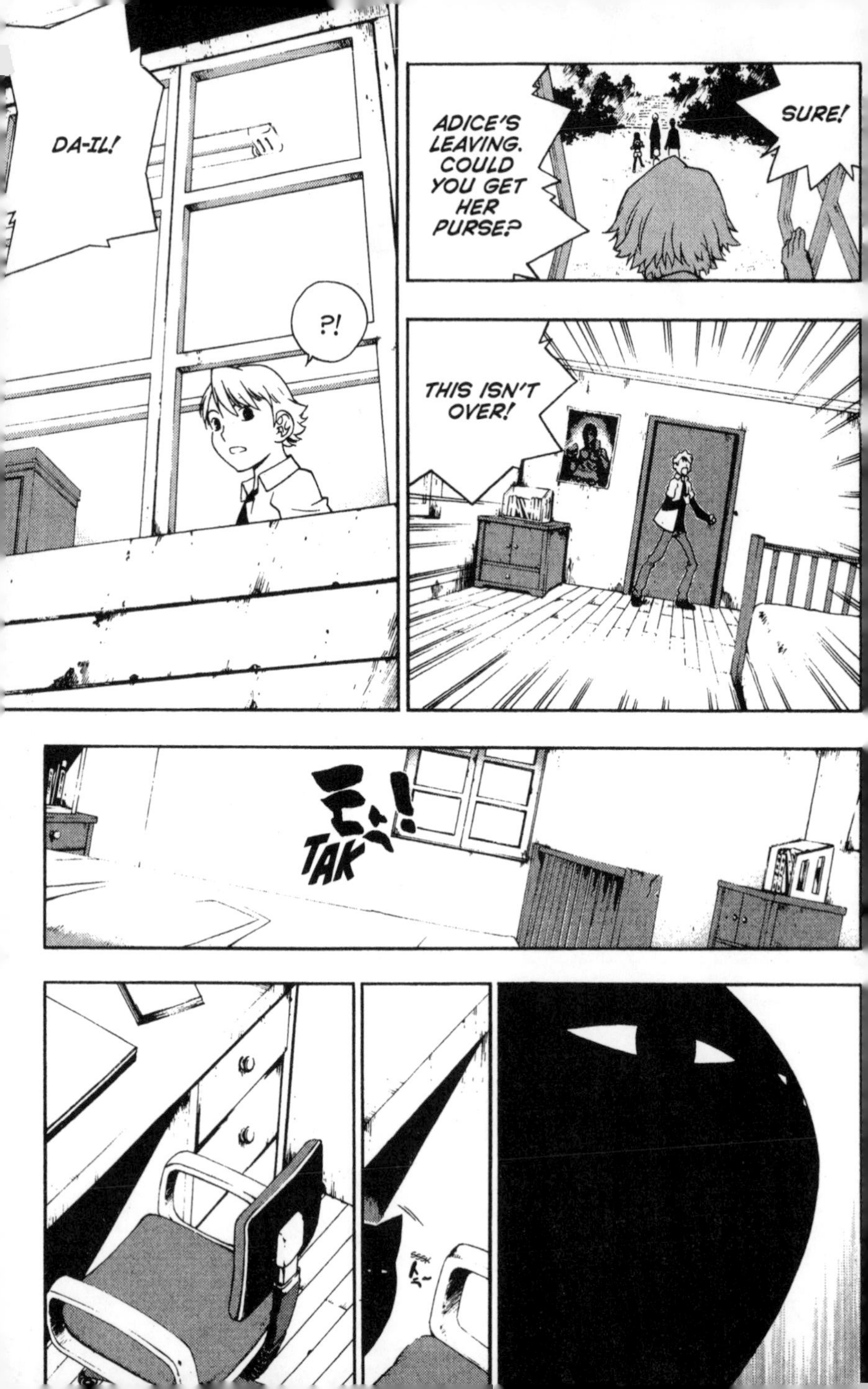
DA-IL!
?!
ADICE'S LEAVING. COULD YOU GET HER PURSE?
SURE!
THIS ISN'T OVER!
TAK
SSSK

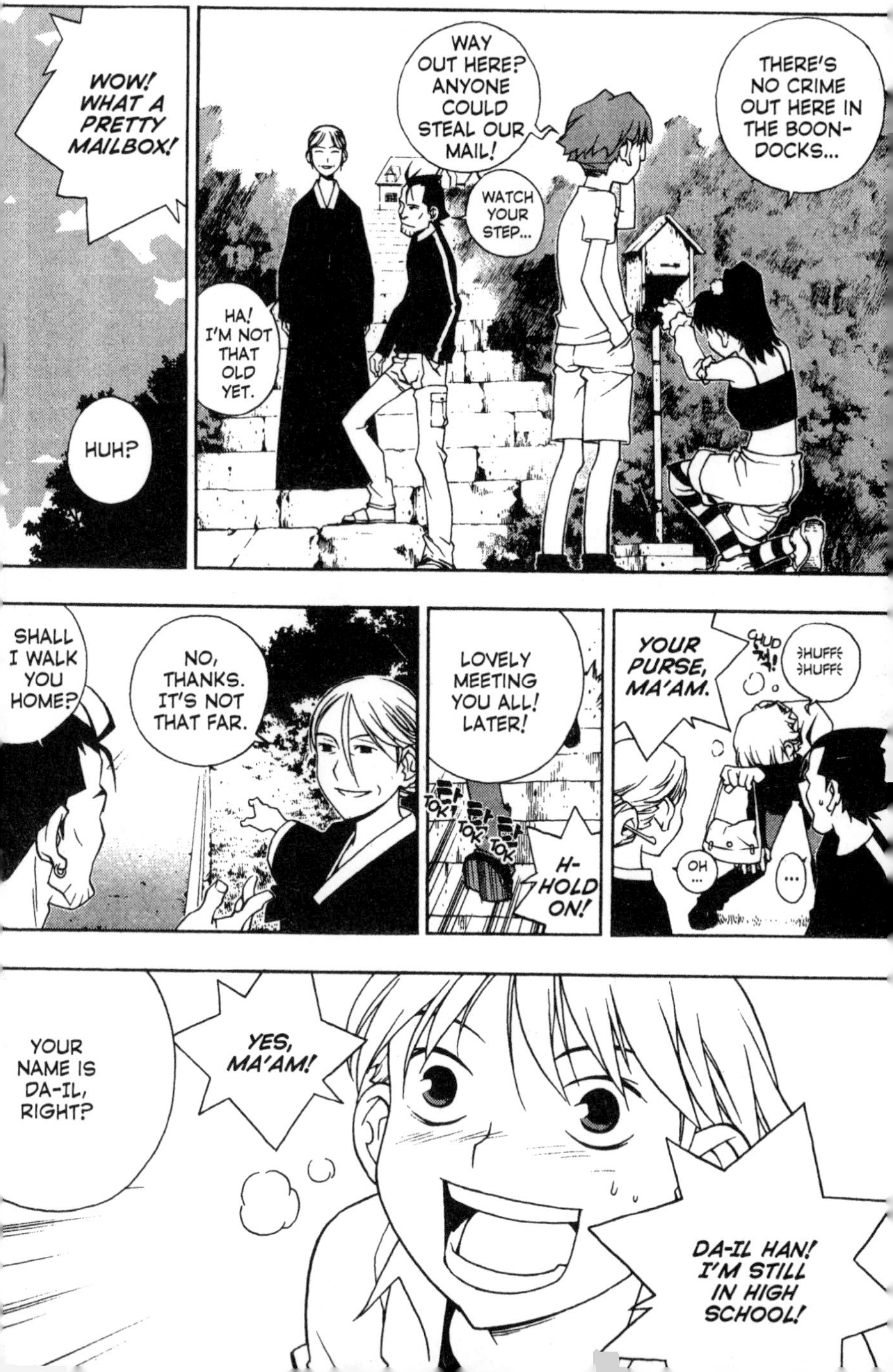
WOW! WHAT A PRETTY MAILBOX!
HUH?
WAY OUT HERE? ANYONE COULD STEAL OUR MAIL!
THERE'S NO CRIME OUT HERE IN THE BOON-DOCKS...
WATCH YOUR STEP...
HA! I'M NOT THAT OLD YET.
SHALL I WALK YOU HOME?
NO, THANKS. IT'S NOT THAT FAR.
LOVELY MEETING YOU ALL! LATER!
TOK TOK TOK TOK
H-HOLD ON!
YOUR PURSE, MA'AM.
CHUD
HUFF HUFF
OH...
...
YOUR NAME IS DA-IL, RIGHT?
YES, MA'AM!
DA-IL HAN! I'M STILL IN HIGH SCHOOL!

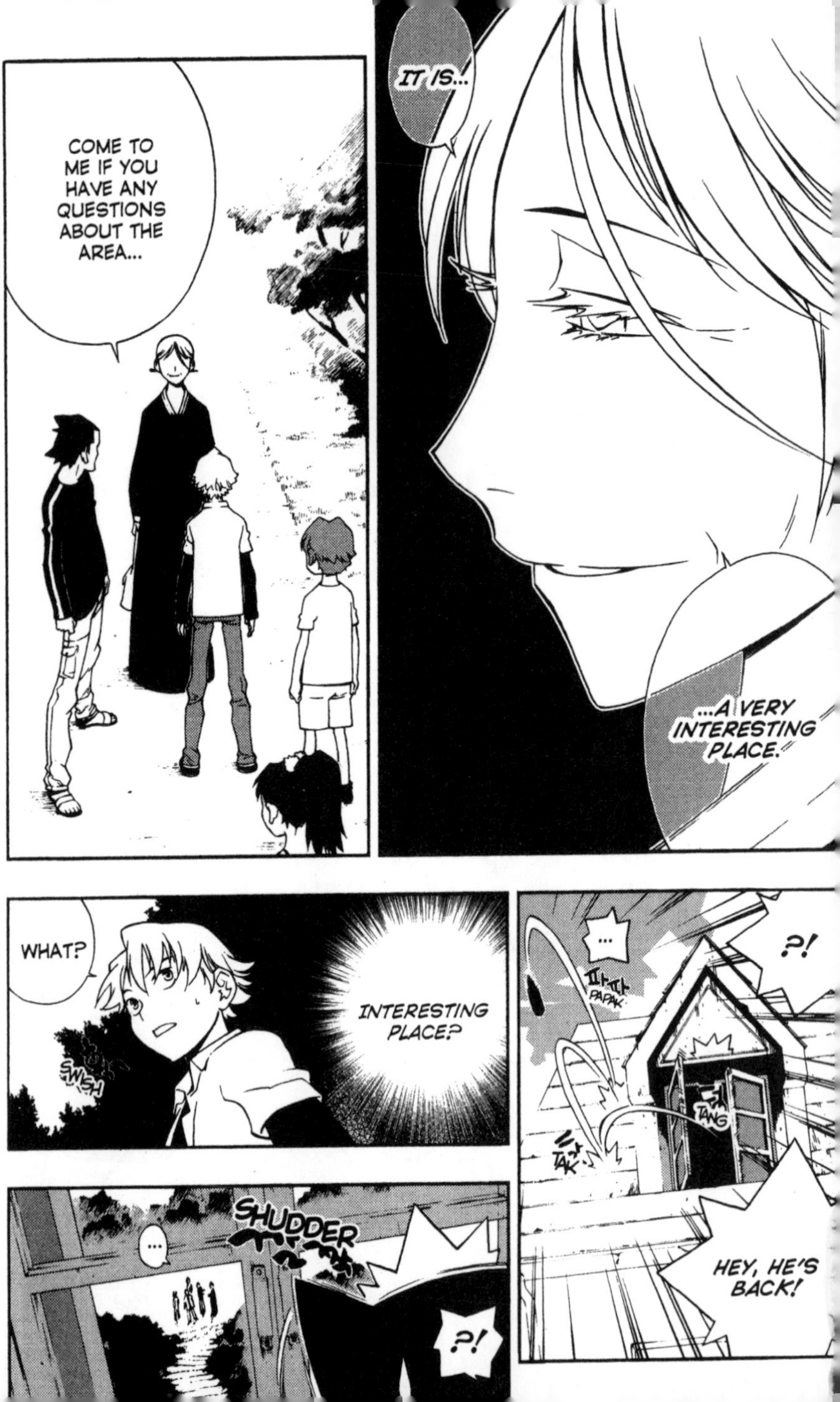
COME TO ME IF YOU HAVE ANY QUESTIONS ABOUT THE AREA...
IT IS...
...A VERY INTERESTING PLACE.
WHAT?
SWISH
INTERESTING PLACE?
...
SHUDDER
?!
...
PAPAK
?!
TANG
TAK
HEY, HE'S BACK!

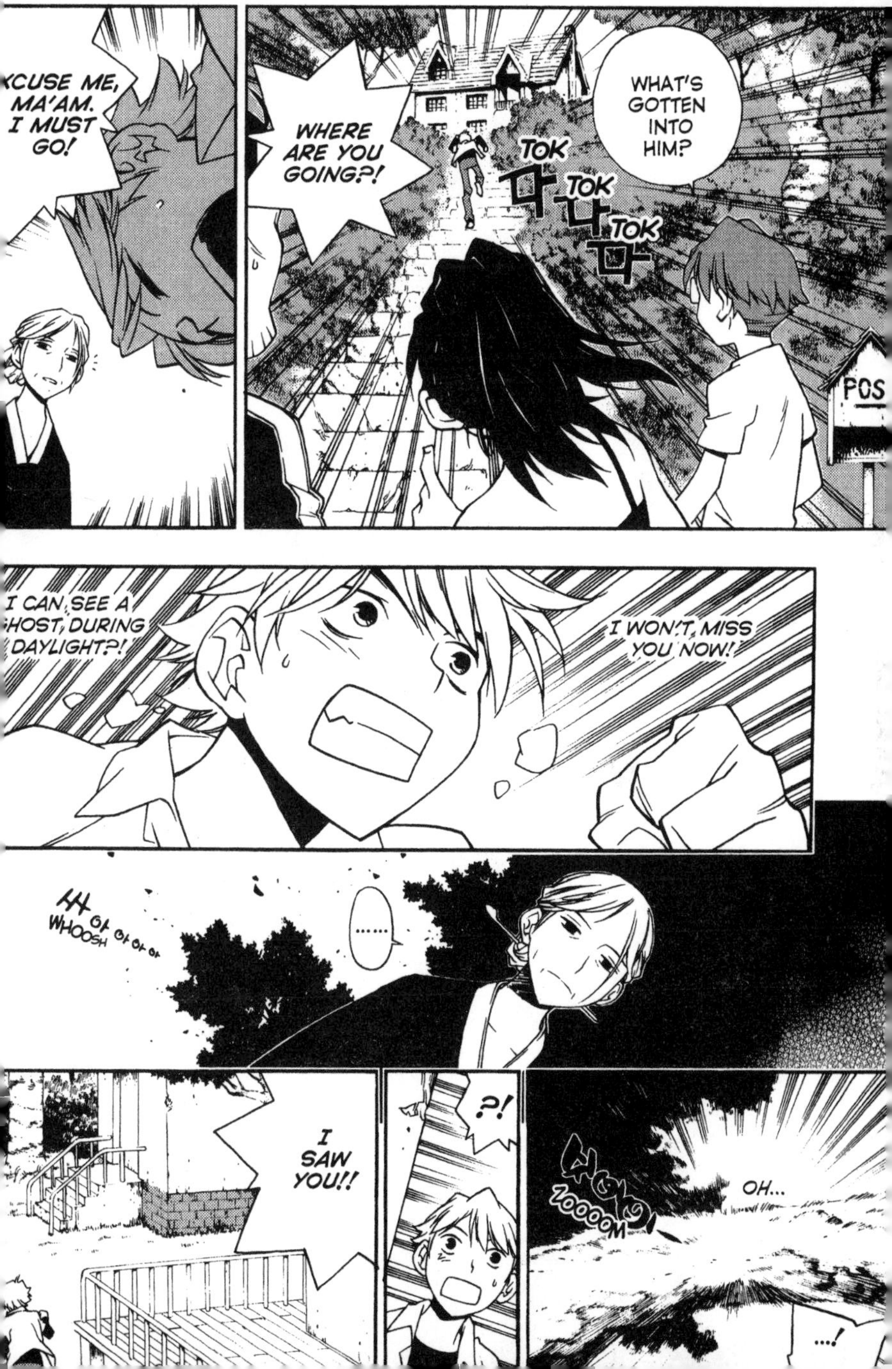
XCUSE ME, MA'AM. I MUST GO!
WHERE ARE YOU GOING?!
TOK
TOK
TOK
WHAT'S GOTTEN INTO HIM?
POS
I CAN SEE A GHOST, DURING DAYLIGHT?!
I WON'T MISS YOU NOW!
WHOOSH
......
I SAW YOU!!
?!
ZOOOOM
OH...
...!

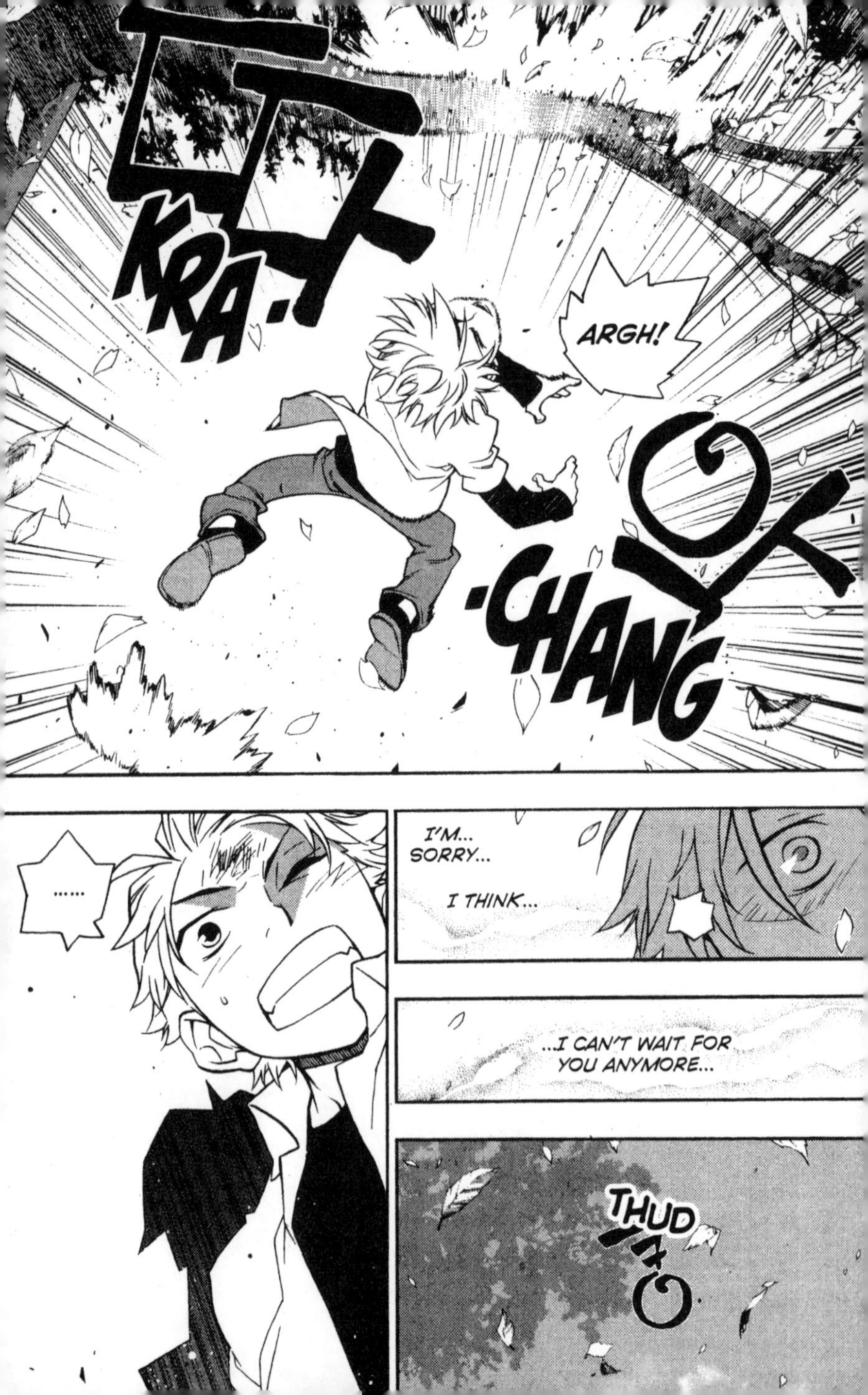

KRA-T
ARGH!
GO-CHANG
I'M... SORRY...
I THINK...
......
...I CAN'T WAIT FOR YOU ANYMORE...
THUD

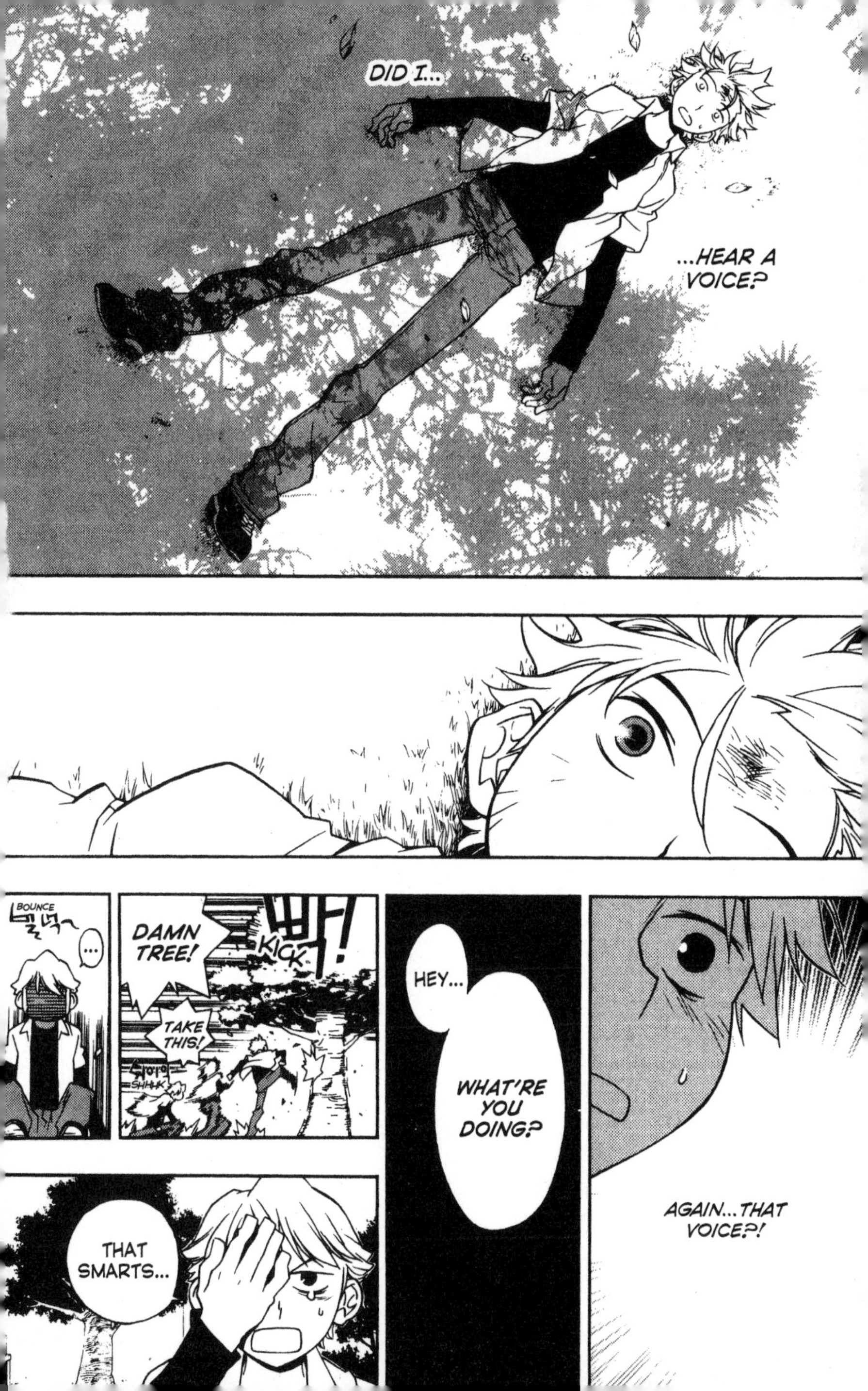
DID I...
...HEAR A VOICE?
AGAIN...THAT VOICE?!
HEY...
WHAT'RE YOU DOING?
KICK
DAMN TREE!
TAKE THIS!
SHHHK
BOUNCE
...
THAT SMARTS...

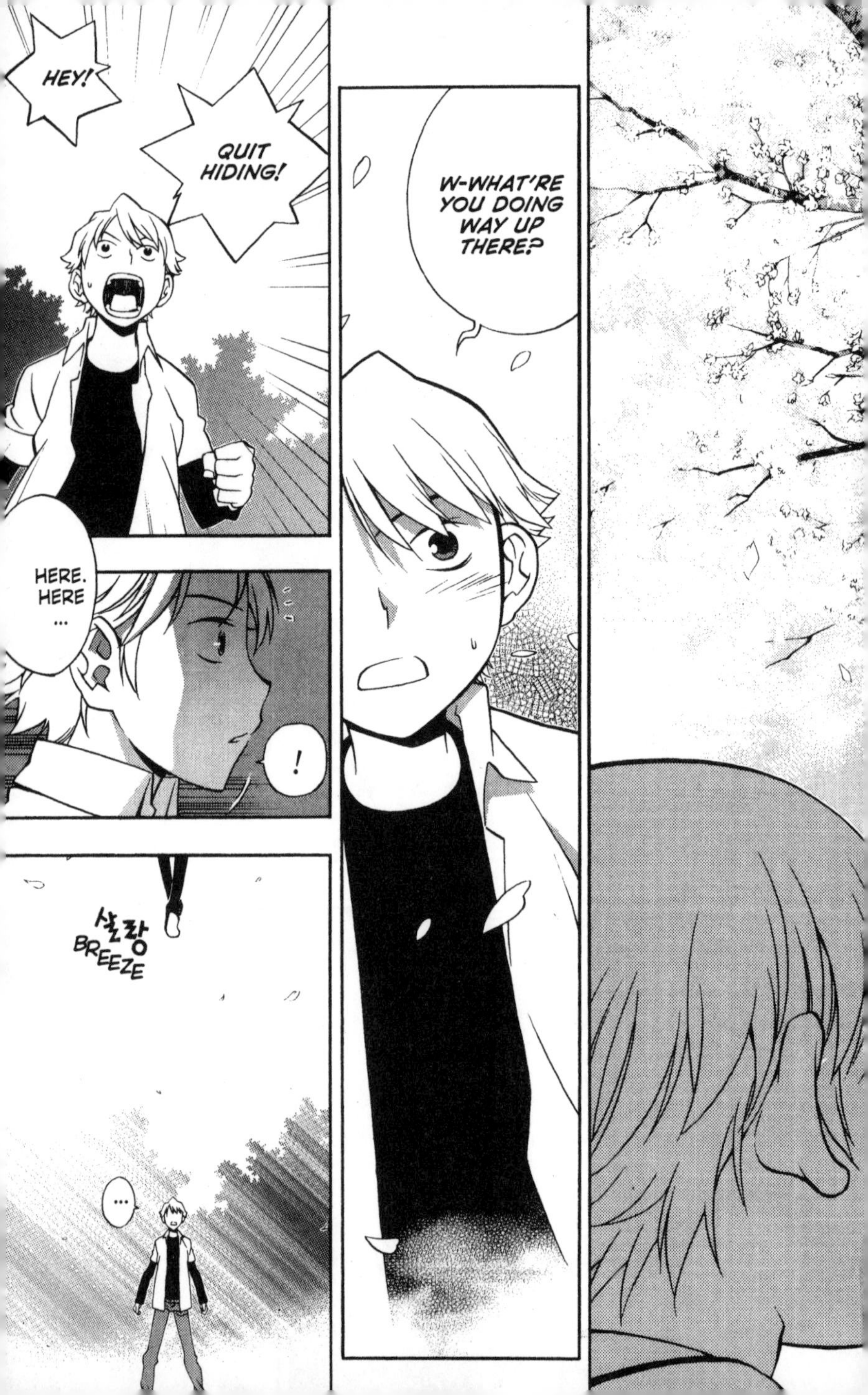
W-WHAT'RE YOU DOING WAY UP THERE?
HEY!
QUIT HIDING!
HERE. HERE ...
!
살랑
BREEZE
...

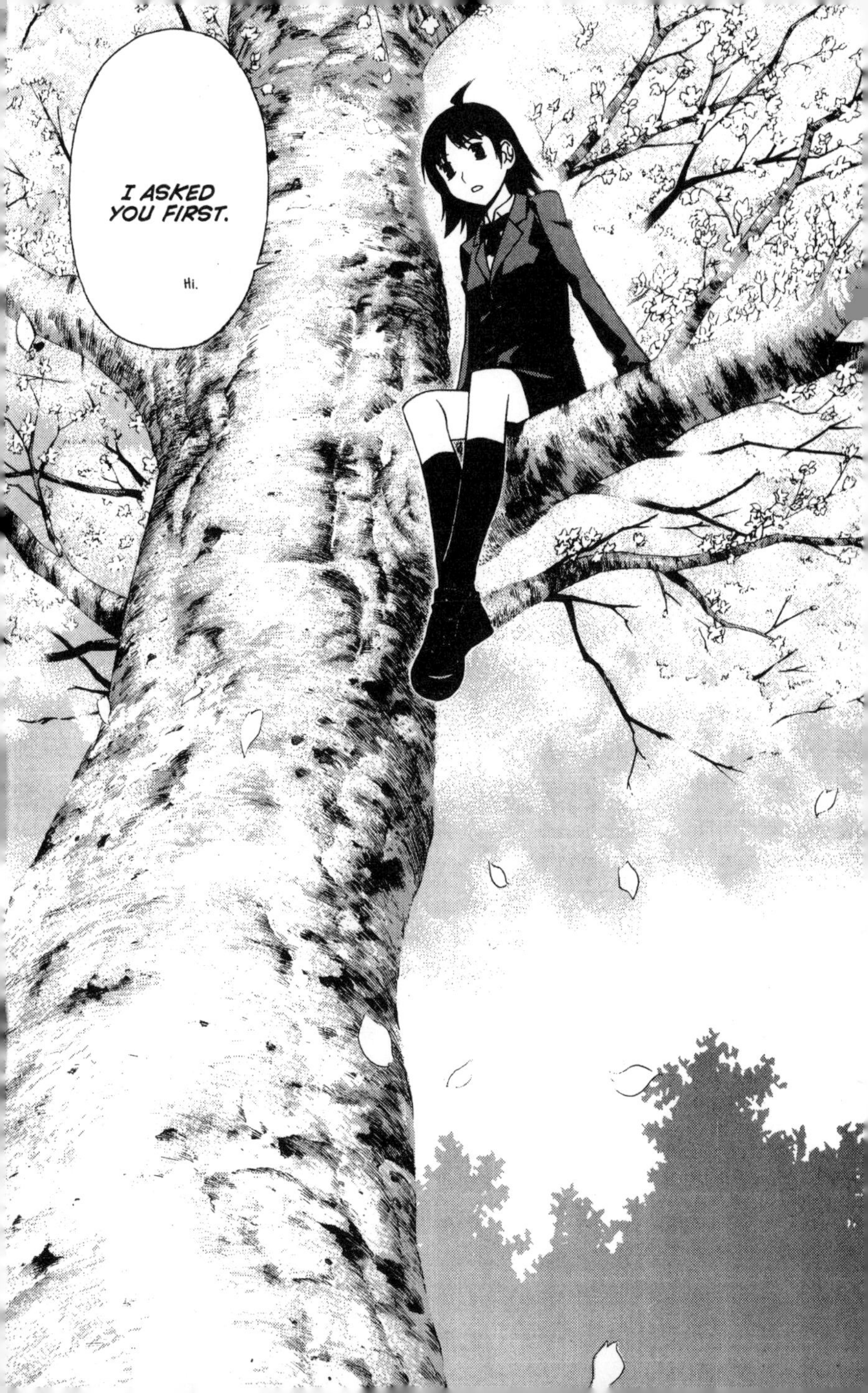
I ASKED YOU FIRST.
Hi.

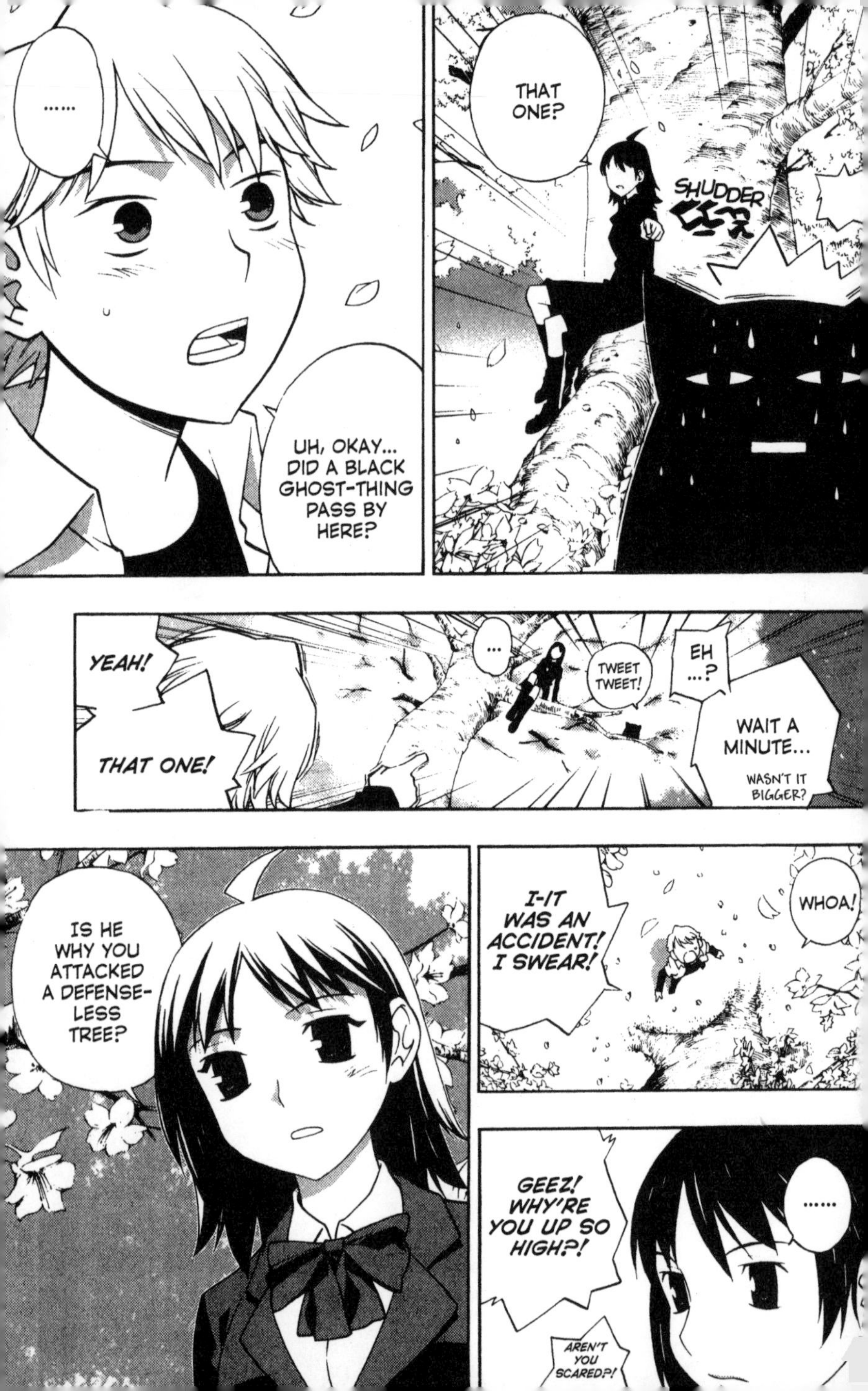
THAT ONE?
SHUDDER
......
UH, OKAY... DID A BLACK GHOST-THING PASS BY HERE?
EH ...?
WAIT A MINUTE...
WASN'T IT BIGGER?
TWEET TWEET!
...
YEAH!
THAT ONE!
WHOA!
I-IT WAS AN ACCIDENT! I SWEAR!
IS HE WHY YOU ATTACKED A DEFENSE-LESS TREE?
......
GEEZ! WHY'RE YOU UP SO HIGH?!
AREN'T YOU SCARED?!

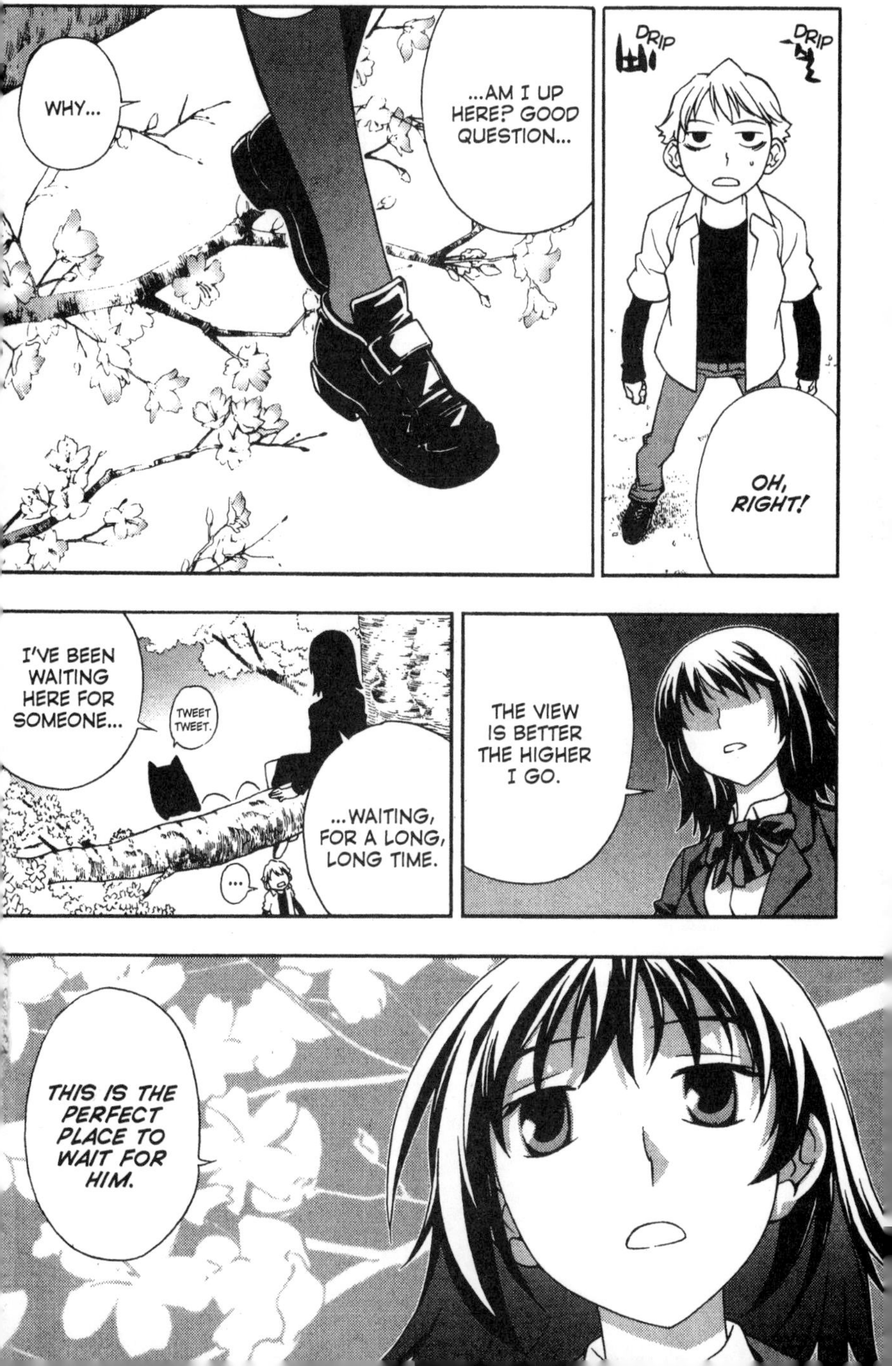
WHY...
...AM I UP HERE? GOOD QUESTION...
DRIP
DRIP
OH, RIGHT!
I'VE BEEN WAITING HERE FOR SOMEONE...
TWEET TWEET.
...WAITING, FOR A LONG, LONG TIME.
...
THE VIEW IS BETTER THE HIGHER I GO.
THIS IS THE PERFECT PLACE TO WAIT FOR HIM.

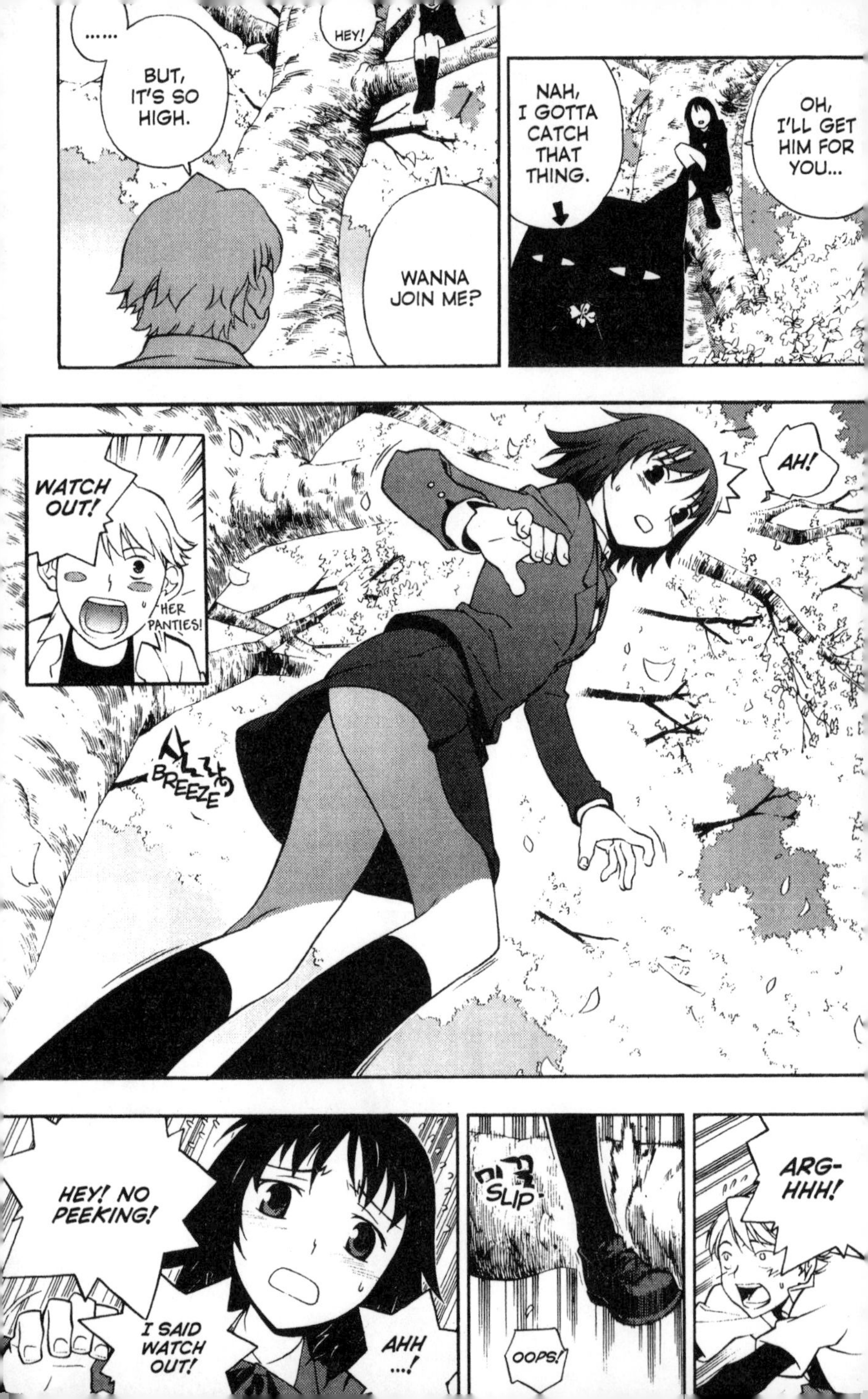
OH, I'LL GET HIM FOR YOU...
NAH, I GOTTA CATCH THAT THING.
HEY!
WANNA JOIN ME?
......
BUT, IT'S SO HIGH.
AH!
BREEZE
WATCH OUT!
HER PANTIES!
ARG-HHH!
SLIP
OOPS!
HEY! NO PEEKING!
I SAID WATCH OUT!
AHH ...!

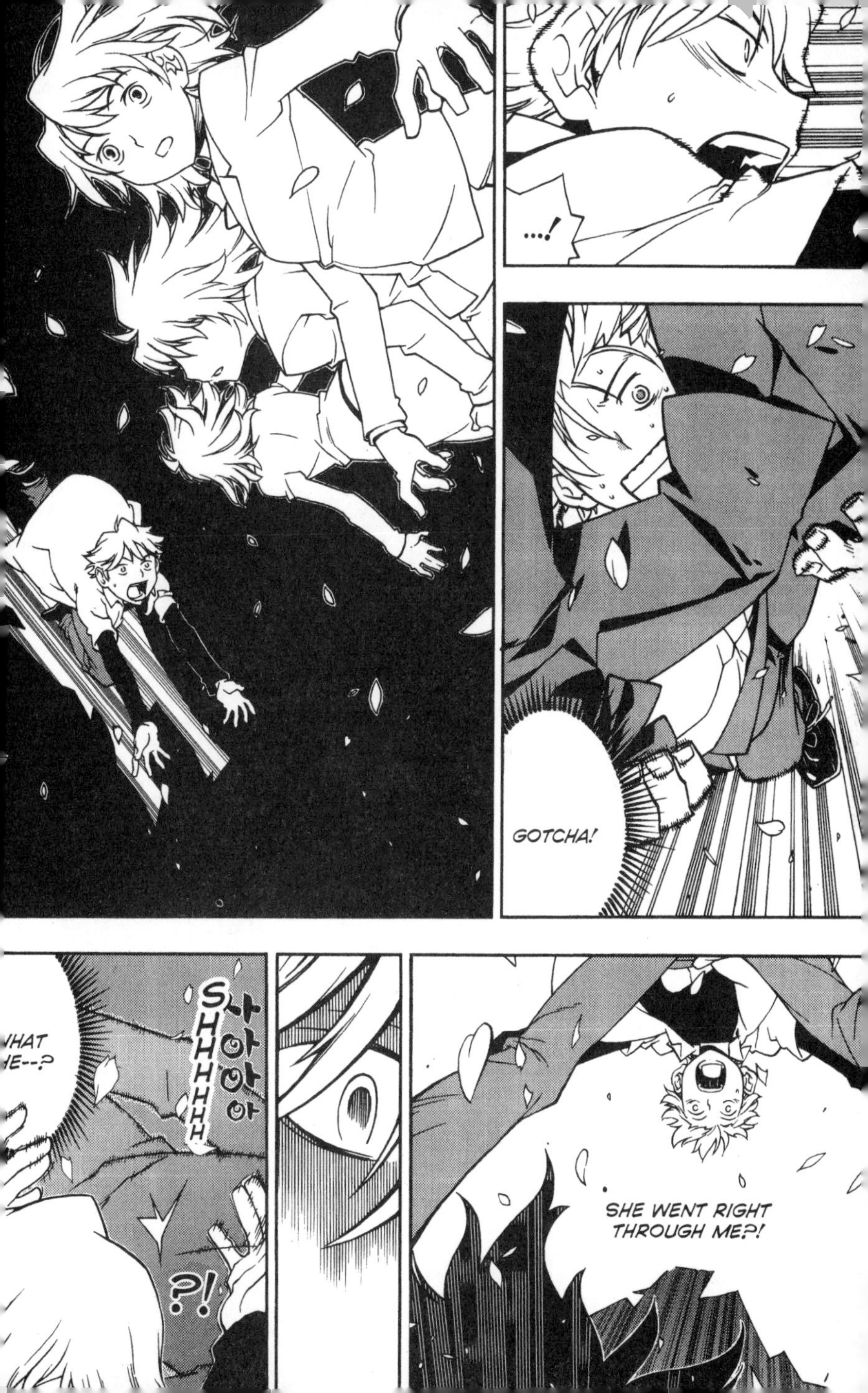
...!
GOTCHA!
SHE WENT RIGHT THROUGH ME?!
SHHHHHH
?!

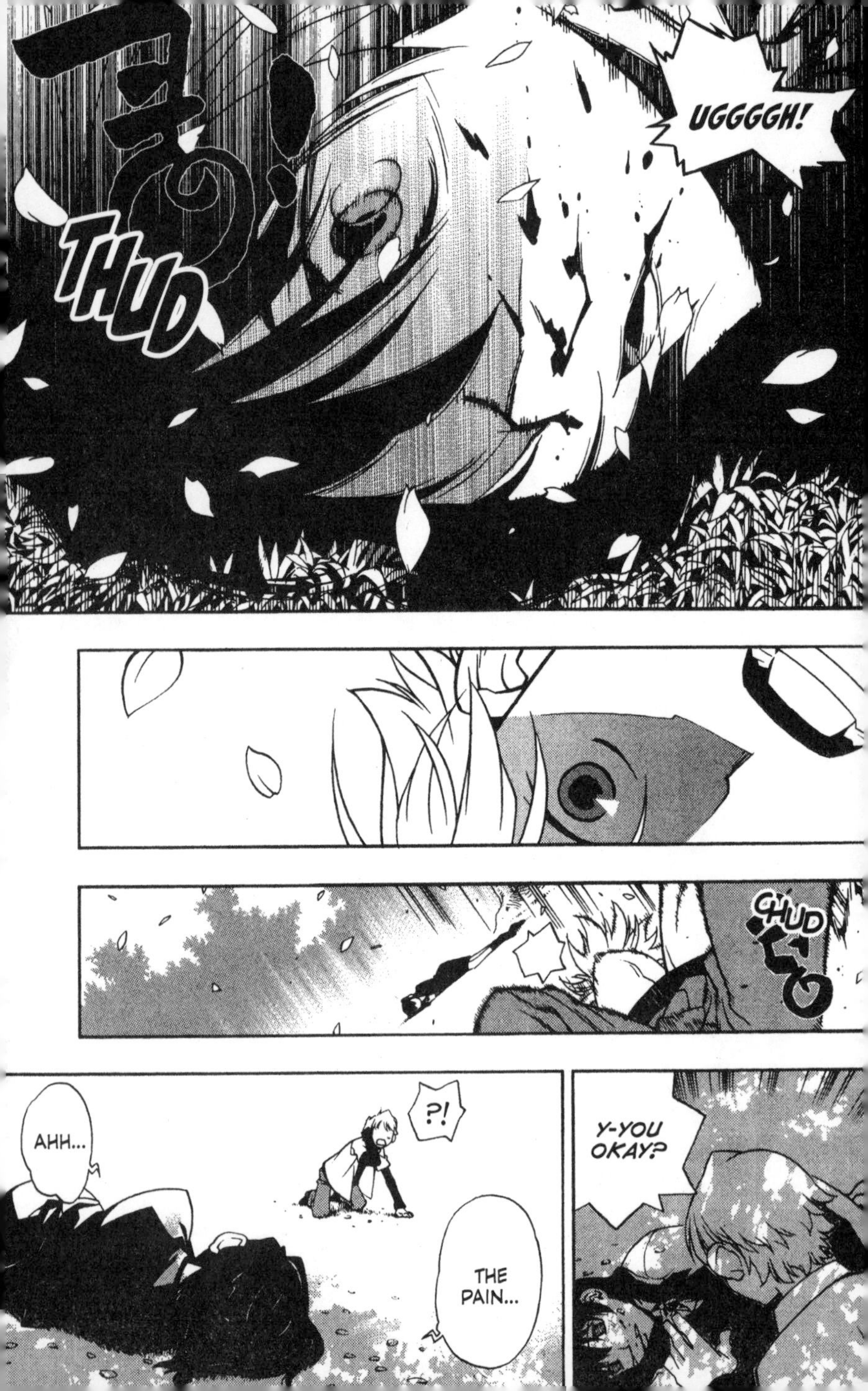
UGGGGH!
THUD
CHUD
Y-YOU OKAY?
?!
AHH...
THE PAIN...

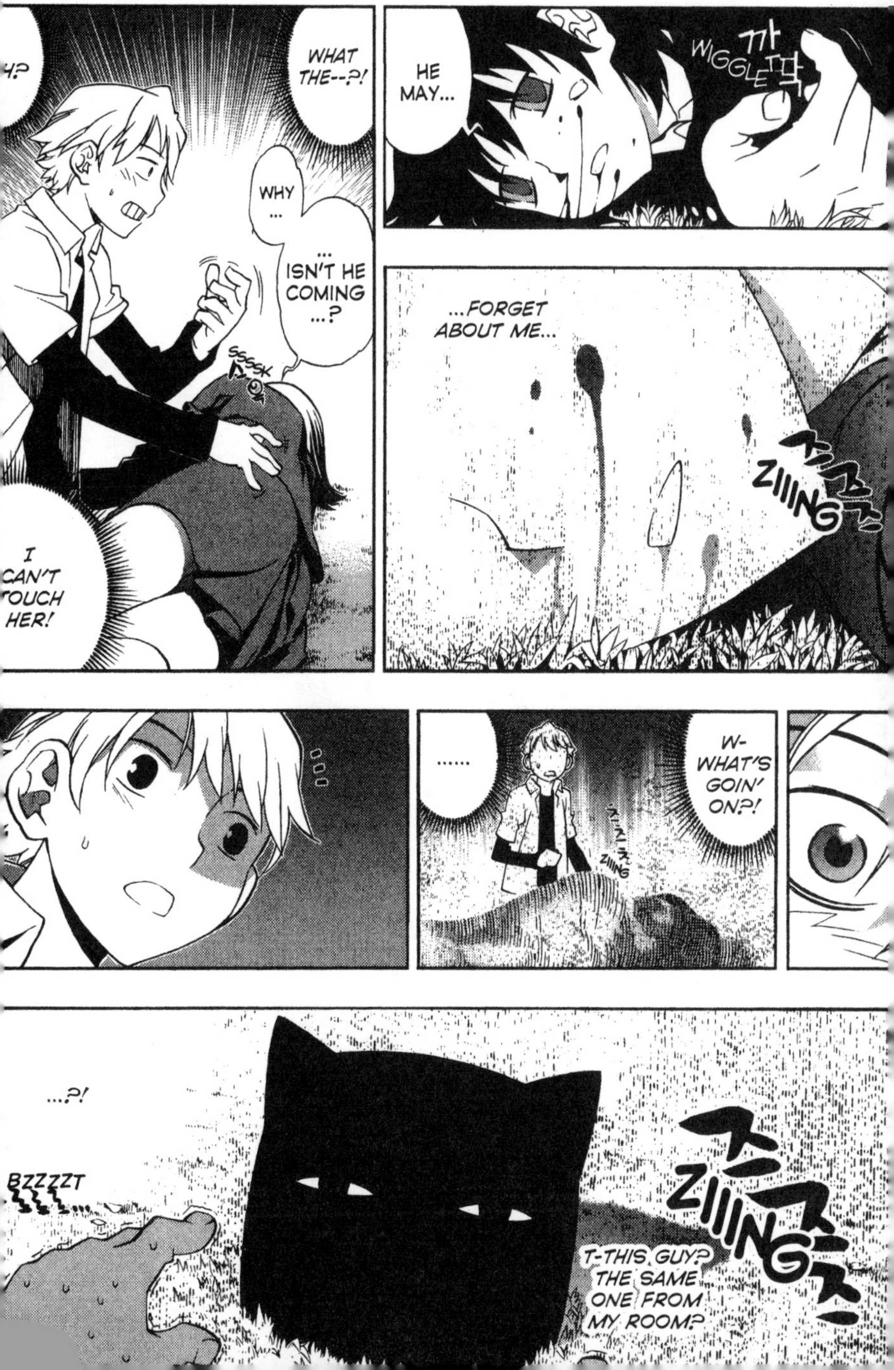
WHAT THE--?!
WHY ...
... ISN'T HE COMING ...?
SSSSK
I CAN'T TOUCH HER!
HE MAY...
WIGGLE
...FORGET ABOUT ME...
ZIIING
......
W-WHAT'S GOIN' ON?!
ZIIING
...?!
BZZZZT
ZIIING
T-THIS GUY? THE SAME ONE FROM MY ROOM?

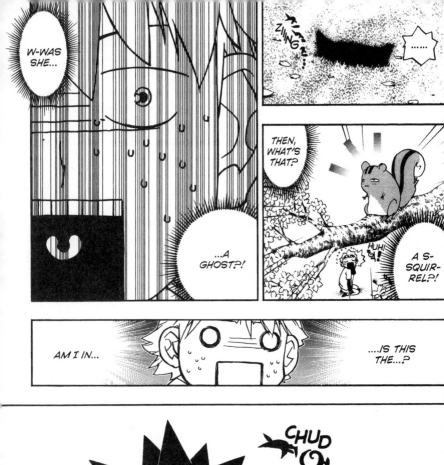

W-WAS SHE...

ZIING...

.....

THEN, WHAT'S THAT?

...A GHOST?!

HUH!

A S-SQUIR-REL?!

AM I IN...

....IS THIS THE...?

CHUD

YUP. THIS IS THE DEAD ZONE. ANOTHER GHOST STORY.

?!

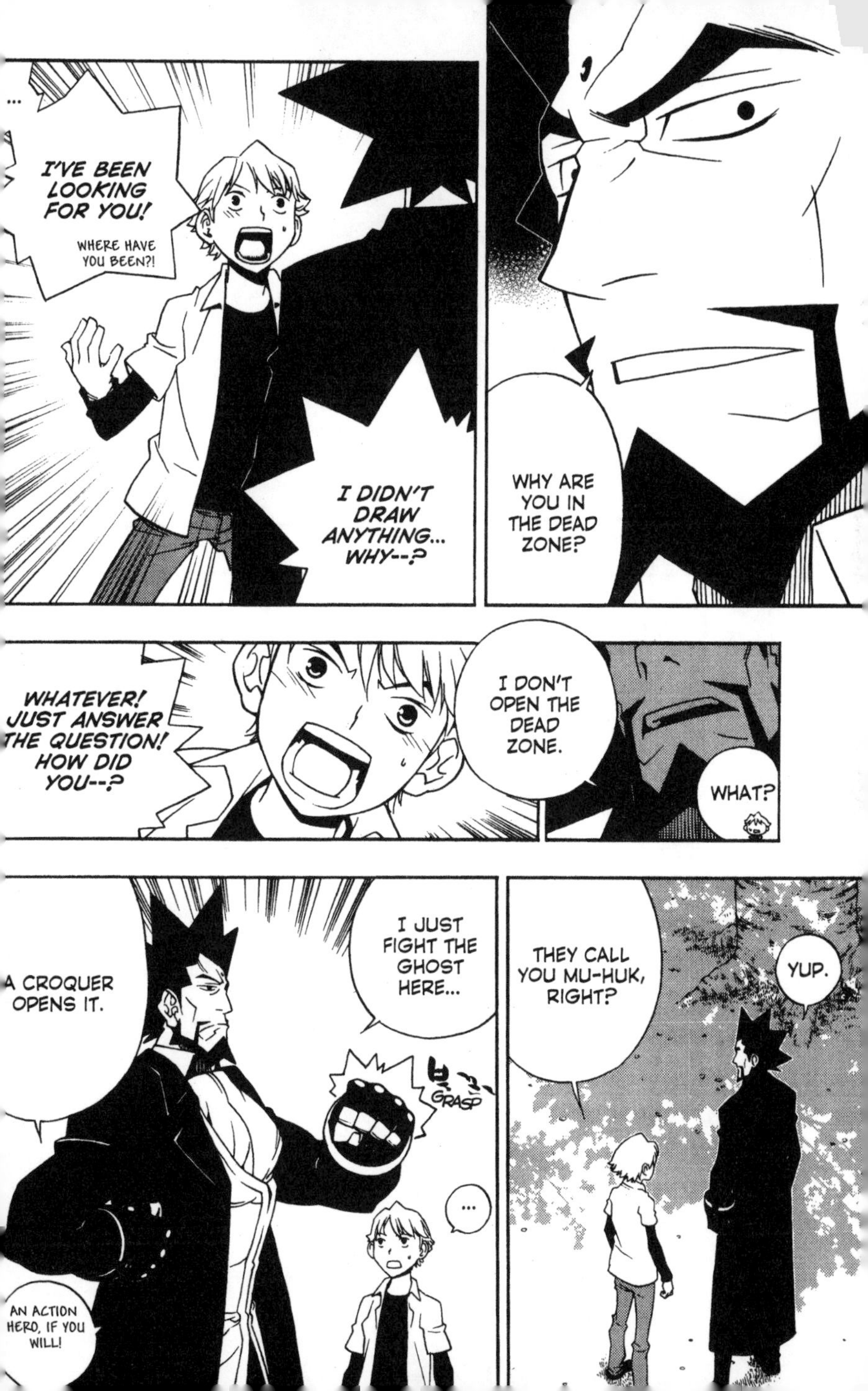
...
I'VE BEEN LOOKING FOR YOU!
WHERE HAVE YOU BEEN?!
I DIDN'T DRAW ANYTHING... WHY--?
WHY ARE YOU IN THE DEAD ZONE?
WHATEVER! JUST ANSWER THE QUESTION! HOW DID YOU--?
I DON'T OPEN THE DEAD ZONE.
WHAT?
A CROQUER OPENS IT.
I JUST FIGHT THE GHOST HERE...
GRASP
...
AN ACTION HERO, IF YOU WILL!
THEY CALL YOU MU-HUK, RIGHT?
YUP.

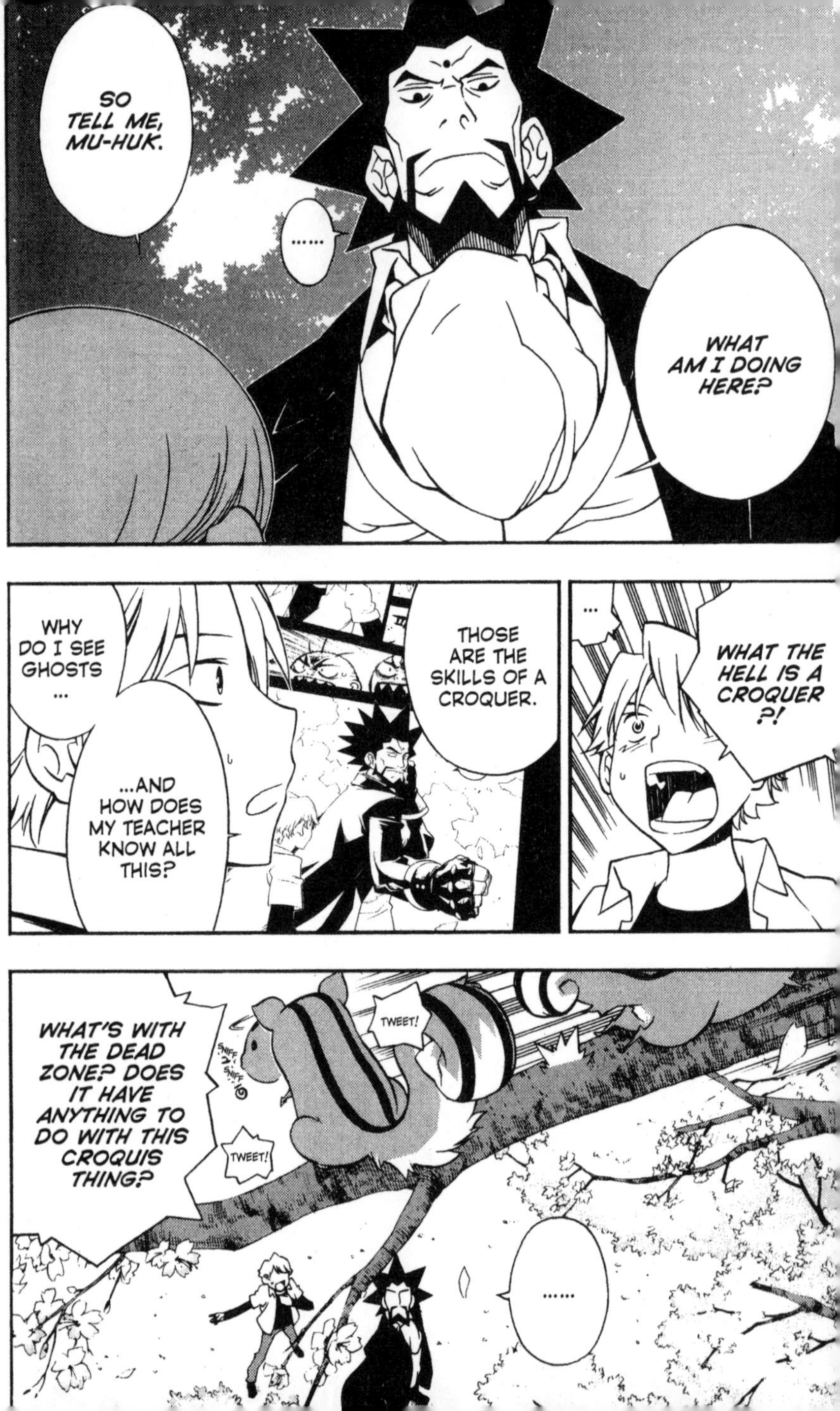
SO TELL ME, MU-HUK.
......
WHAT AM I DOING HERE?
...
WHAT THE HELL IS A CROQUER ?!
THOSE ARE THE SKILLS OF A CROQUER.
WHY DO I SEE GHOSTS ...
...AND HOW DOES MY TEACHER KNOW ALL THIS?
TWEET!
SNIFF SNIFF
WHAT'S WITH THE DEAD ZONE? DOES IT HAVE ANYTHING TO DO WITH THIS CROQUIS THING?
TWEET!
......

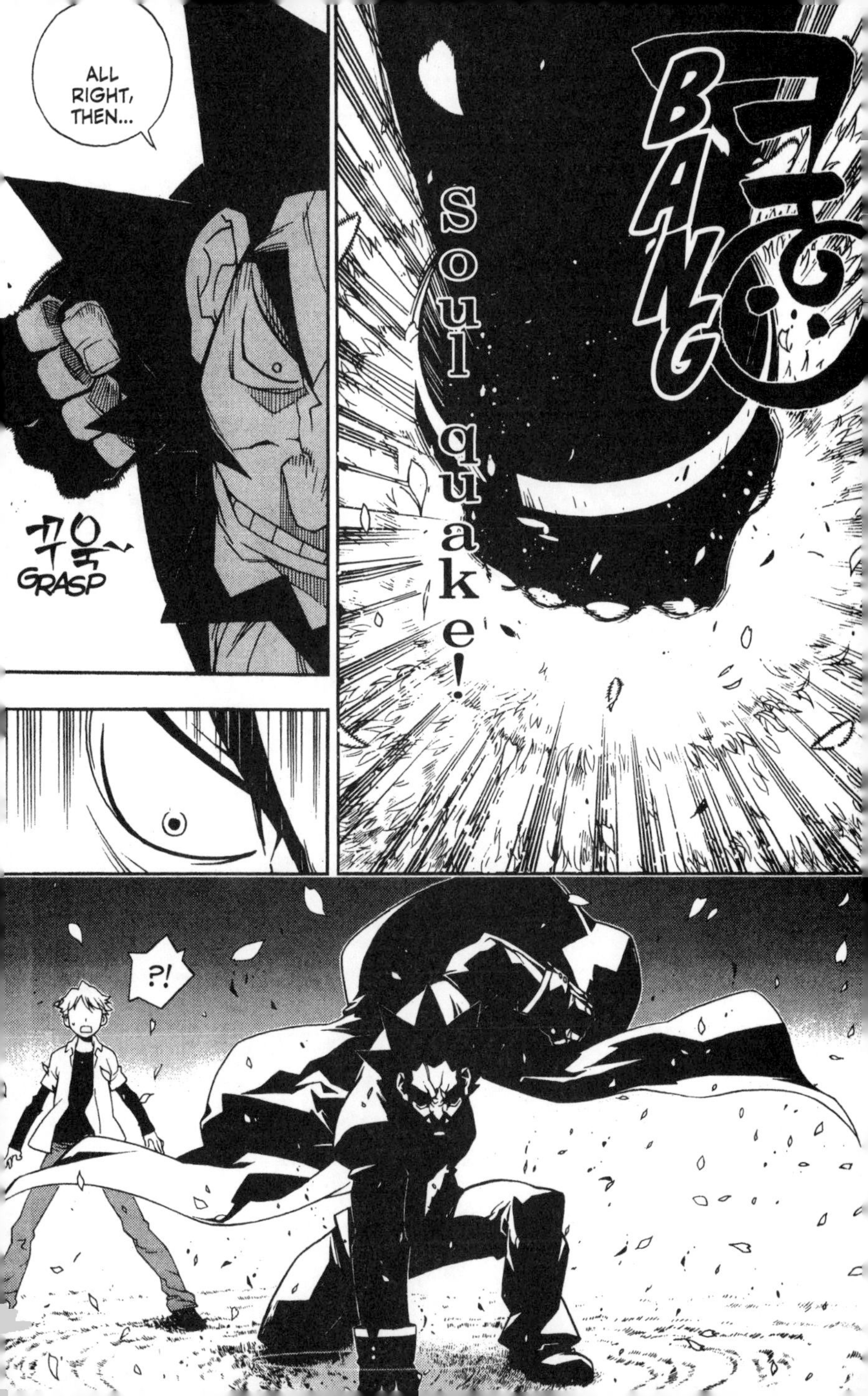
BANG
soul quake!
ALL RIGHT, THEN...
꾸욱
GRASP
?!

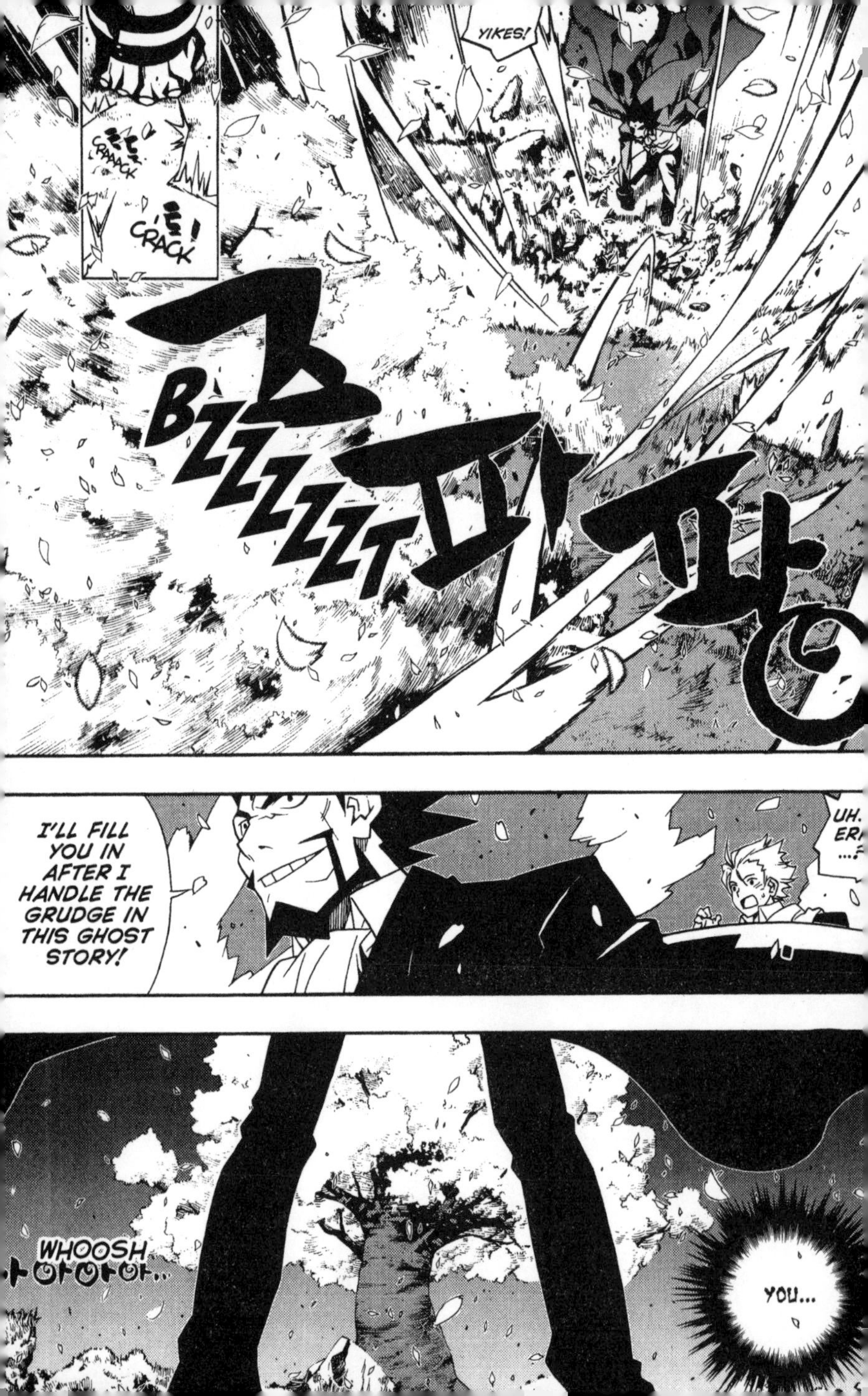
YIKES!
CRAAACK
CRACK
BZZZZZZT
I'LL FILL YOU IN AFTER I HANDLE THE GRUDGE IN THIS GHOST STORY!
UH... ER...?!
WHOOSH
YOU...

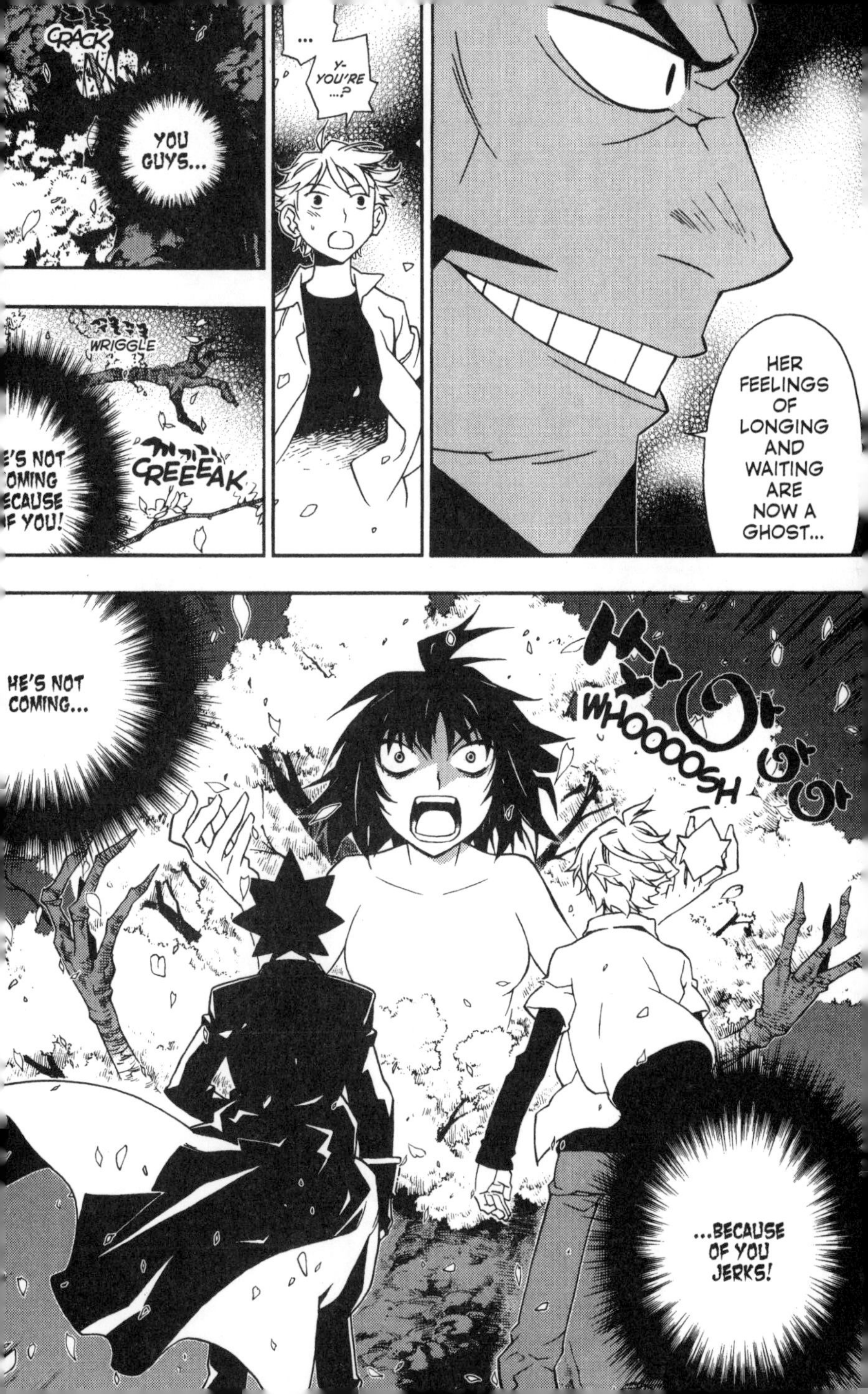

HER FEELINGS OF LONGING AND WAITING ARE NOW A GHOST...
...
Y-YOU'RE ...?
CRACK
YOU GUYS...
WRIGGLE
CREEEAK
E'S NOT COMING ECAUSE F YOU!
WHOOOOOSH
HE'S NOT COMING...
...BECAUSE OF YOU JERKS!

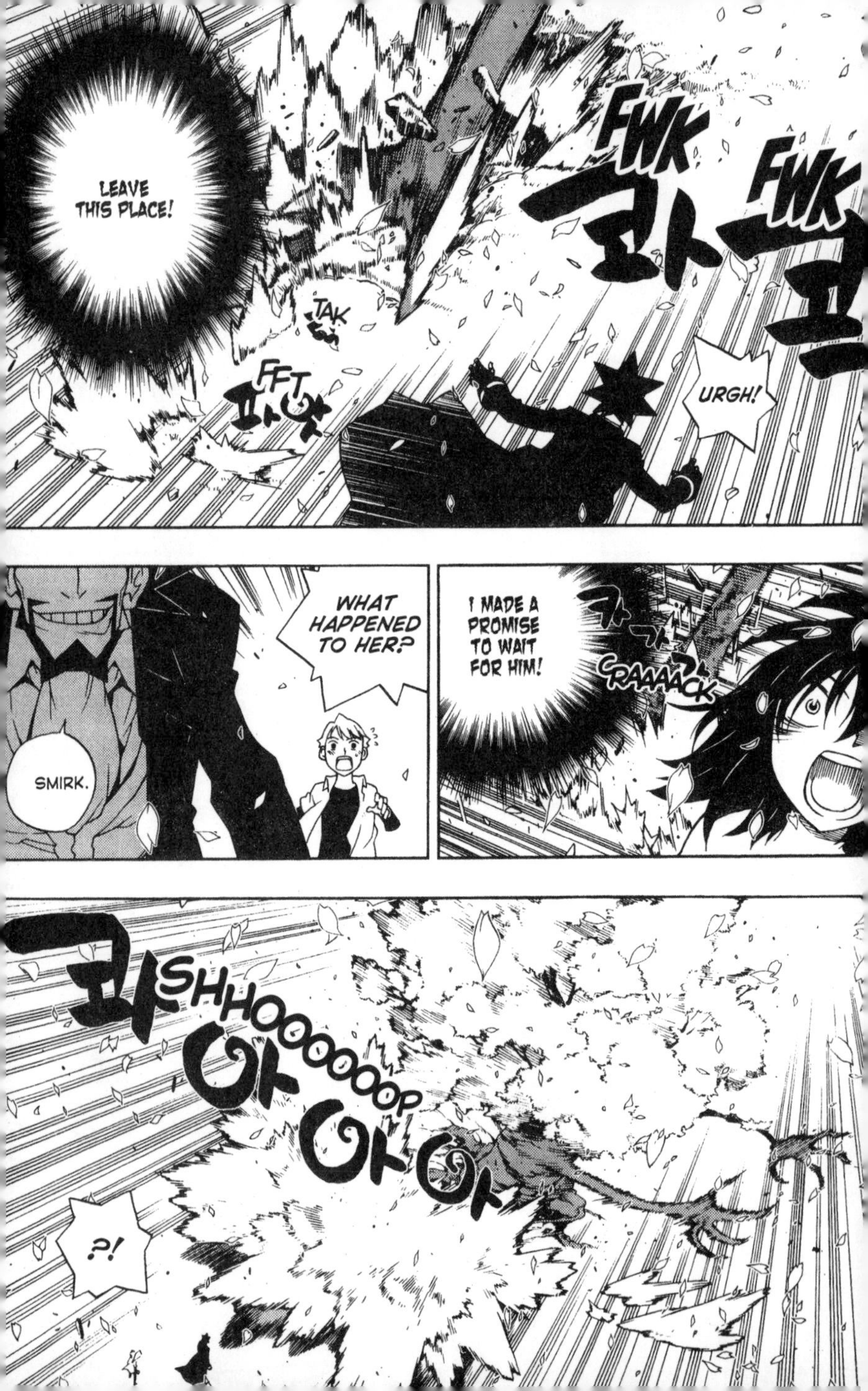
LEAVE THIS PLACE!
FWK
FWK
TAK
FFT
URGH!
WHAT HAPPENED TO HER?
SMIRK.
I MADE A PROMISE TO WAIT FOR HIM!
CRAAAACK
SHHOOOOOOOP
?!

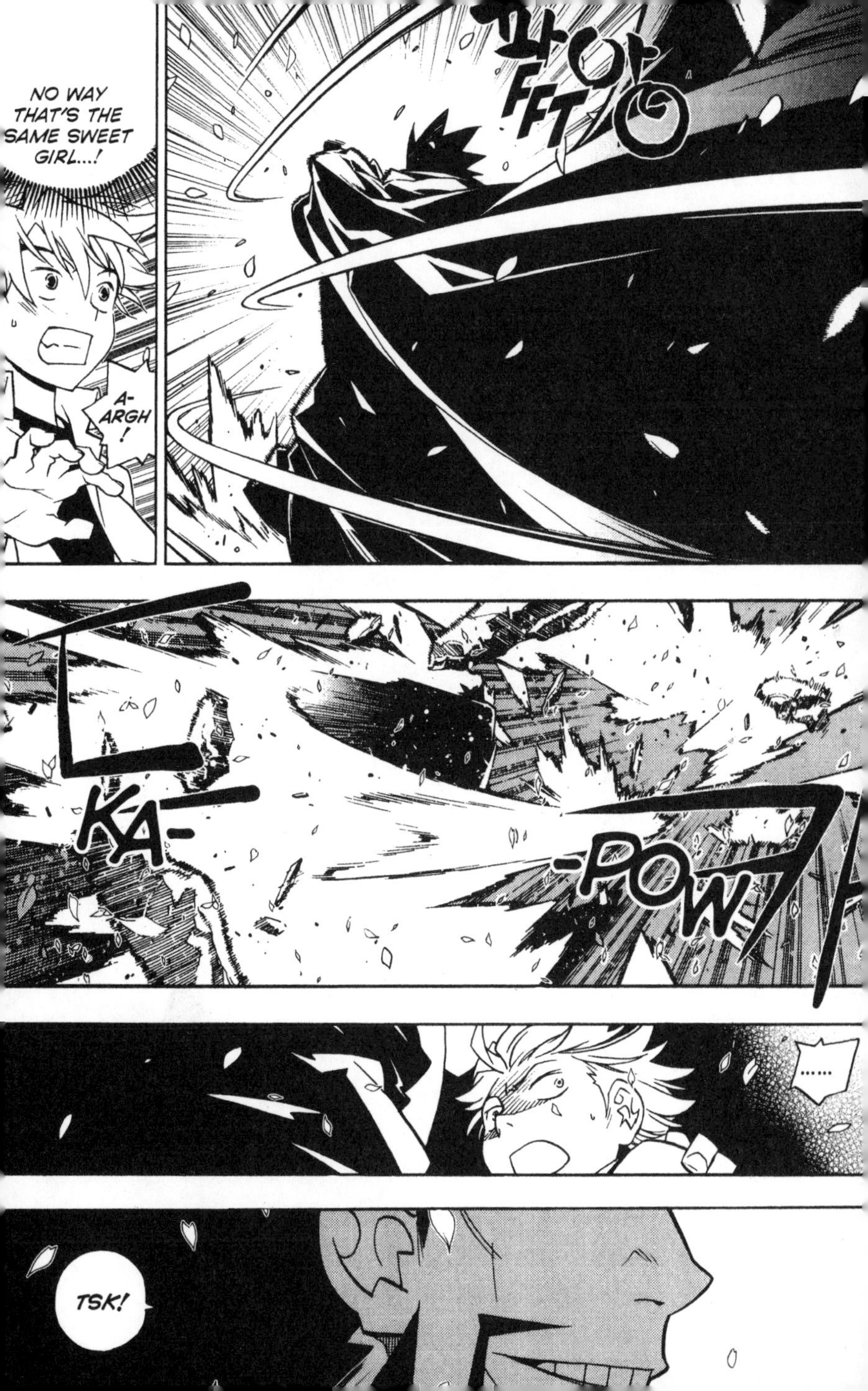
FFT
NO WAY THAT'S THE SAME SWEET GIRL...!
A-ARGH!
KA-
-POW
......
TSK!

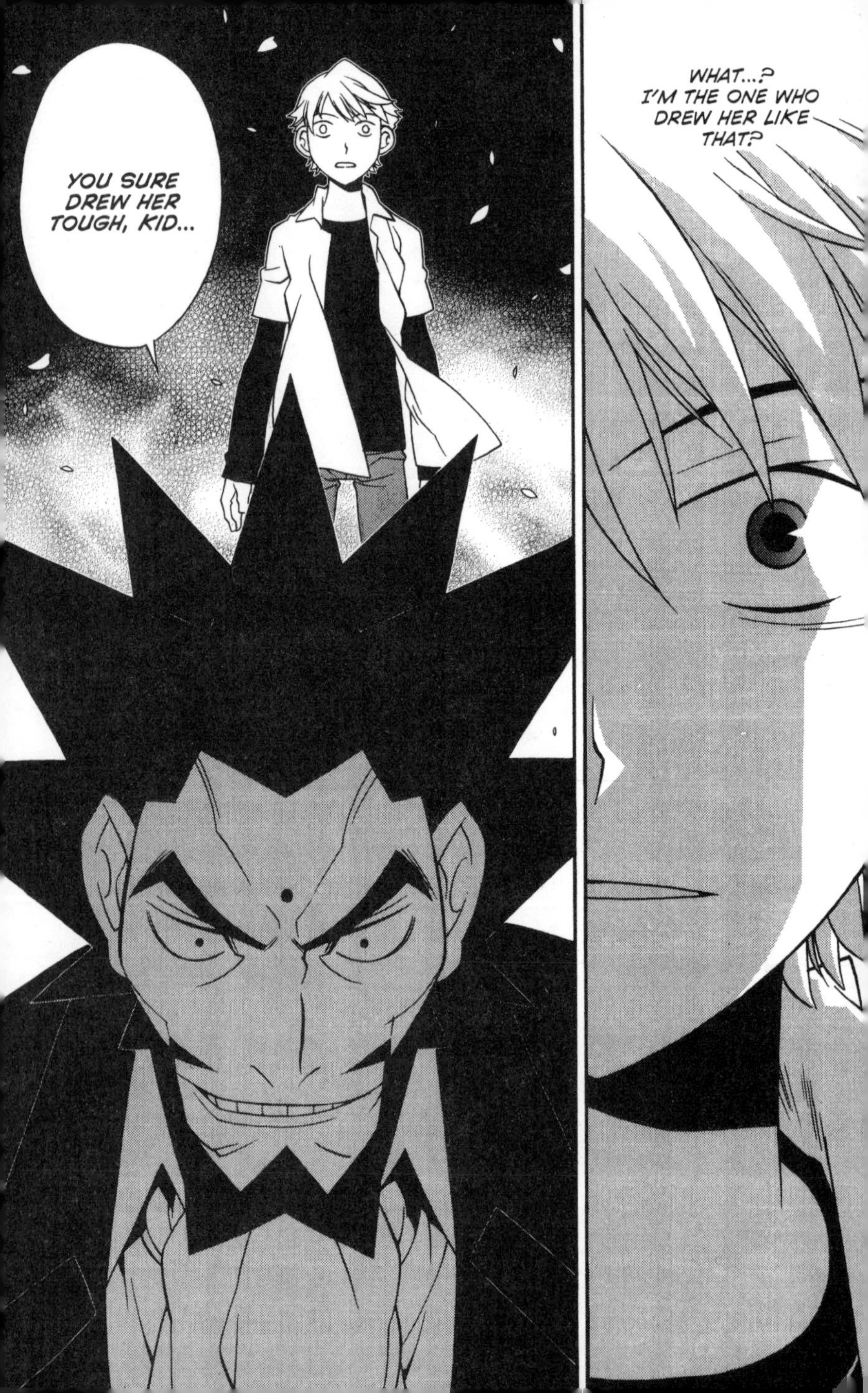
WHAT...? I'M THE ONE WHO DREW HER LIKE THAT?
YOU SURE DREW HER TOUGH, KID...

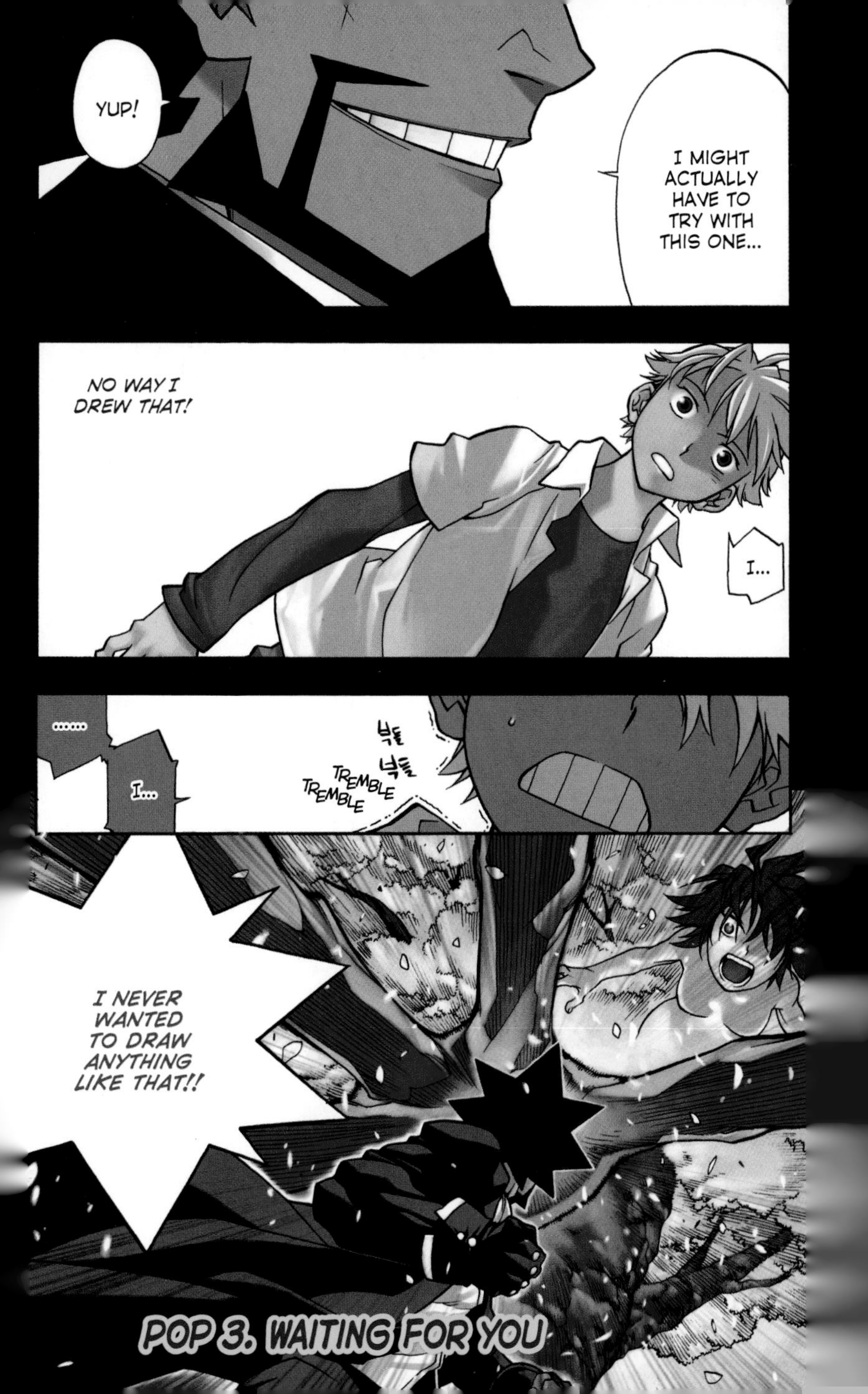
I MIGHT ACTUALLY HAVE TO TRY WITH THIS ONE...
YUP!
NO WAY I DREW THAT!
I...
......
I...
TREMBLE
TREMBLE
I NEVER WANTED TO DRAW ANYTHING LIKE THAT!!
POP 3. WAITING FOR YOU

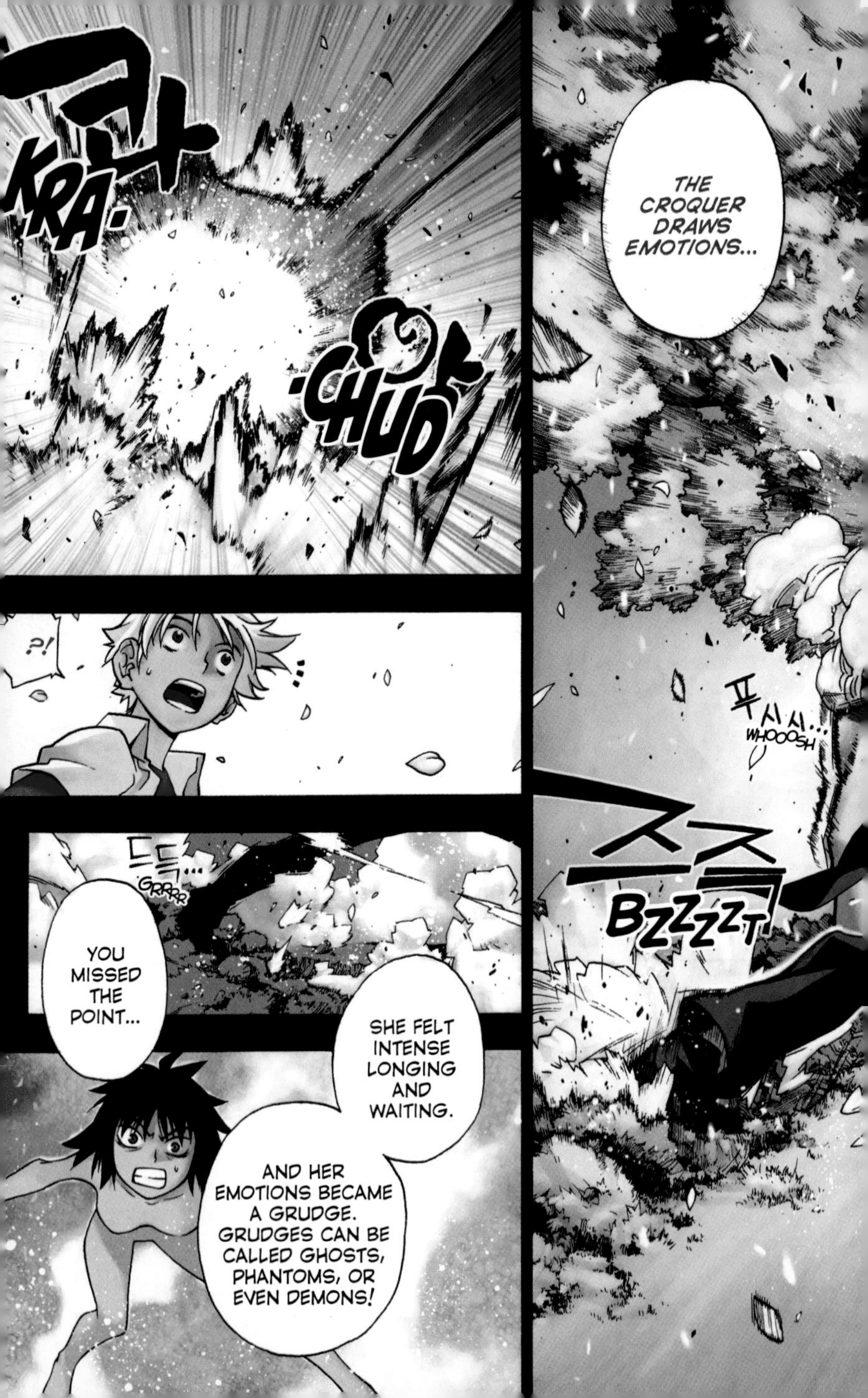
KRA-
-CHUD
?!
드득...
GRRRR
YOU MISSED THE POINT...
SHE FELT INTENSE LONGING AND WAITING.
AND HER EMOTIONS BECAME A GRUDGE. GRUDGES CAN BE CALLED GHOSTS, PHANTOMS, OR EVEN DEMONS!
THE CROQUER DRAWS EMOTIONS...
푸시시...
WHOOOSH
BZZZZT

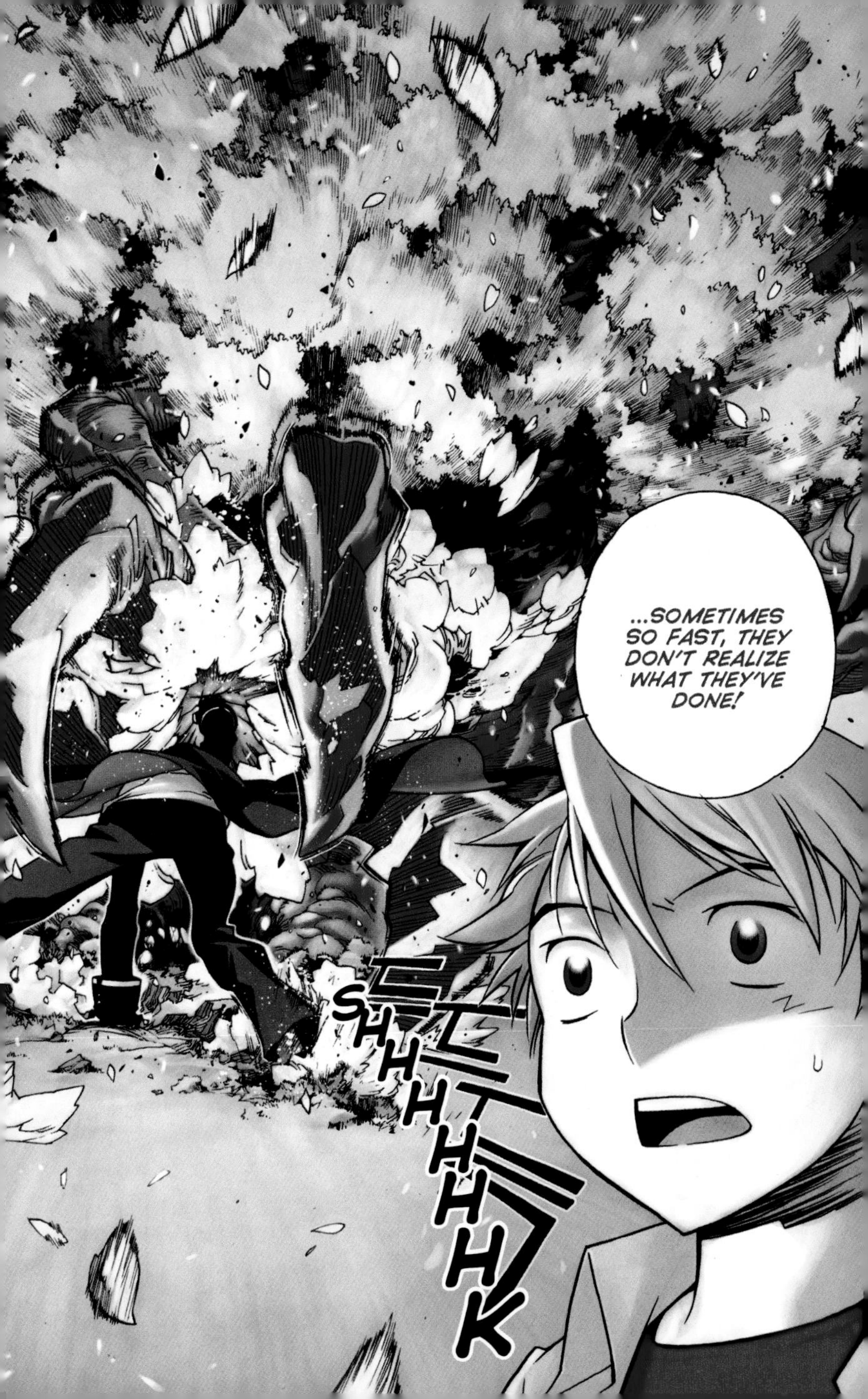
...SOMETIMES SO FAST, THEY DON'T REALIZE WHAT THEY'VE DONE!
SHHHHHHK

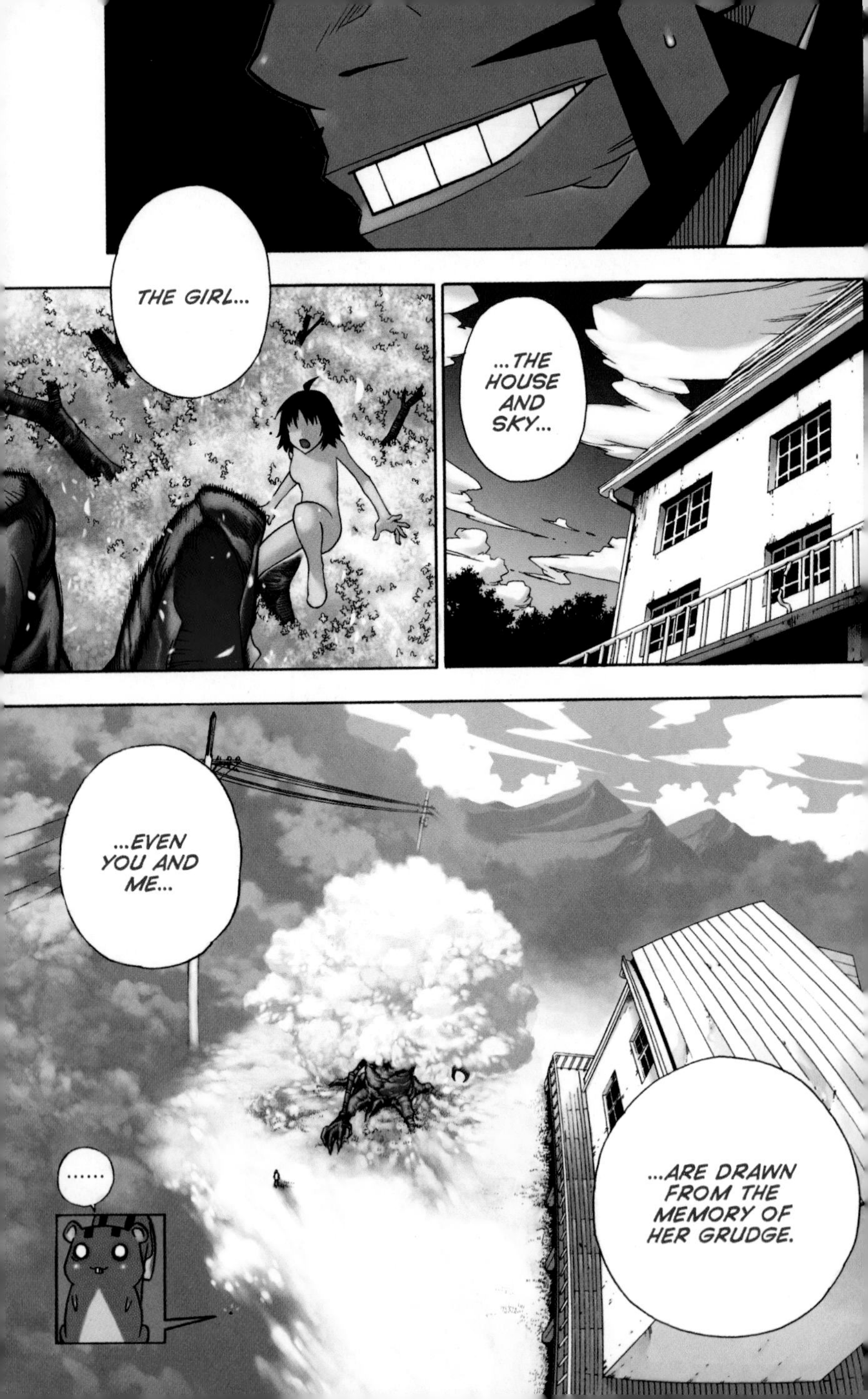
THE GIRL...
...THE HOUSE AND SKY...
...EVEN YOU AND ME...
...ARE DRAWN FROM THE MEMORY OF HER GRUDGE.
......

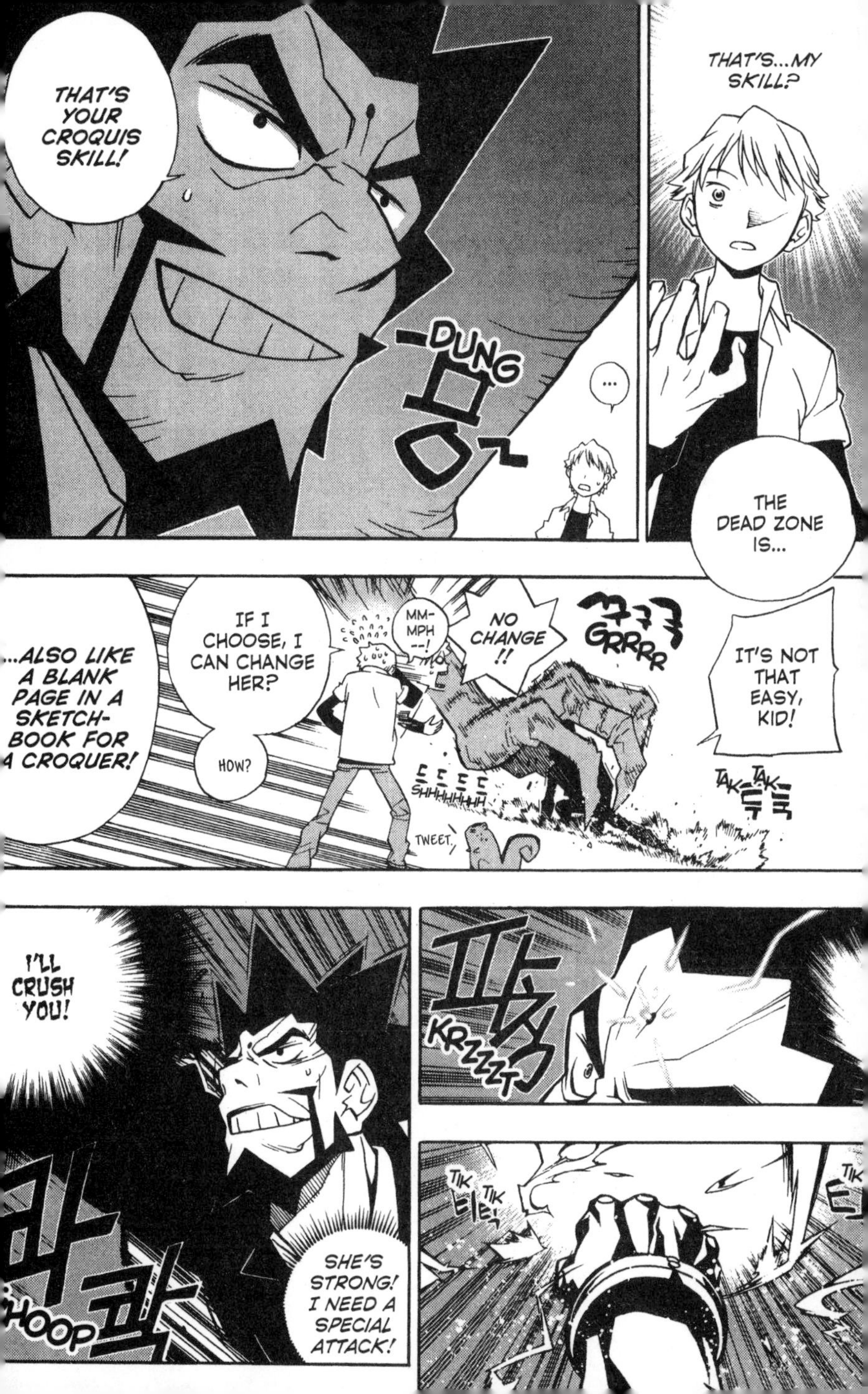

THAT'S YOUR CROQUIS SKILL!
-DUNG
...
THAT'S...MY SKILL?
THE DEAD ZONE IS...
...ALSO LIKE A BLANK PAGE IN A SKETCH-BOOK FOR A CROQUER!
IF I CHOOSE, I CAN CHANGE HER?
HOW?
MM-MPH--!
NO CHANGE!!
GRRRR
SHHHHHHHH
TWEET
IT'S NOT THAT EASY, KID!
TAK TAK
I'LL CRUSH YOU!
SHE'S STRONG! I NEED A SPECIAL ATTACK!
HOOP
KRZZZT
TIK TIK
TIK

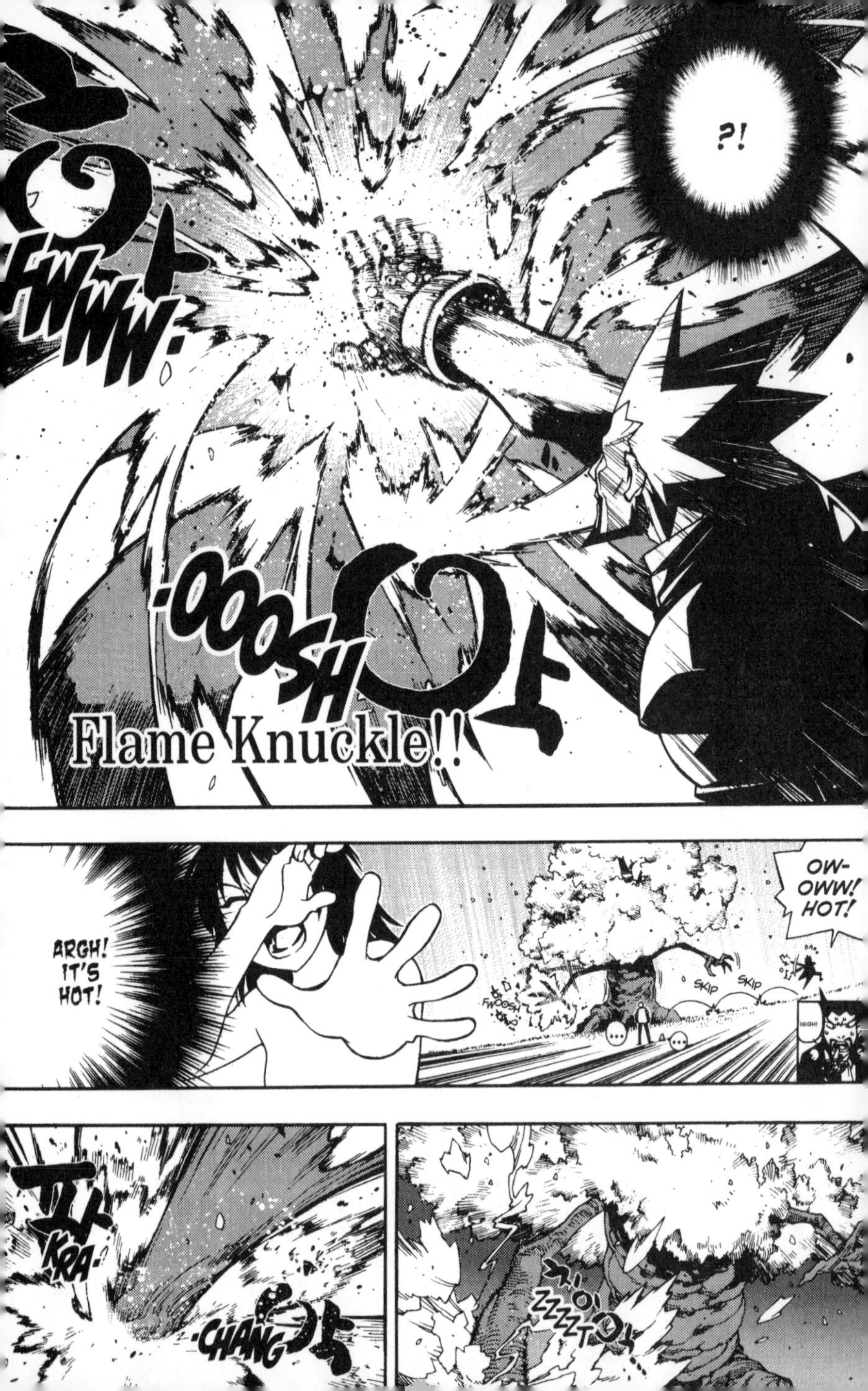
?!
FWWWW-OOOSH
Flame Knuckle!!
OW-OWW! HOT!
SKIP
SKIP
FWOOSH
...
...
ARGH! IT'S HOT!
ZZZZT
KRA-CHANG

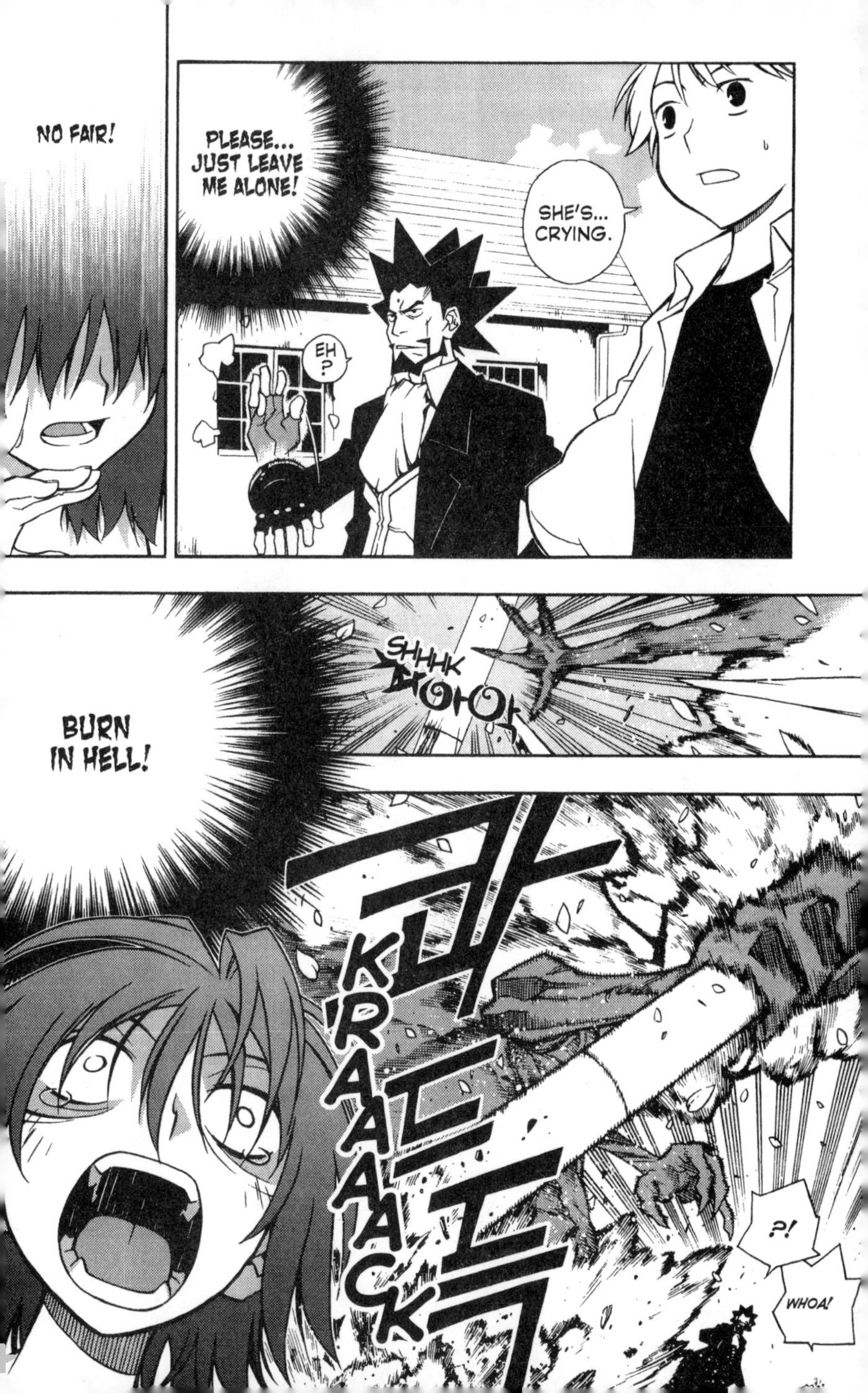
SHE'S... CRYING.
PLEASE... JUST LEAVE ME ALONE!
EH?
NO FAIR!
SHHHK
BURN IN HELL!
KRAAAACK
?!
WHOA!

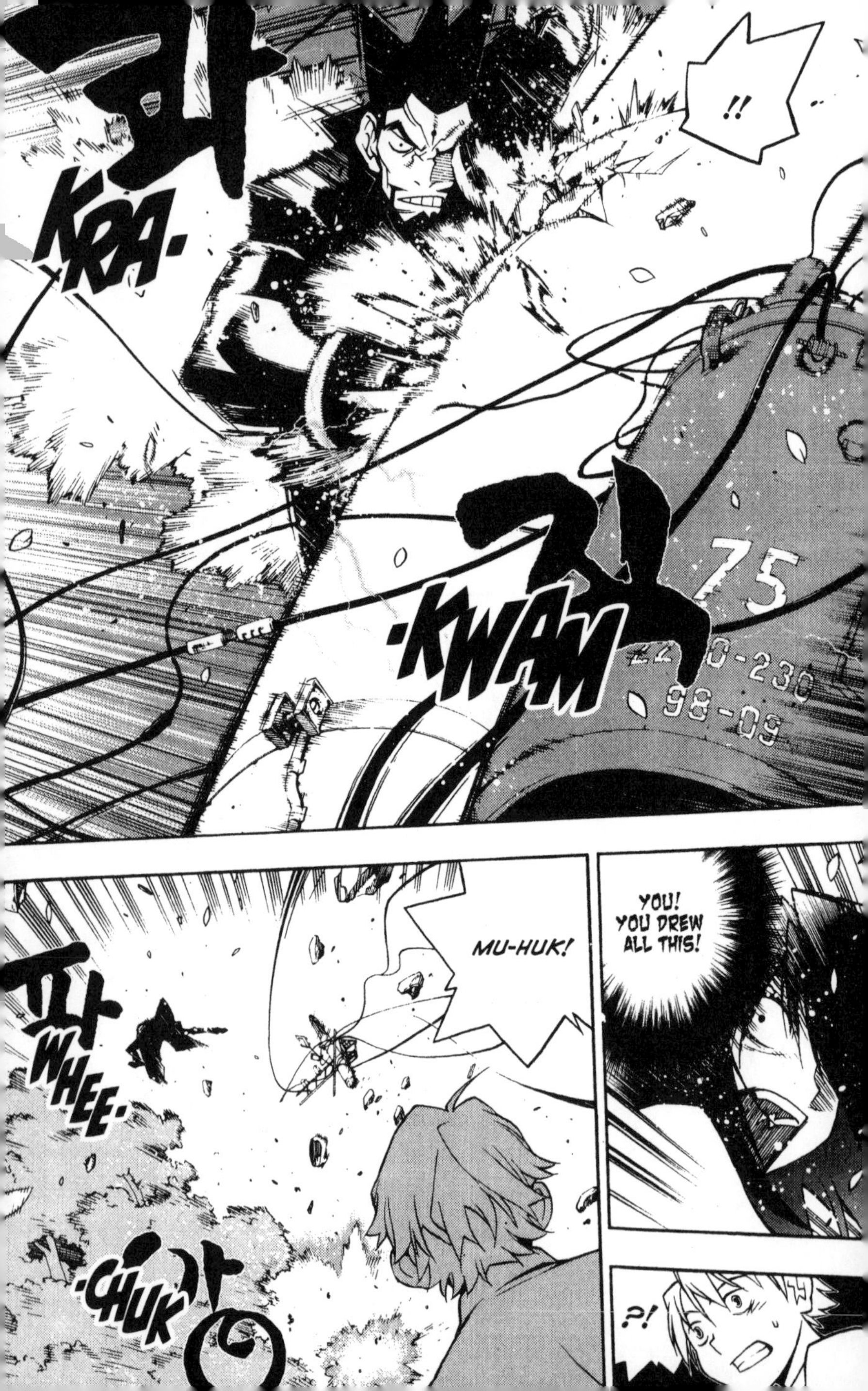
KRA-
!!
-KWAM
75
98-09
WHEE-
MU-HUK!
-CHUK
YOU! YOU DREW ALL THIS!
?!

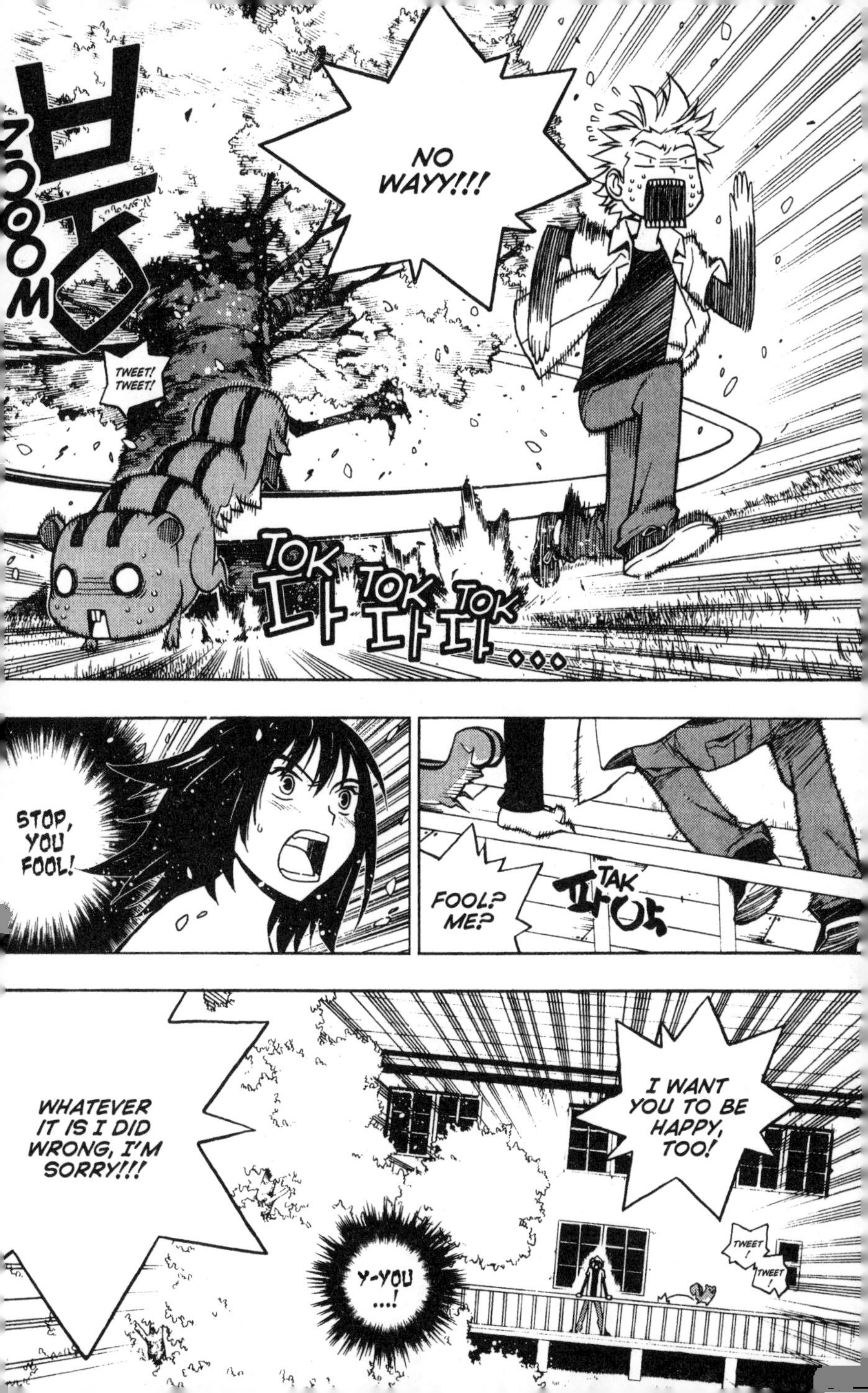
ZOOOM
NO WAYY!!!
TWEET! TWEET!
TOK TOK TOK...
STOP, YOU FOOL!
FOOL? ME?
TAK
WHATEVER IT IS I DID WRONG, I'M SORRY!!!
I WANT YOU TO BE HAPPY, TOO!
Y-YOU ...!
TWEET!
TWEET!

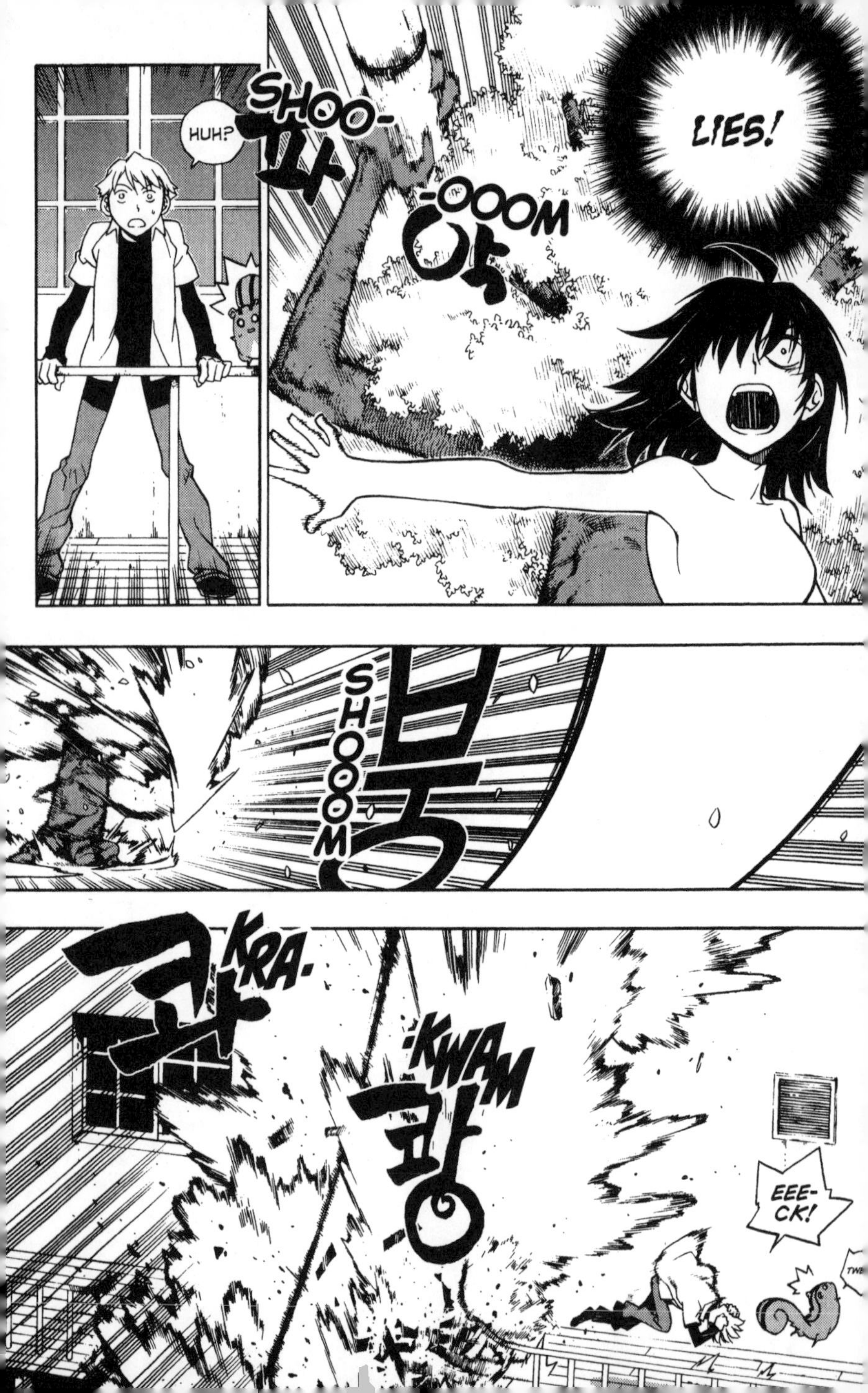
HUH?
SHOO-
-OOOM
LIES!
SHOOOOOM
KRA-
-KWAM
EEE-CK!

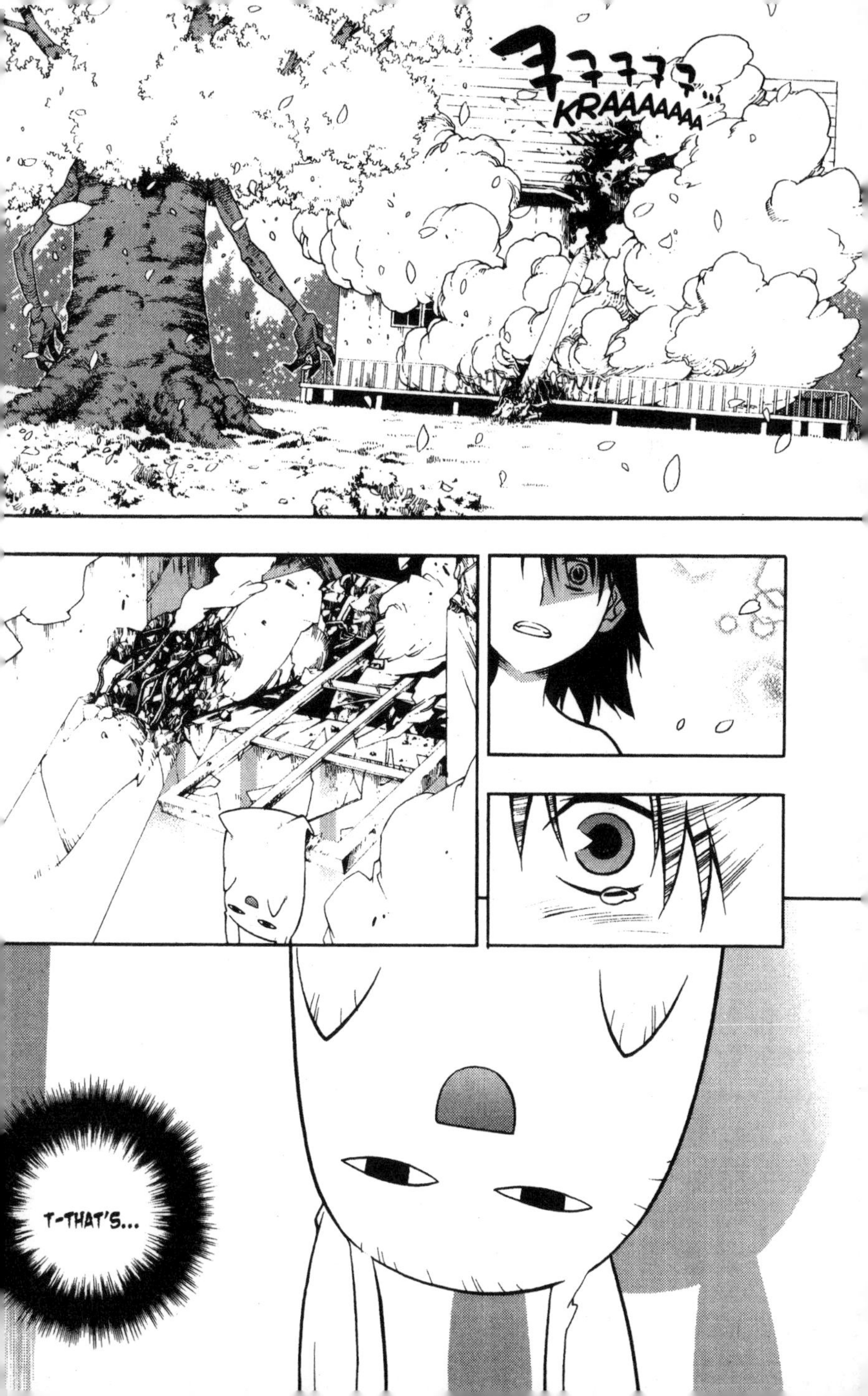

KRAAAAAAA
T-THAT'S...

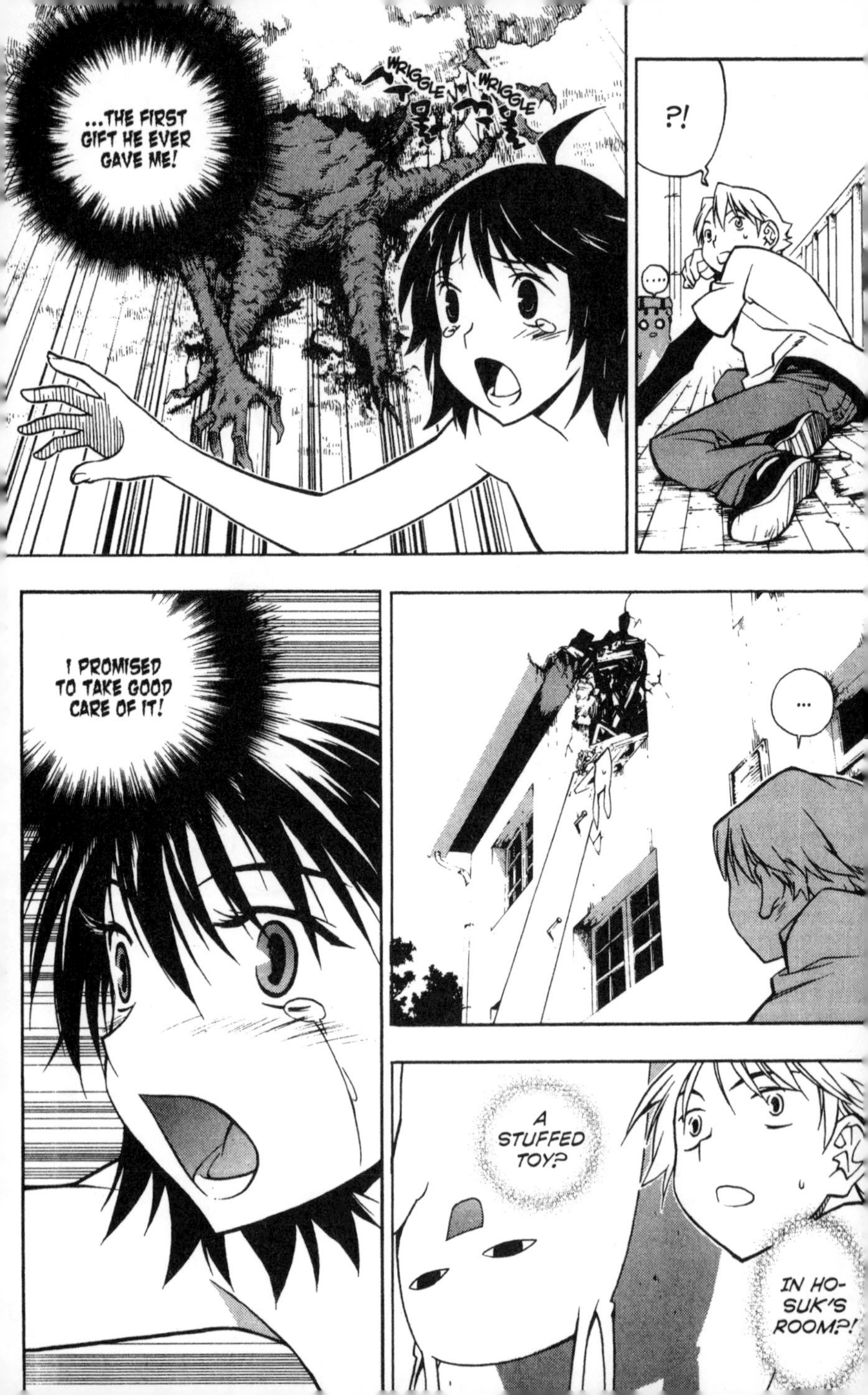
?!
....
WRIGGLE WRIGGLE
...THE FIRST GIFT HE EVER GAVE ME!
...
A STUFFED TOY?
IN HO-SUK'S ROOM?!
I PROMISED TO TAKE GOOD CARE OF IT!

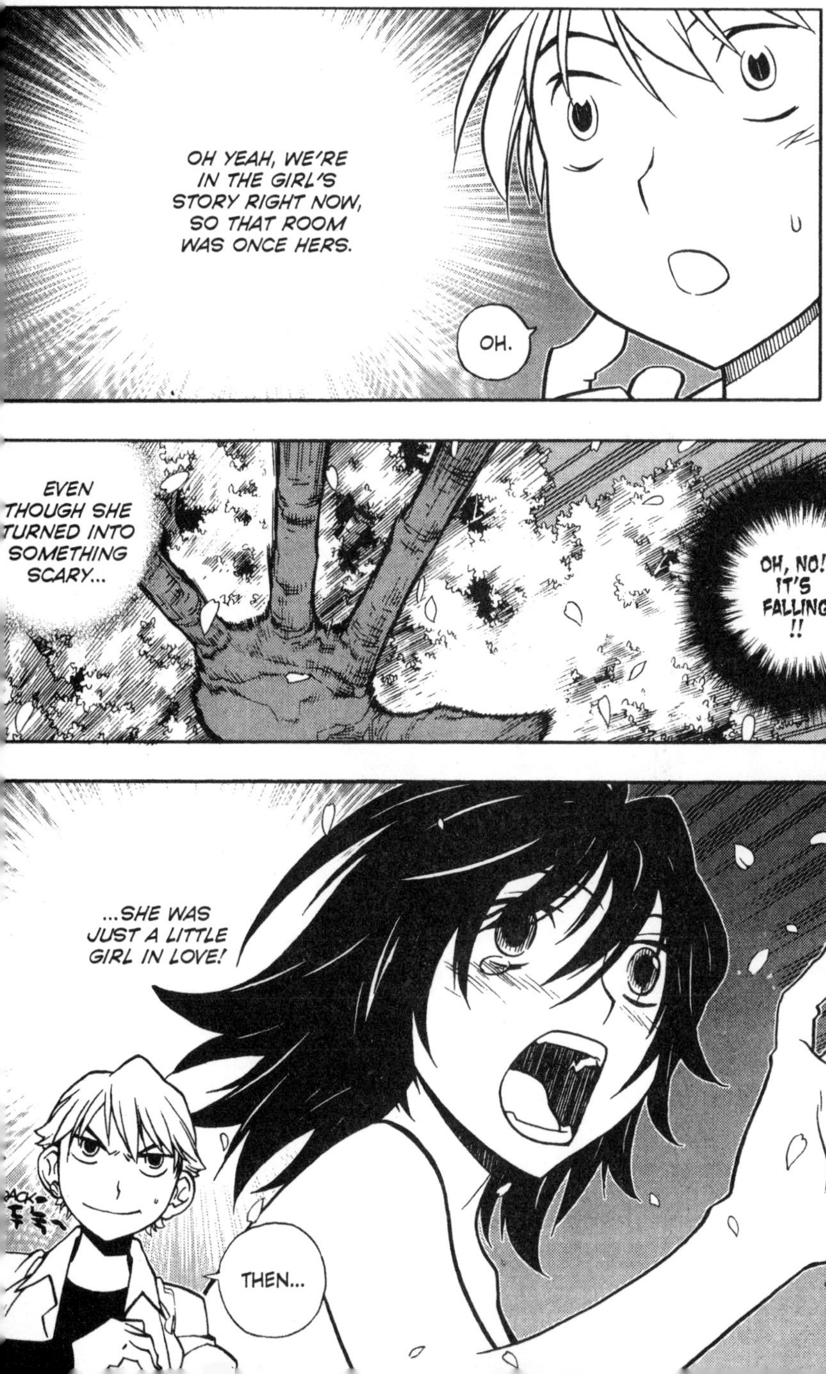
OH.
OH YEAH, WE'RE IN THE GIRL'S STORY RIGHT NOW, SO THAT ROOM WAS ONCE HERS.
OH, NO! IT'S FALLING!!
EVEN THOUGH SHE TURNED INTO SOMETHING SCARY...
...SHE WAS JUST A LITTLE GIRL IN LOVE!
THEN...

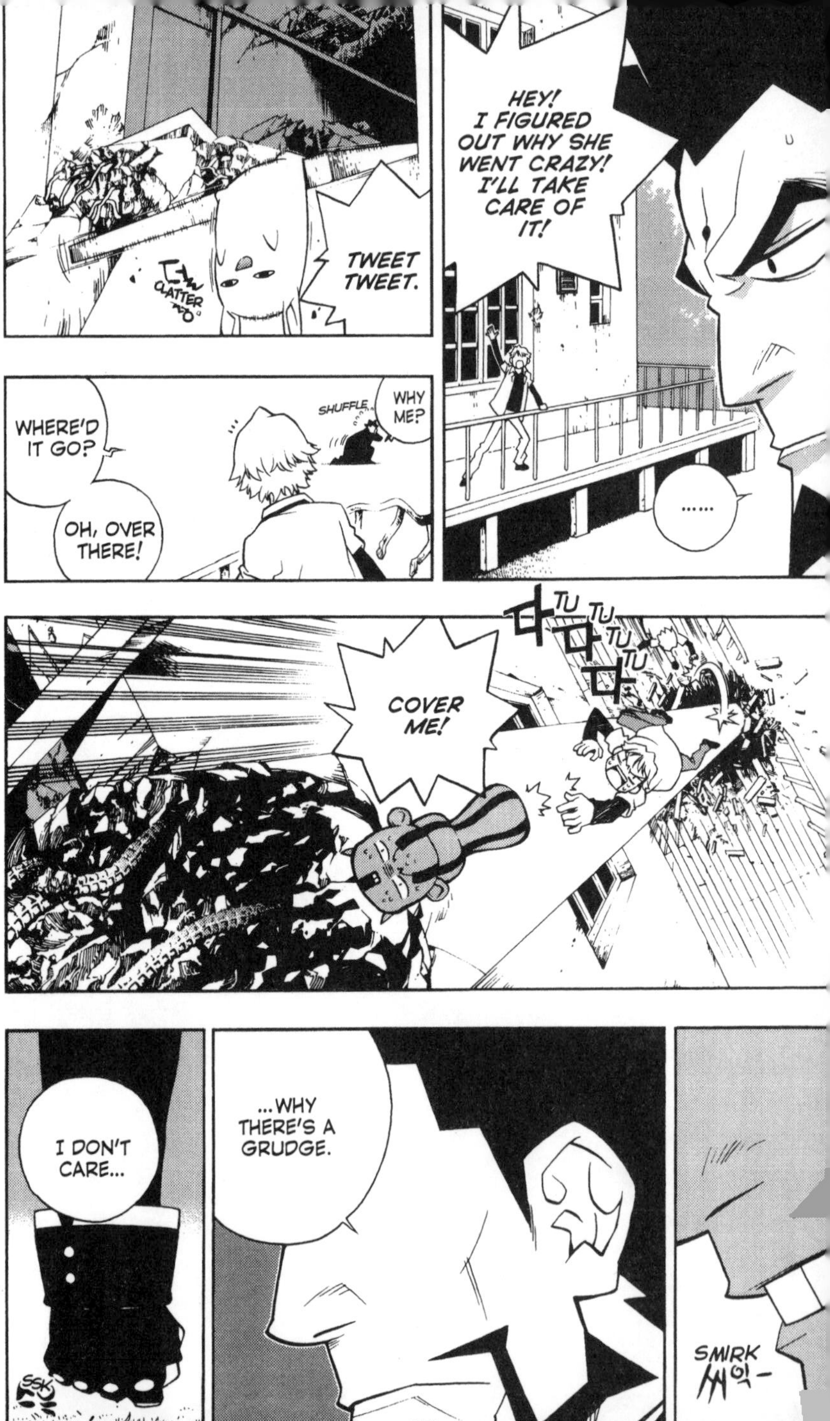
CLATTER
TWEET TWEET.
WHERE'D IT GO?
OH, OVER THERE!
SHUFFLE
WHY ME?
HEY! I FIGURED OUT WHY SHE WENT CRAZY! I'LL TAKE CARE OF IT!
......
TU TU TU TU
COVER ME!
I DON'T CARE...
SSK
...WHY THERE'S A GRUDGE.
SMIRK
씨익-

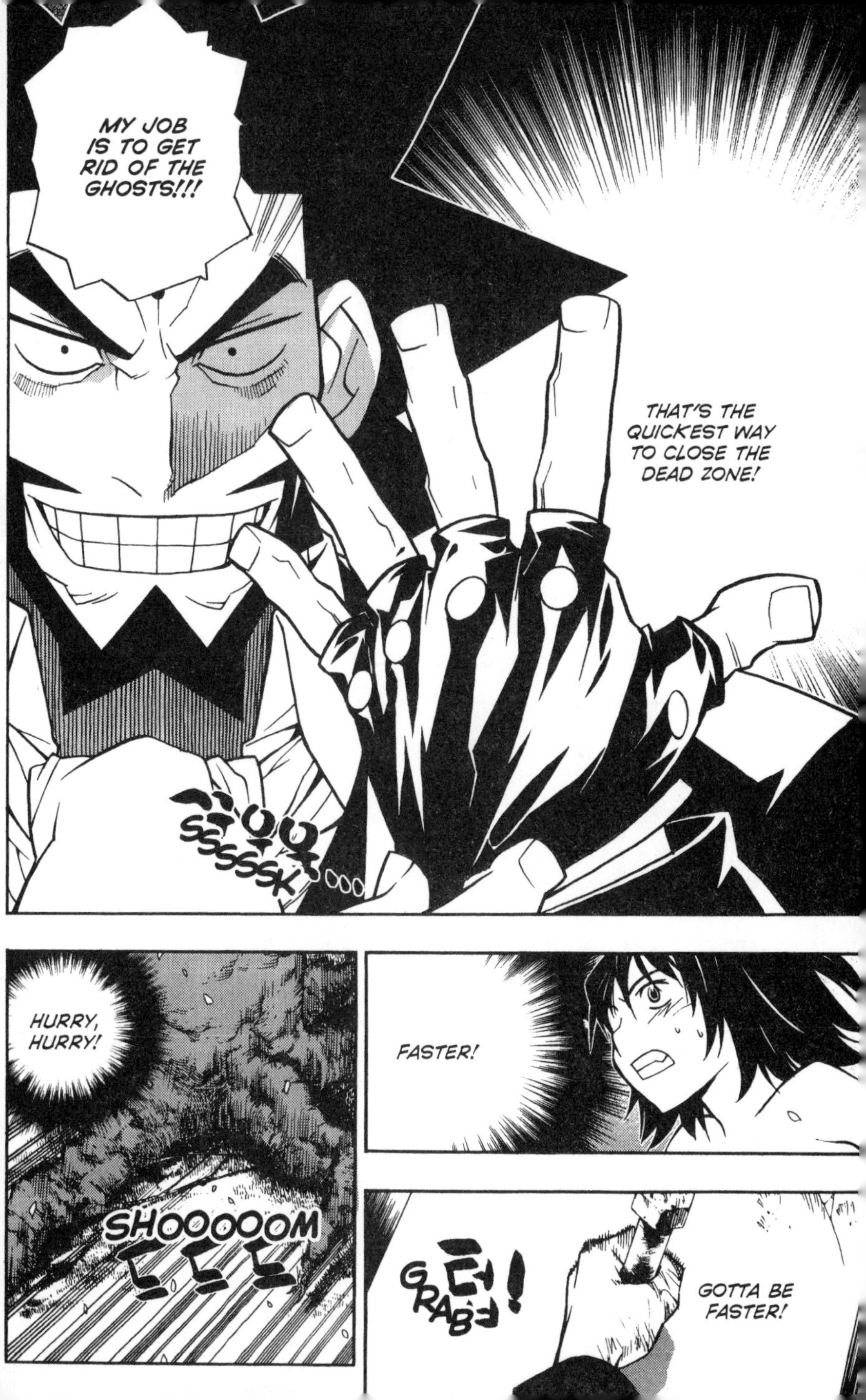

MY JOB IS TO GET RID OF THE GHOSTS!!!
THAT'S THE QUICKEST WAY TO CLOSE THE DEAD ZONE!
SSSSSSK
FASTER!
HURRY, HURRY!
SHOOOOOM
GOTTA BE FASTER!
GRAB!

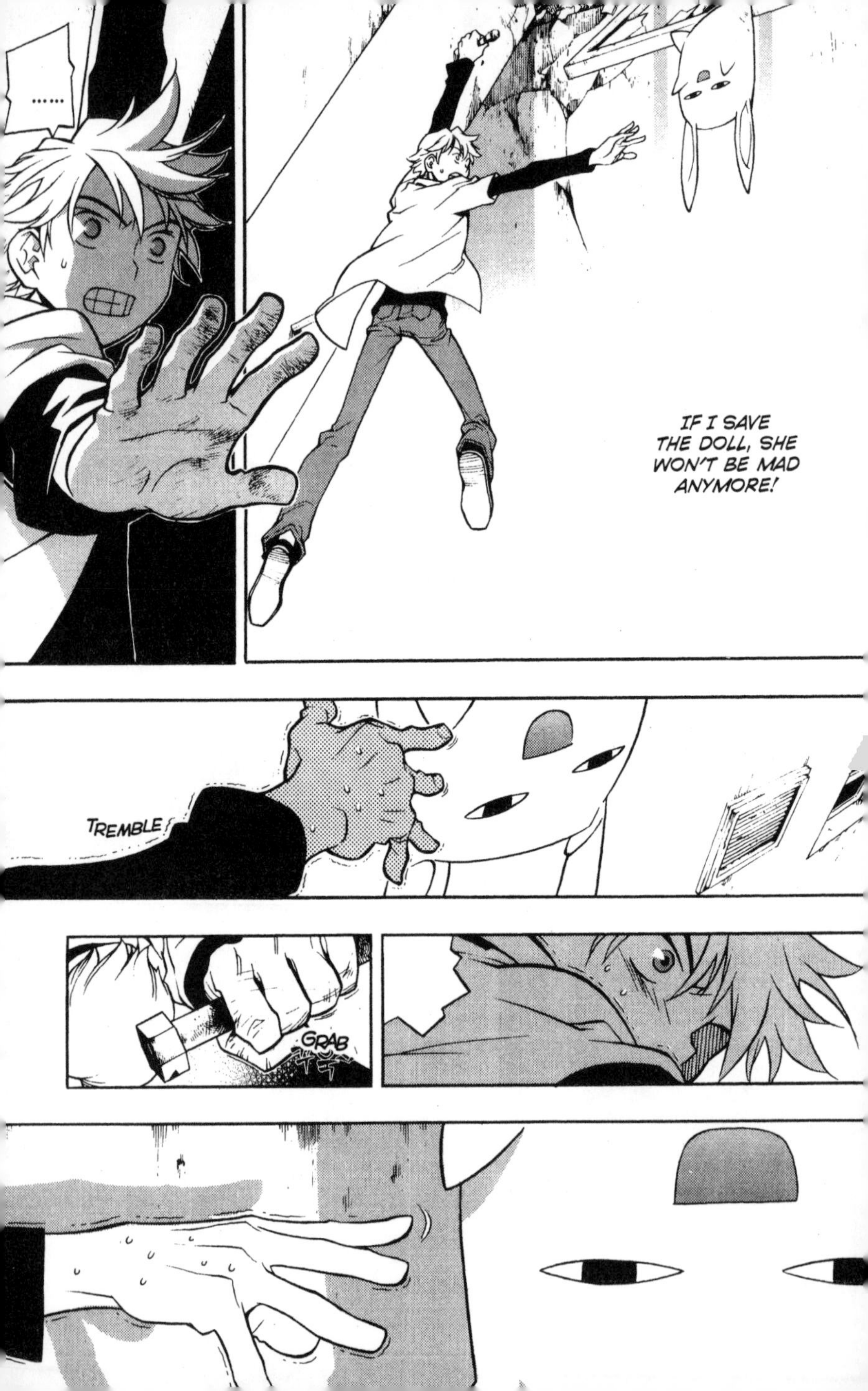
IF I SAVE THE DOLL, SHE WON'T BE MAD ANYMORE!
......
TREMBLE
GRAB

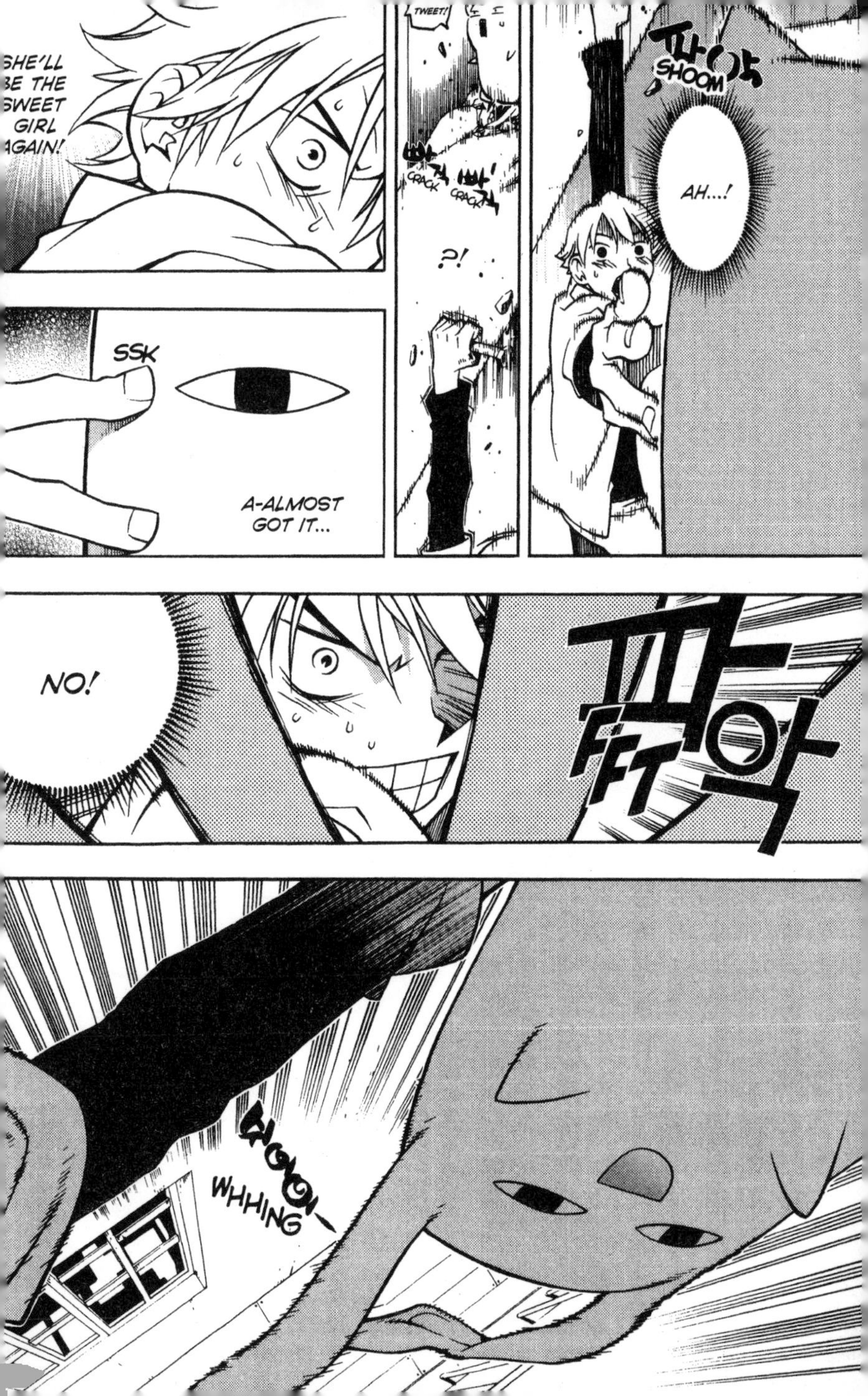

SHE'LL BE THE SWEET GIRL AGAIN!
TWEET!
CRACK
CRACK
?!
SHOOM
AH...!
SSK
A-ALMOST GOT IT...
NO!
FFT
WHHING

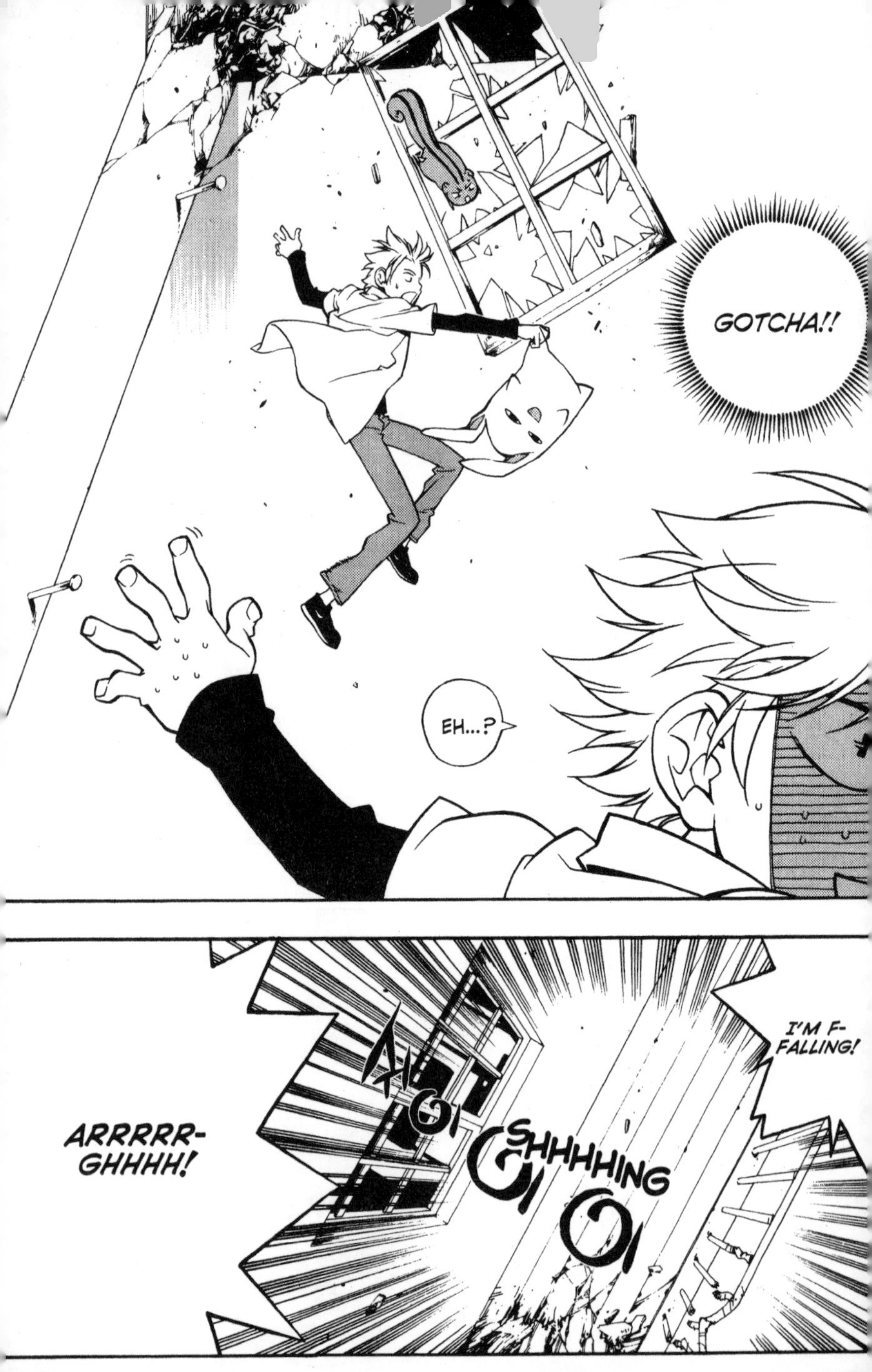
GOTCHA!!
EH...?
I'M F-FALLING!
SHHHHING
ARRRRR-GHHHH!

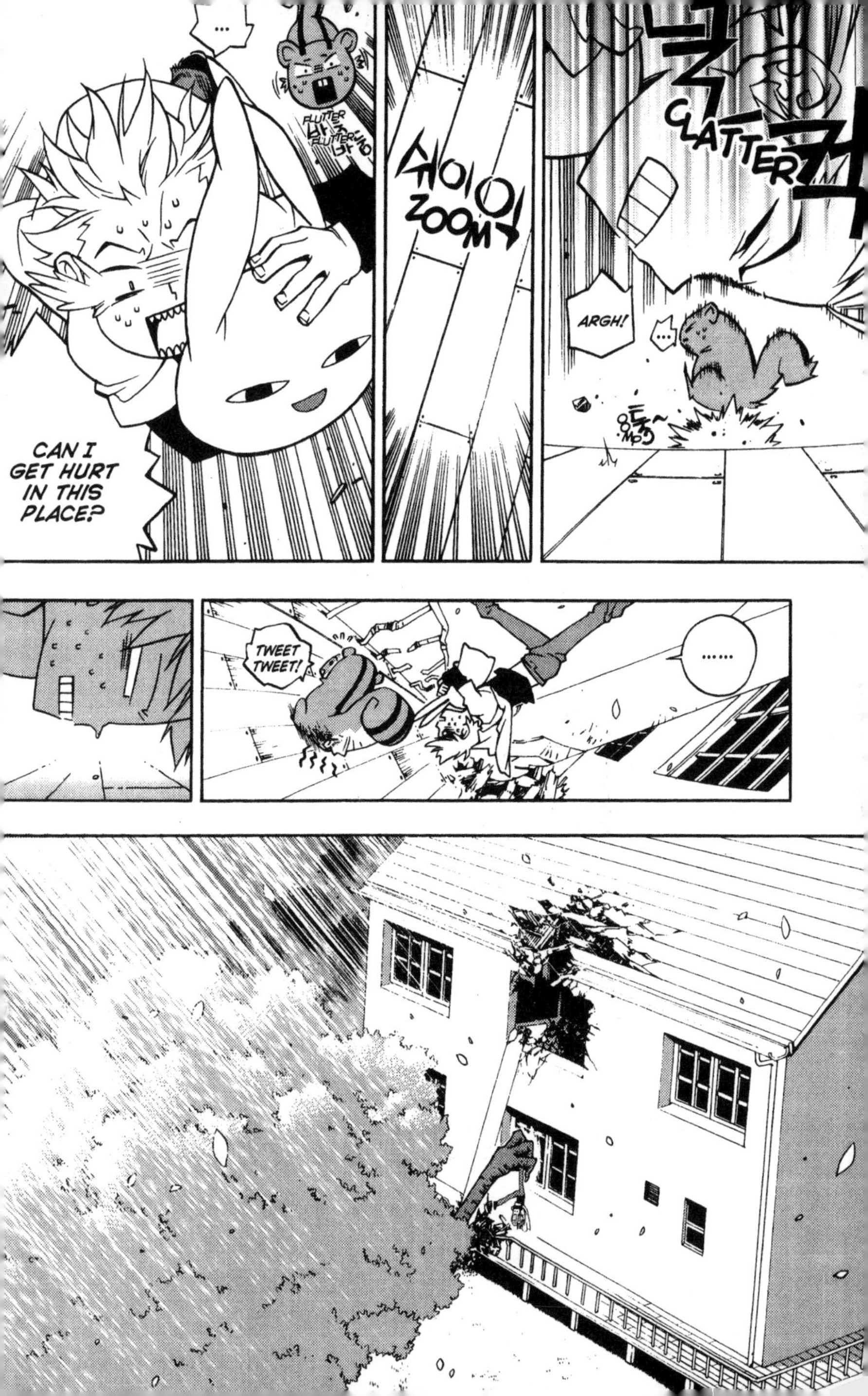
...
FLUTTER FLUTTER
CAN I GET HURT IN THIS PLACE?
ZOOM
CLATTER
ARGH!
...
TWEET TWEET!
......

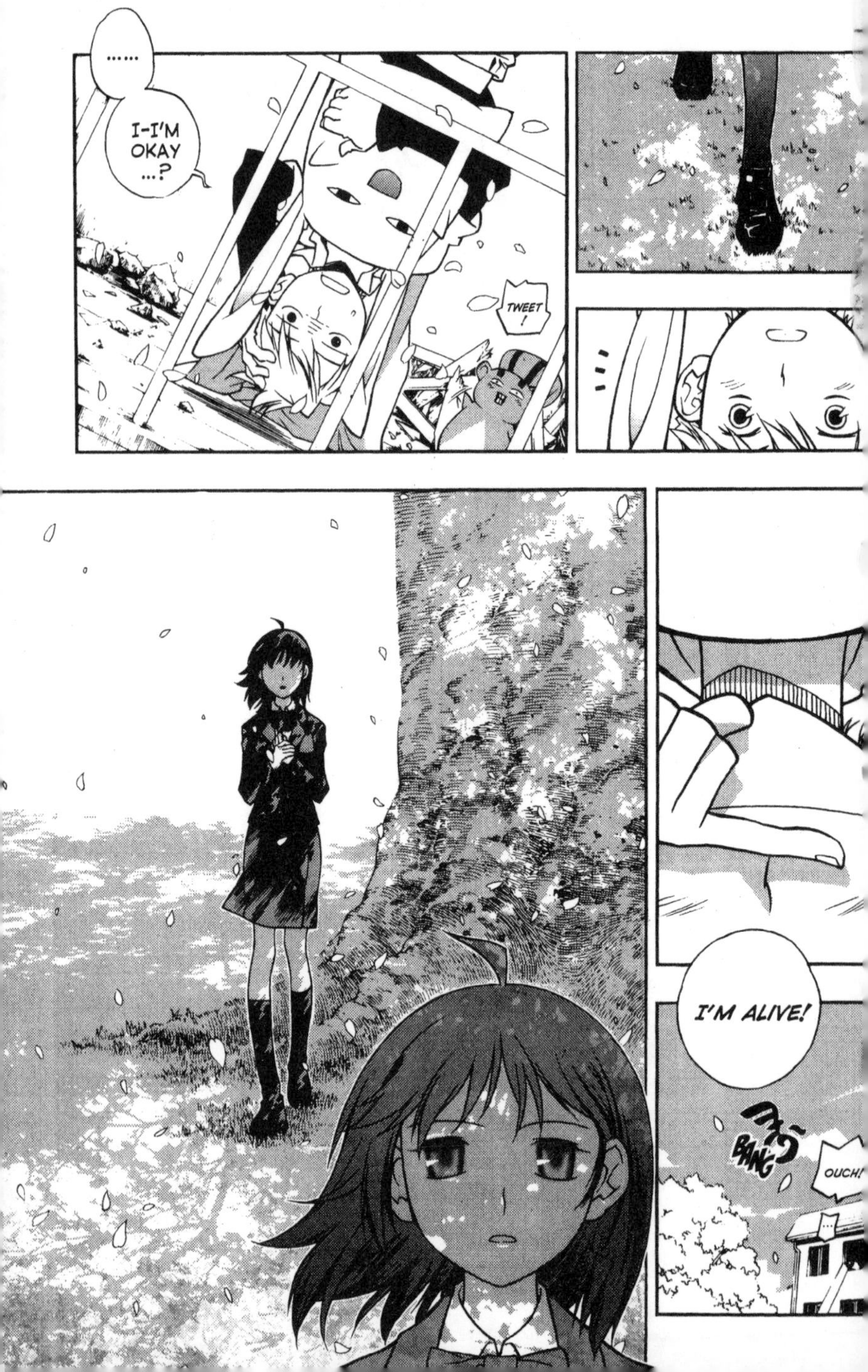
......
I-I'M OKAY ...?
TWEET!
I'M ALIVE!
BANG
OUCH!

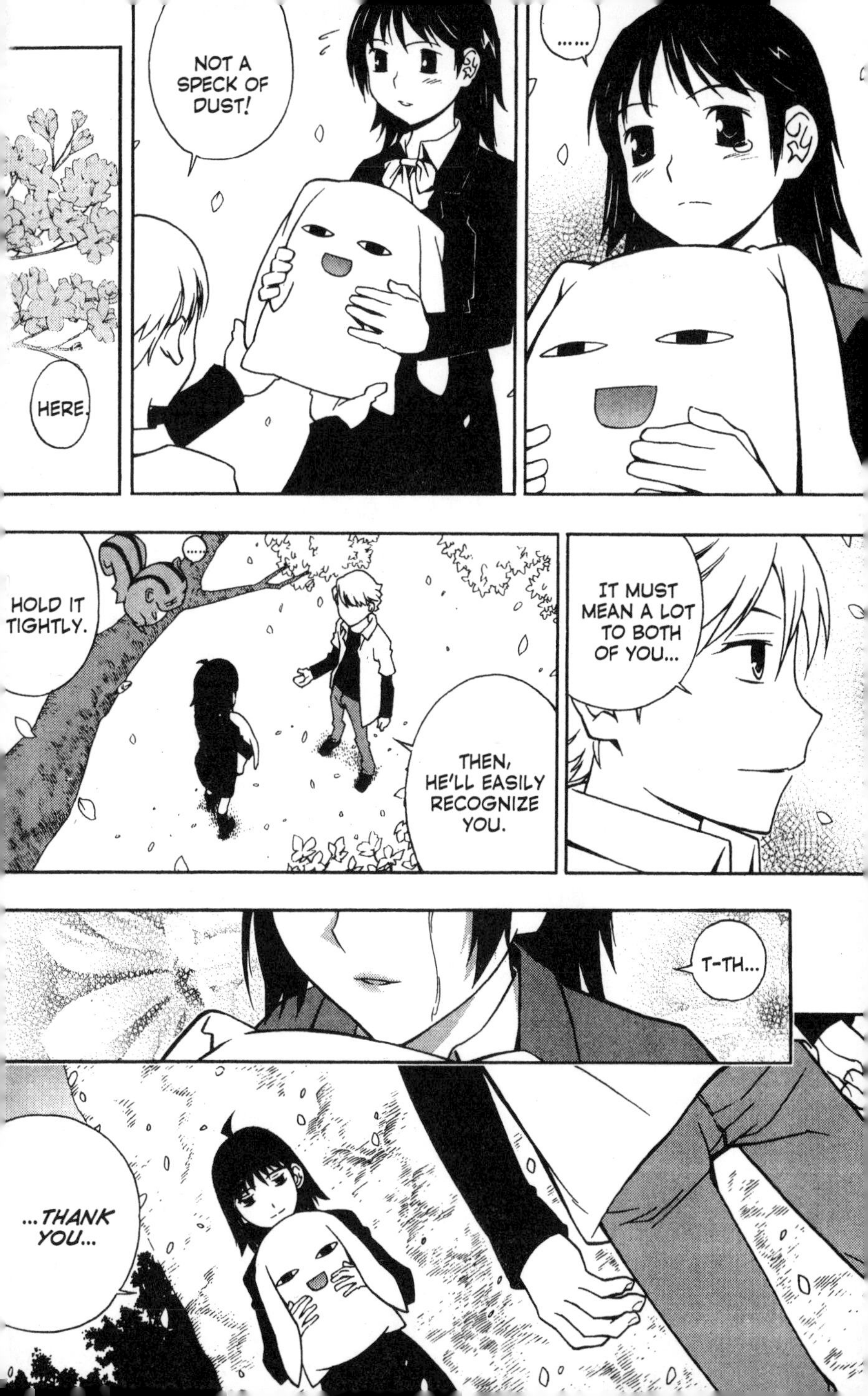
HERE.
NOT A SPECK OF DUST!
......
HOLD IT TIGHTLY.
......
THEN, HE'LL EASILY RECOGNIZE YOU.
IT MUST MEAN A LOT TO BOTH OF YOU...
T-TH...
...THANK YOU...

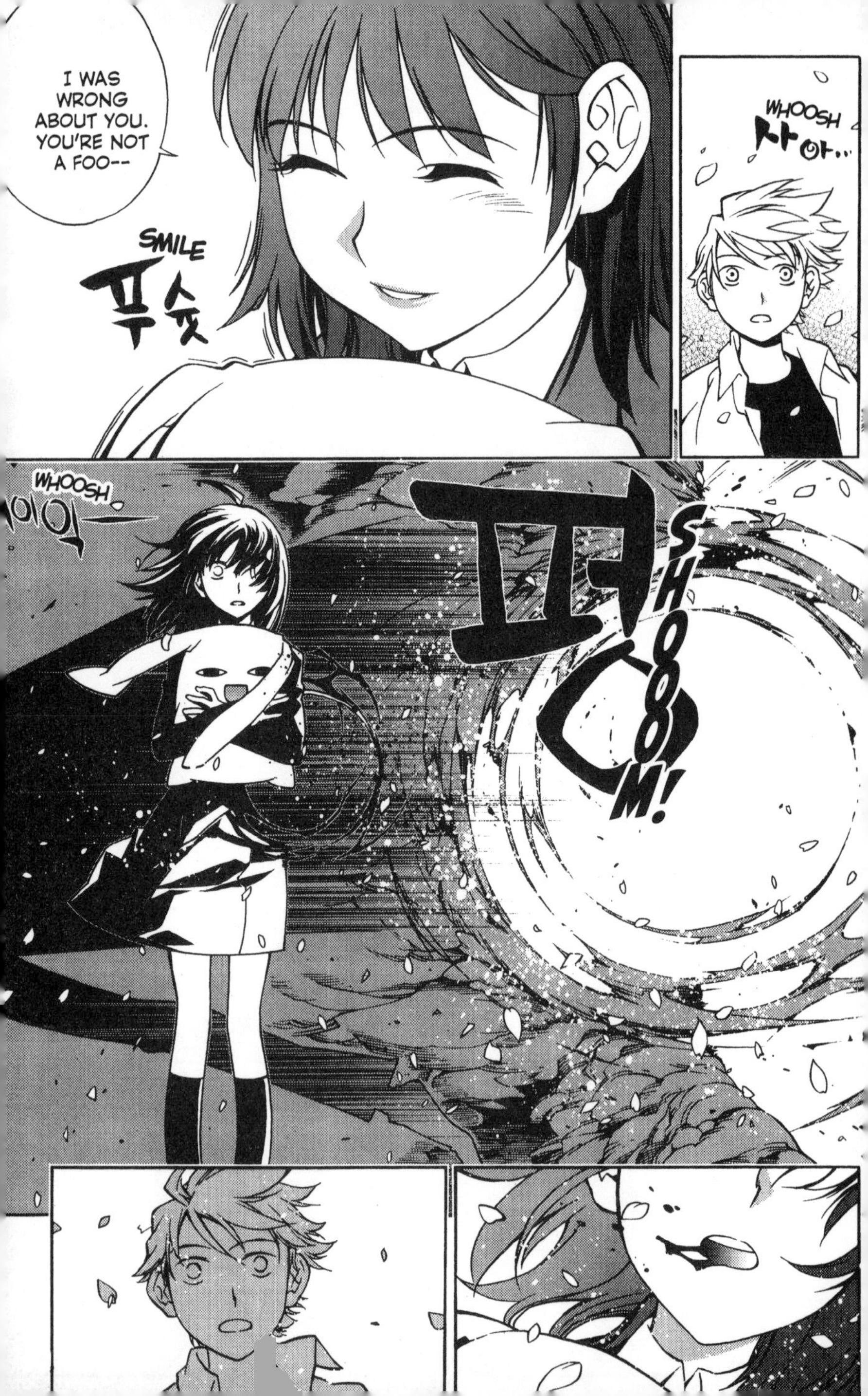

WHOOSH
사아...
I WAS WRONG ABOUT YOU. YOU'RE NOT A FOO--
SMILE
푸슷
WHOOSH
SHOOOOM!

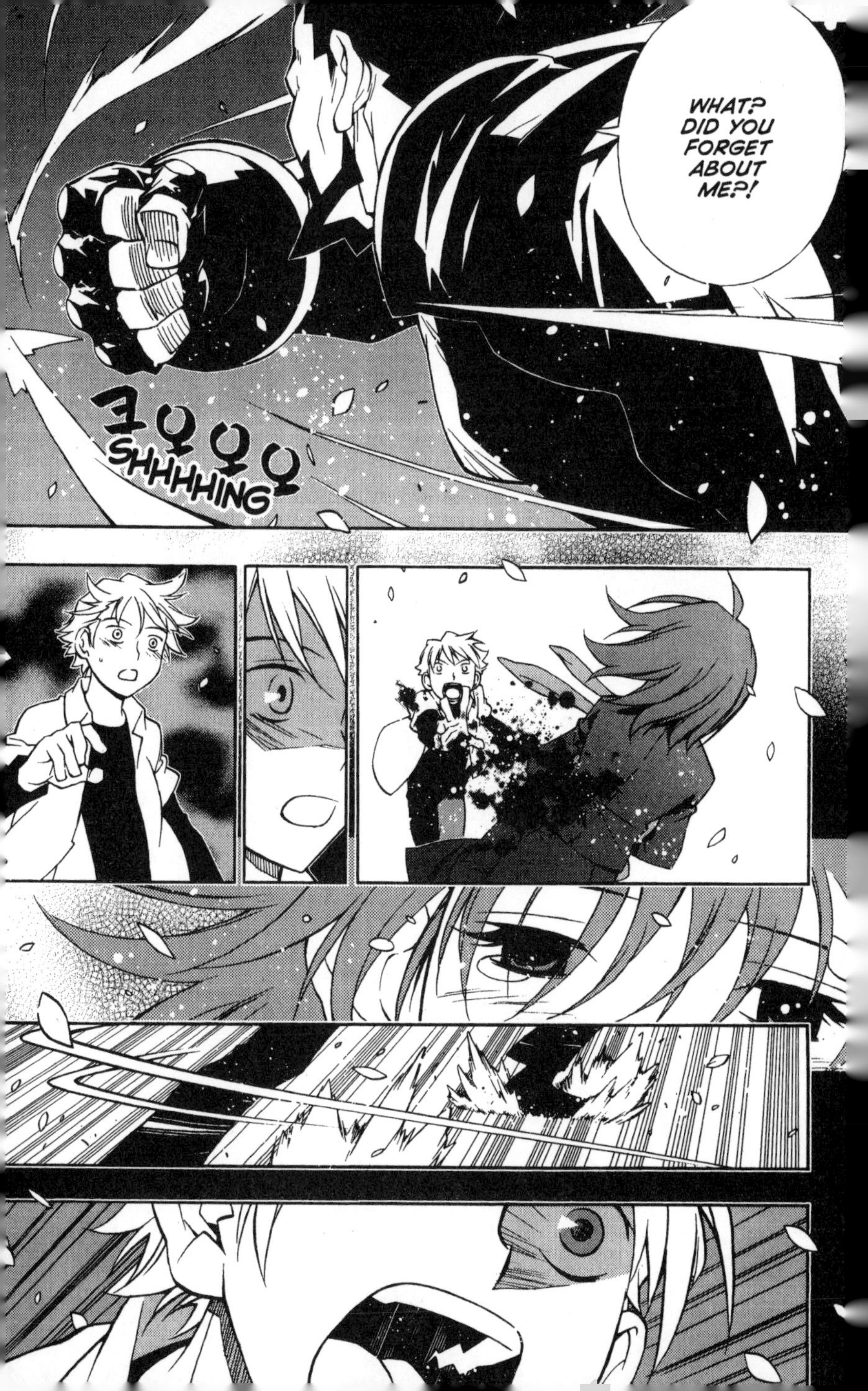
WHAT? DID YOU FORGET ABOUT ME?!
쉬우우우
SHHHHING

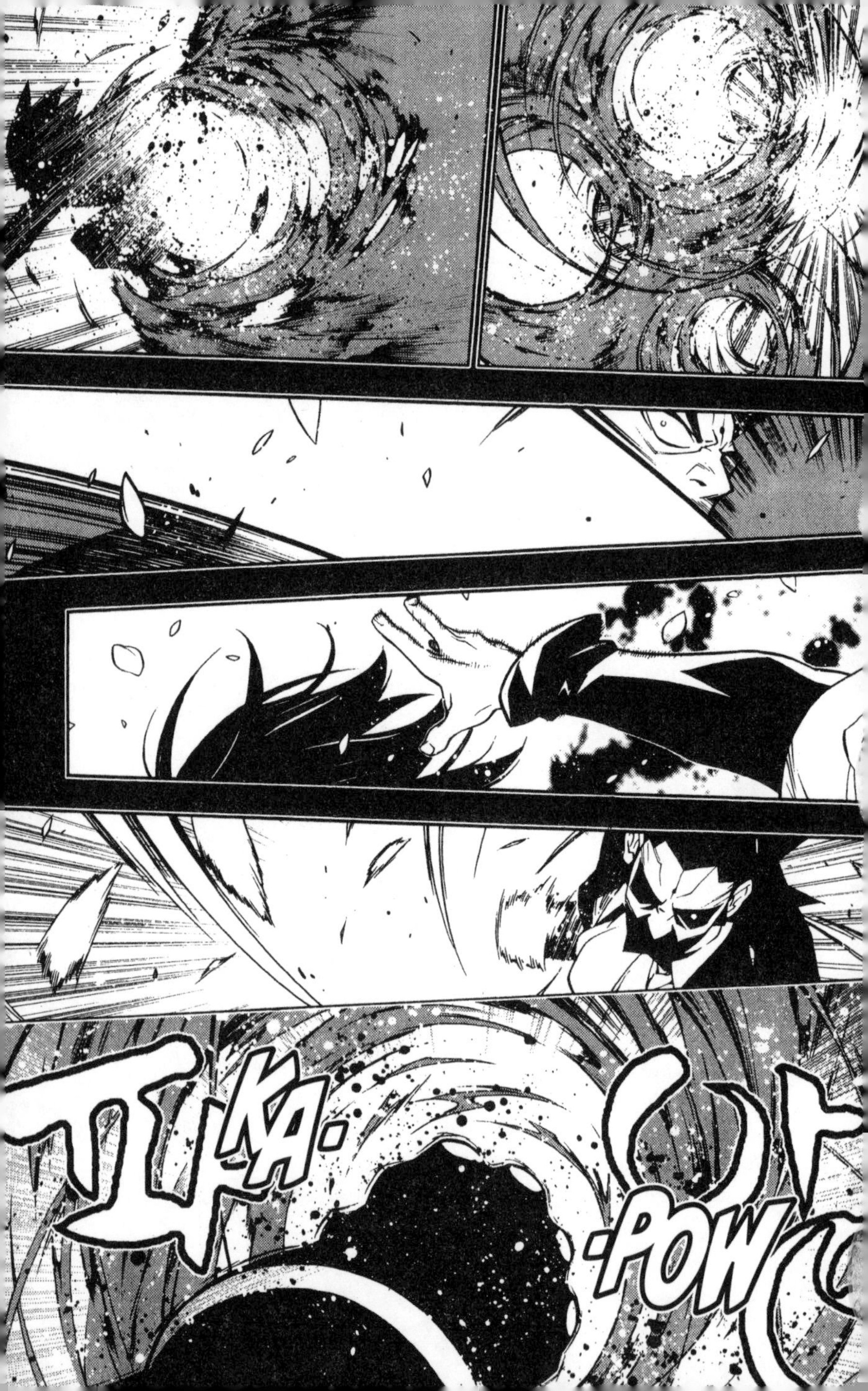
KA-POW

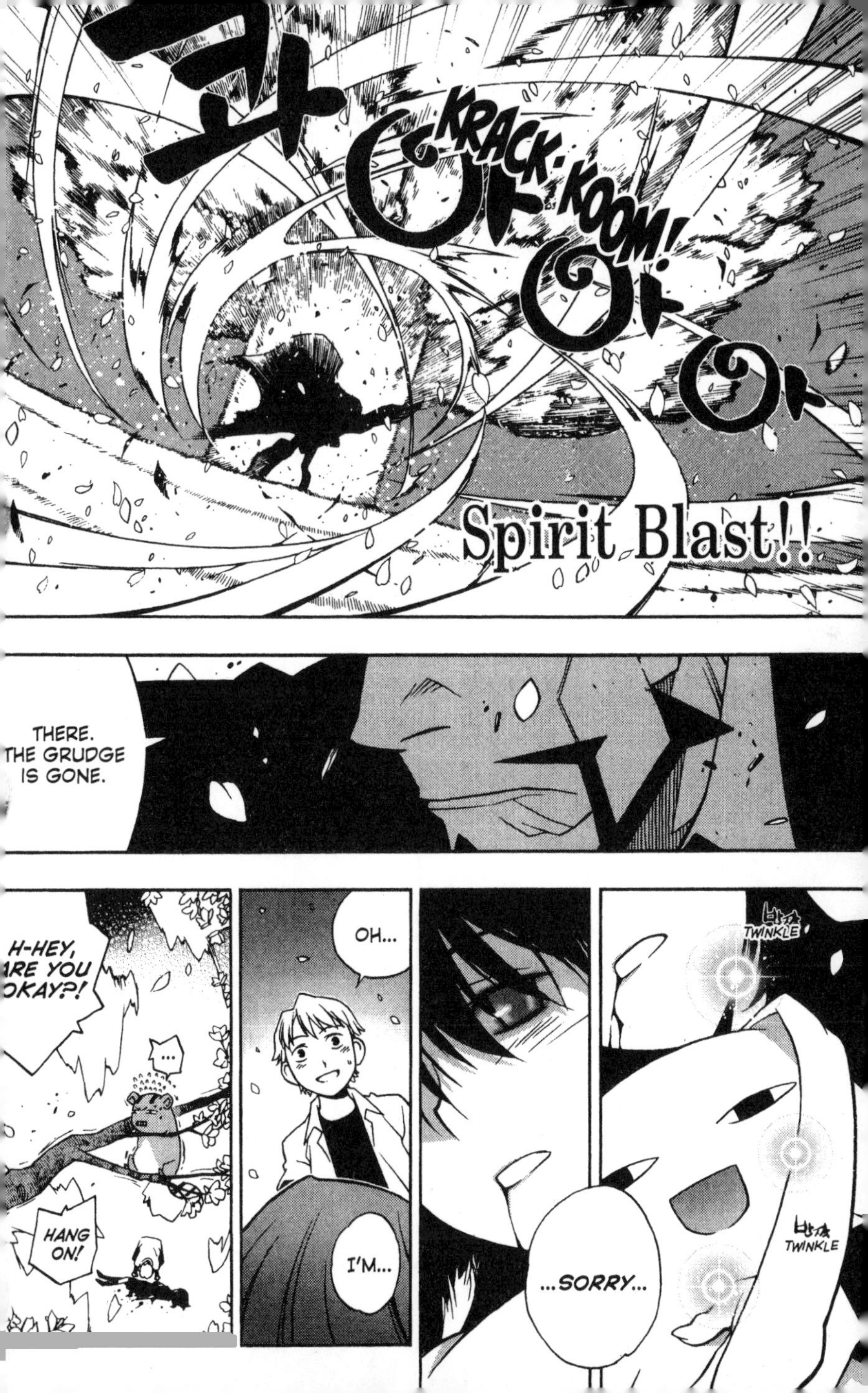
KRACK-KOOM!
Spirit Blast!!
THERE. THE GRUDGE IS GONE.
TWINKLE
TWINKLE
...SORRY...
OH...
I'M...
H-HEY, ARE YOU OKAY?!
...
HANG ON!

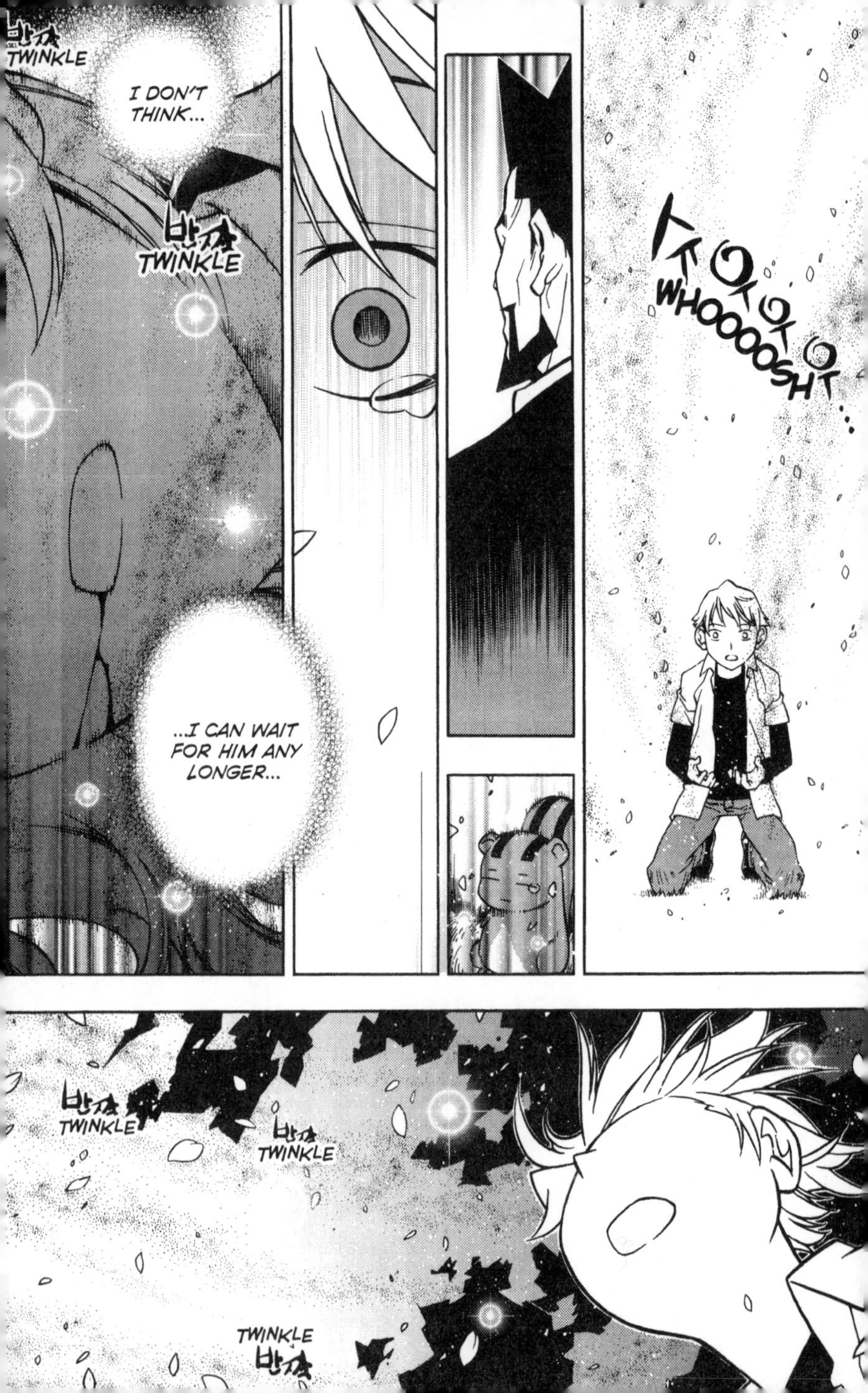

WHOOOOOSH...
반짝
TWINKLE
I DON'T THINK...
반짝
TWINKLE
...I CAN WAIT FOR HIM ANY LONGER...
반짝
TWINKLE
반짝
TWINKLE
TWINKLE
반짝

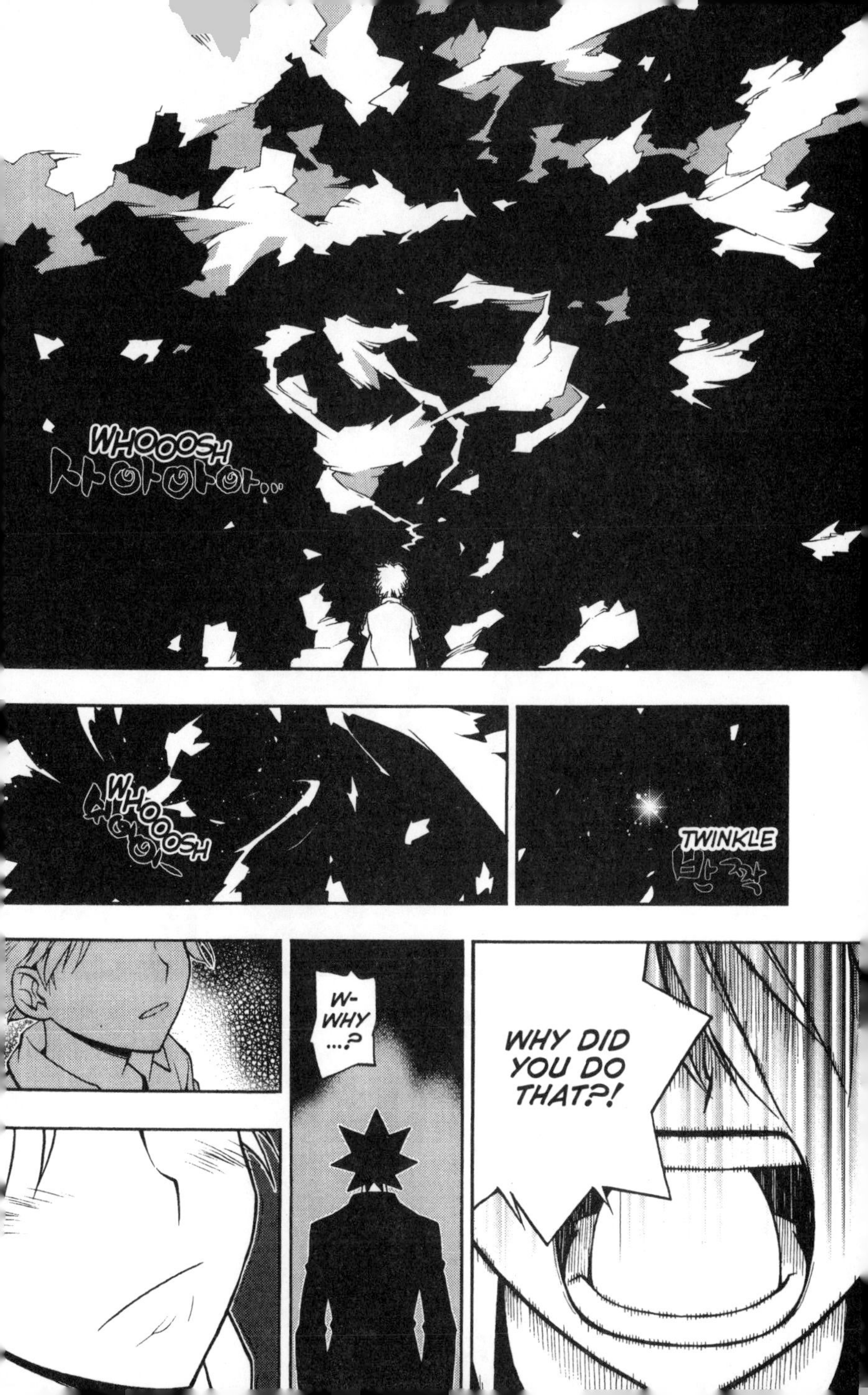
WHOOOSH
사아아아아..
WHOOOSH
TWINKLE
반짝
W-WHY ...?
WHY DID YOU DO THAT?!

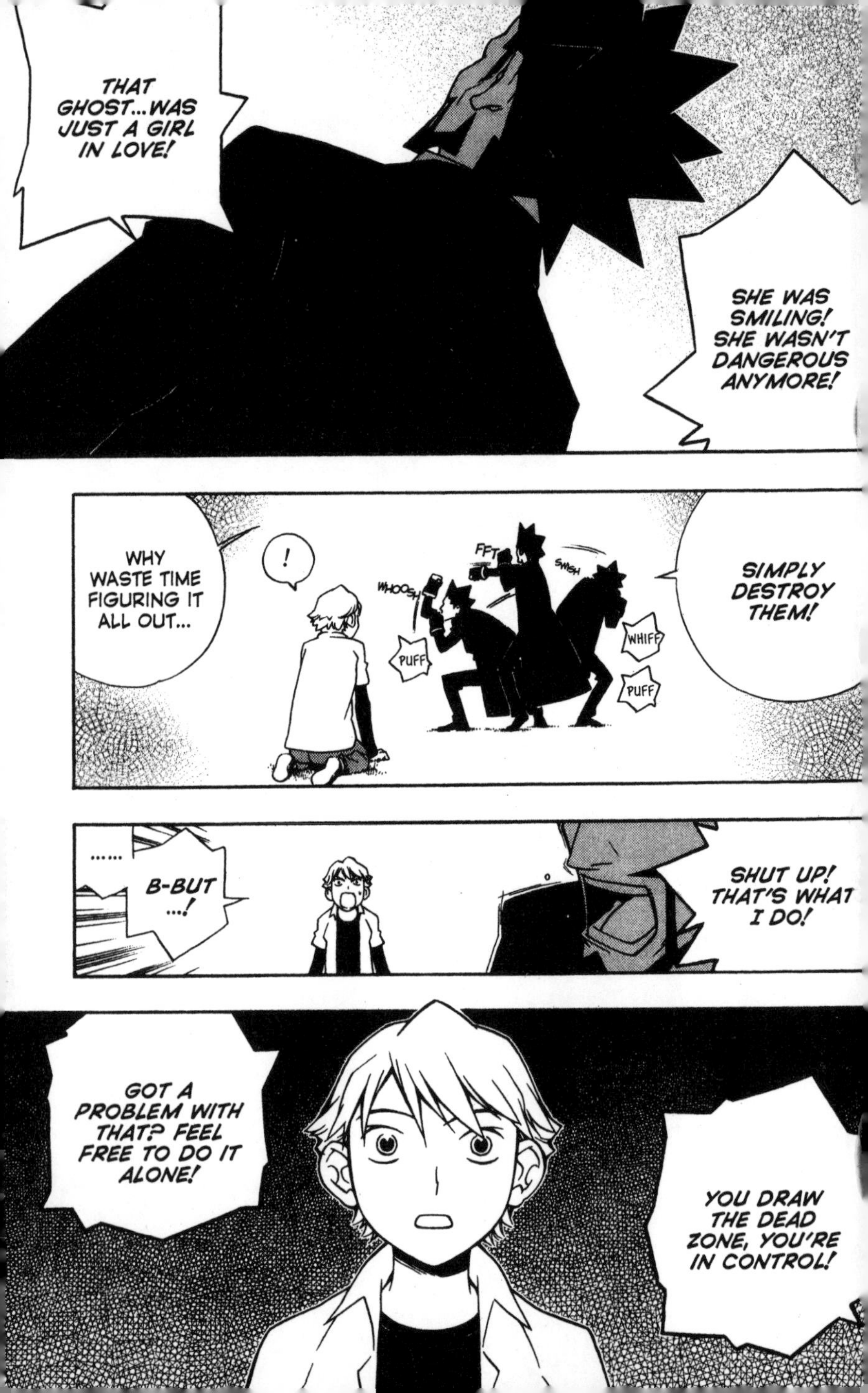
THAT GHOST...WAS JUST A GIRL IN LOVE!
SHE WAS SMILING! SHE WASN'T DANGEROUS ANYMORE!
SIMPLY DESTROY THEM!
SWISH
FFT
WHOOSH
!
WHY WASTE TIME FIGURING IT ALL OUT...
WHIFF
PUFF
PUFF
SHUT UP! THAT'S WHAT I DO!
B-BUT ...!
......
YOU DRAW THE DEAD ZONE, YOU'RE IN CONTROL!
GOT A PROBLEM WITH THAT? FEEL FREE TO DO IT ALONE!

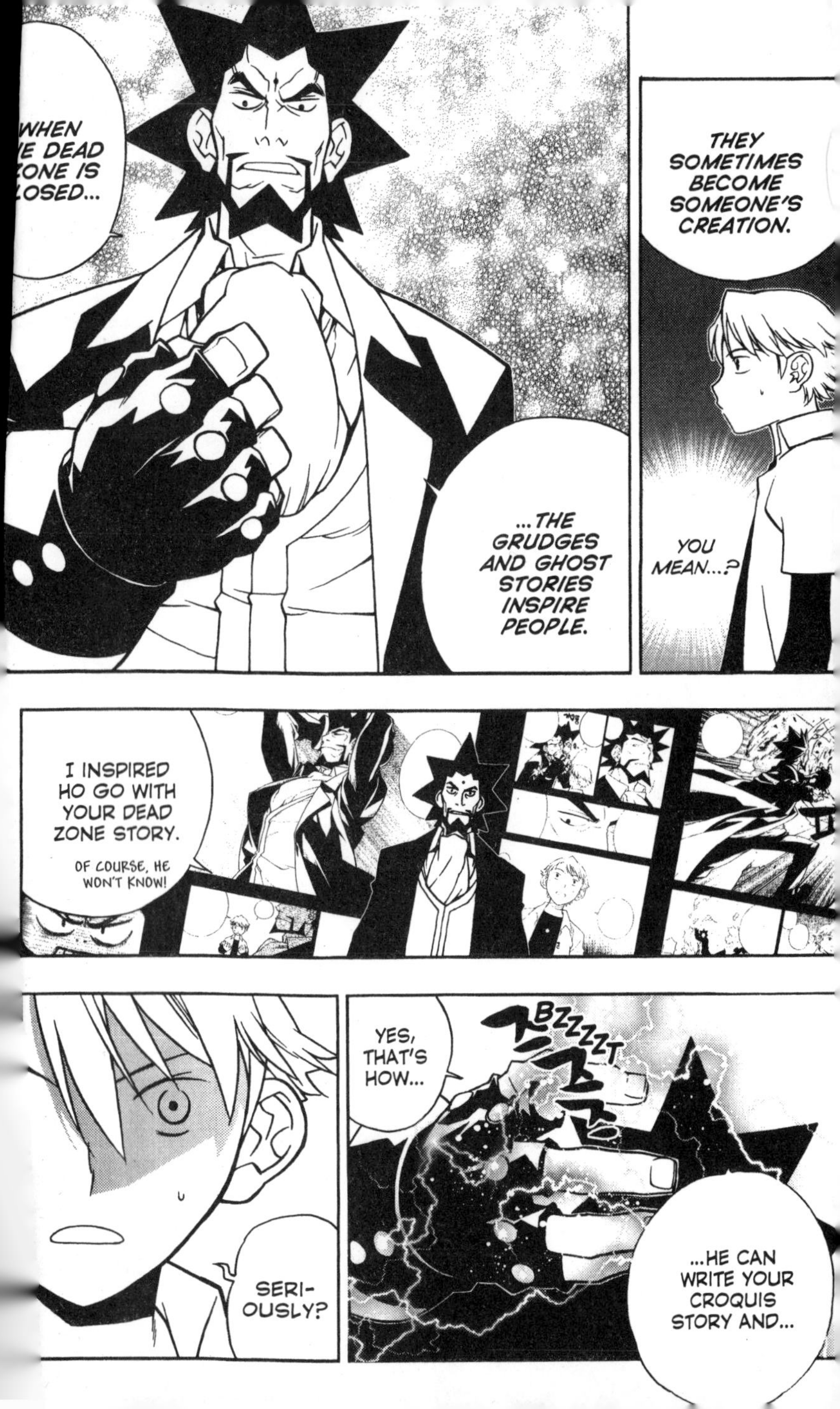
WHEN
E DEAD
ZONE IS
LOSED...
...THE GRUDGES AND GHOST STORIES INSPIRE PEOPLE.
THEY SOMETIMES BECOME SOMEONE'S CREATION.
YOU MEAN...?
I INSPIRED HO GO WITH YOUR DEAD ZONE STORY.
OF COURSE, HE WON'T KNOW!
SERI-OUSLY?
YES, THAT'S HOW...
BZZZZZT
...HE CAN WRITE YOUR CROQUIS STORY AND...

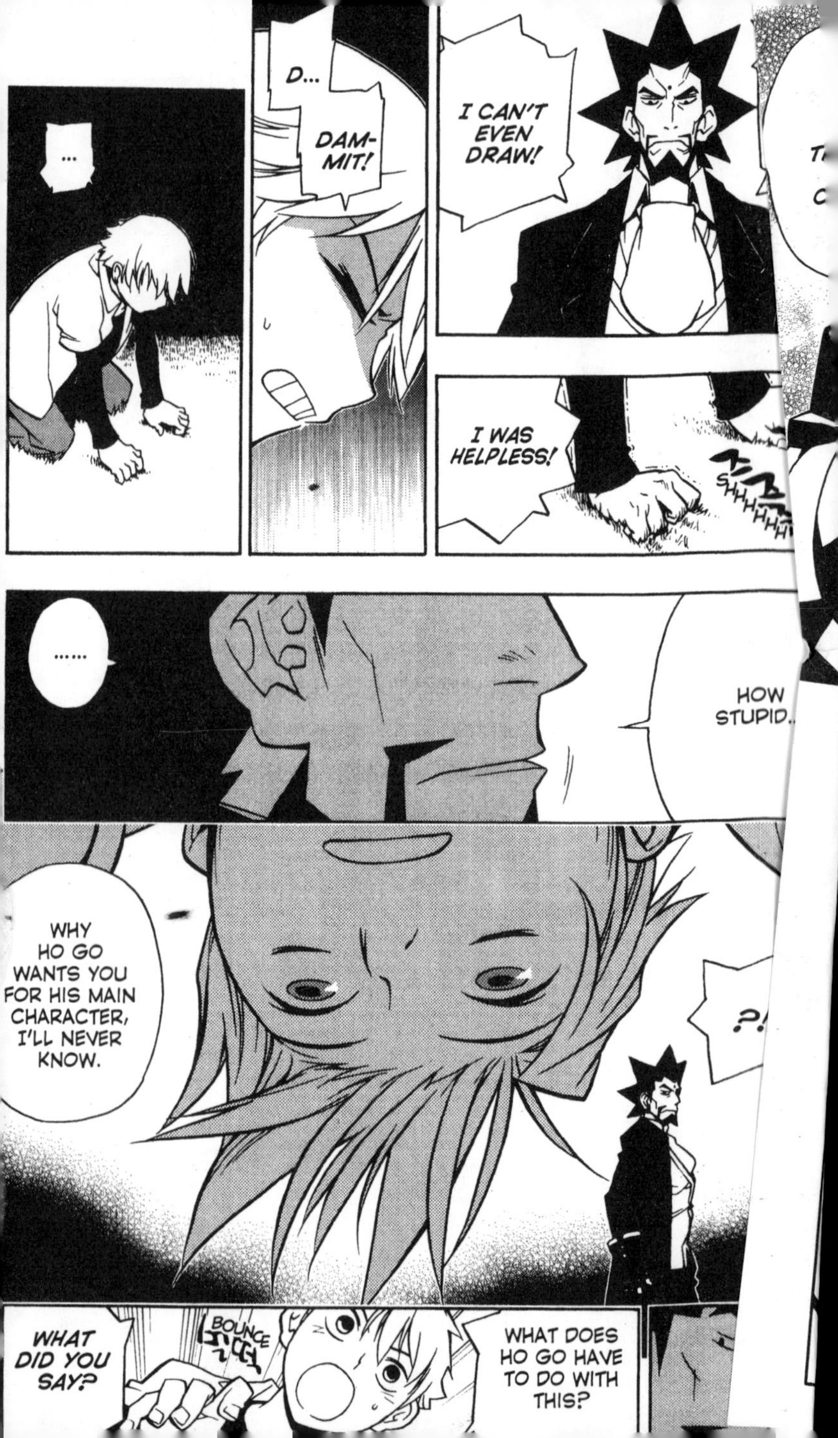
...
D...
DAM-MIT!
I CAN'T EVEN DRAW!
I WAS HELPLESS!
SHHHHH
......
HOW STUPID...
WHY HO GO WANTS YOU FOR HIS MAIN CHARACTER, I'LL NEVER KNOW.
?!
WHAT DID YOU SAY?
BOUNCE
WHAT DOES HO GO HAVE TO DO WITH THIS?

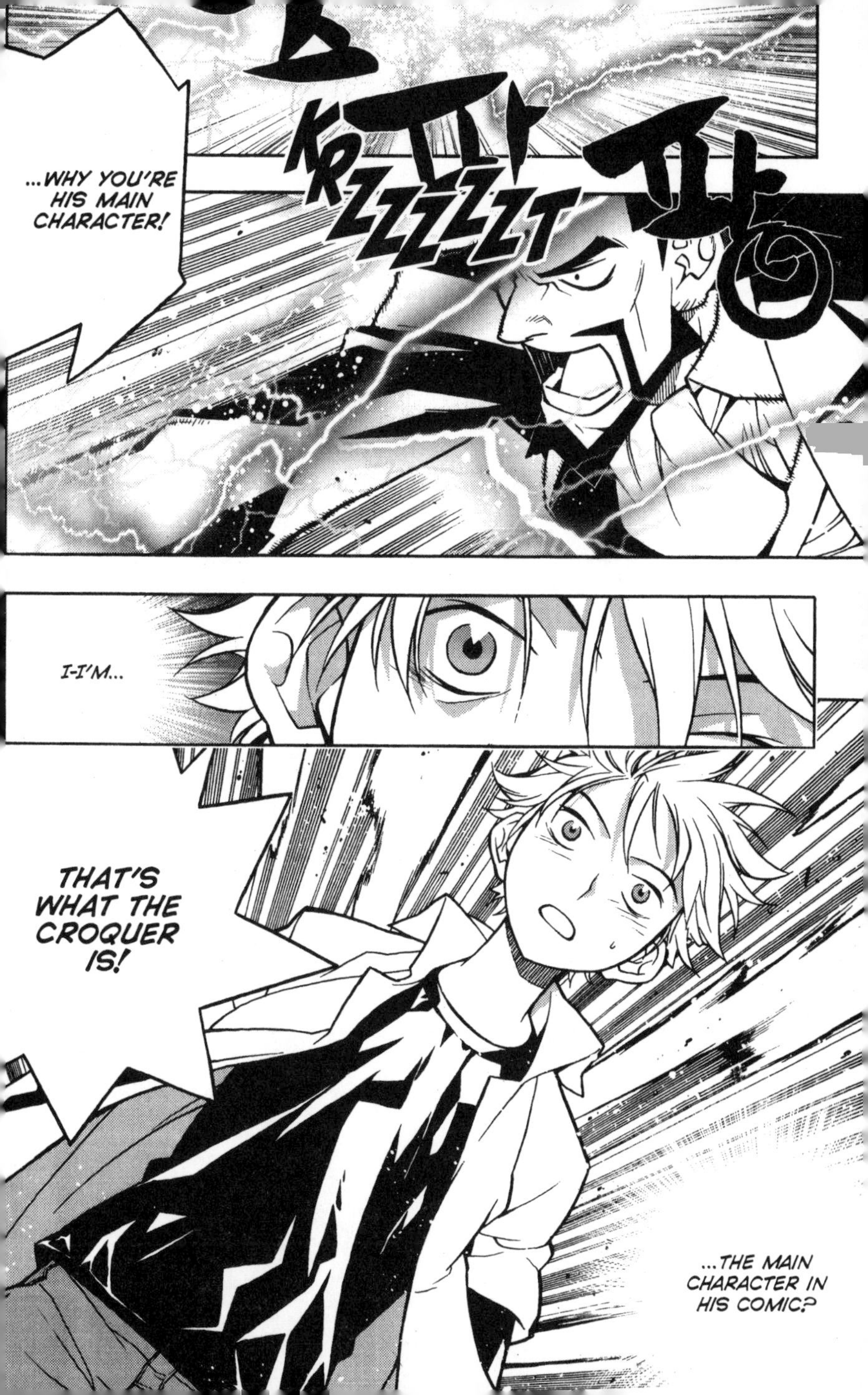
...WHY YOU'RE HIS MAIN CHARACTER!
KRZZZZZT
I-I'M...
...THE MAIN CHARACTER IN HIS COMIC?
THAT'S WHAT THE CROQUER IS!

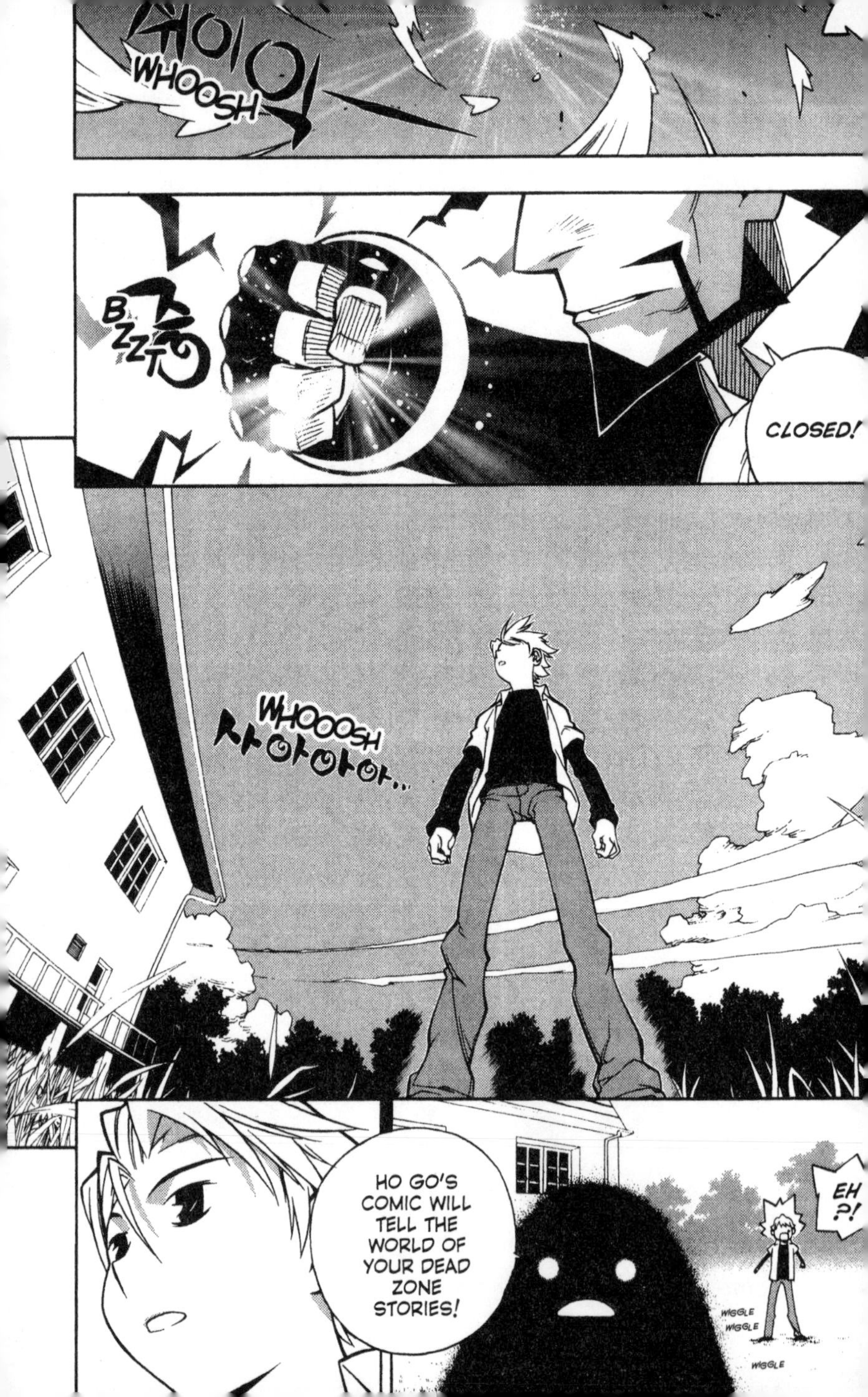
WHOOSH
BZZZT
CLOSED!
WHOOOSH
HO GO'S COMIC WILL TELL THE WORLD OF YOUR DEAD ZONE STORIES!
EH ?!
WIGGLE
WIGGLE
WIGGLE

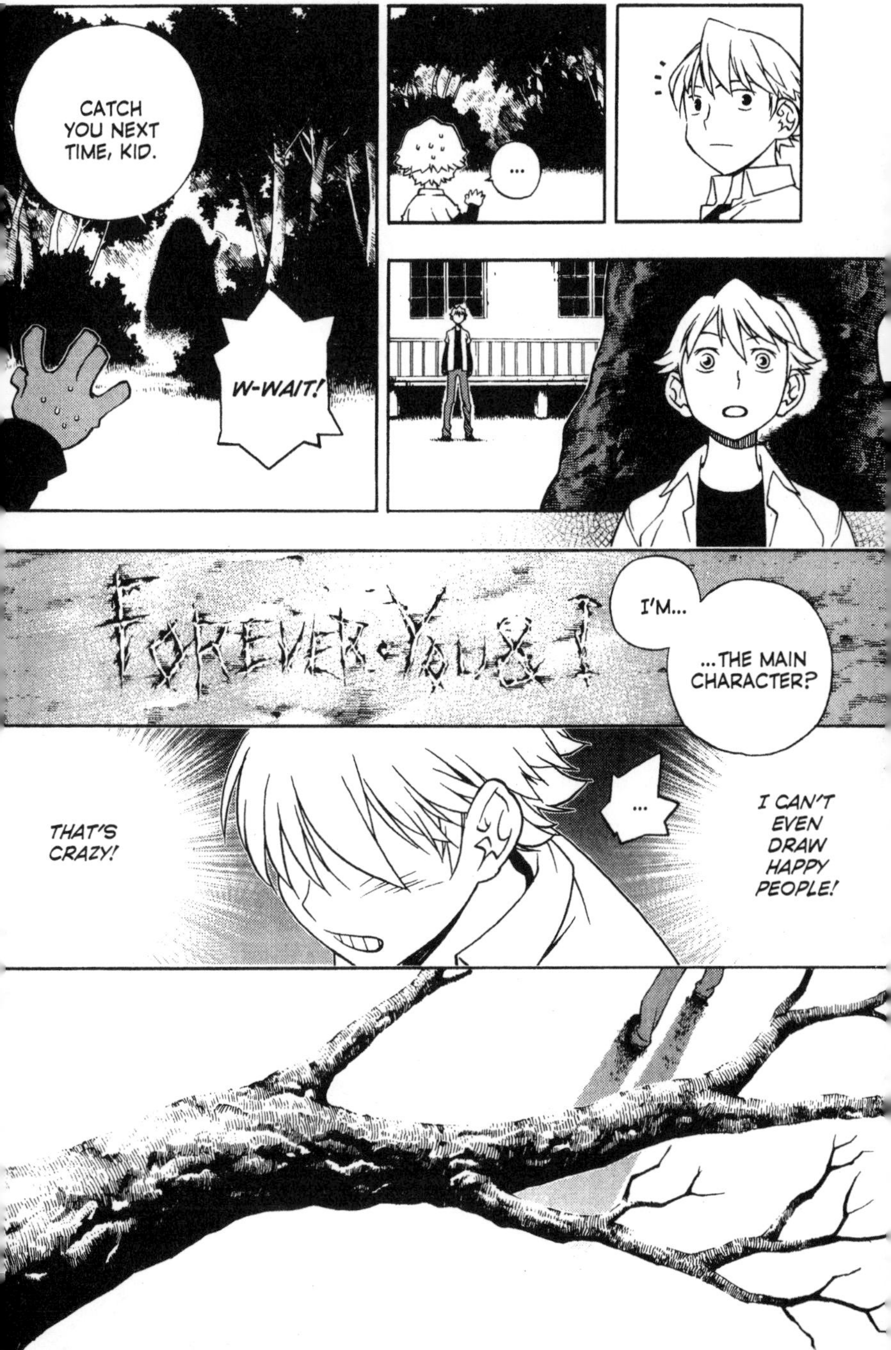

...
CATCH YOU NEXT TIME, KID.
W-WAIT!
FOREVER YOU & I
I'M...
...THE MAIN CHARACTER?
I CAN'T EVEN DRAW HAPPY PEOPLE!
...
THAT'S CRAZY!

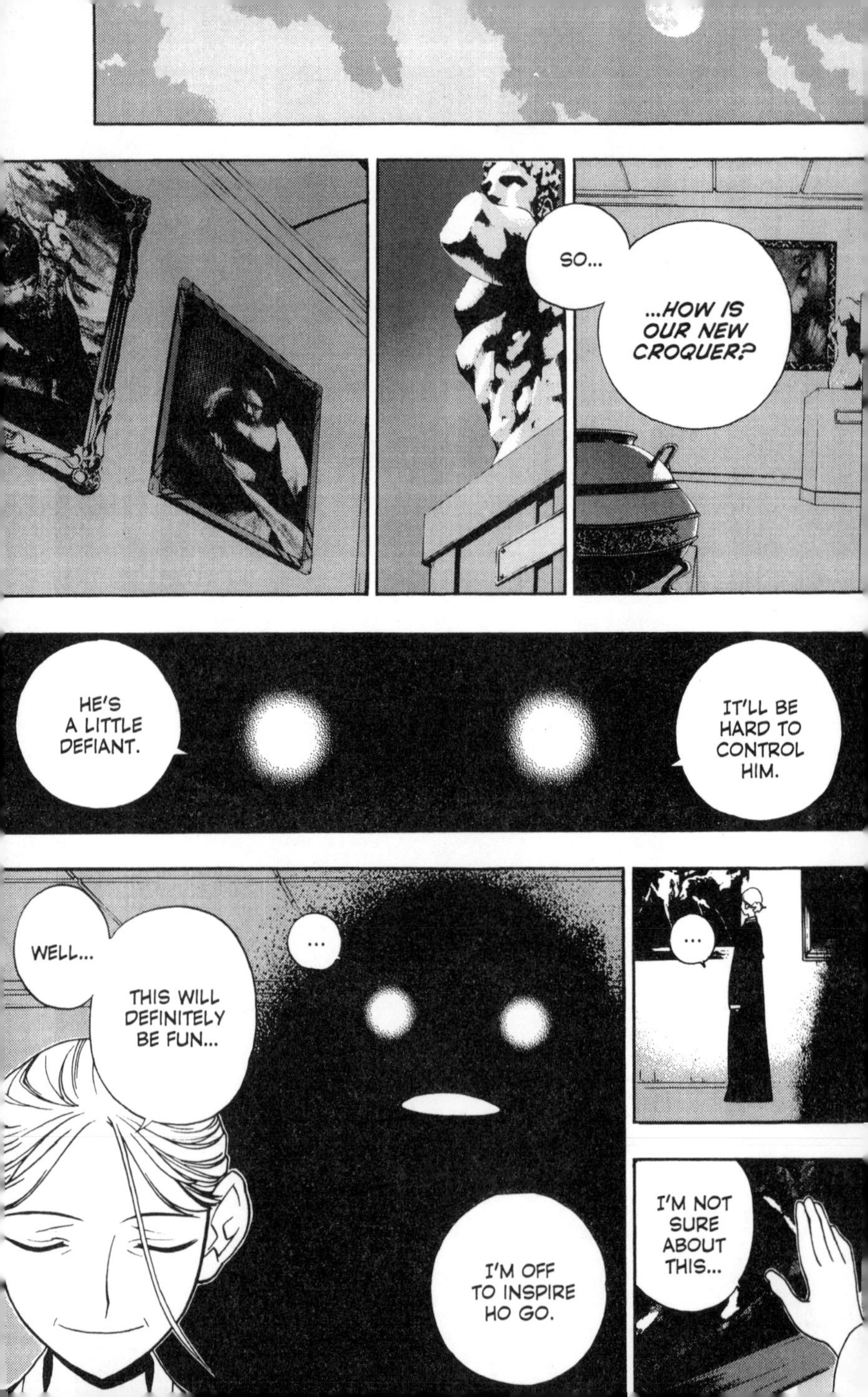
SO...
...HOW IS OUR NEW CROQUER?
HE'S A LITTLE DEFIANT.
IT'LL BE HARD TO CONTROL HIM.
WELL...
THIS WILL DEFINITELY BE FUN...
...
I'M OFF TO INSPIRE HO GO.
...
I'M NOT SURE ABOUT THIS...

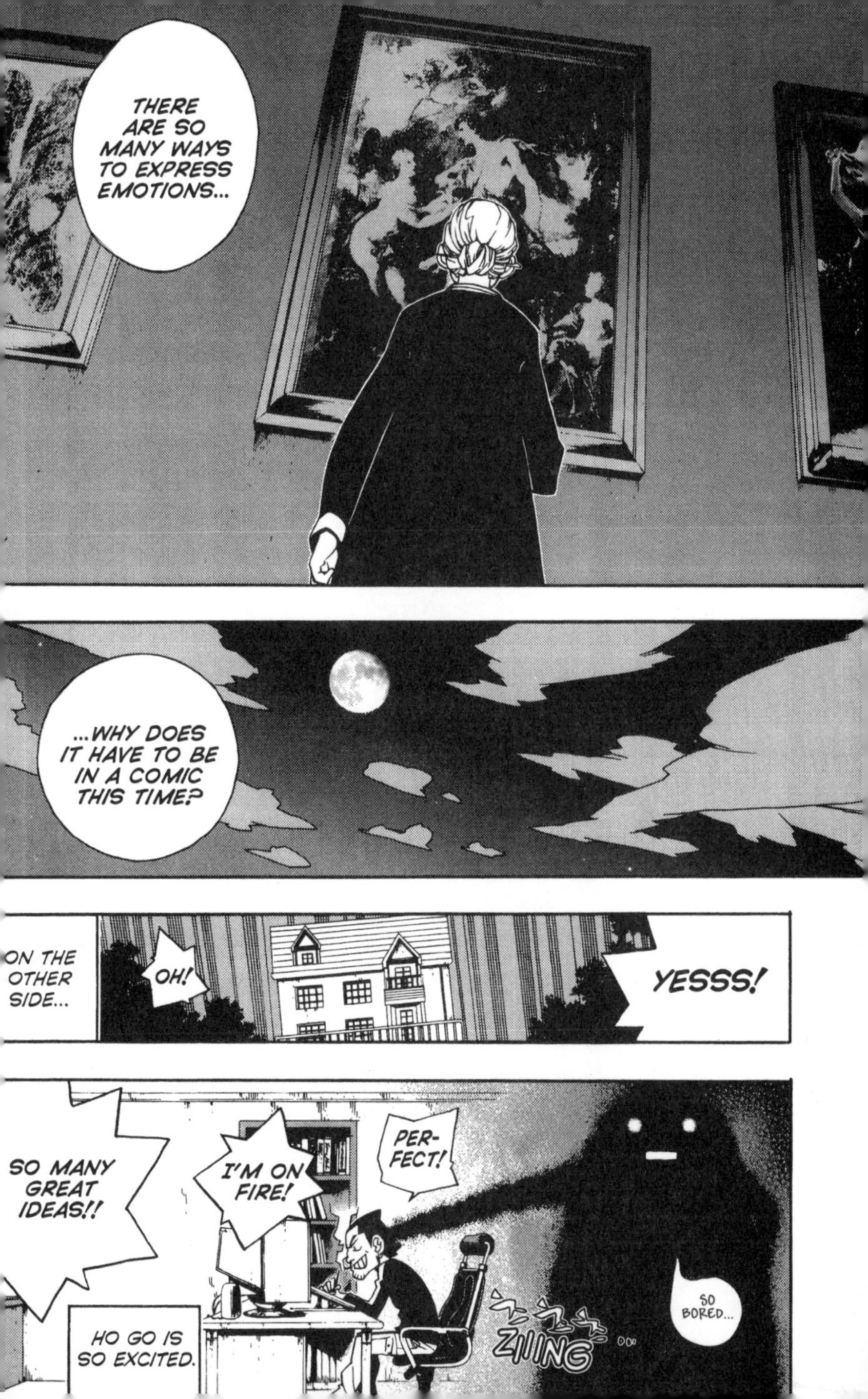
THERE ARE SO MANY WAYS TO EXPRESS EMOTIONS...
...WHY DOES IT HAVE TO BE IN A COMIC THIS TIME?
ON THE OTHER SIDE...
OH!
YESSS!
SO MANY GREAT IDEAS!!
I'M ON FIRE!
PER-FECT!
HO GO IS SO EXCITED.
ZIIING
SO BORED...

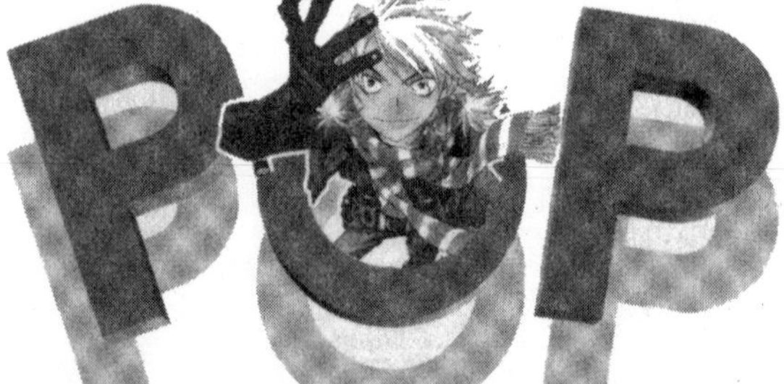
POP

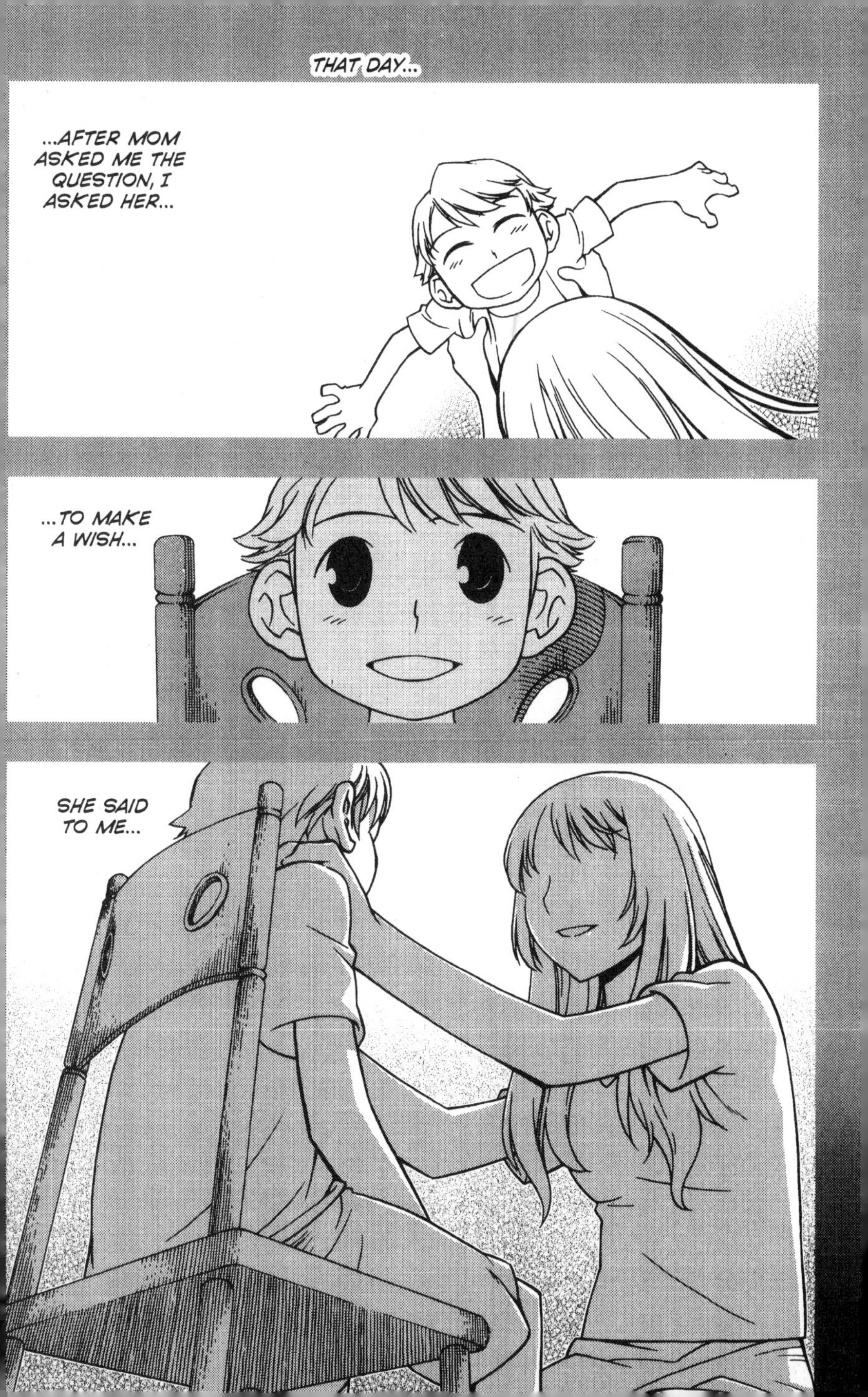
THAT DAY...
...AFTER MOM ASKED ME THE QUESTION, I ASKED HER...
...TO MAKE A WISH...
SHE SAID TO ME...

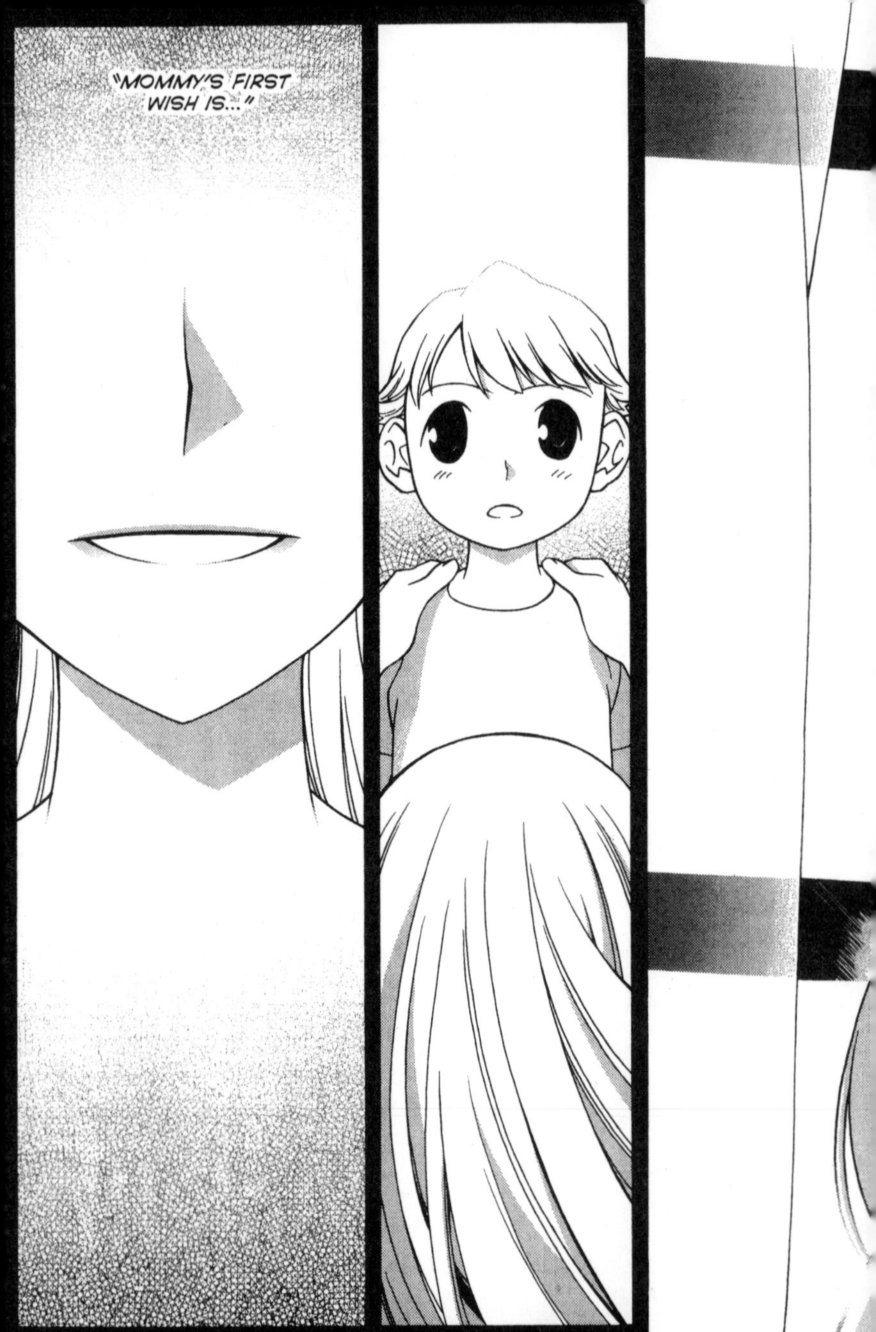
"MOMMY'S FIRST WISH IS..."

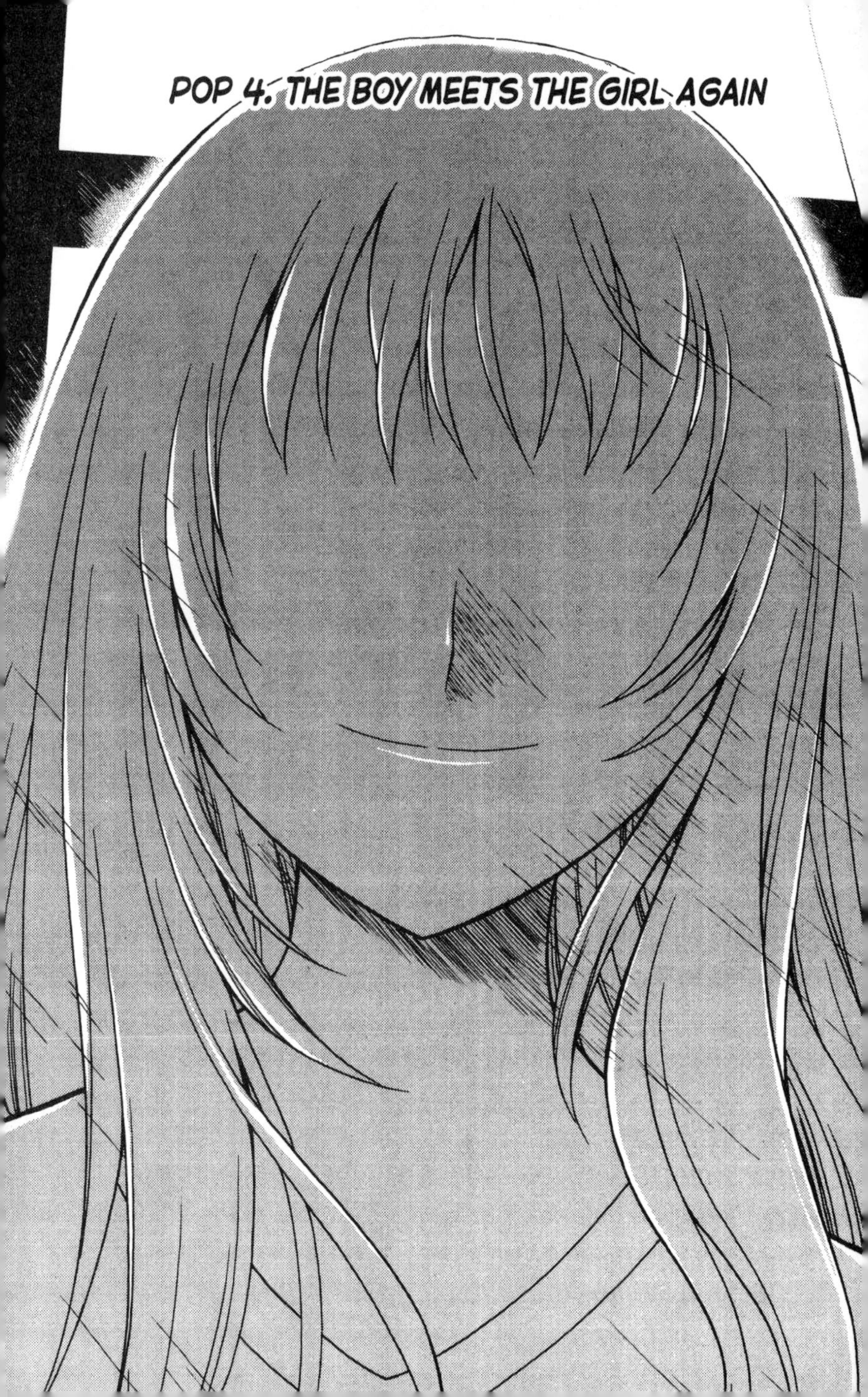
POP 4. THE BOY MEETS THE GIRL AGAIN

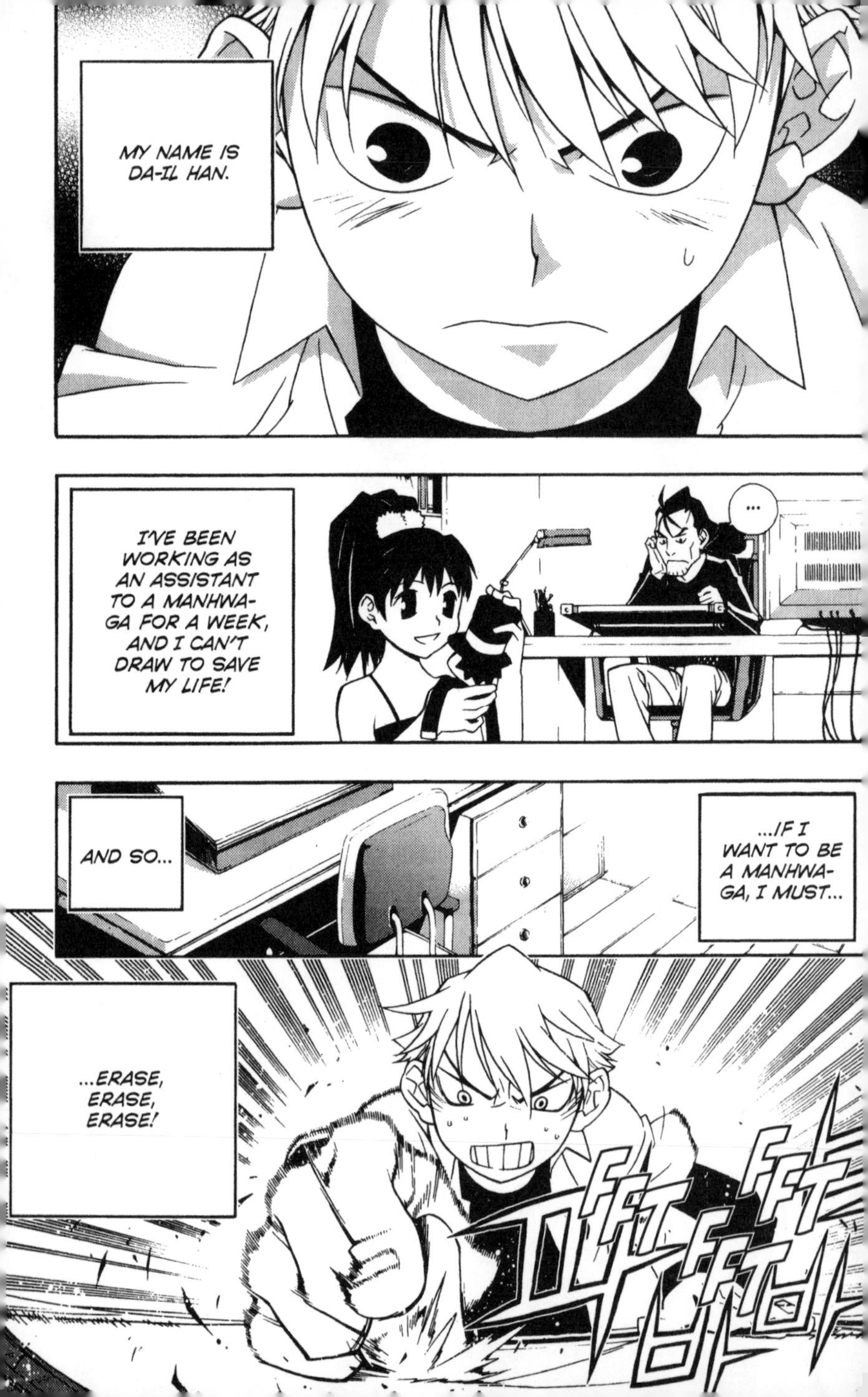
MY NAME IS DA-IL HAN.
I'VE BEEN WORKING AS AN ASSISTANT TO A MANHWA-GA FOR A WEEK, AND I CAN'T DRAW TO SAVE MY LIFE!
...
AND SO...
...IF I WANT TO BE A MANHWA-GA, I MUST...
...ERASE, ERASE, ERASE!

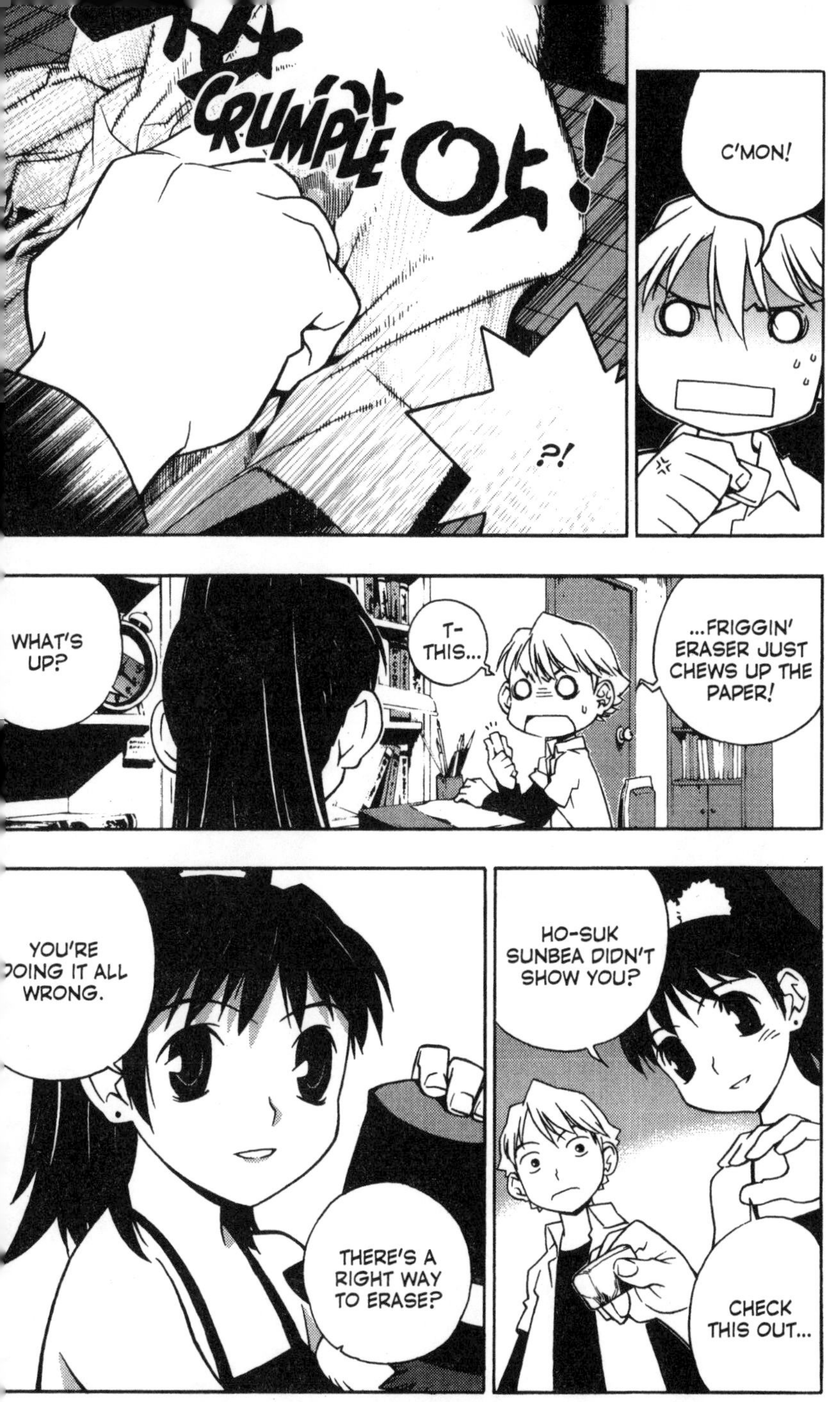
CRUMPLE
?!
C'MON!
WHAT'S UP?
T- THIS...
...FRIGGIN' ERASER JUST CHEWS UP THE PAPER!
YOU'RE DOING IT ALL WRONG.
THERE'S A RIGHT WAY TO ERASE?
HO-SUK SUNBEA DIDN'T SHOW YOU?
CHECK THIS OUT...

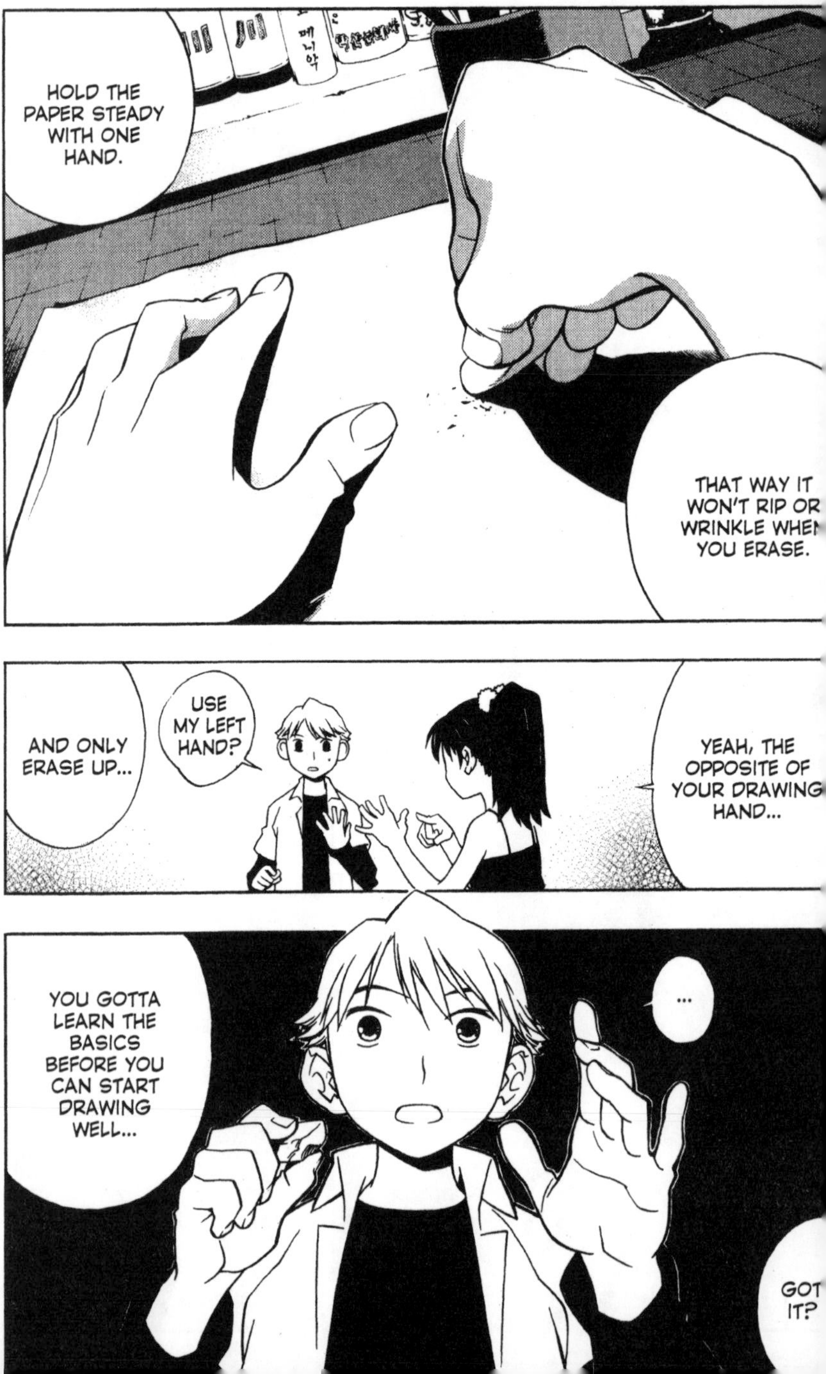

HOLD THE PAPER STEADY WITH ONE HAND.
THAT WAY IT WON'T RIP OR WRINKLE WHEN YOU ERASE.
USE MY LEFT HAND?
YEAH, THE OPPOSITE OF YOUR DRAWING HAND...
AND ONLY ERASE UP...
YOU GOTTA LEARN THE BASICS BEFORE YOU CAN START DRAWING WELL...
...
GOT IT?

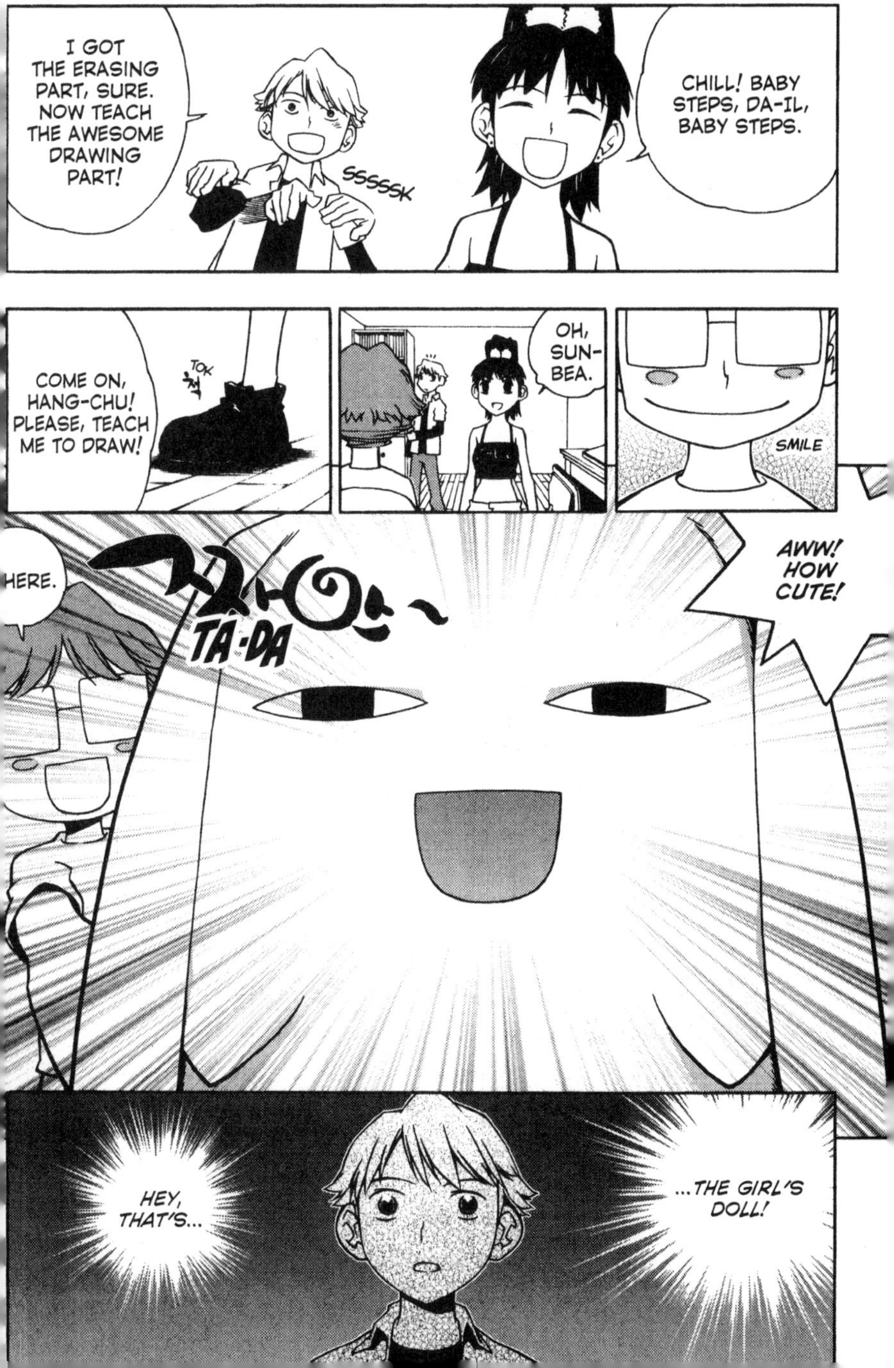
I GOT THE ERASING PART, SURE. NOW TEACH THE AWESOME DRAWING PART!
SSSSSK
CHILL! BABY STEPS, DA-IL, BABY STEPS.
COME ON, HANG-CHU! PLEASE, TEACH ME TO DRAW!
TOK
OH, SUN-BEA.
SMILE
HERE.
TA-DA
AWW! HOW CUTE!
HEY, THAT'S...
...THE GIRL'S DOLL!

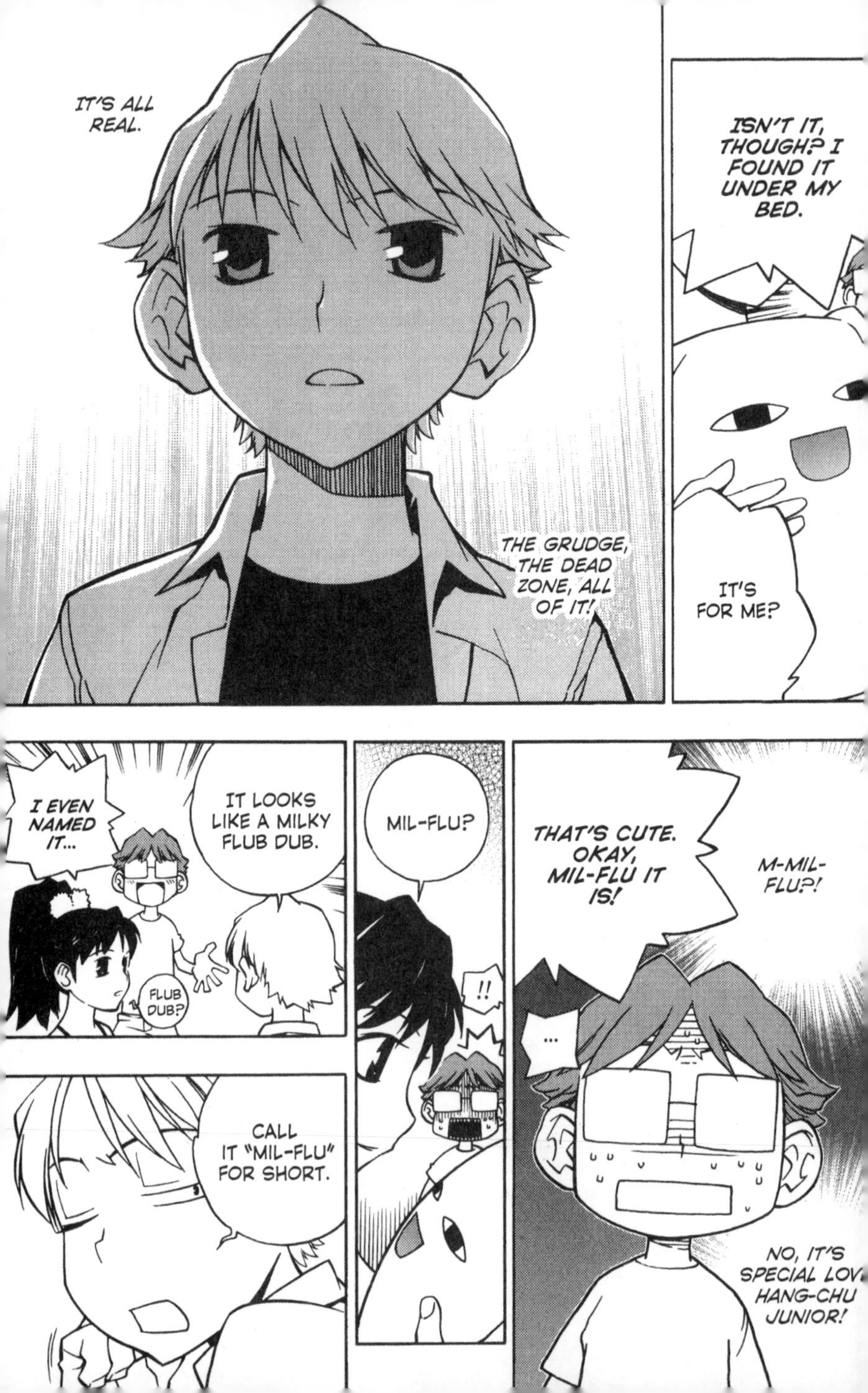

IT'S ALL REAL.
THE GRUDGE, THE DEAD ZONE, ALL OF IT!
ISN'T IT, THOUGH? I FOUND IT UNDER MY BED.
IT'S FOR ME?
I EVEN NAMED IT...
IT LOOKS LIKE A MILKY FLUB DUB.
FLUB DUB?
CALL IT "MIL-FLU" FOR SHORT.
MIL-FLU?
!!
THAT'S CUTE. OKAY, MIL-FLU IT IS!
M-MIL-FLU?!
...
NO, IT'S SPECIAL LOV HANG-CHU JUNIOR!

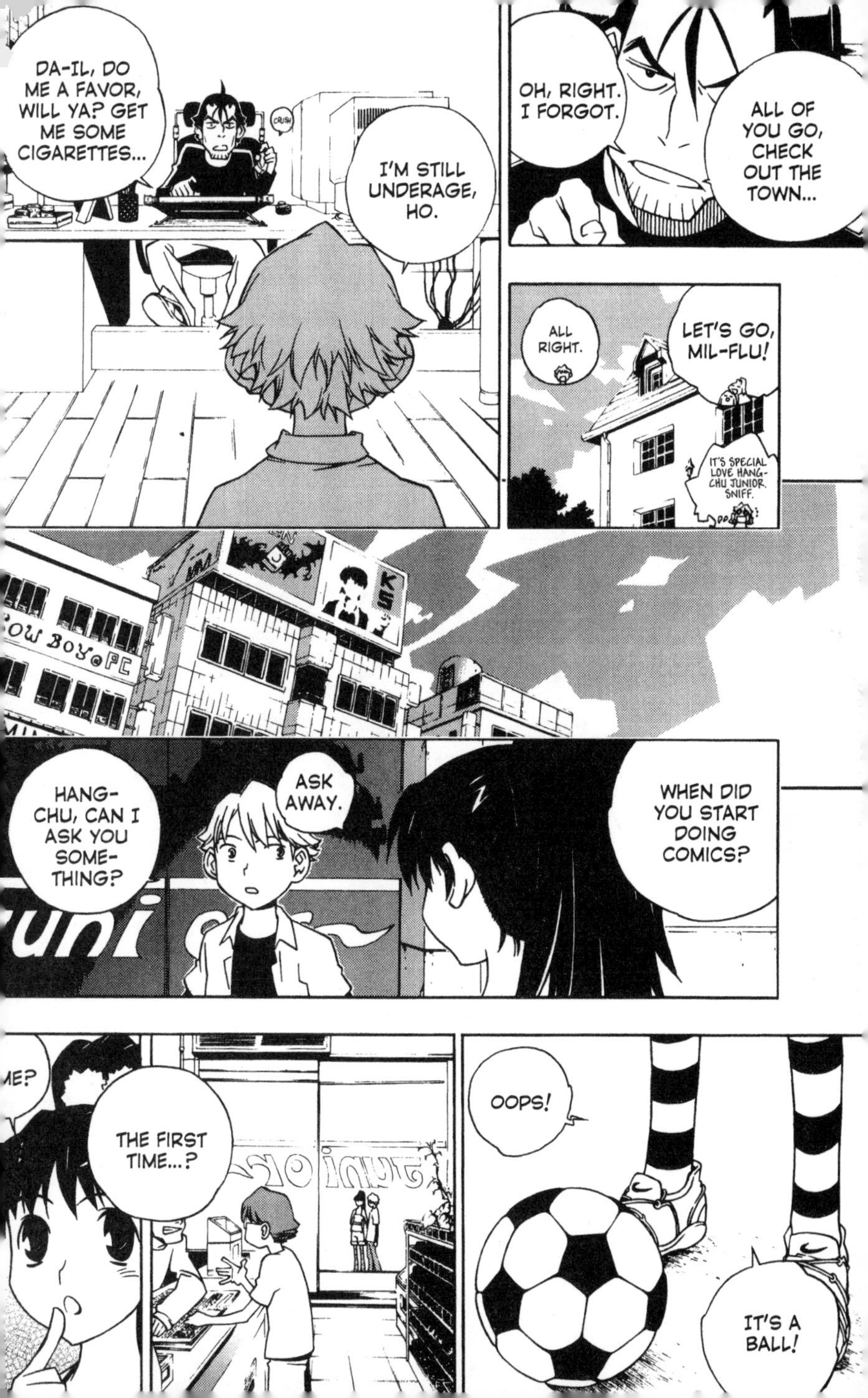
DA-IL, DO ME A FAVOR, WILL YA? GET ME SOME CIGARETTES...
CRUSH
I'M STILL UNDERAGE, HO.
OH, RIGHT. I FORGOT.
ALL OF YOU GO, CHECK OUT THE TOWN...
LET'S GO, MIL-FLU!
ALL RIGHT.
IT'S SPECIAL LOVE HANG-CHU JUNIOR. SNIFF.
KS
HANG-CHU, CAN I ASK YOU SOME-THING?
ASK AWAY.
WHEN DID YOU START DOING COMICS?
ME?
THE FIRST TIME...?
OOPS!
IT'S A BALL!

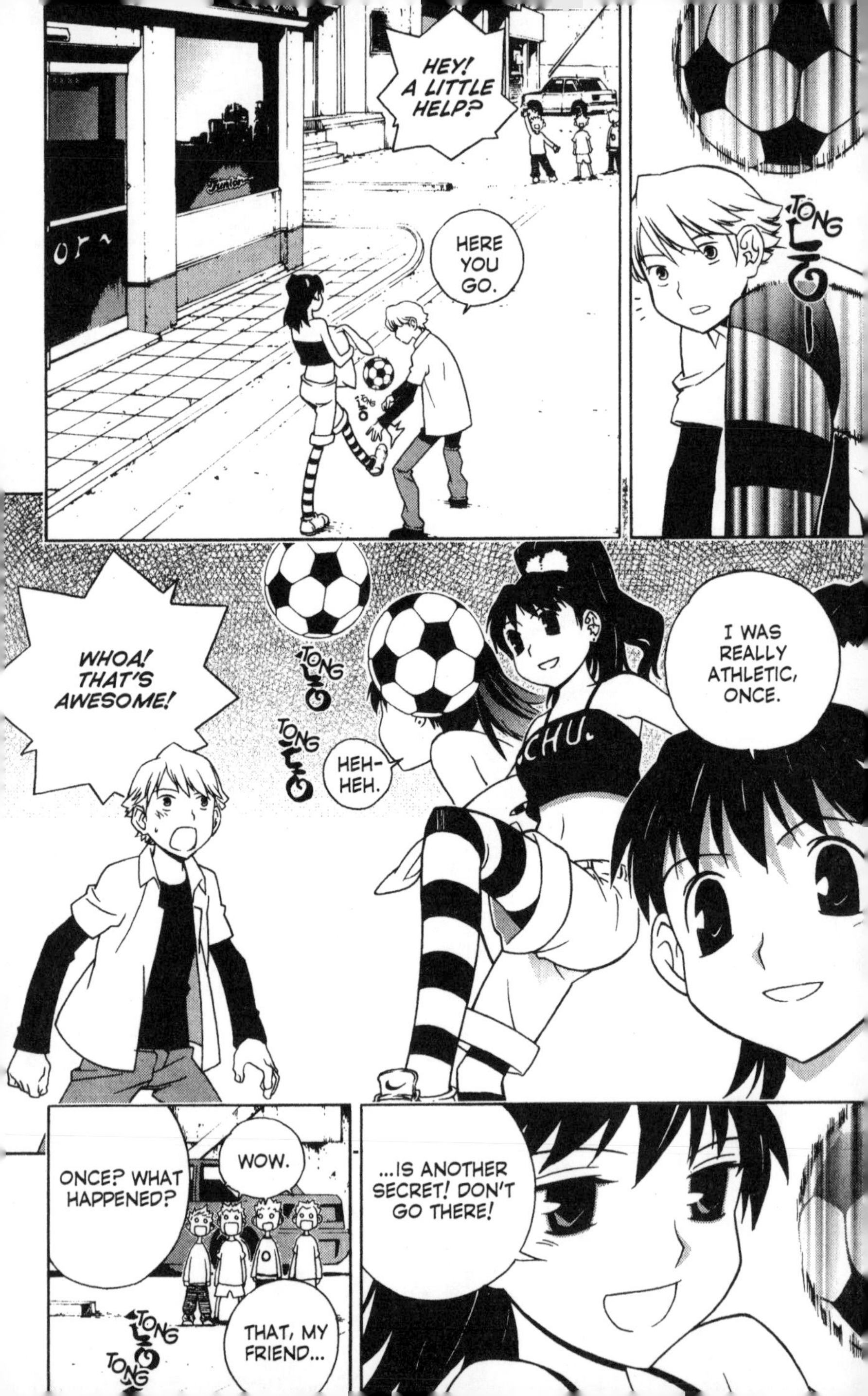
HEY! A LITTLE HELP?
HERE YOU GO.
TONG
TONG
WHOA! THAT'S AWESOME!
TONG
TONG
HEH-HEH.
I WAS REALLY ATHLETIC, ONCE.
CHU
ONCE? WHAT HAPPENED?
WOW.
TONG
TONG
THAT, MY FRIEND...
...IS ANOTHER SECRET! DON'T GO THERE!

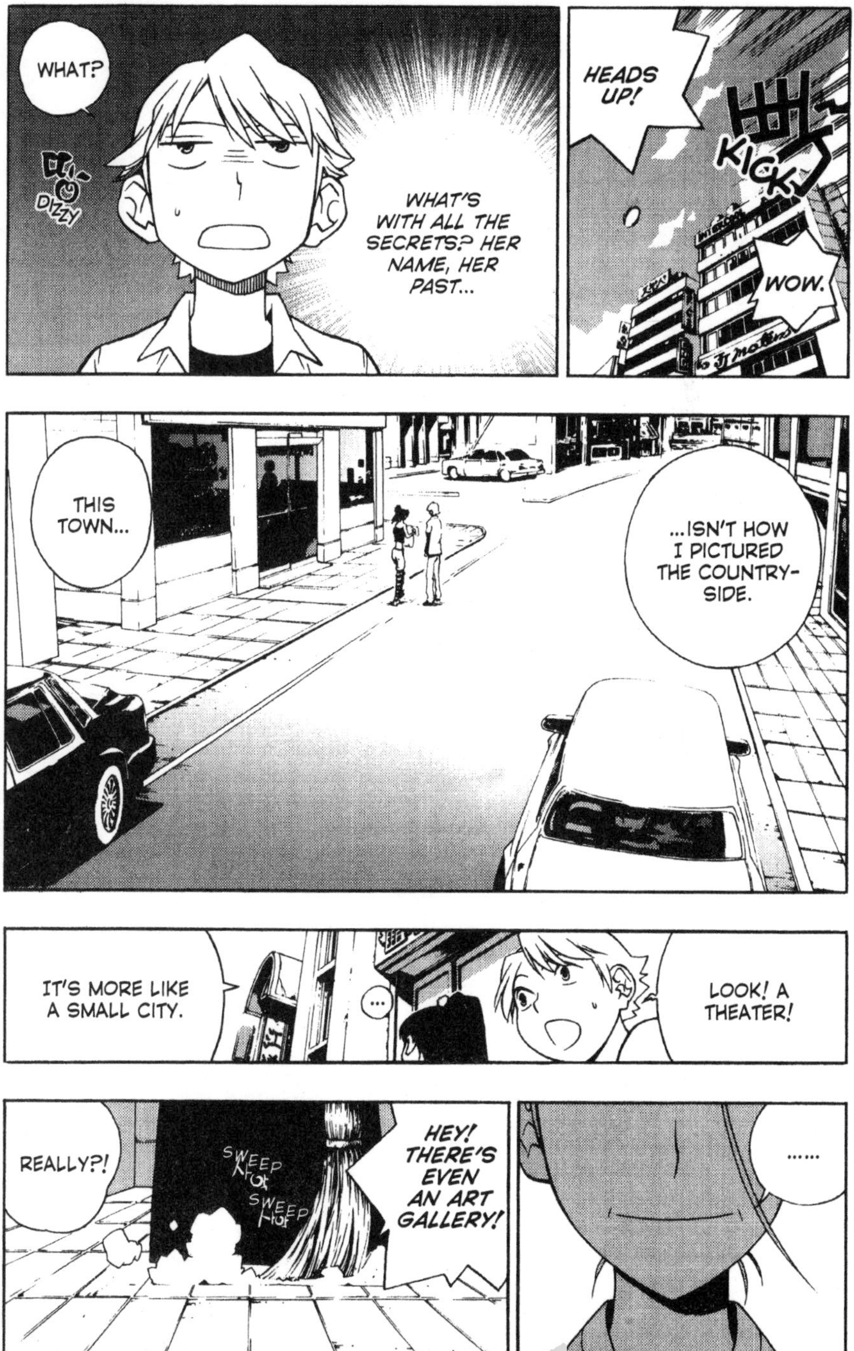
HEADS UP!
KICK
WOW.
WHAT?
DIZZY
WHAT'S WITH ALL THE SECRETS? HER NAME, HER PAST...
THIS TOWN...
...ISN'T HOW I PICTURED THE COUNTRY-SIDE.
LOOK! A THEATER!
...
IT'S MORE LIKE A SMALL CITY.
......
HEY! THERE'S EVEN AN ART GALLERY!
SWEEP SWEEP
REALLY?!

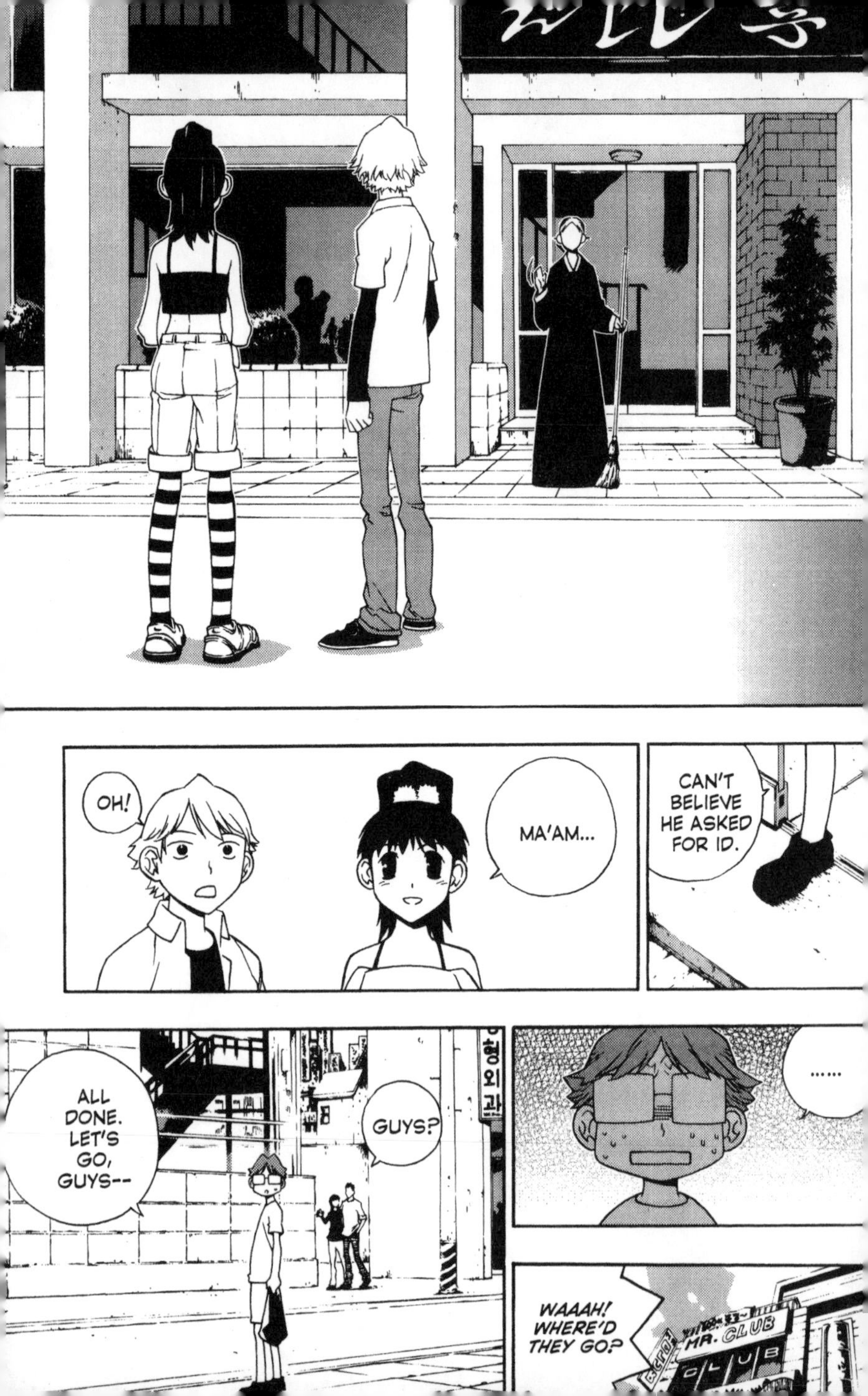
OH!
MA'AM...
CAN'T BELIEVE HE ASKED FOR ID.
형외과
ALL DONE. LET'S GO, GUYS--
GUYS?
......
WAAAH! WHERE'D THEY GO?
MR. CLUB
CLUB

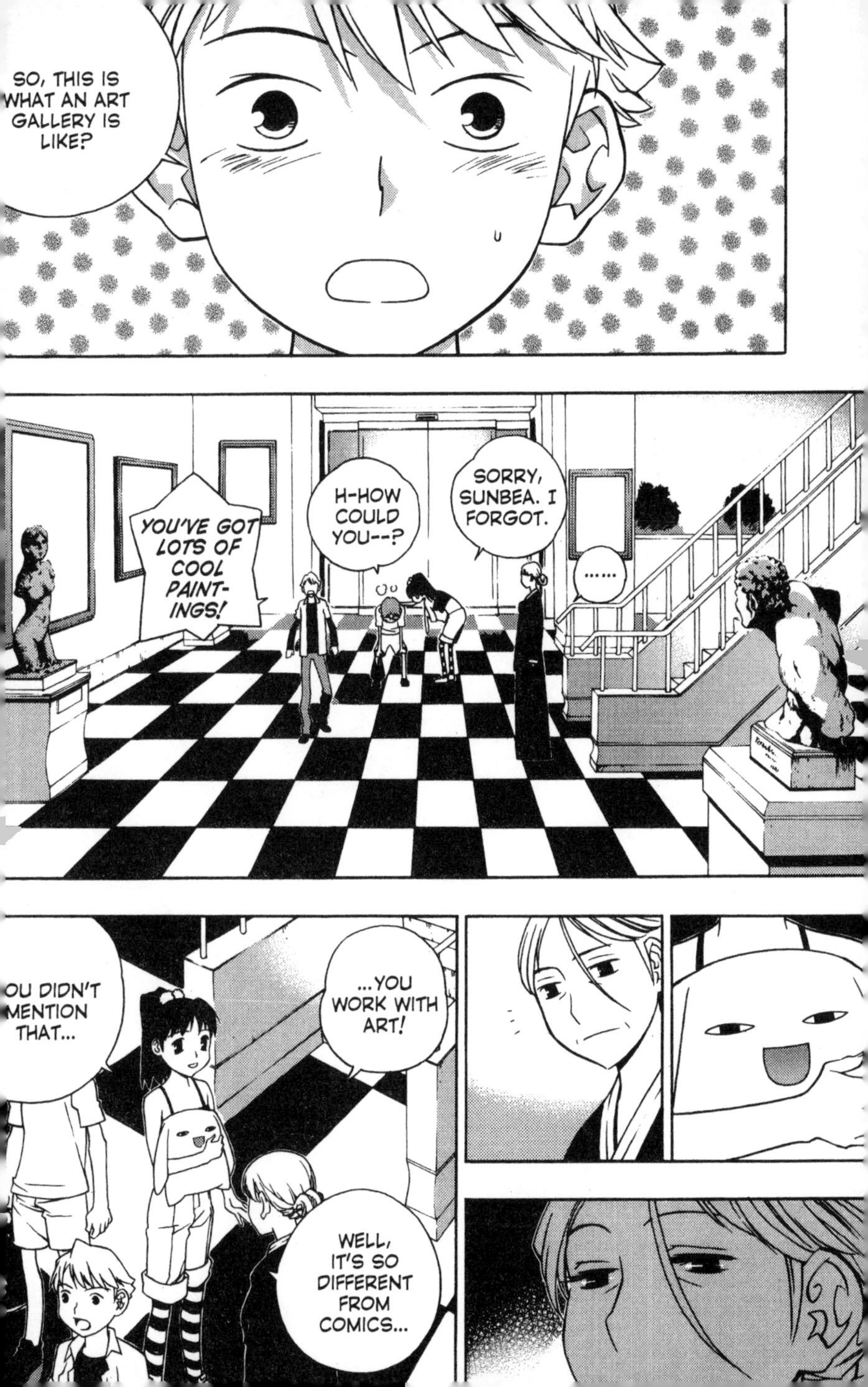
SO, THIS IS WHAT AN ART GALLERY IS LIKE?
YOU'VE GOT LOTS OF COOL PAINT-INGS!
H-HOW COULD YOU--?
SORRY, SUNBEA. I FORGOT.
......
OU DIDN'T MENTION THAT...
...YOU WORK WITH ART!
WELL, IT'S SO DIFFERENT FROM COMICS...

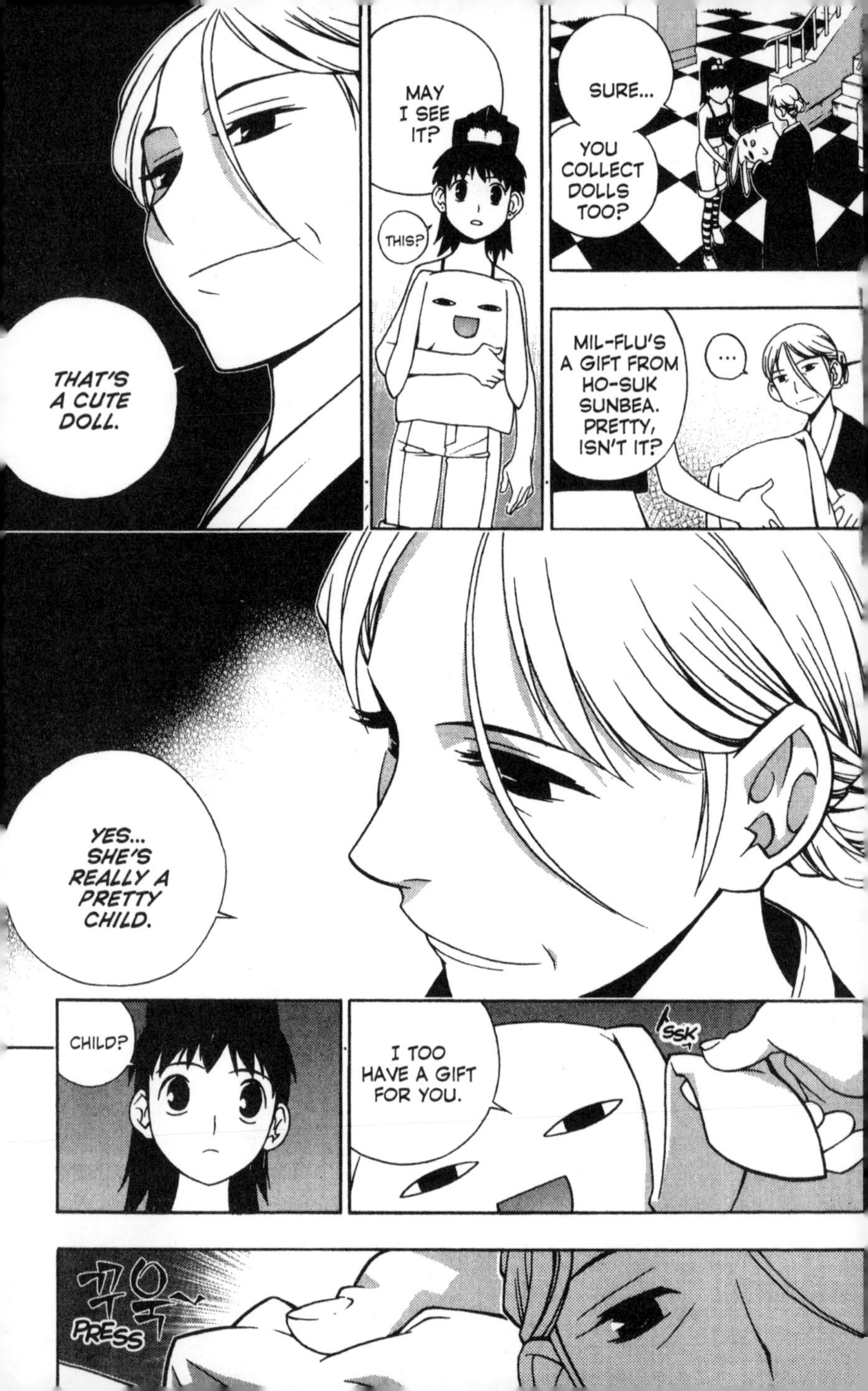
THAT'S A CUTE DOLL.
MAY I SEE IT?
THIS?
SURE...
YOU COLLECT DOLLS TOO?
MIL-FLU'S A GIFT FROM HO-SUK SUNBEA. PRETTY, ISN'T IT?
...
YES... SHE'S REALLY A PRETTY CHILD.
CHILD?
I TOO HAVE A GIFT FOR YOU.
SSK
PRESS

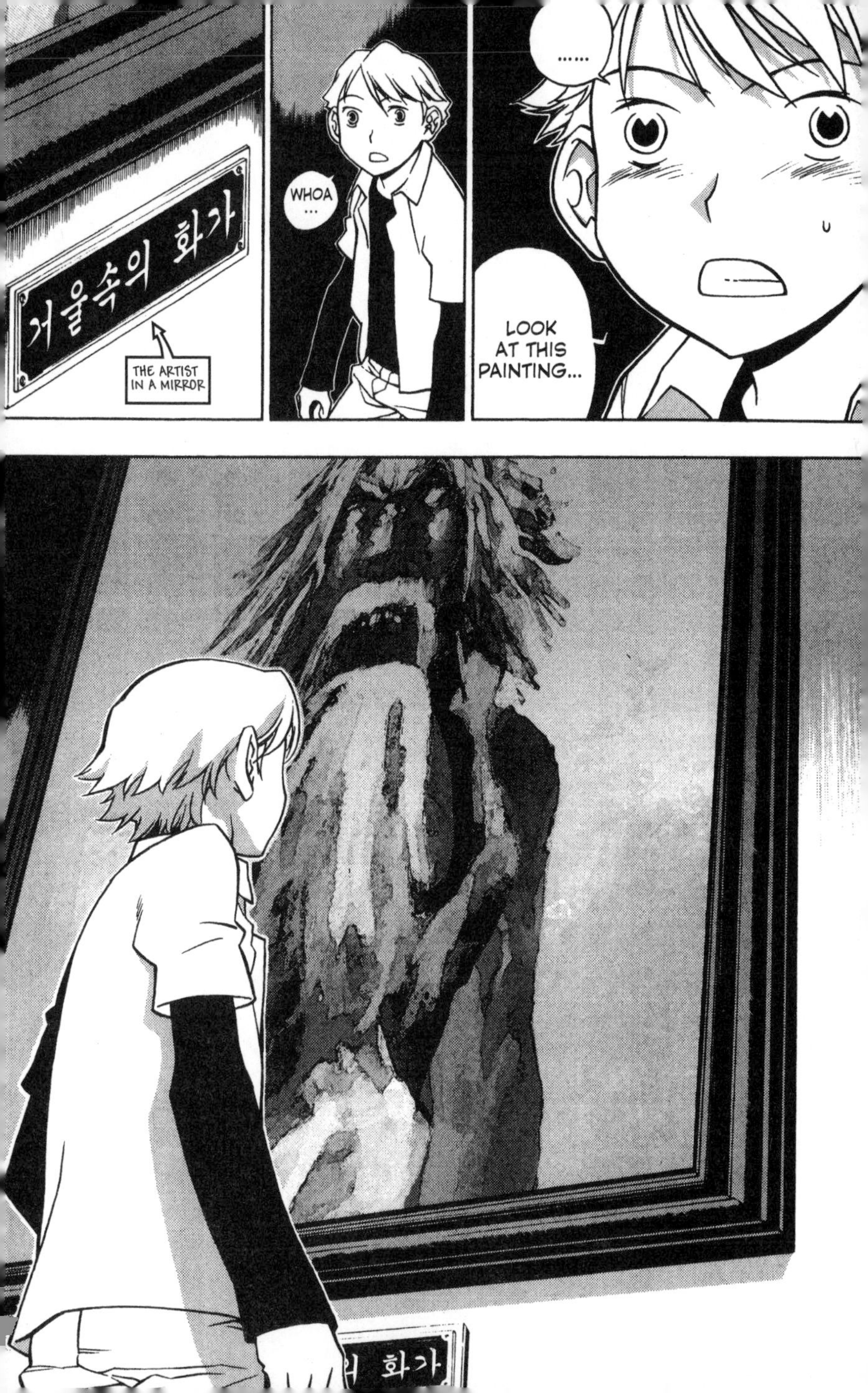

거울속의 화가
THE ARTIST IN A MIRROR
WHOA ...
......
LOOK AT THIS PAINTING...

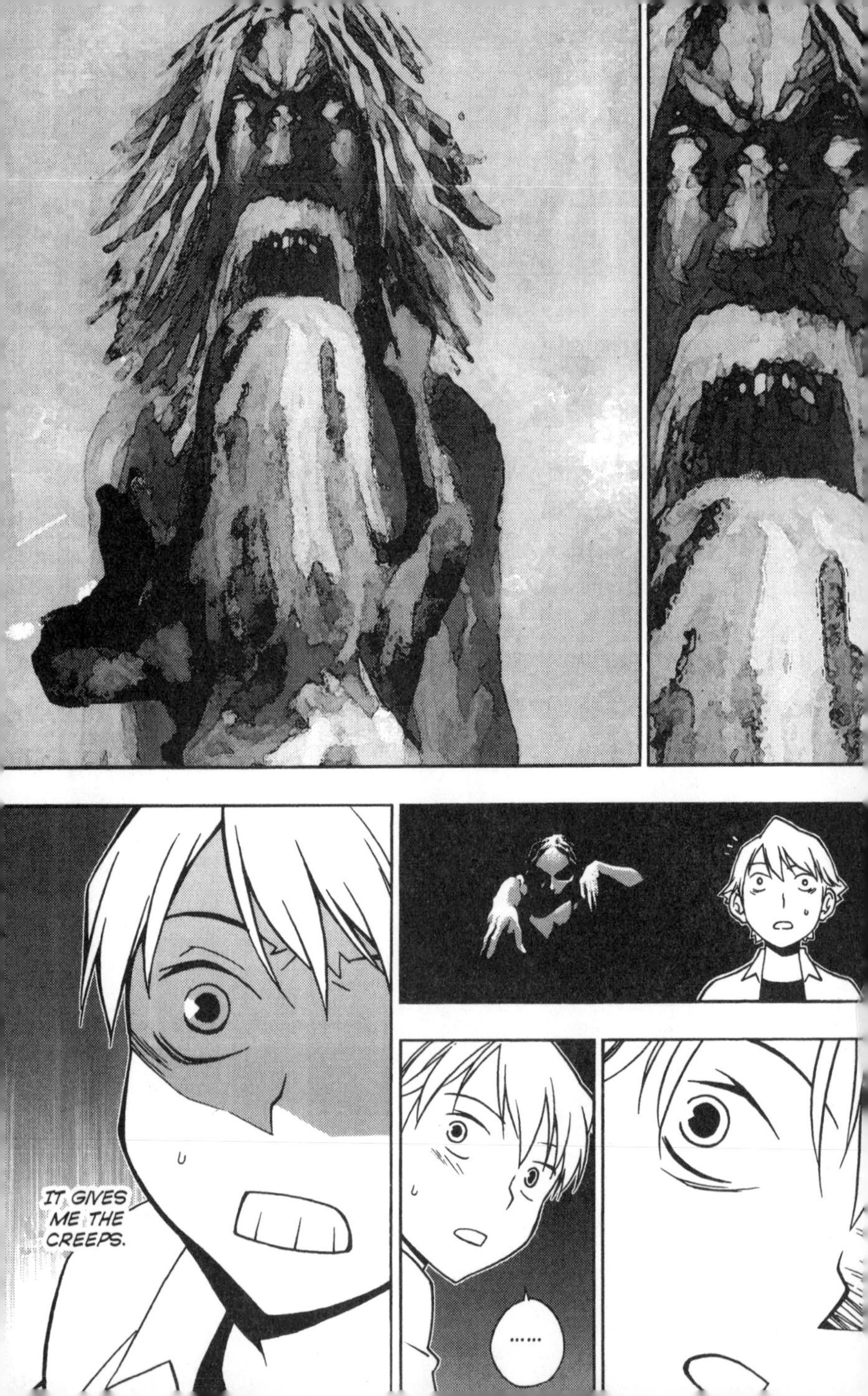
IT GIVES ME THE CREEPS.
......

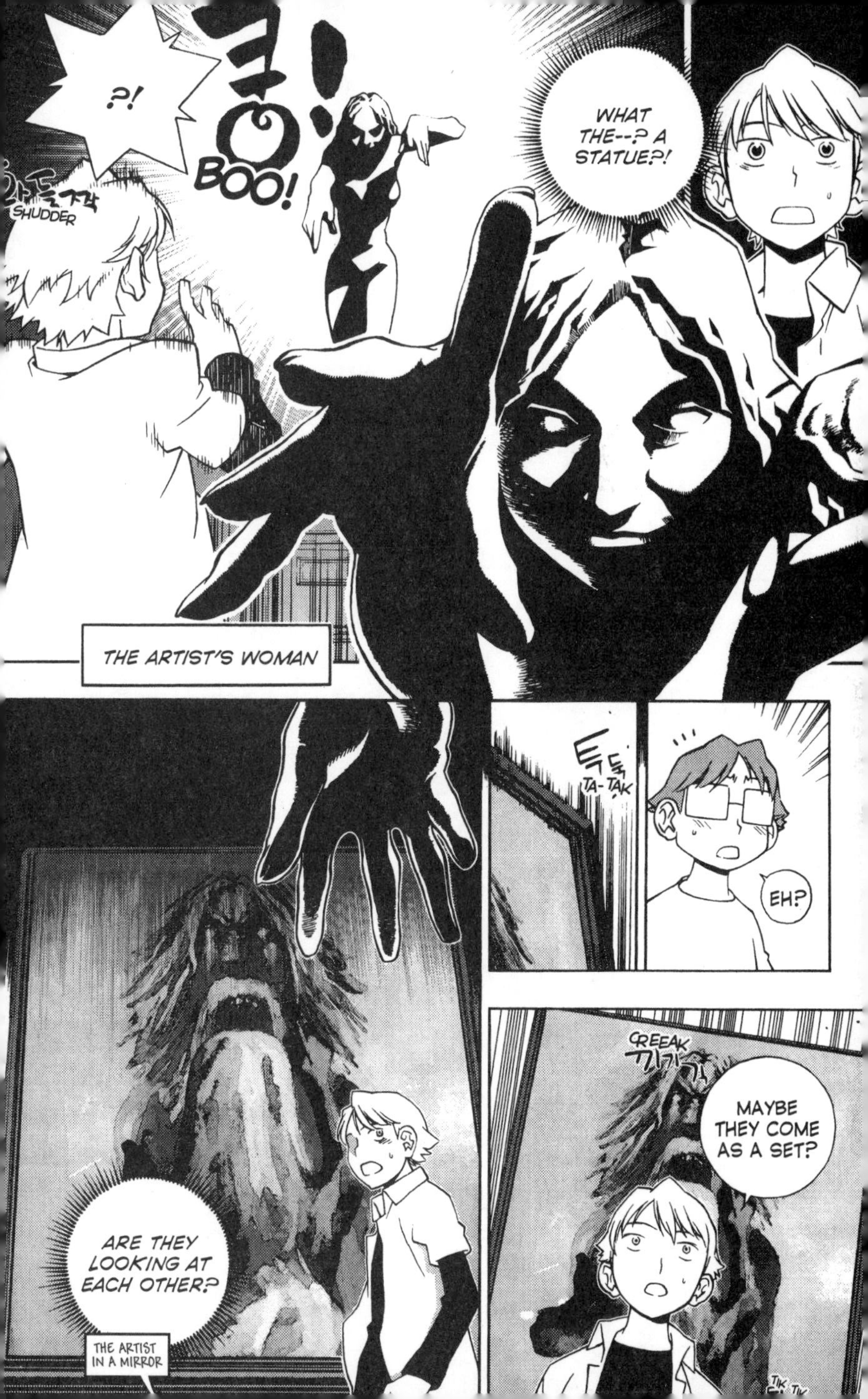
?!
BOO!
SHUDDER
WHAT THE--? A STATUE?!
THE ARTIST'S WOMAN
TA-TAK
EH?
ARE THEY LOOKING AT EACH OTHER?
THE ARTIST IN A MIRROR
CREEAK
MAYBE THEY COME AS A SET?

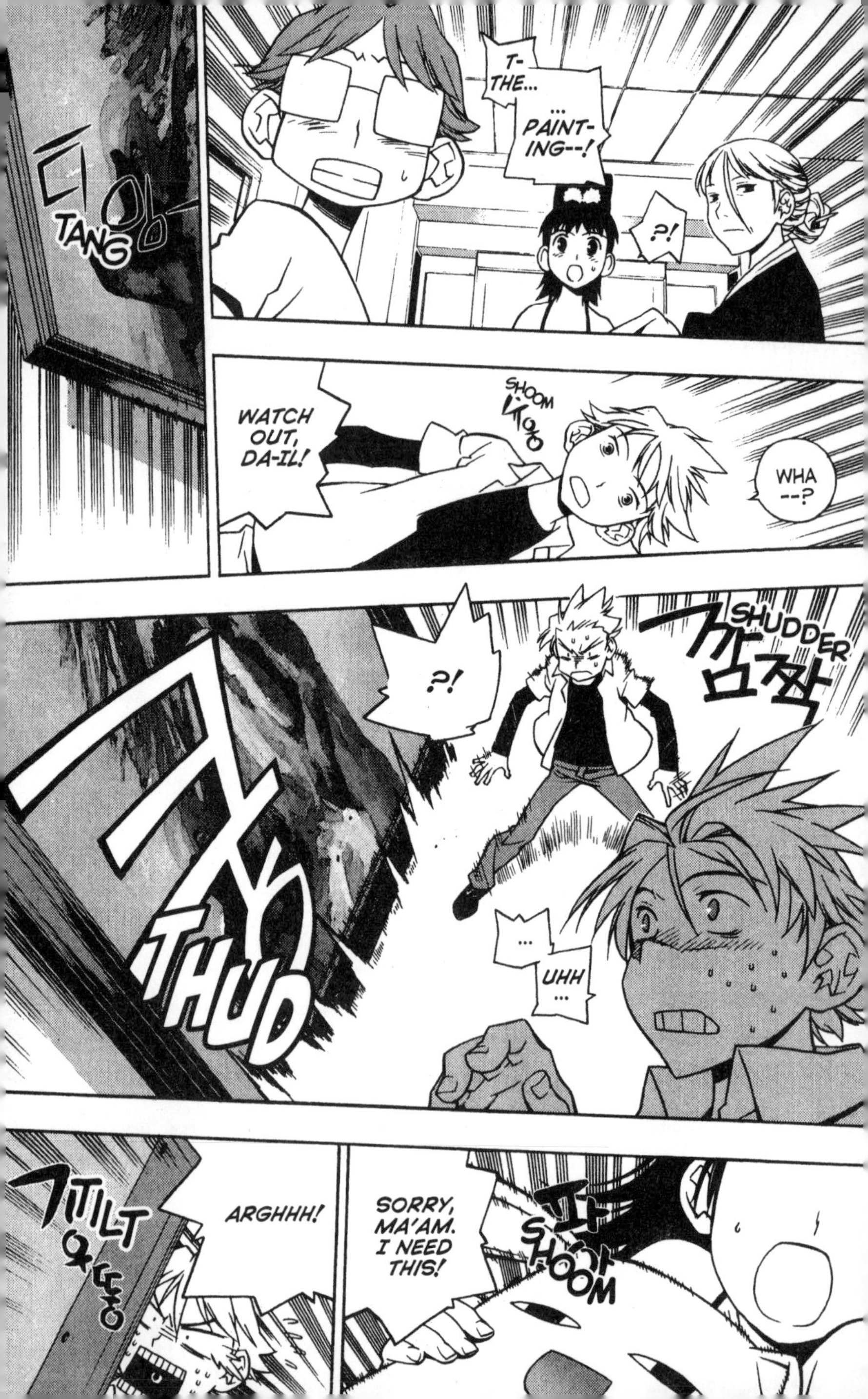

T-THE...
... PAINT-ING--!
?!
TANG
WATCH OUT, DA-IL!
SHOOM
WHA --?
SHUDDER
?!
THUD
...
UHH ...
TILT
ARGHHH!
SORRY, MA'AM. I NEED THIS!
SHOOM

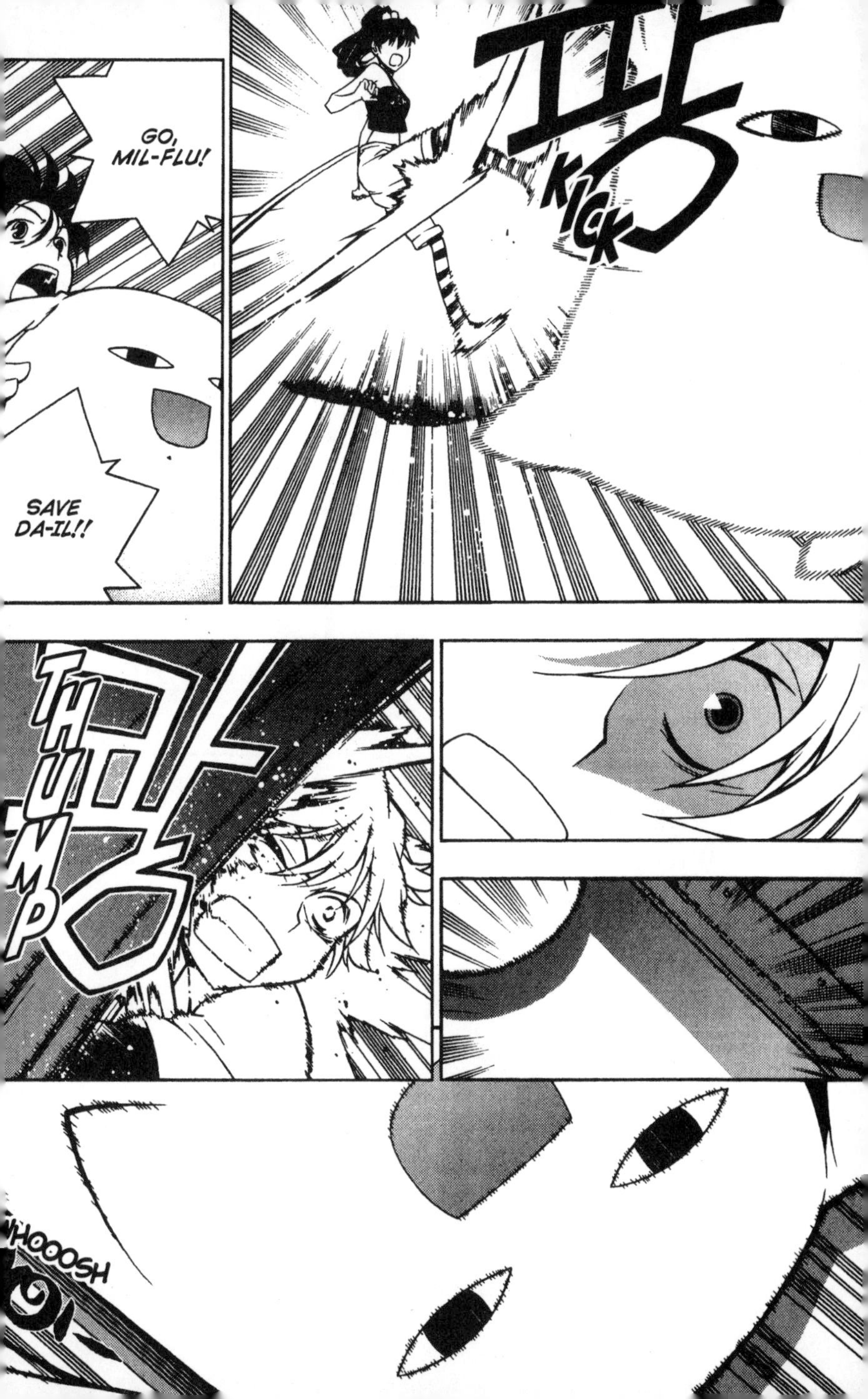

GO, MIL-FLU!
SAVE DA-IL!!
KICK
THUMP
WHOOOOSH

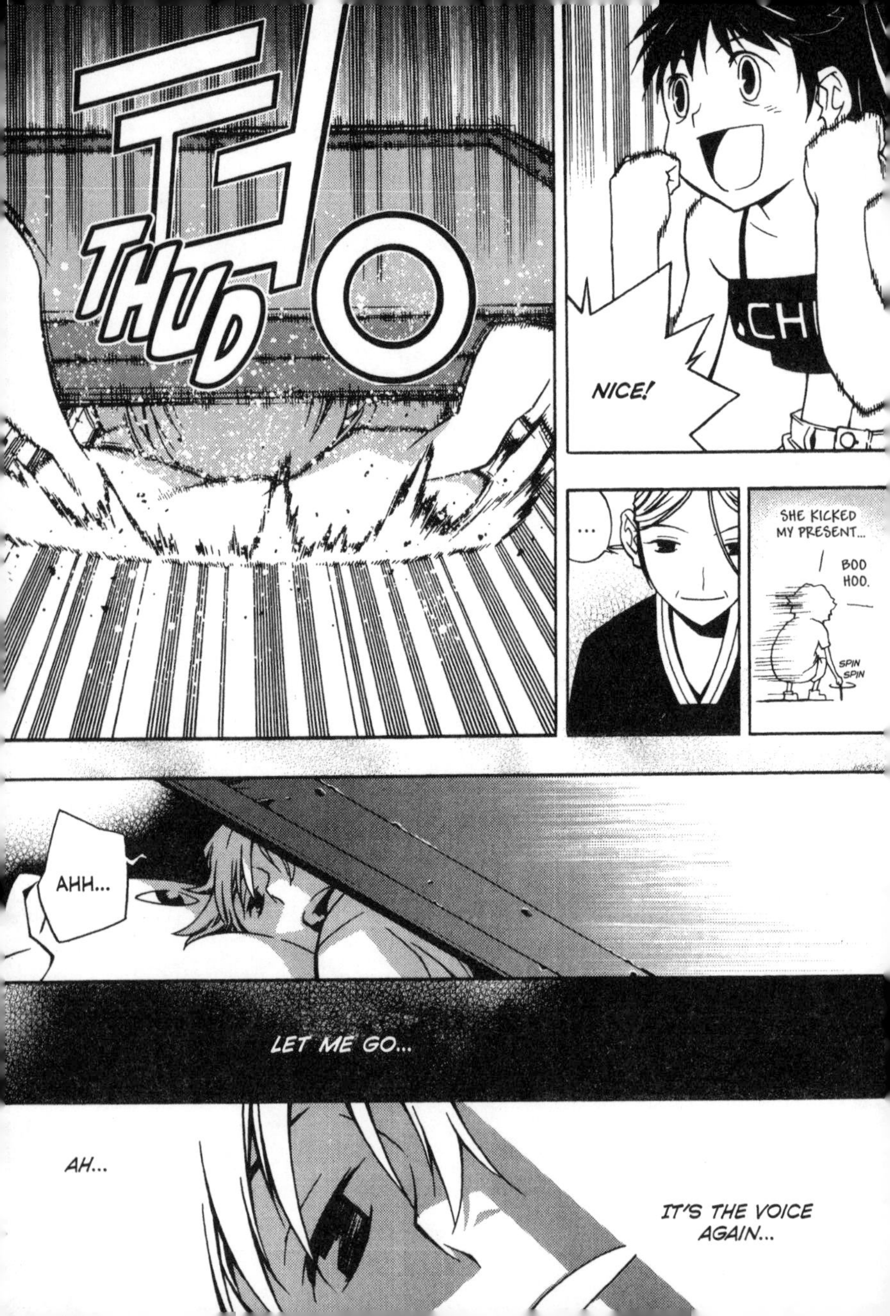
THUD
NICE!
...
SHE KICKED MY PRESENT...
BOO HOO.
SPIN SPIN
AHH...
LET ME GO...
AH...
IT'S THE VOICE AGAIN...

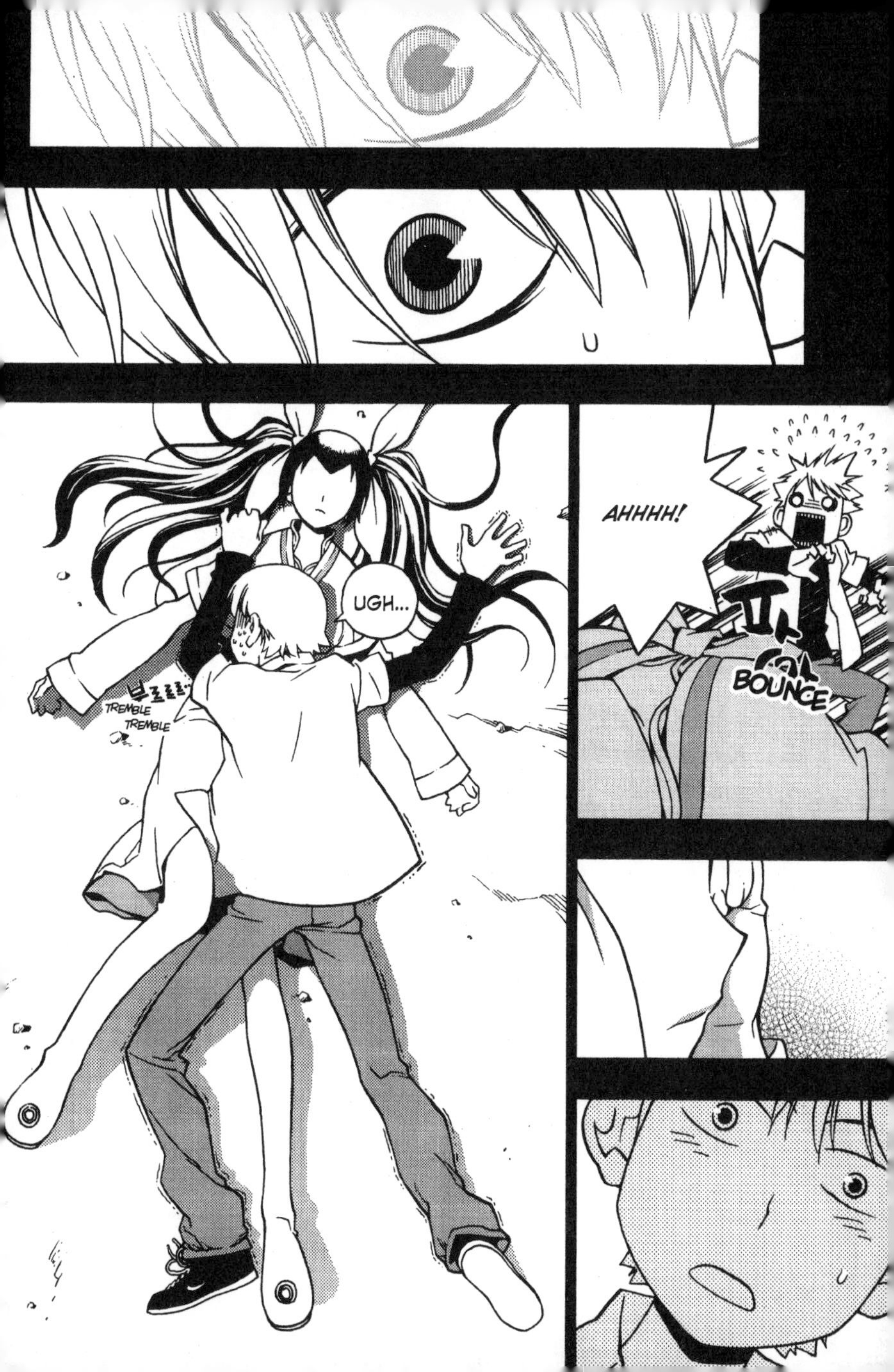

UGH...
TREMBLE
TREMBLE
AHHHH!
BOUNCE

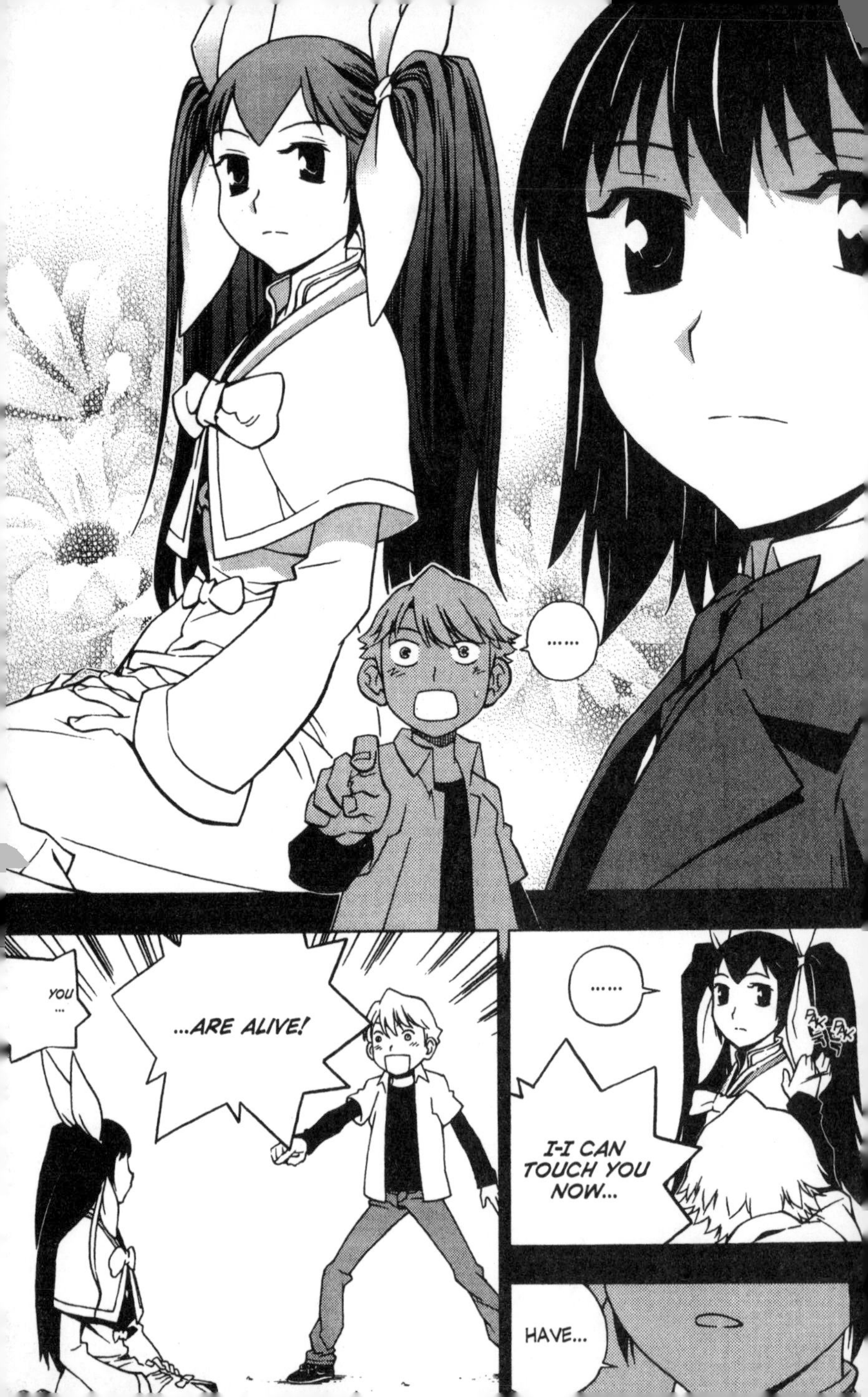
......
YOU ...
...ARE ALIVE!
......
PAK PAK
I-I CAN TOUCH YOU NOW...
HAVE...

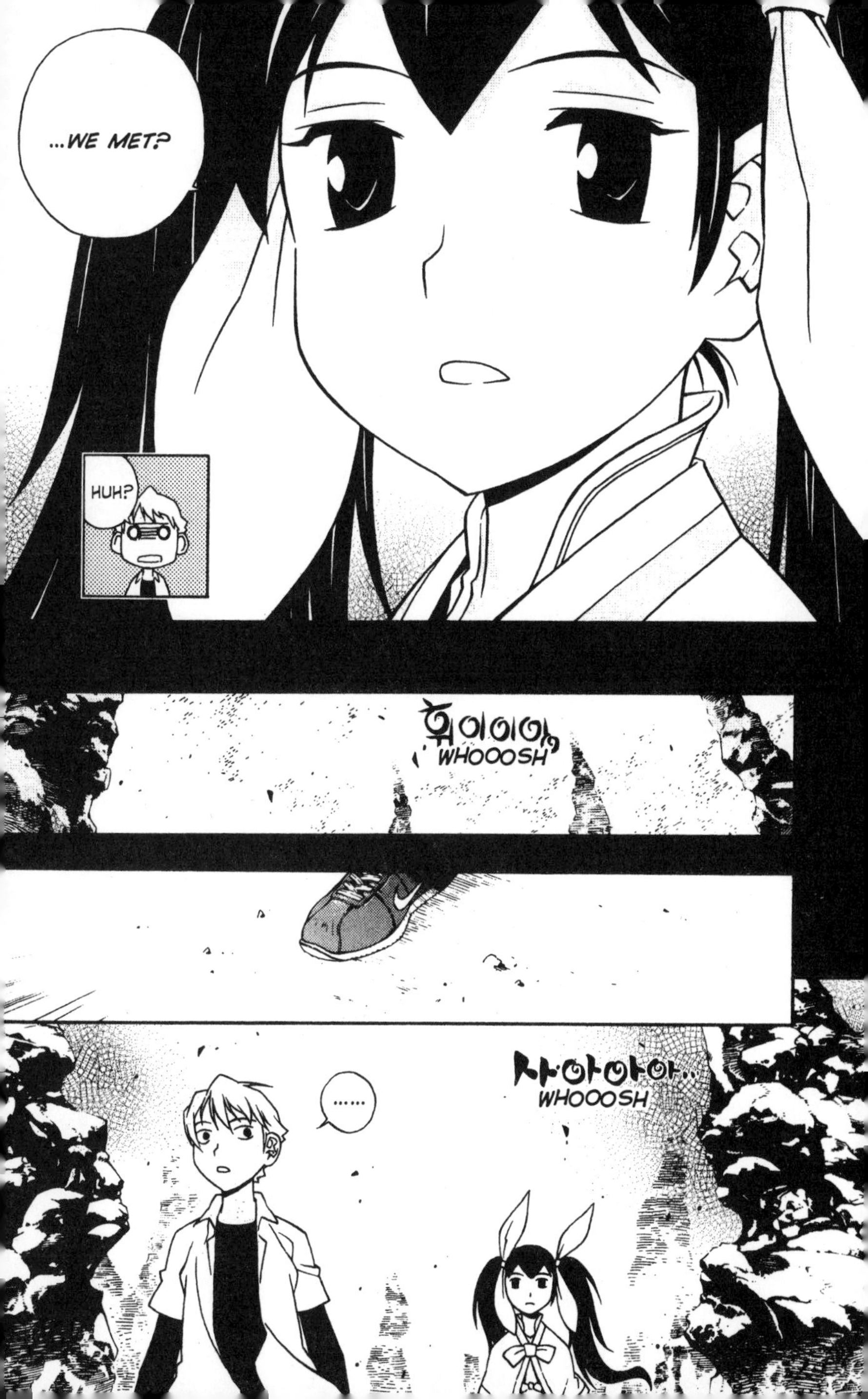
...WE MET?
HUH?
훼이이잉
WHOOOSH
사아아아...
WHOOOSH
......

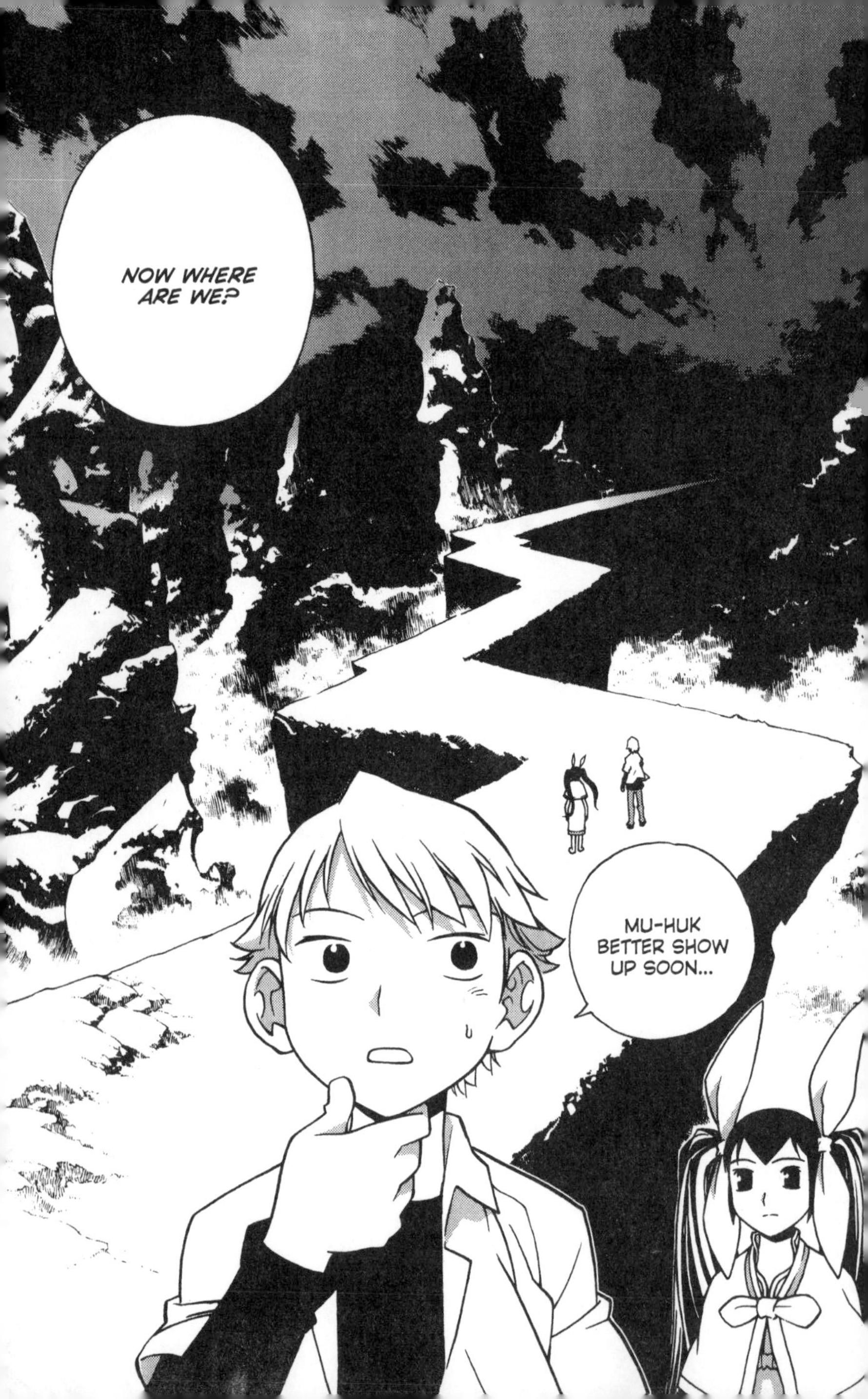
NOW WHERE ARE WE?
MU-HUK BETTER SHOW UP SOON...

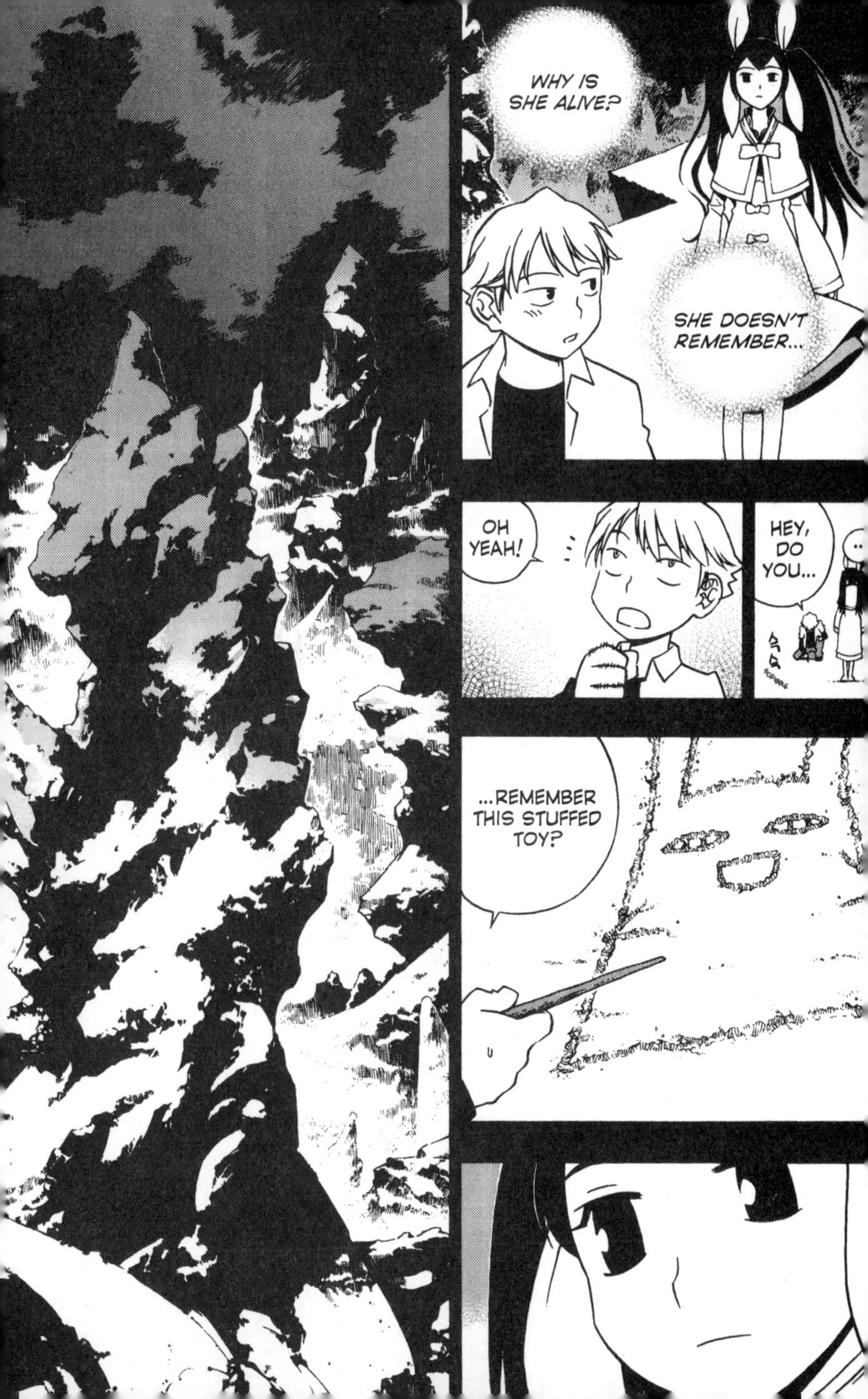
WHY IS SHE ALIVE?
SHE DOESN'T REMEMBER...
HEY, DO YOU...
OH YEAH!
...REMEMBER THIS STUFFED TOY?

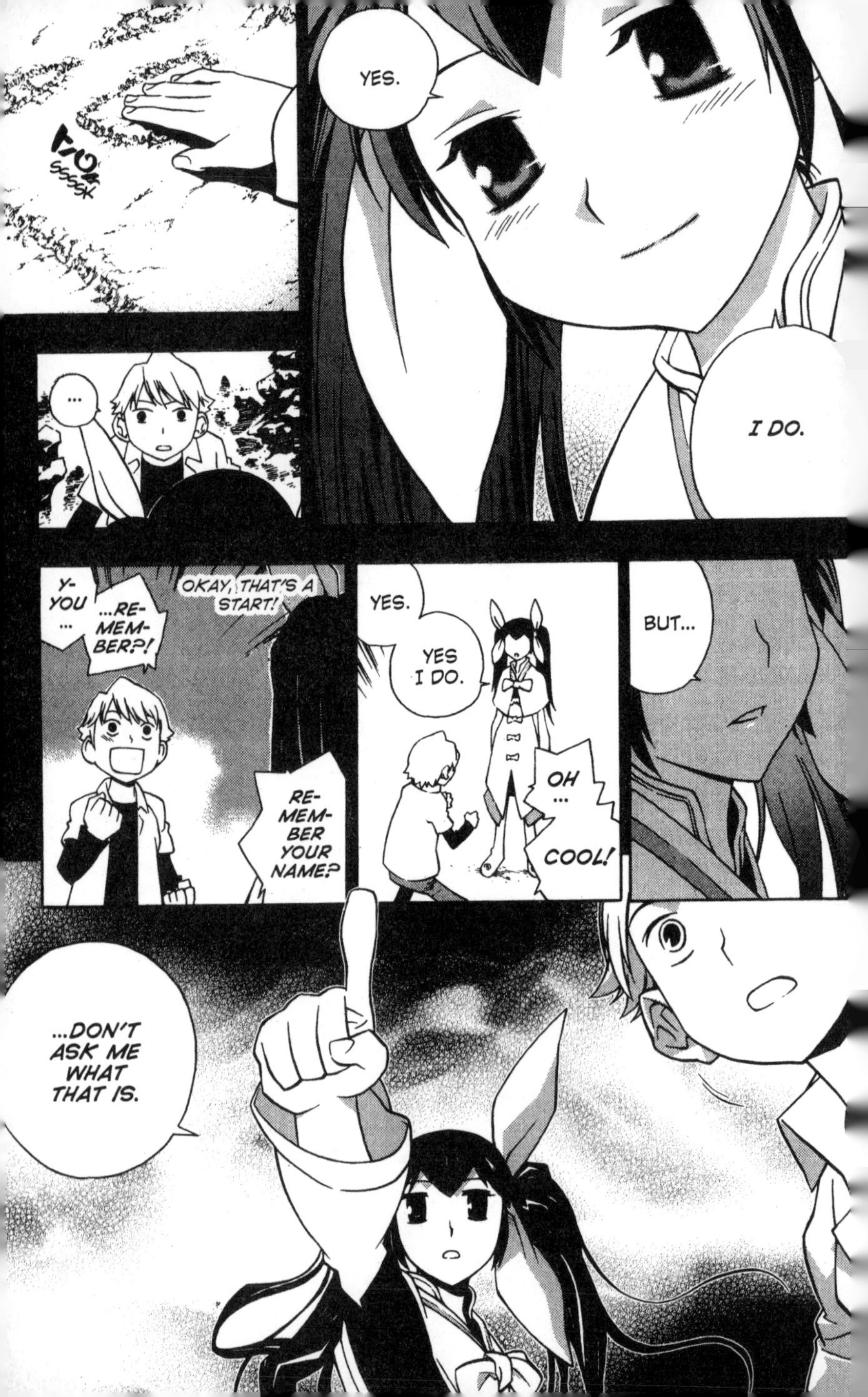
YES.
I DO.
SSSSK
...
BUT...
YES.
YES I DO.
OH ... COOL!
Y-YOU ...
...RE-MEMBER?!
OKAY, THAT'S A START!
RE-MEMBER YOUR NAME?
...DON'T ASK ME WHAT THAT IS.

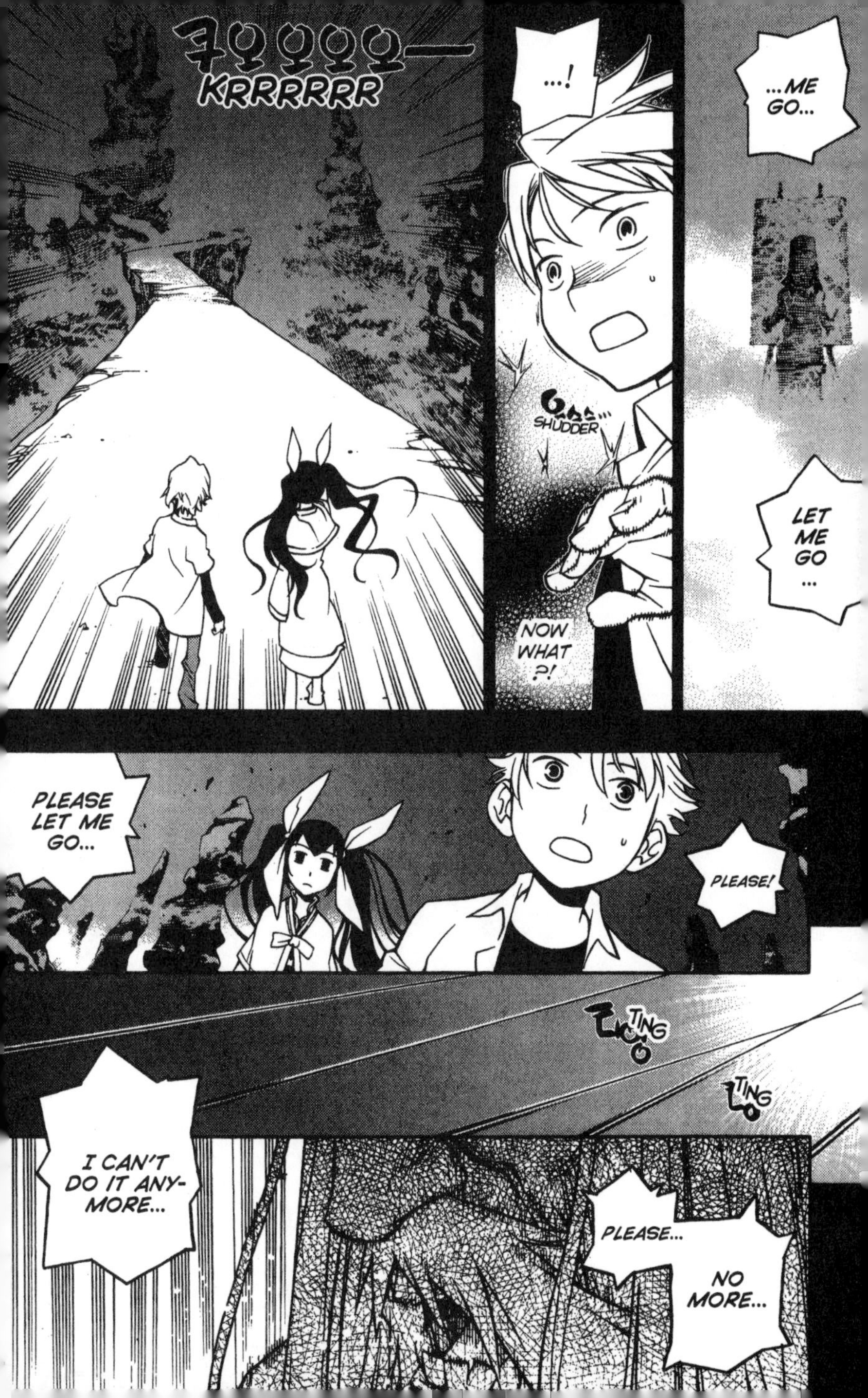

쿠오오오오—
KRRRRRR
...!
SHUDDER
NOW WHAT?!
...ME GO...
LET ME GO...
PLEASE LET ME GO...
PLEASE!
TING
TING
I CAN'T DO IT ANYMORE...
PLEASE...
NO MORE...

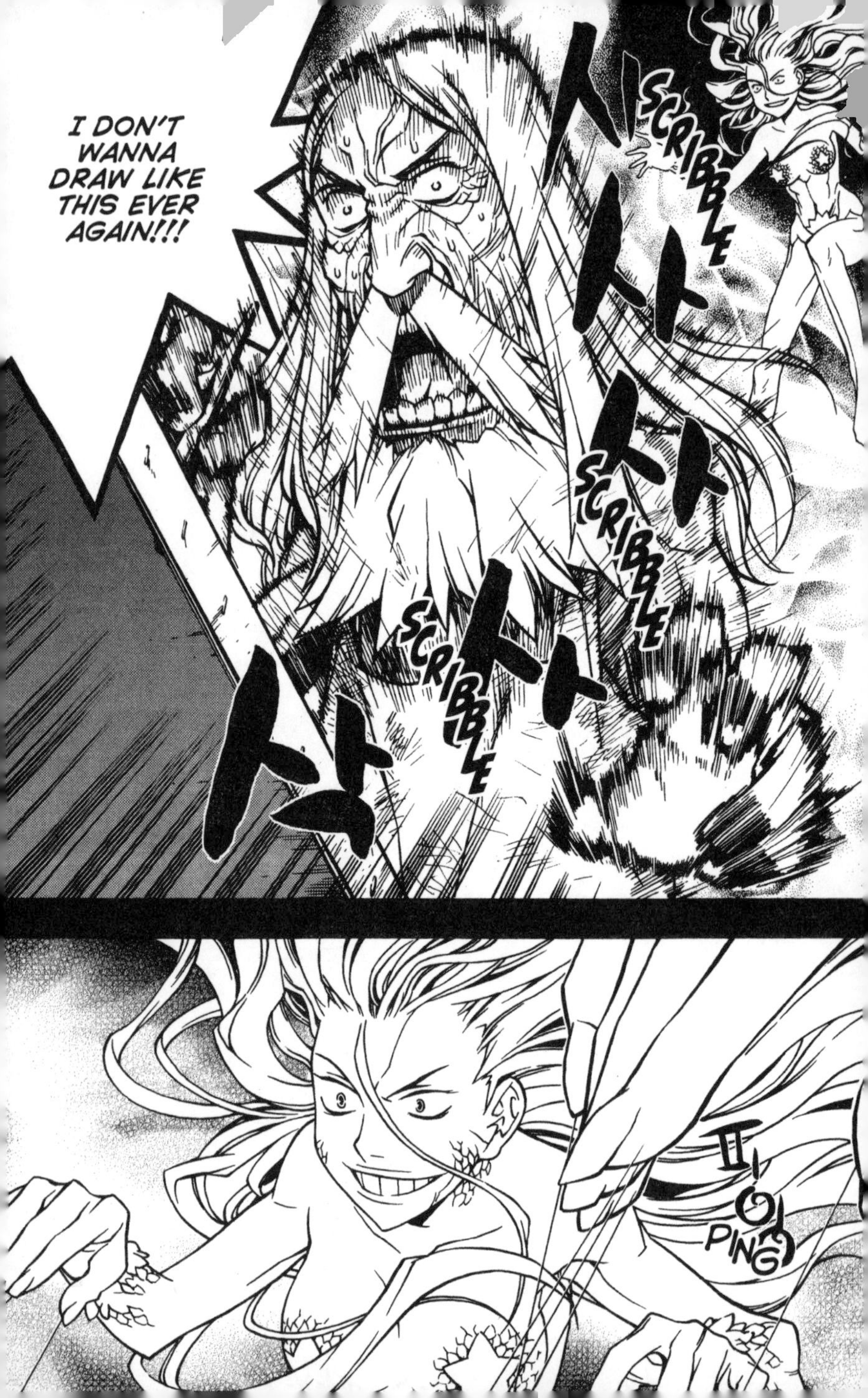
I DON'T WANNA DRAW LIKE THIS EVER AGAIN!!!
SCRIBBBLE
SCRIBBBLE
SCRIBBBLE
PING

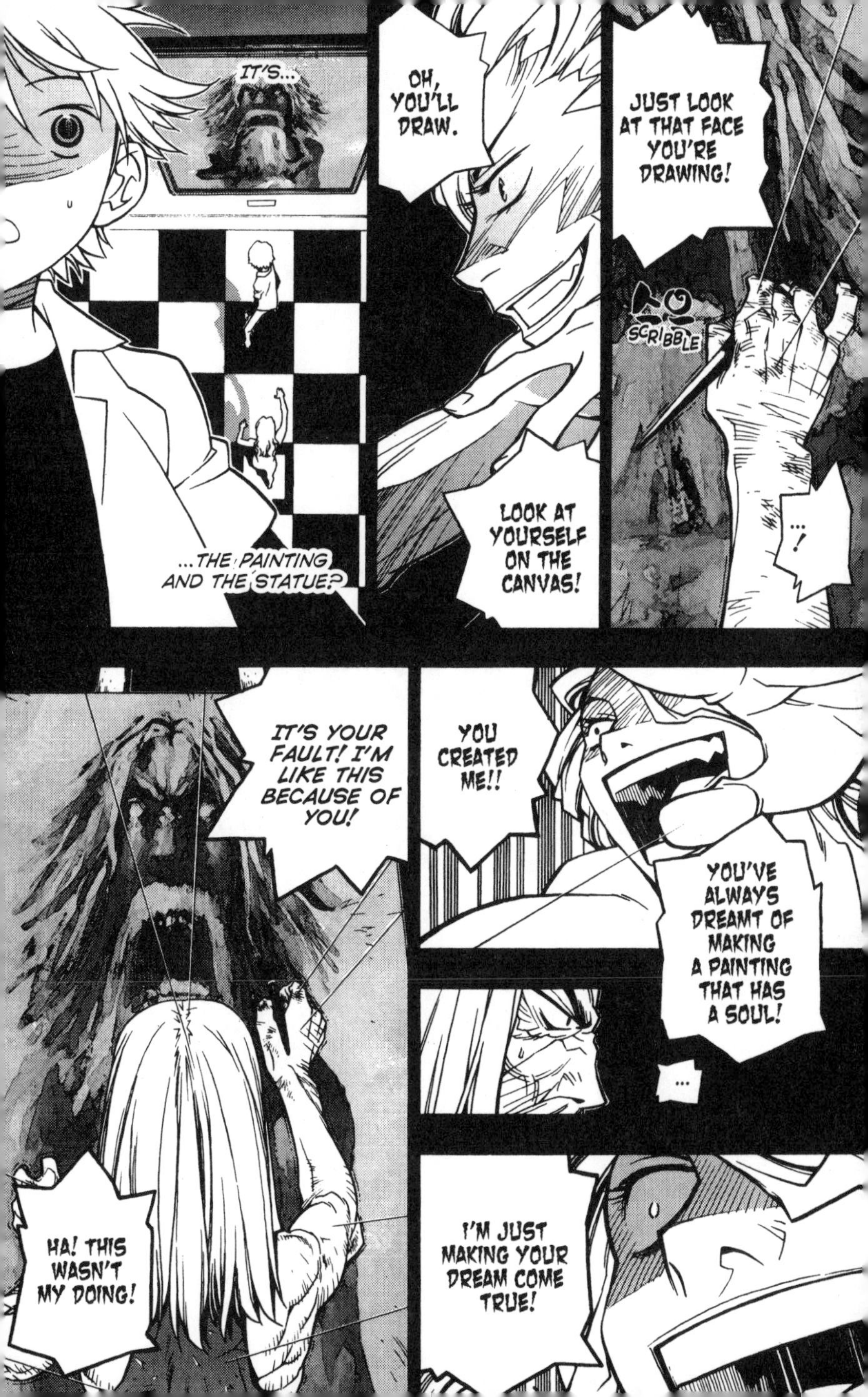

IT'S...
...THE PAINTING AND THE STATUE?
OH, YOU'LL DRAW.
LOOK AT YOURSELF ON THE CANVAS!
JUST LOOK AT THAT FACE YOU'RE DRAWING!
SCRIBBLE
...!
IT'S YOUR FAULT! I'M LIKE THIS BECAUSE OF YOU!
HA! THIS WASN'T MY DOING!
YOU CREATED ME!!
YOU'VE ALWAYS DREAMT OF MAKING A PAINTING THAT HAS A SOUL!
...
I'M JUST MAKING YOUR DREAM COME TRUE!

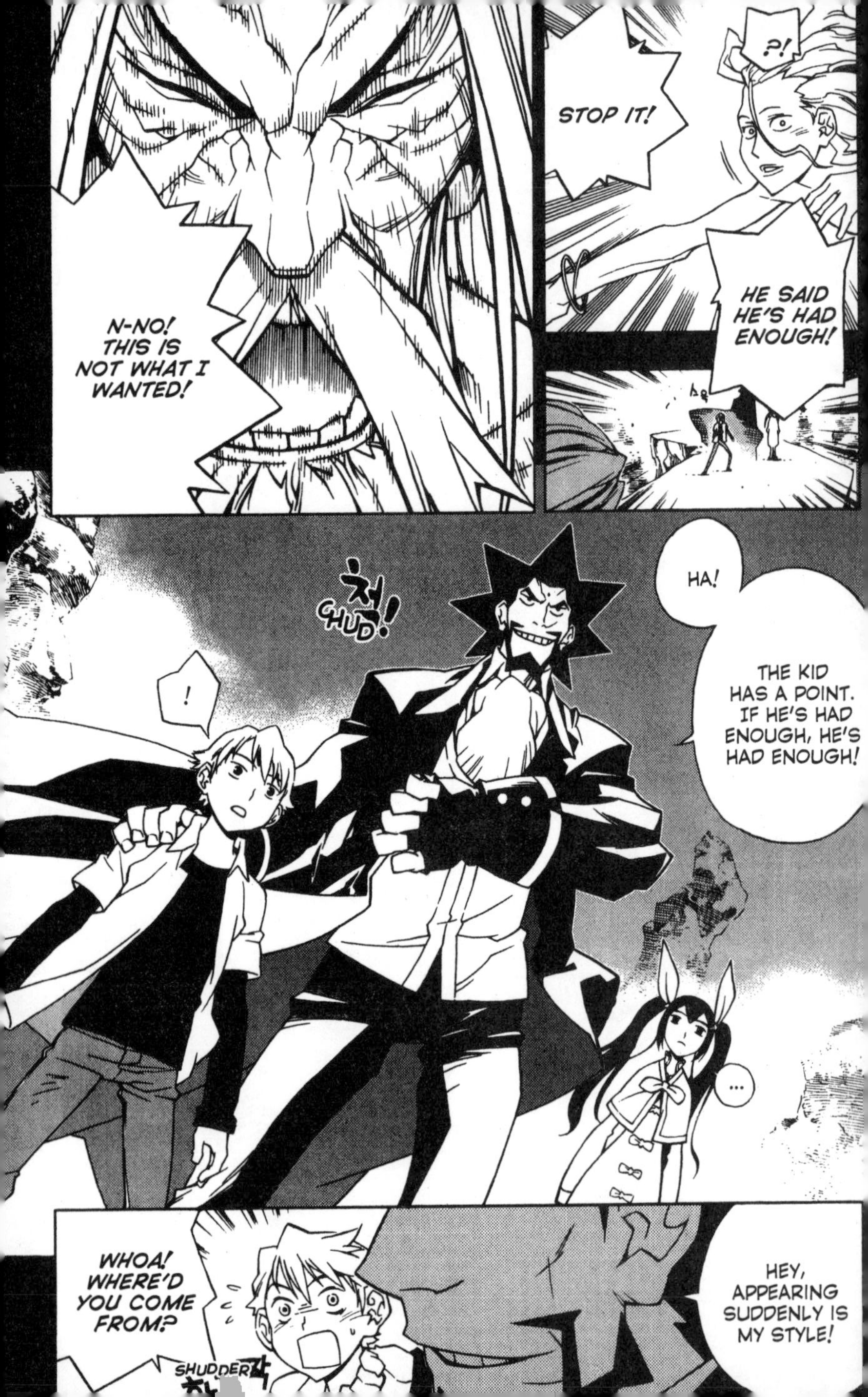
N-NO! THIS IS NOT WHAT I WANTED!
STOP IT!
?!
HE SAID HE'S HAD ENOUGH!
CHUD!
!
HA!
THE KID HAS A POINT. IF HE'S HAD ENOUGH, HE'S HAD ENOUGH!
...
WHOA! WHERE'D YOU COME FROM?
HEY, APPEARING SUDDENLY IS MY STYLE!
SHUDDER

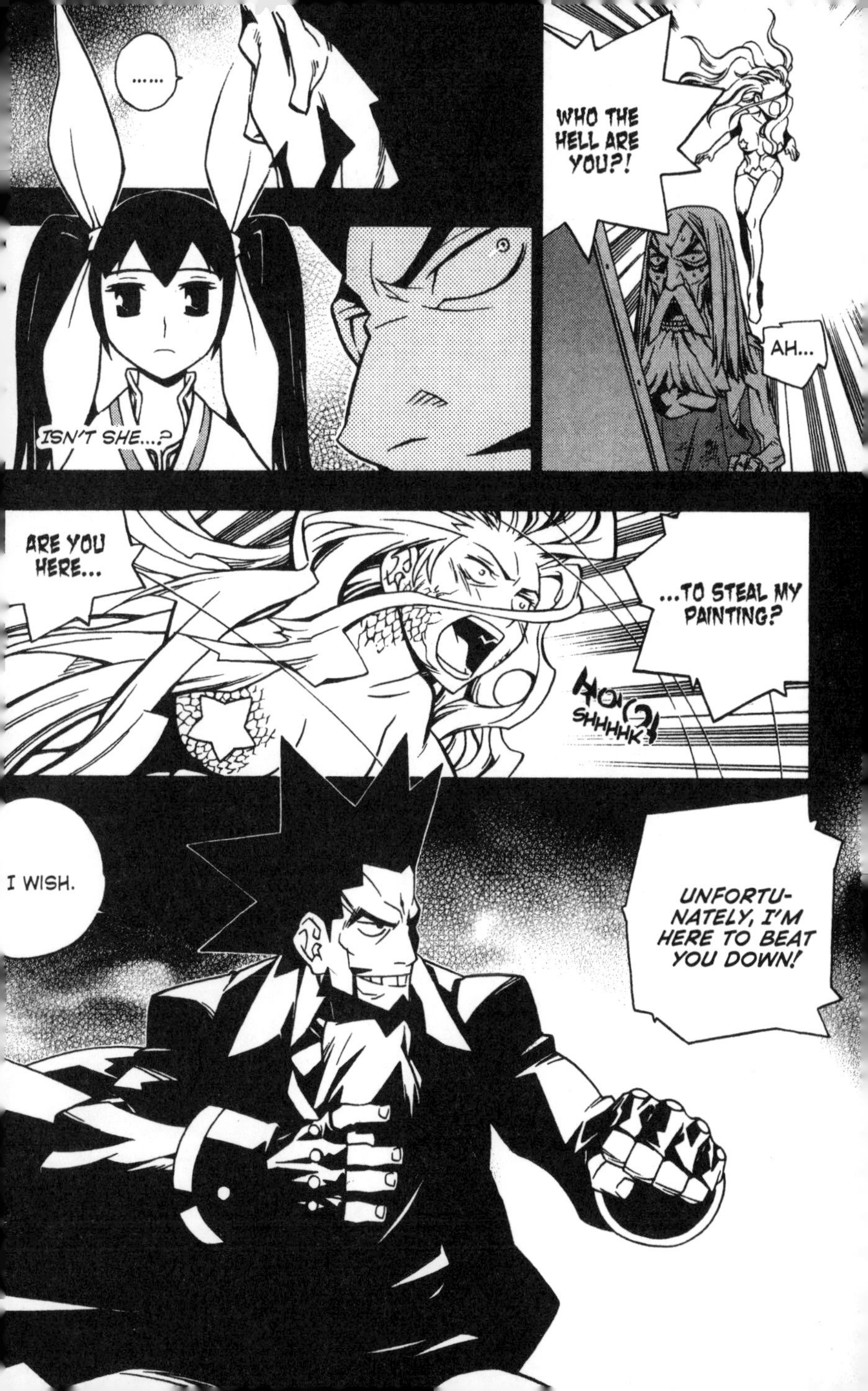
......
ISN'T SHE...?
WHO THE HELL ARE YOU?!
AH...
ARE YOU HERE...
...TO STEAL MY PAINTING?
SHHHHK
I WISH.
UNFORTUNATELY, I'M HERE TO BEAT YOU DOWN!

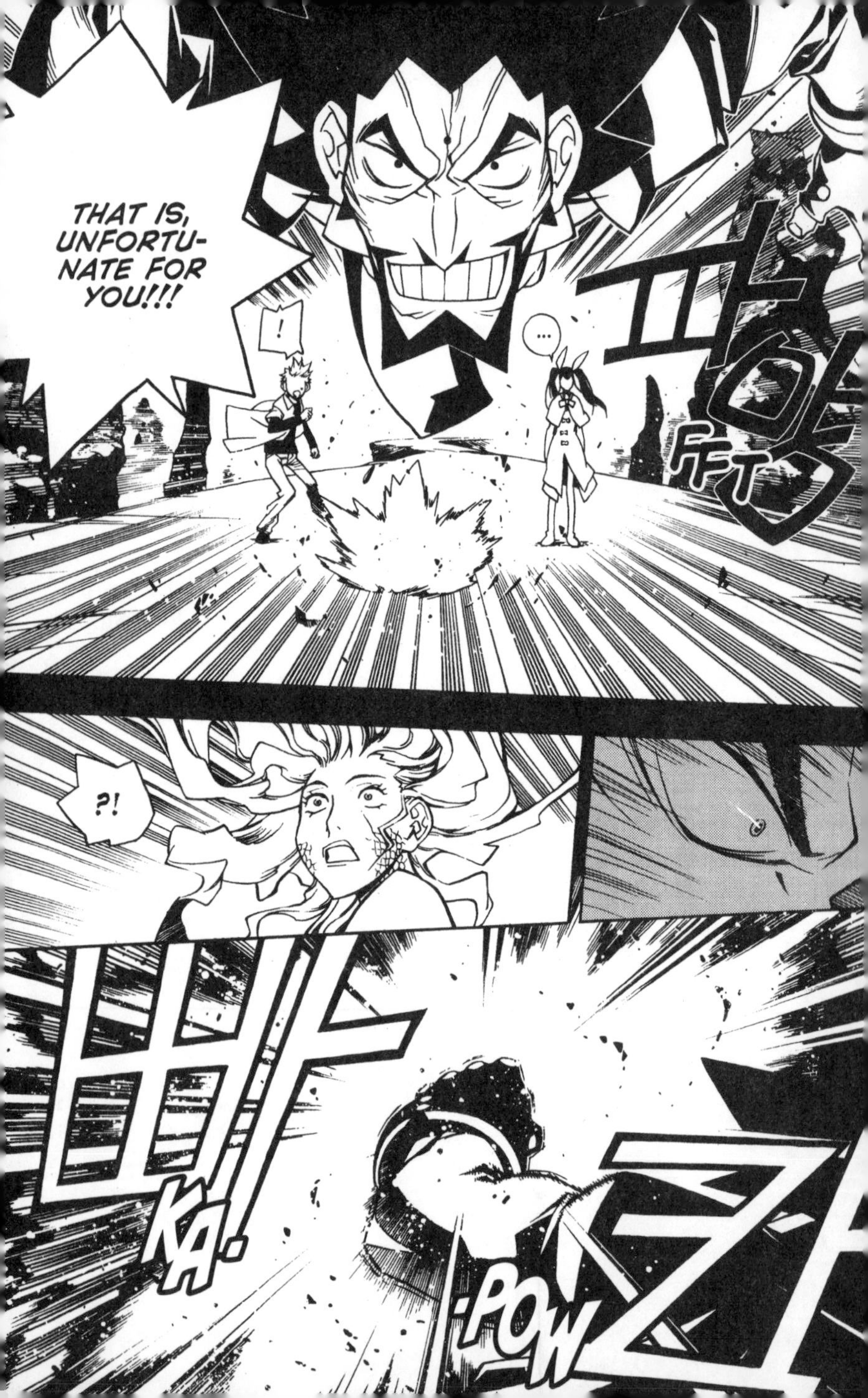
THAT IS, UNFORTU-NATE FOR YOU!!!
!
...
FFT
?!
KA.
POW

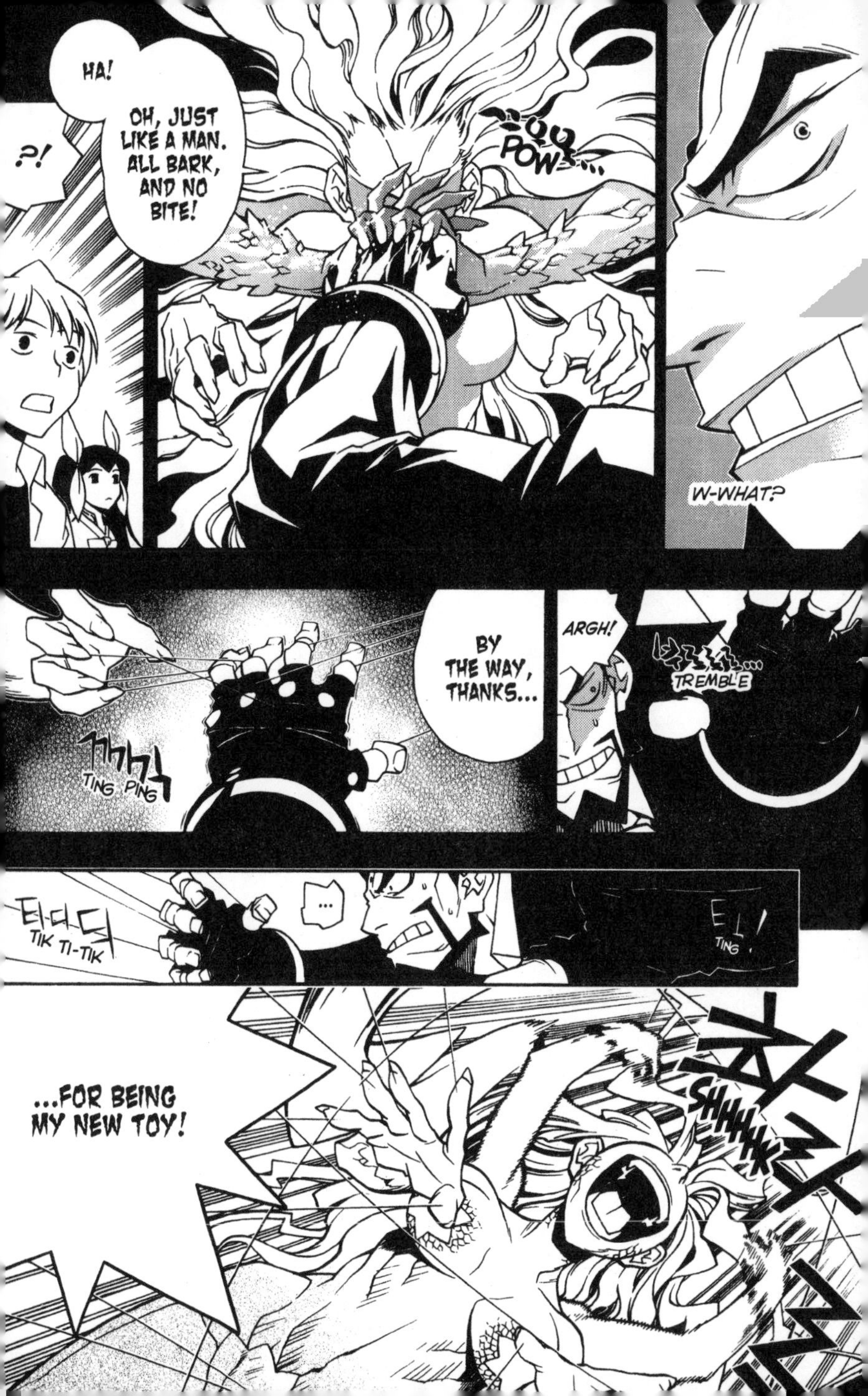

HA!
OH, JUST LIKE A MAN. ALL BARK, AND NO BITE!
?!
POW...
W-WHAT?
BY THE WAY, THANKS...
ARGH!
TREMBLE
TING PING
...
TIK TI-TIK
TING
...FOR BEING MY NEW TOY!
SHHHKK

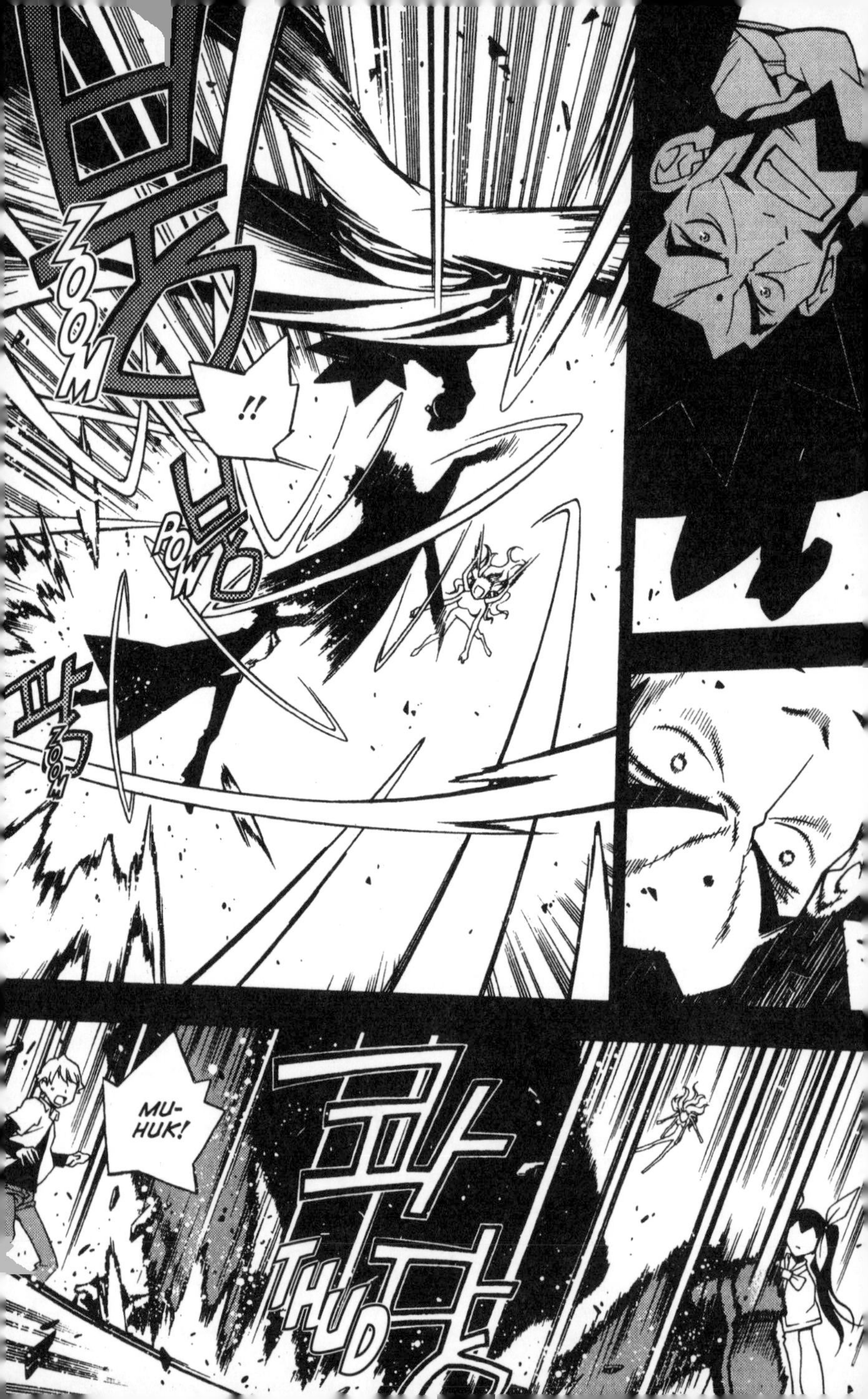

ZOOM
!!
POW
ZOOM
MU-
HUK!
THUD

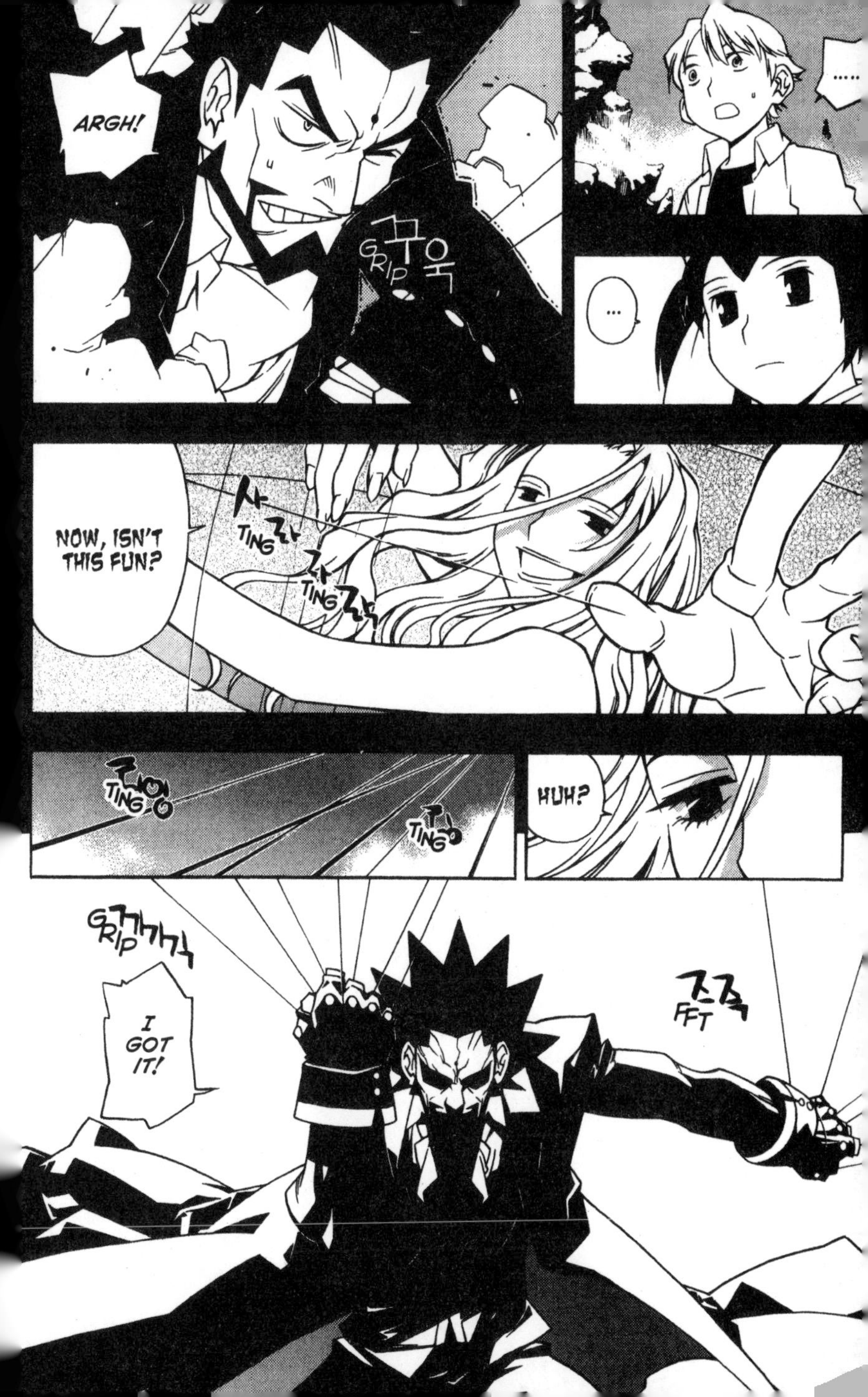
ARGH!
GRIP
......
...
NOW, ISN'T THIS FUN?
TING
TING
TING
TING
HUH?
GRIP
I GOT IT!
FFT

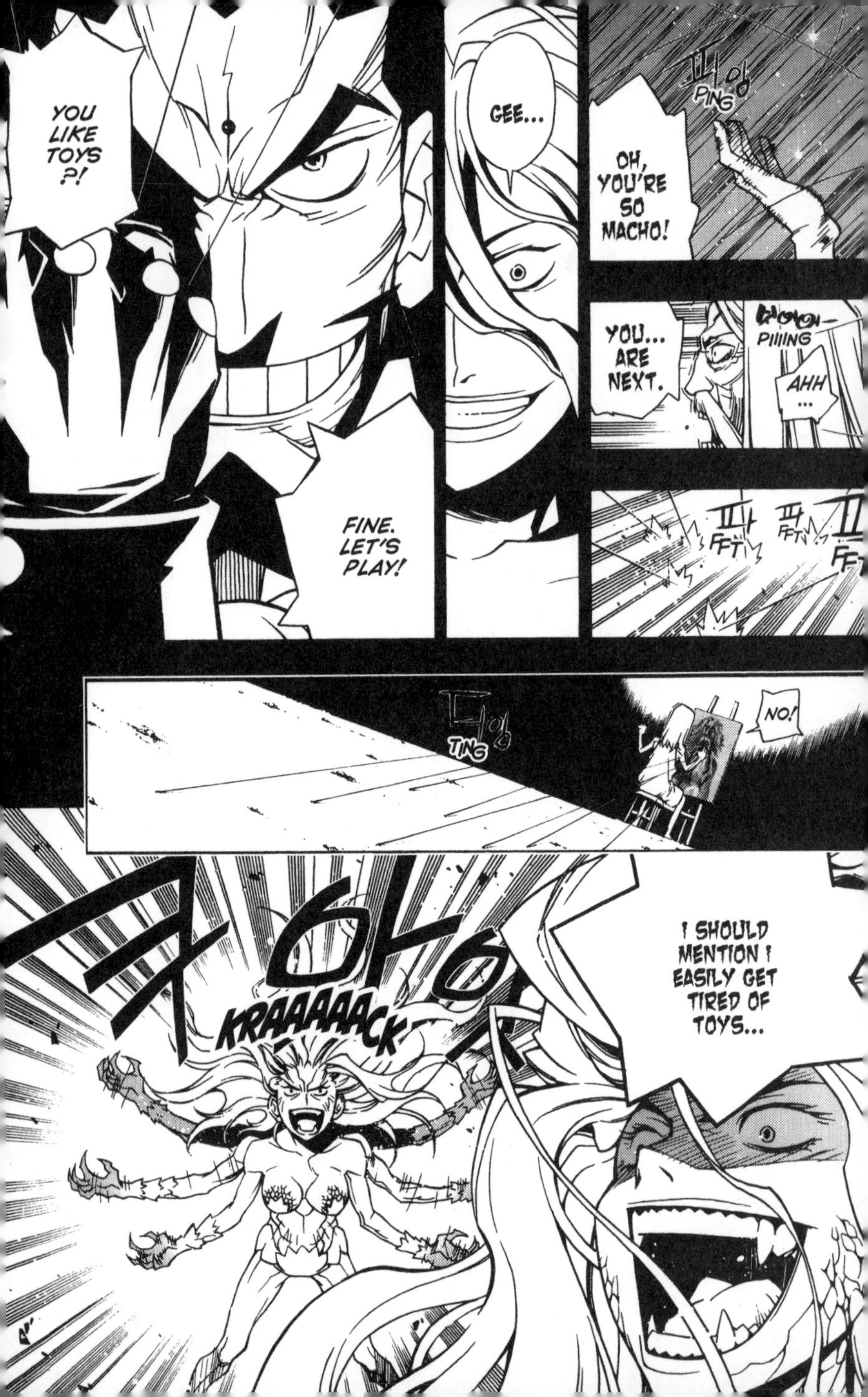
YOU LIKE TOYS ?!
FINE. LET'S PLAY!
GEE...
OH, YOU'RE SO MACHO!
PING
YOU... ARE NEXT.
PIIING
AHH ...
FFT
FFT
FF
TING
NO!
KRAAAAACK
I SHOULD MENTION I EASILY GET TIRED OF TOYS...

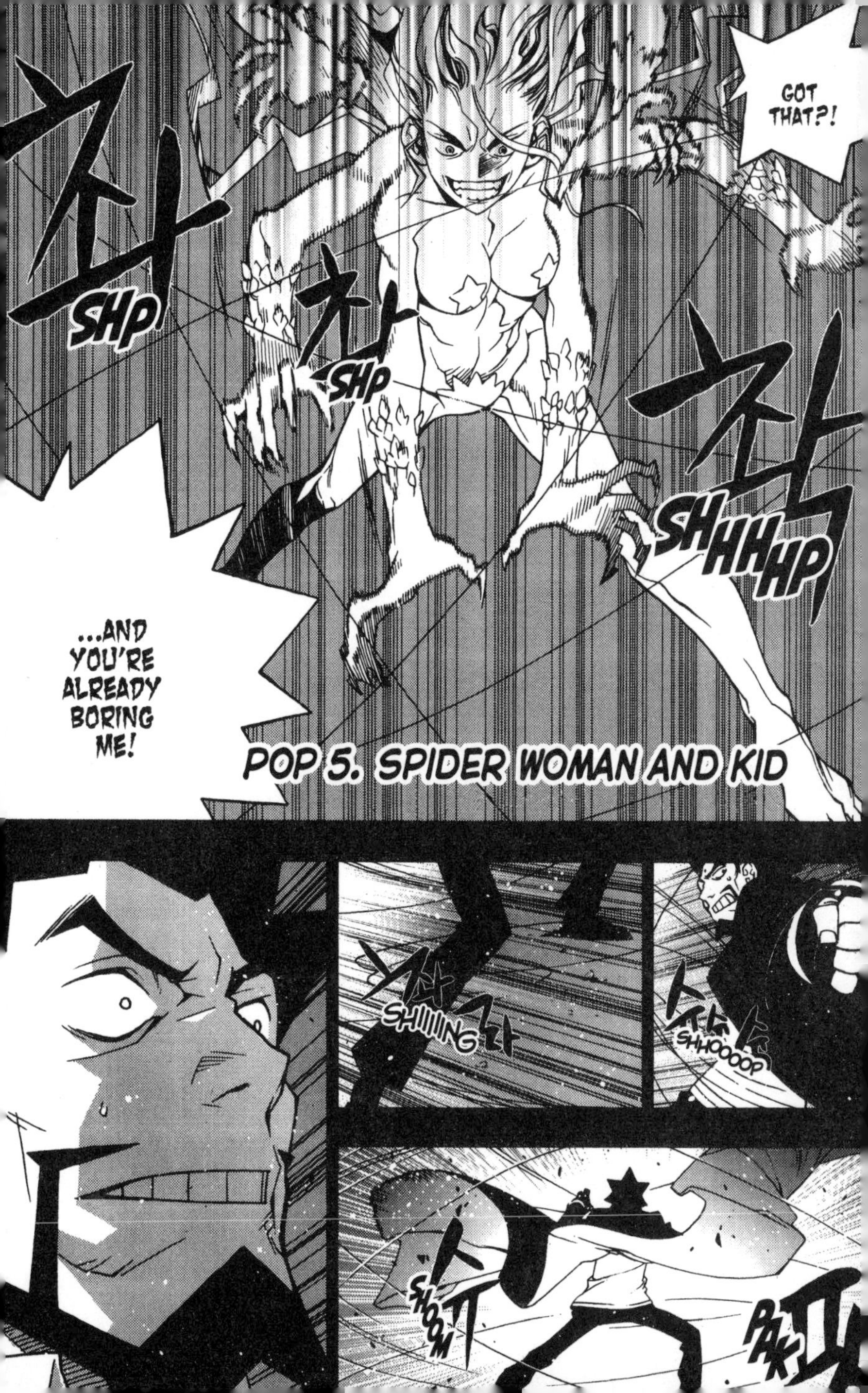
GOT THAT?!
SHP
SHP
SHHHHP
...AND YOU'RE ALREADY BORING ME!
POP 5. SPIDER WOMAN AND KID
SHHOOOOP
SHIIIING
PAK
SHOOM

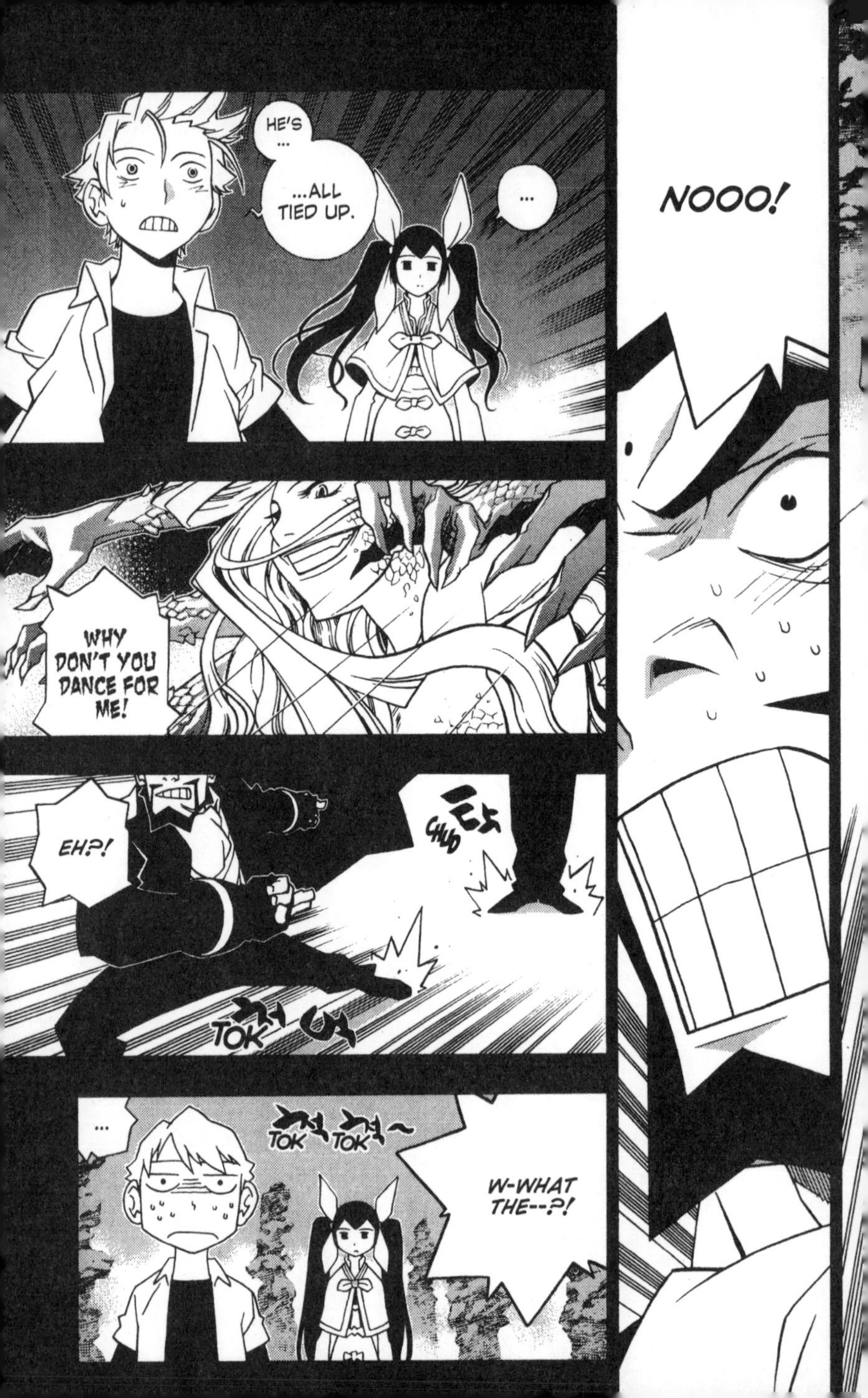
HE'S ...
...ALL TIED UP.
...
WHY DON'T YOU DANCE FOR ME!
EH?!
CHUD
TOK
...
TOK TOK
W-WHAT THE--?!
NOOO!

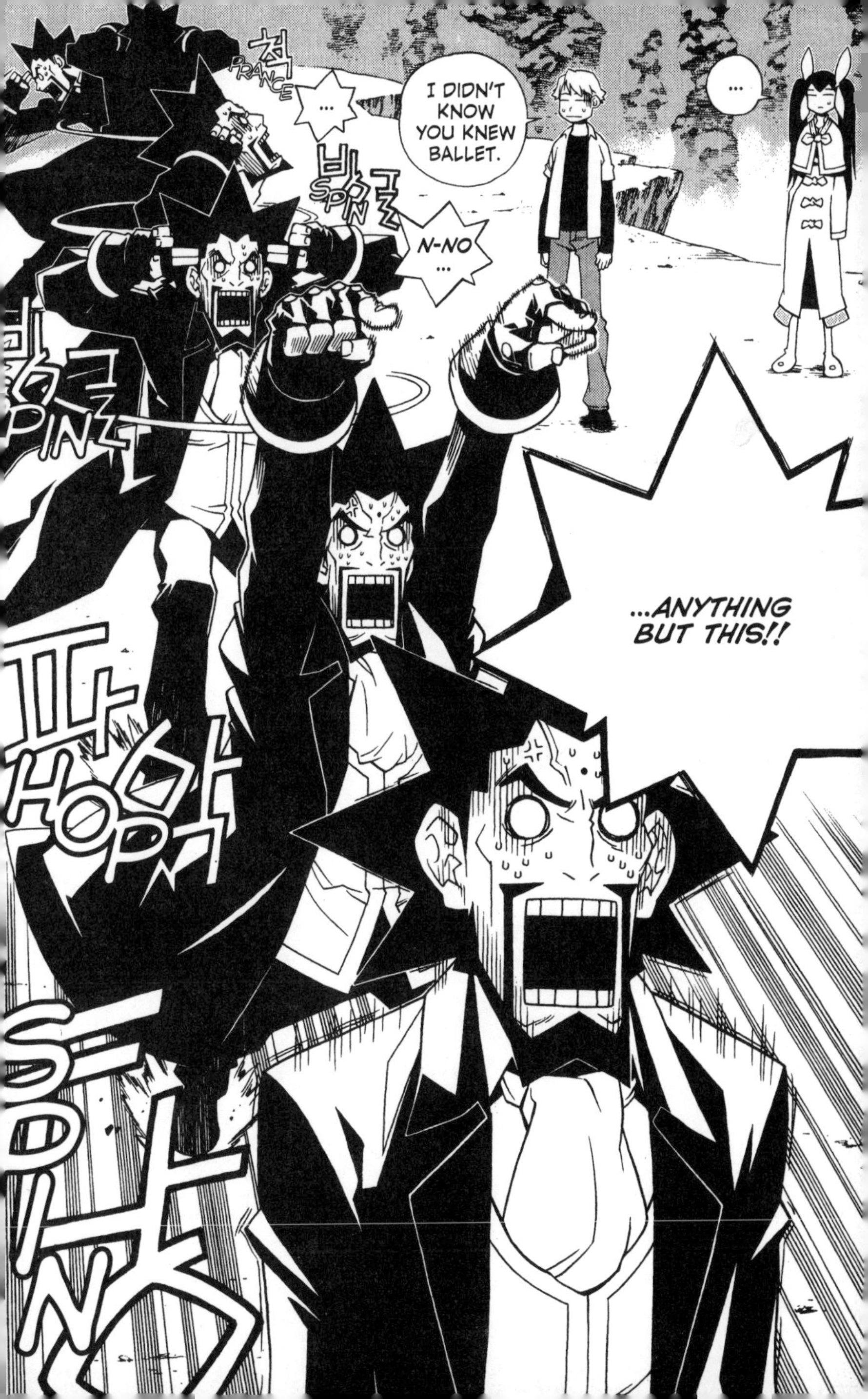

PRANCE
...
I DIDN'T KNOW YOU KNEW BALLET.
...
SPIN
N-NO ...
SPIN
HOP
...ANYTHING BUT THIS!!
SPIN

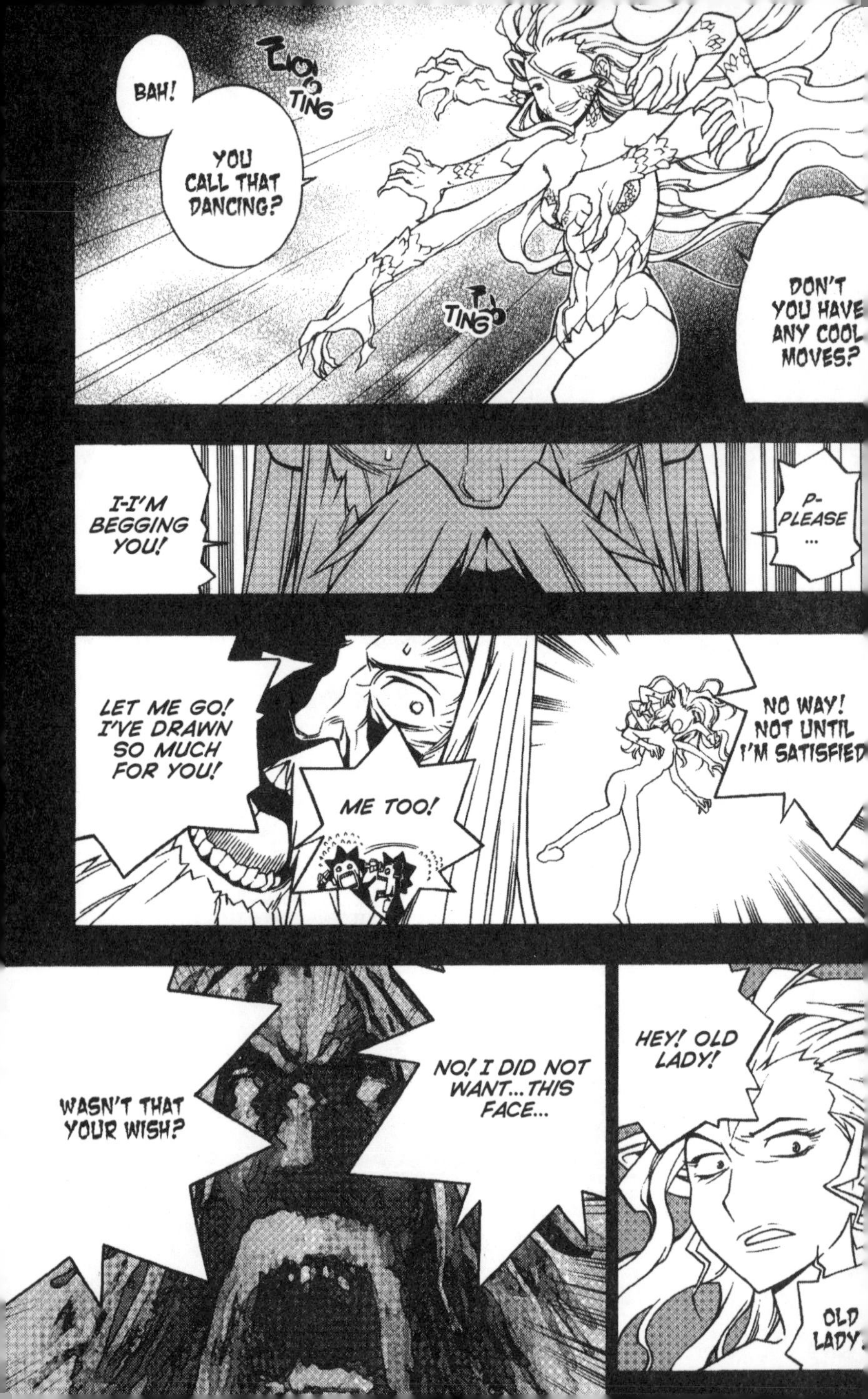
DON'T YOU HAVE ANY COOL MOVES?
TING
BAH!
YOU CALL THAT DANCING?
TING
P-PLEASE ...
I-I'M BEGGING YOU!
NO WAY! NOT UNTIL I'M SATISFIED
ME TOO!
LET ME GO! I'VE DRAWN SO MUCH FOR YOU!
HEY! OLD LADY!
OLD LADY.
NO! I DID NOT WANT...THIS FACE...
WASN'T THAT YOUR WISH?

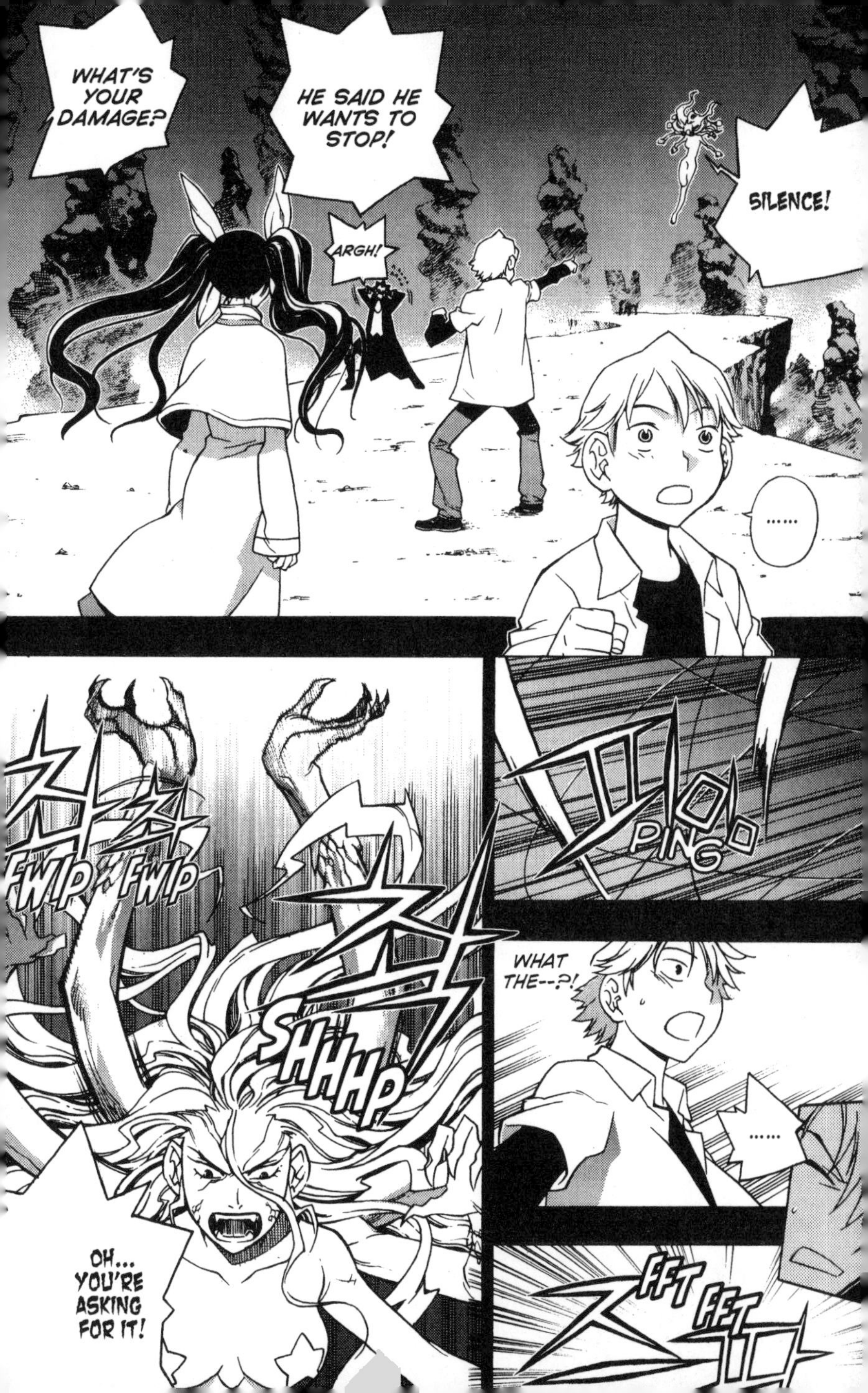
WHAT'S YOUR DAMAGE?
HE SAID HE WANTS TO STOP!
ARGH!
SILENCE!
......
PING
WHAT THE--?!
......
FFT FFT
FWIP FWIP
SHHHP
OH... YOU'RE ASKING FOR IT!

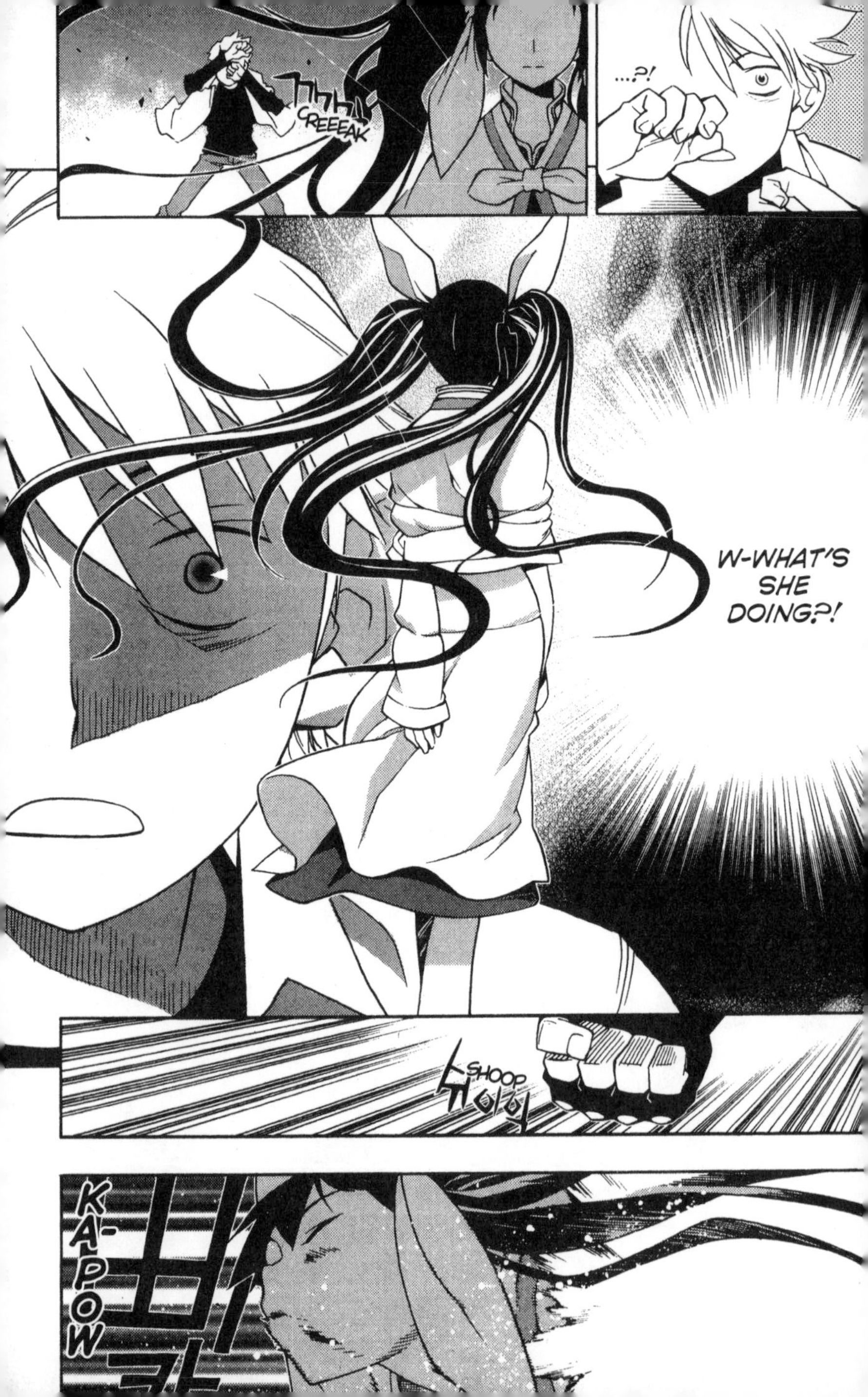
CREEEAK
...?!
W-WHAT'S SHE DOING?!
SHOOP
KA-POW

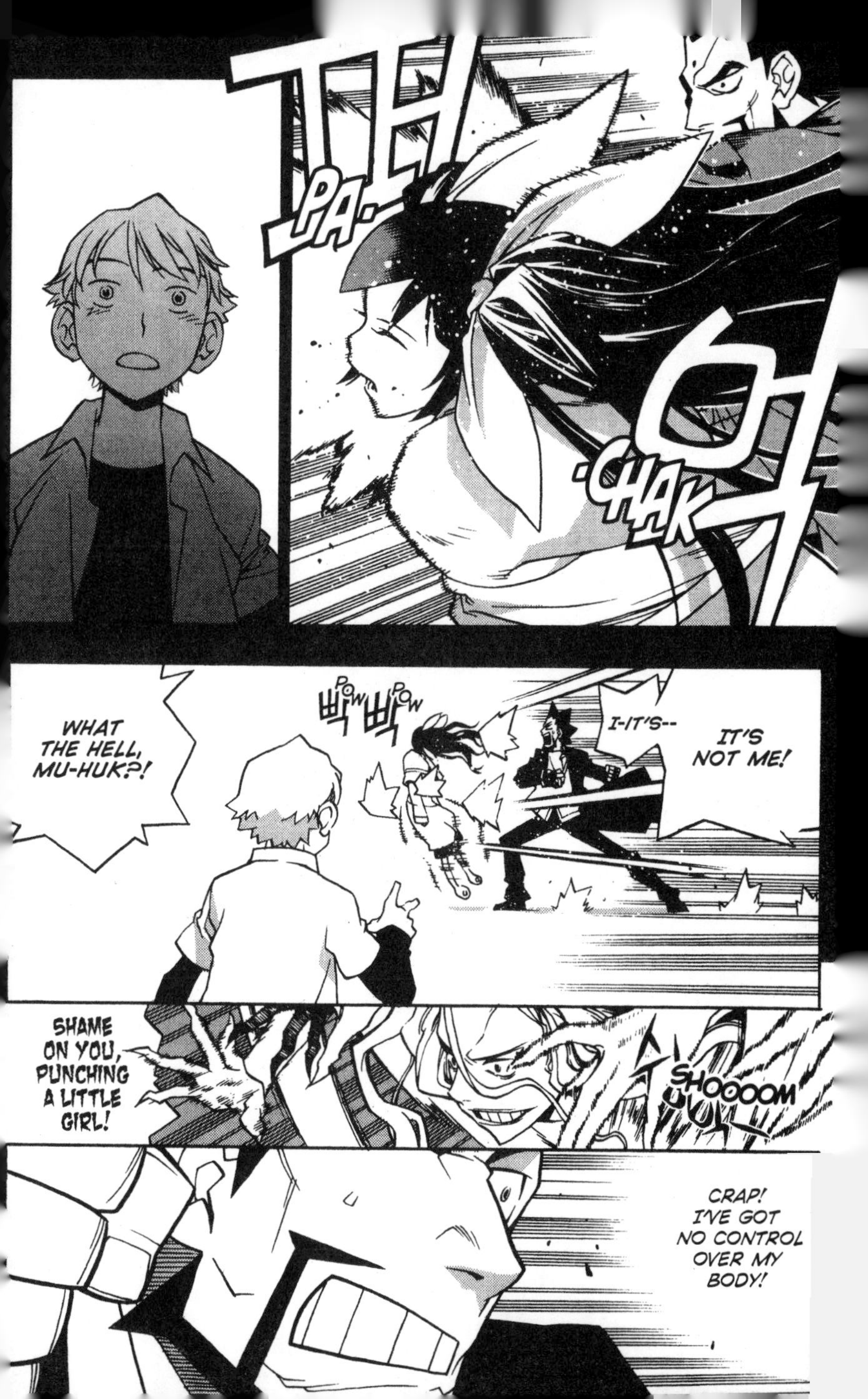

TTH
PA-
CHAK
WHAT THE HELL, MU-HUK?!
POW POW
I-IT'S--
IT'S NOT ME!
SHAME ON YOU, PUNCHING A LITTLE GIRL!
SHOOOOM
CRAP! I'VE GOT NO CONTROL OVER MY BODY!

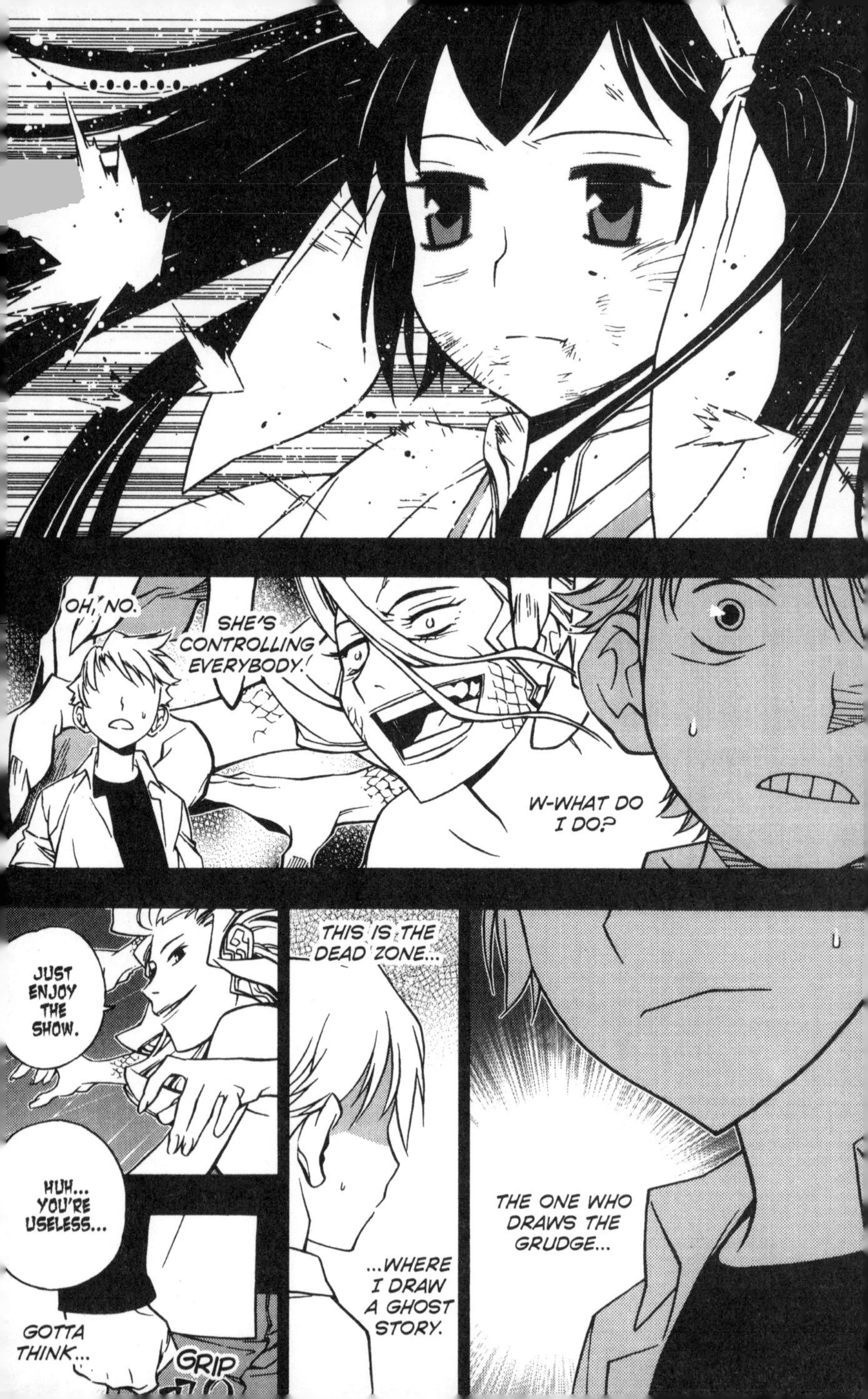
OH, NO.
SHE'S CONTROLLING EVERYBODY.
W-WHAT DO I DO?
THE ONE WHO DRAWS THE GRUDGE...
THIS IS THE DEAD ZONE...
...WHERE I DRAW A GHOST STORY.
JUST ENJOY THE SHOW.
HUH... YOU'RE USELESS...
GOTTA THINK...
GRIP

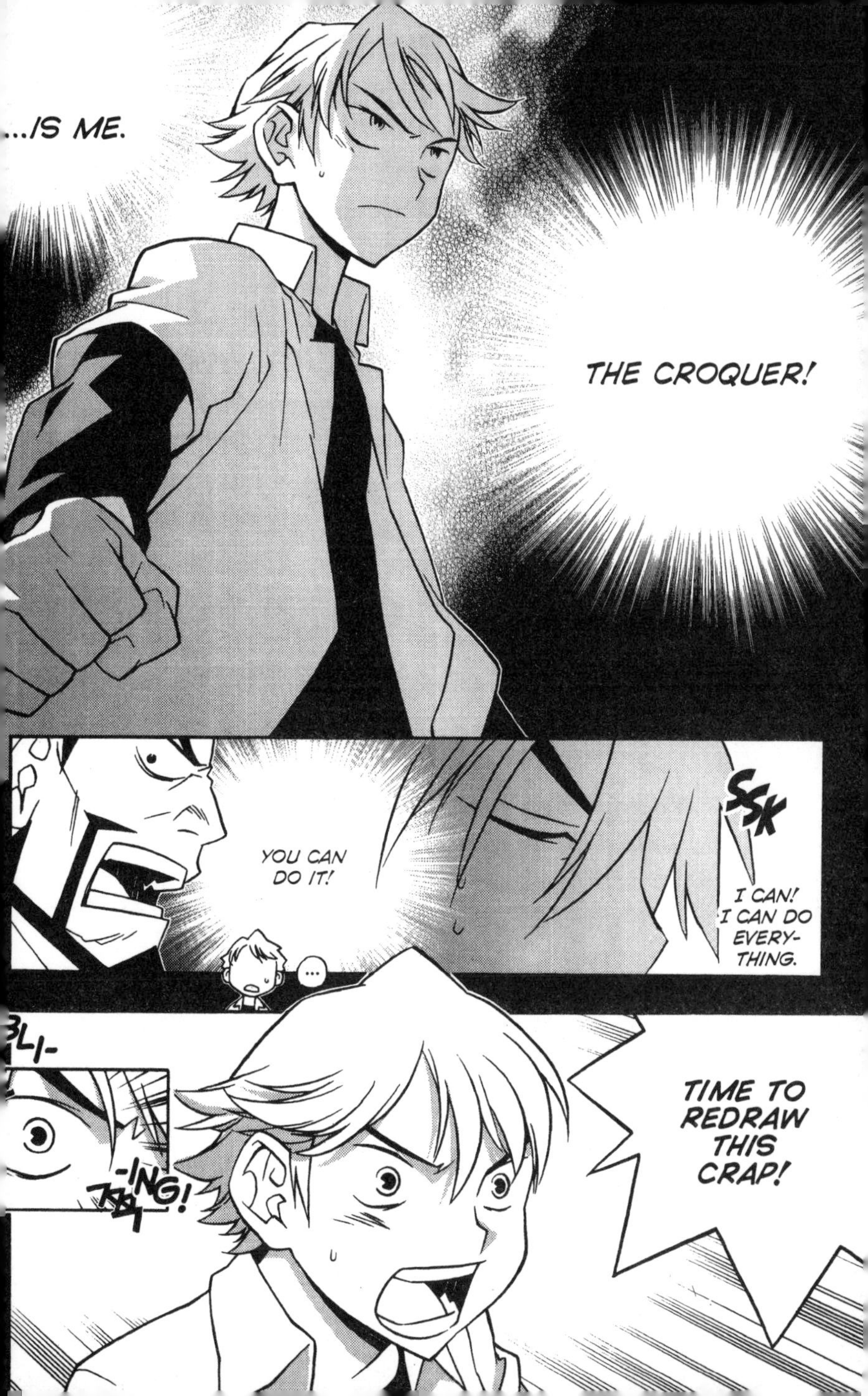
...IS ME.
THE CROQUER!
SSK
I CAN! I CAN DO EVERYTHING.
YOU CAN DO IT!
...
TIME TO REDRAW THIS CRAP!
BLI-
-ING!

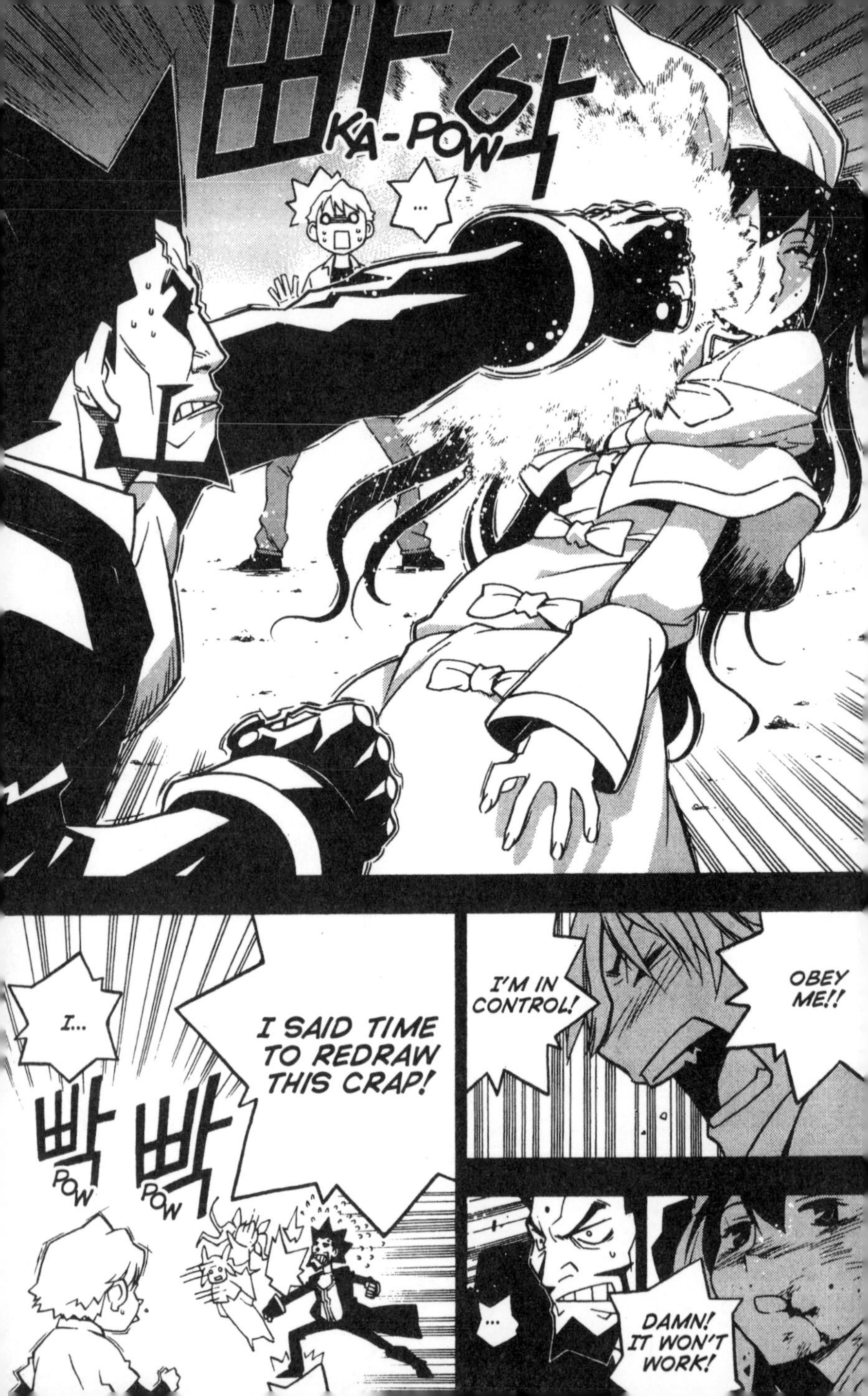

빠악
KA-POW
...
I...
I SAID TIME TO REDRAW THIS CRAP!
빠 POW
빠 POW
I'M IN CONTROL!
OBEY ME!!
...
DAMN! IT WON'T WORK!

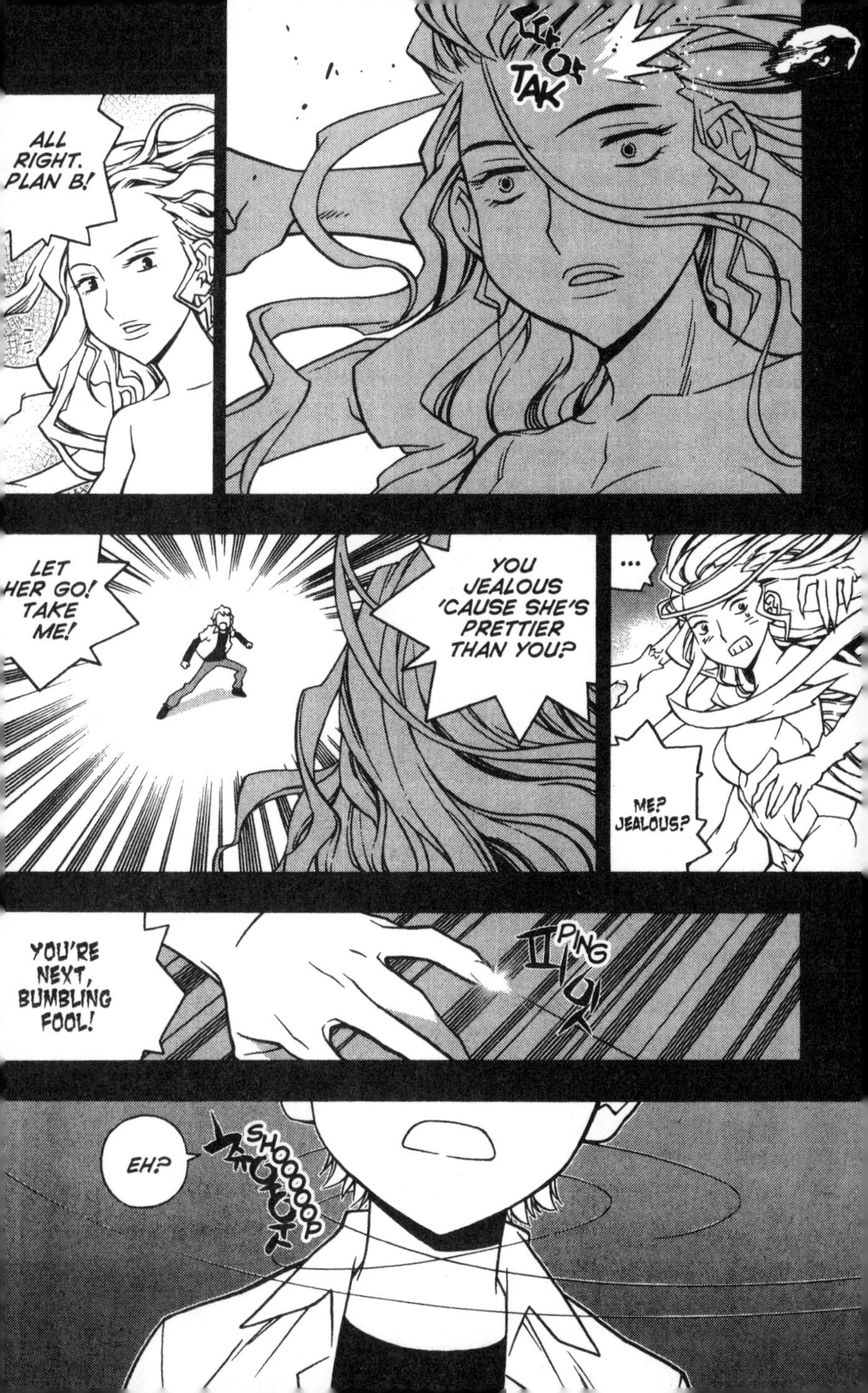
TAK
ALL RIGHT. PLAN B!
LET HER GO! TAKE ME!
YOU JEALOUS 'CAUSE SHE'S PRETTIER THAN YOU?
...
ME? JEALOUS?
YOU'RE NEXT, BUMBLING FOOL!
PING
EH?
SHOOOOOP

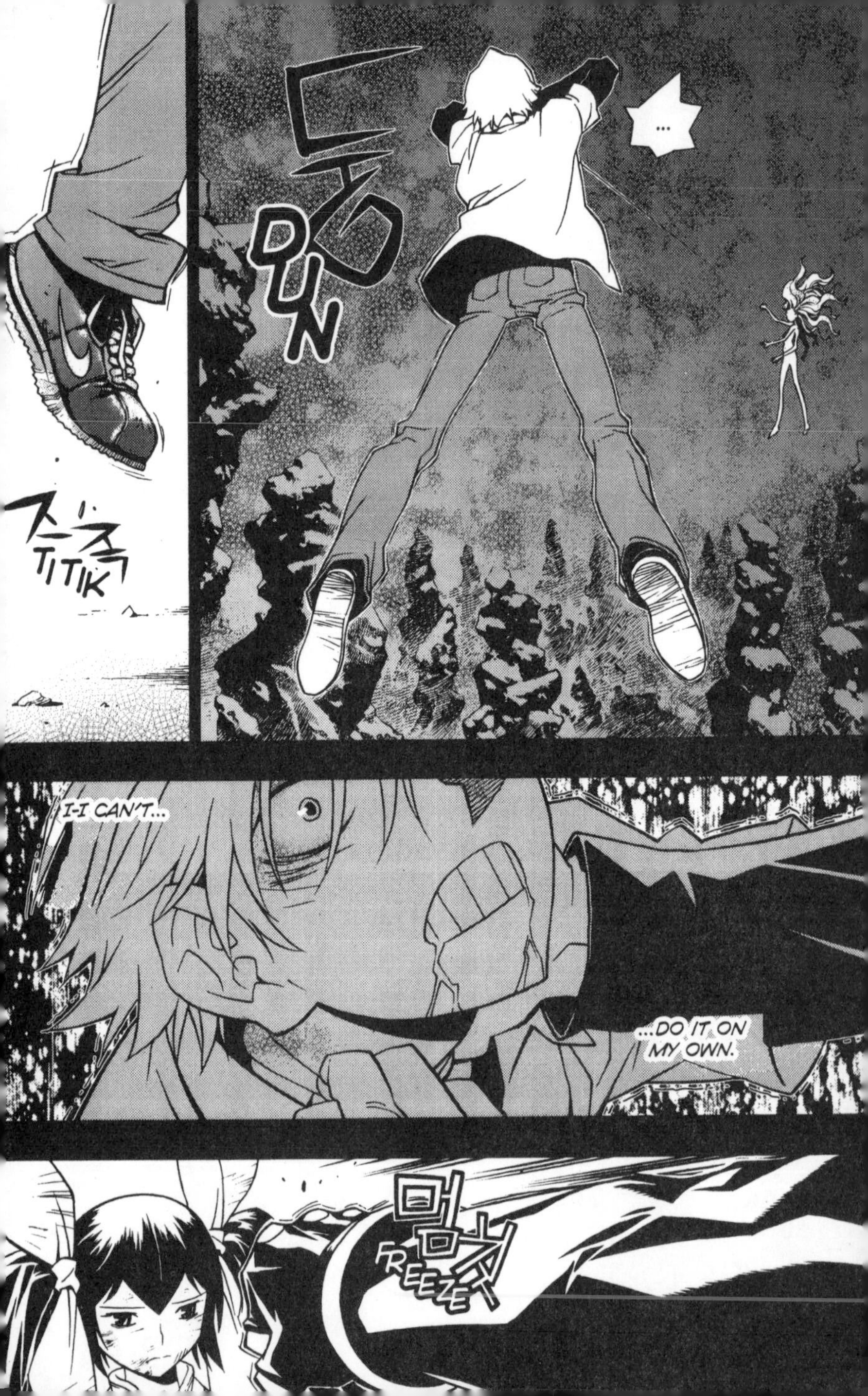

DUN
...
TITIK
I-I CAN'T...
...DO IT ON MY OWN.
FREEZE

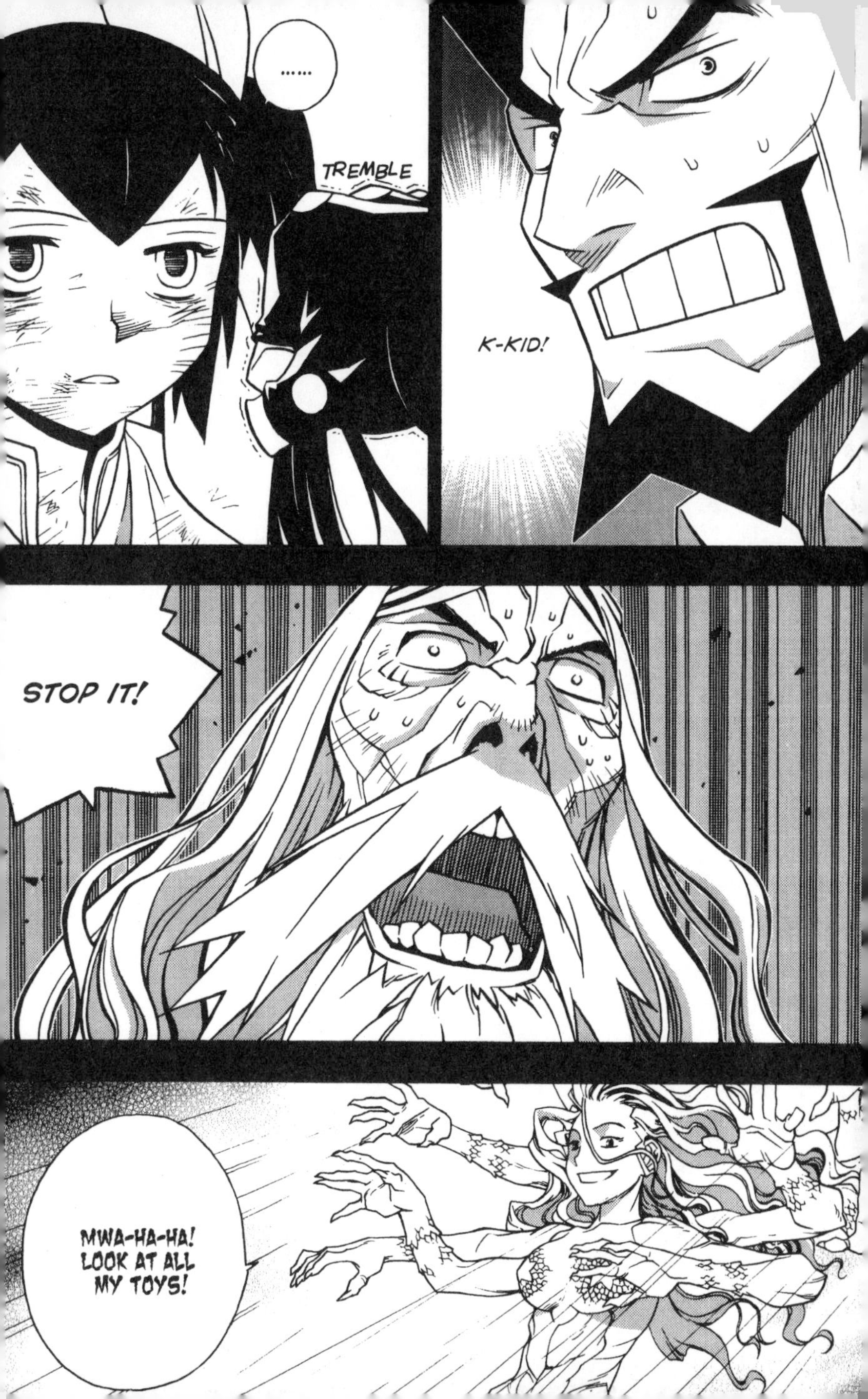
K-KID!
......
TREMBLE
STOP IT!
MWA-HA-HA! LOOK AT ALL MY TOYS!

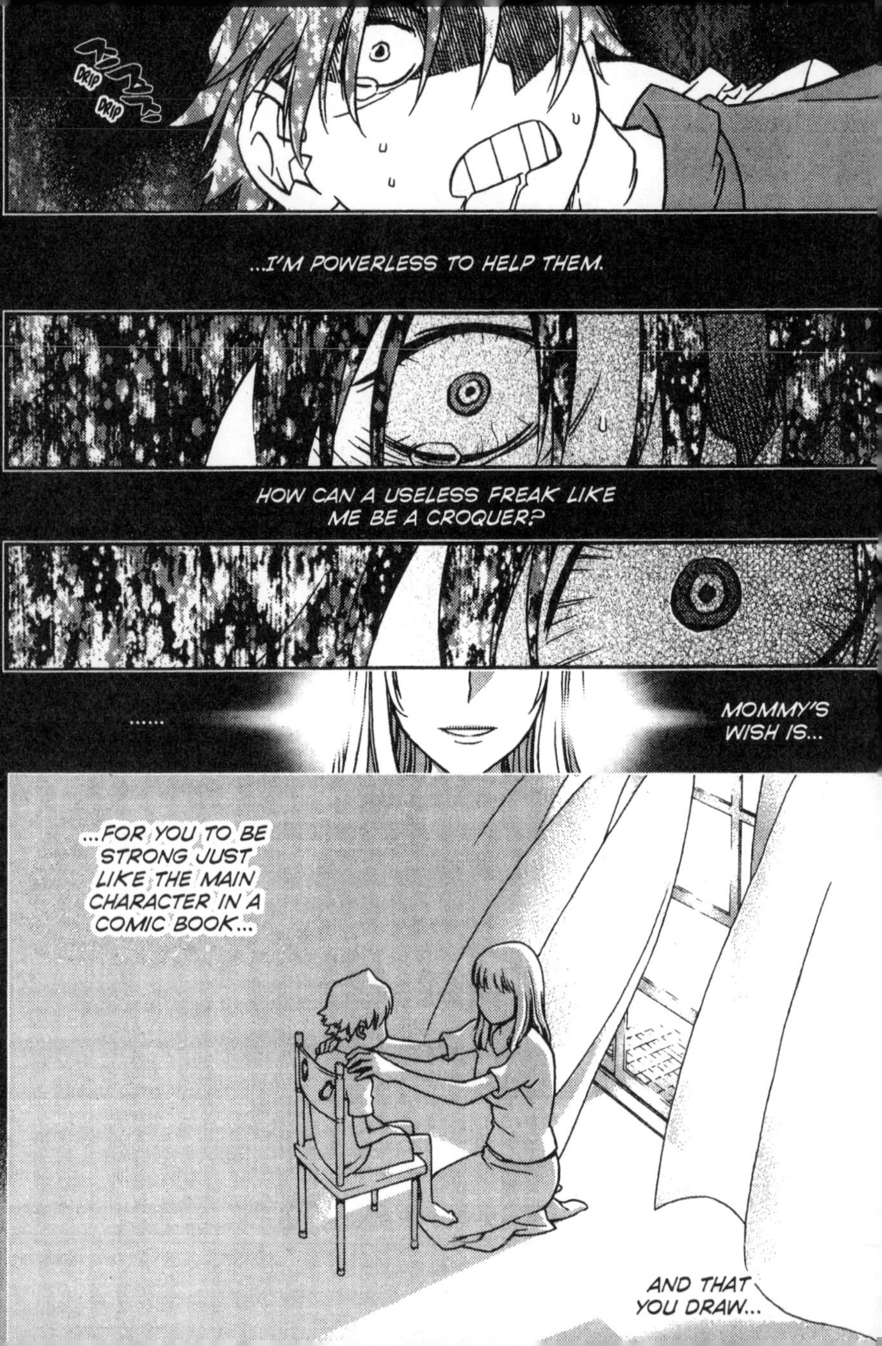
DRIP
DRIP
...I'M POWERLESS TO HELP THEM.
HOW CAN A USELESS FREAK LIKE ME BE A CROQUER?
......
MOMMY'S WISH IS...
...FOR YOU TO BE STRONG JUST LIKE THE MAIN CHARACTER IN A COMIC BOOK...
AND THAT YOU DRAW...

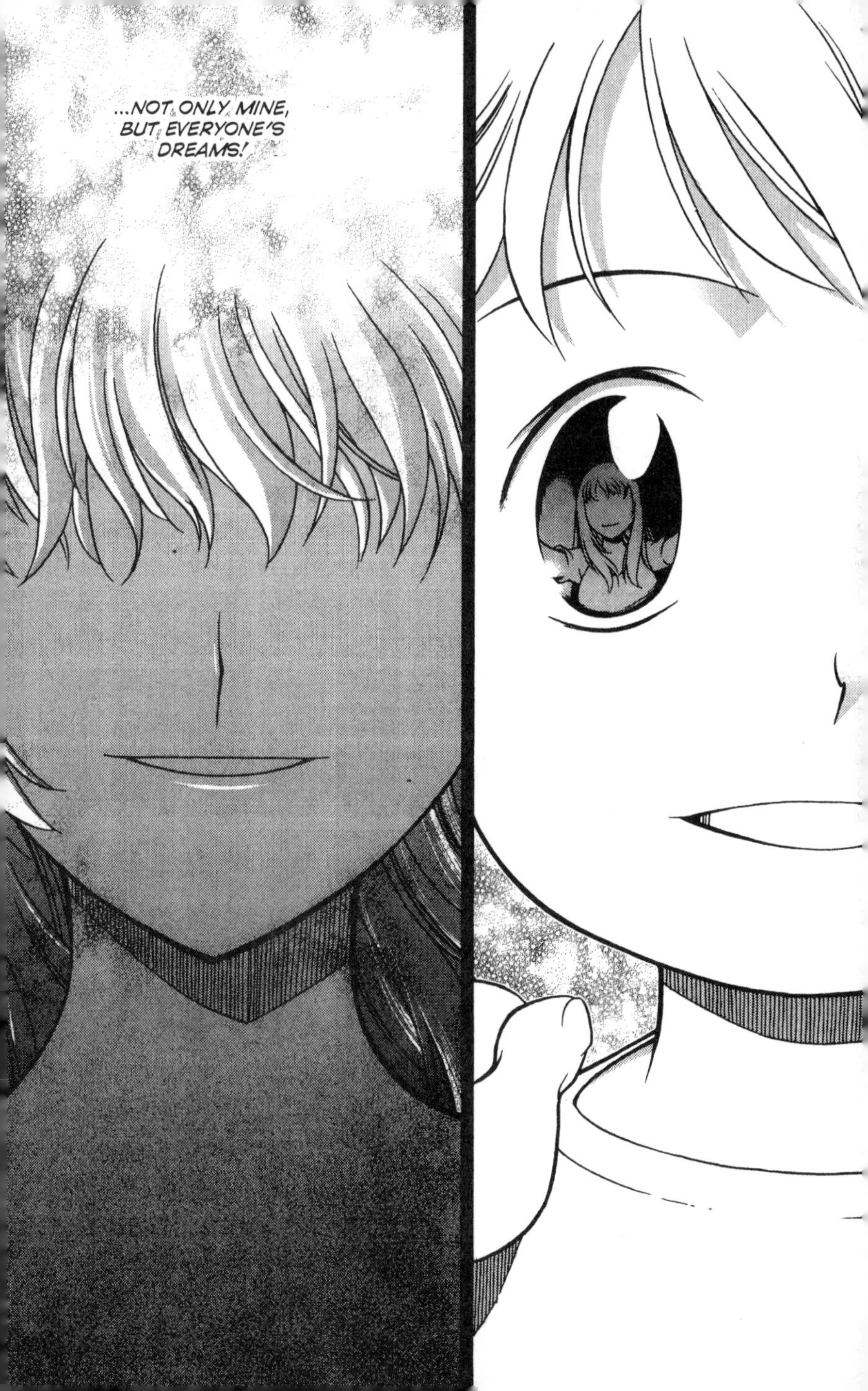
...NOT ONLY MINE, BUT EVERYONE'S DREAMS!

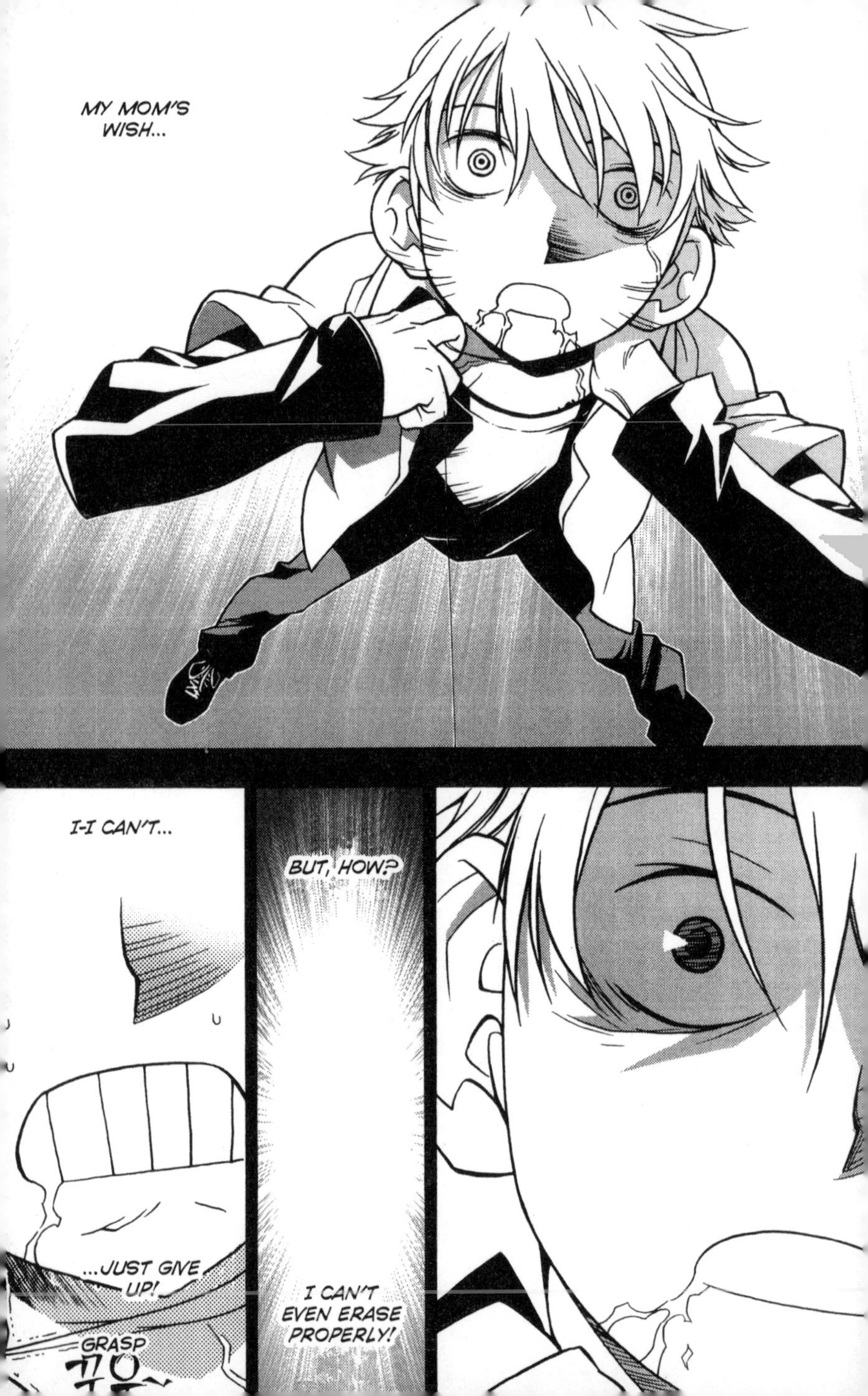
MY MOM'S WISH...
BUT, HOW?
I CAN'T EVEN ERASE PROPERLY!
I-I CAN'T...
...JUST GIVE UP!
GRASP

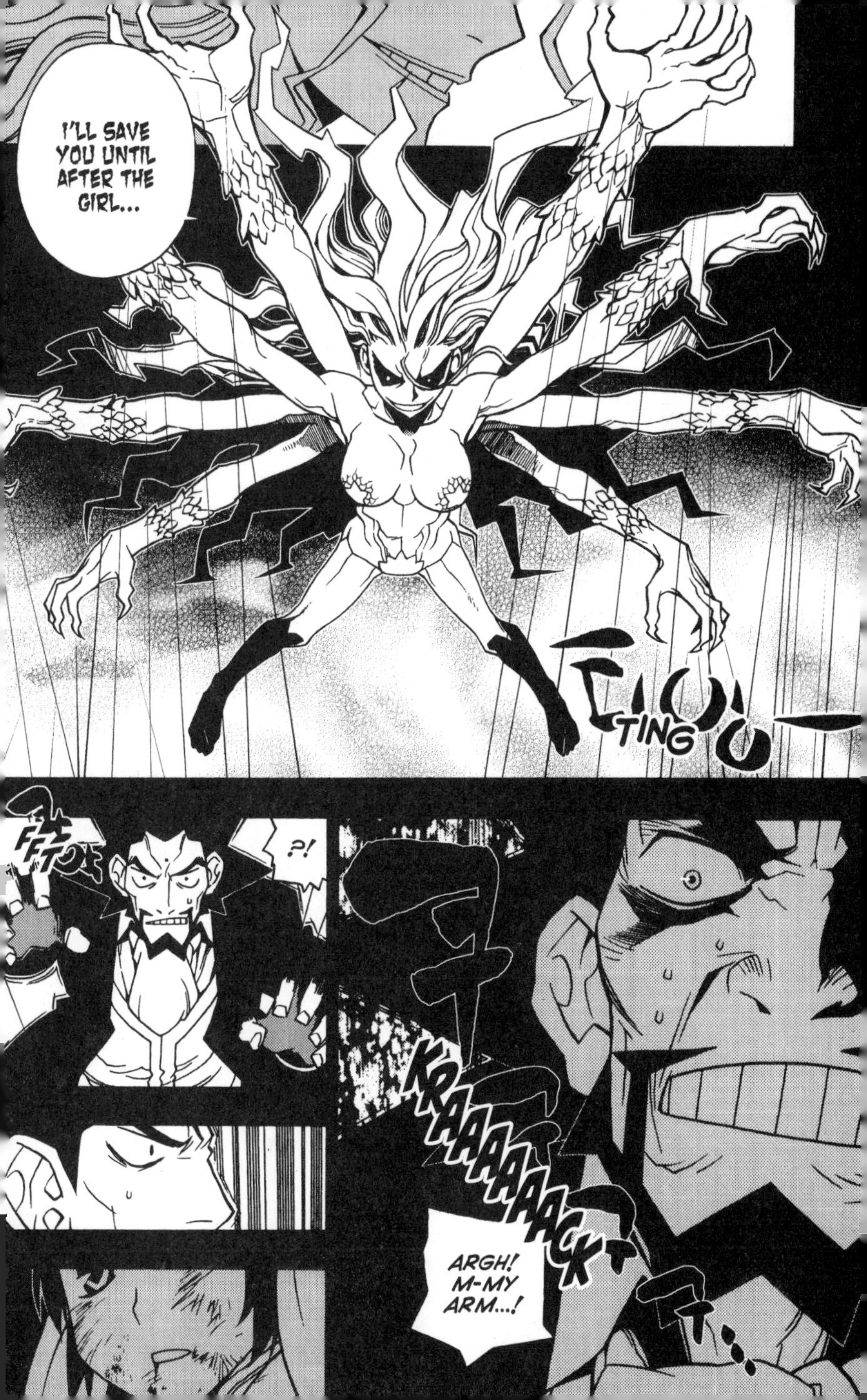
I'LL SAVE YOU UNTIL AFTER THE GIRL...
TING
KRAAAAAAACK
ARGH! M-MY ARM...!
FFT
?!

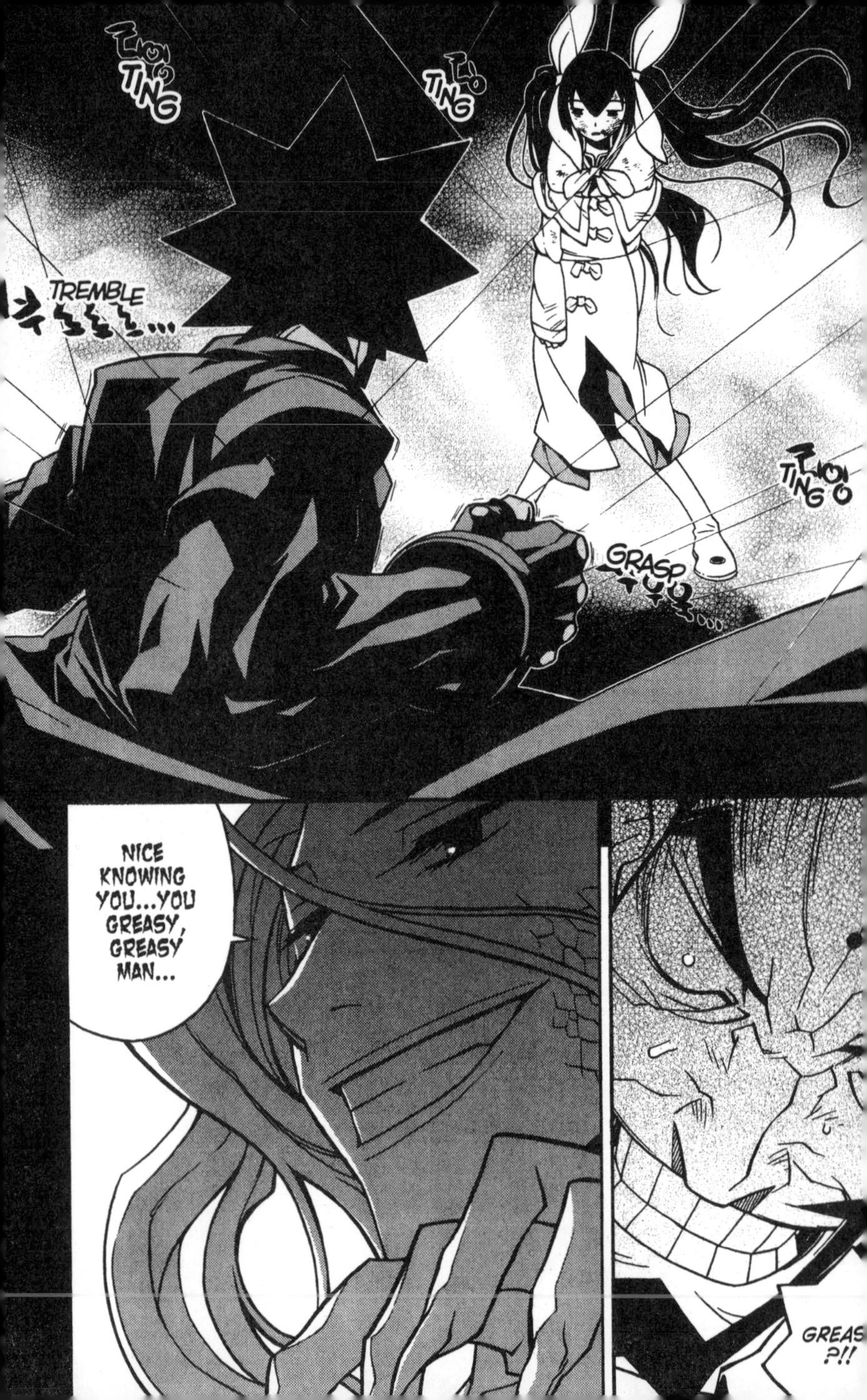
TING
TING
TREMBLE
TING
GRASP
NICE KNOWING YOU...YOU GREASY, GREASY MAN...
GREAS ?!!

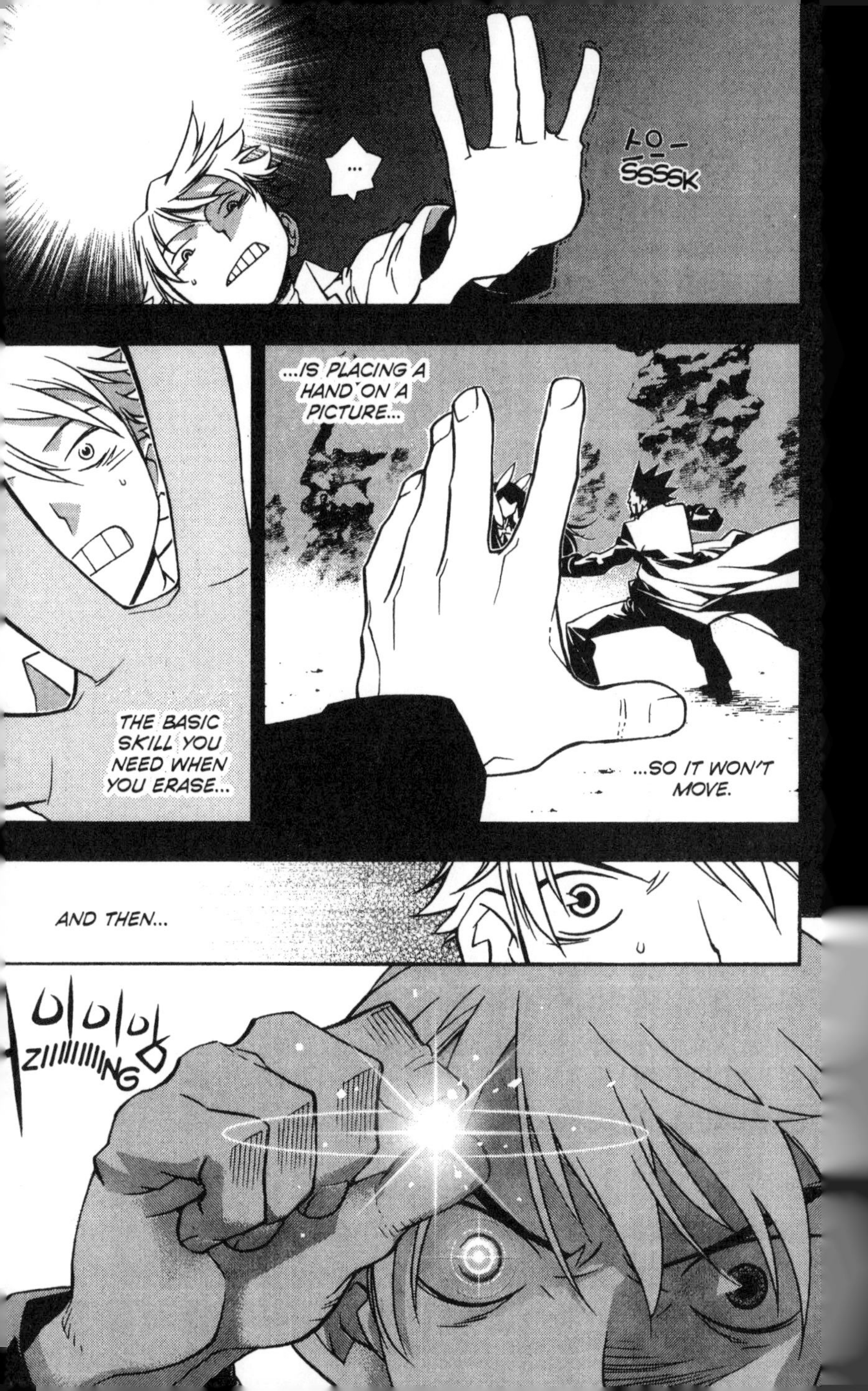
SSSSK
...
THE BASIC SKILL YOU NEED WHEN YOU ERASE...
...IS PLACING A HAND ON A PICTURE...
...SO IT WON'T MOVE.
AND THEN...
ZIIIIIIIING

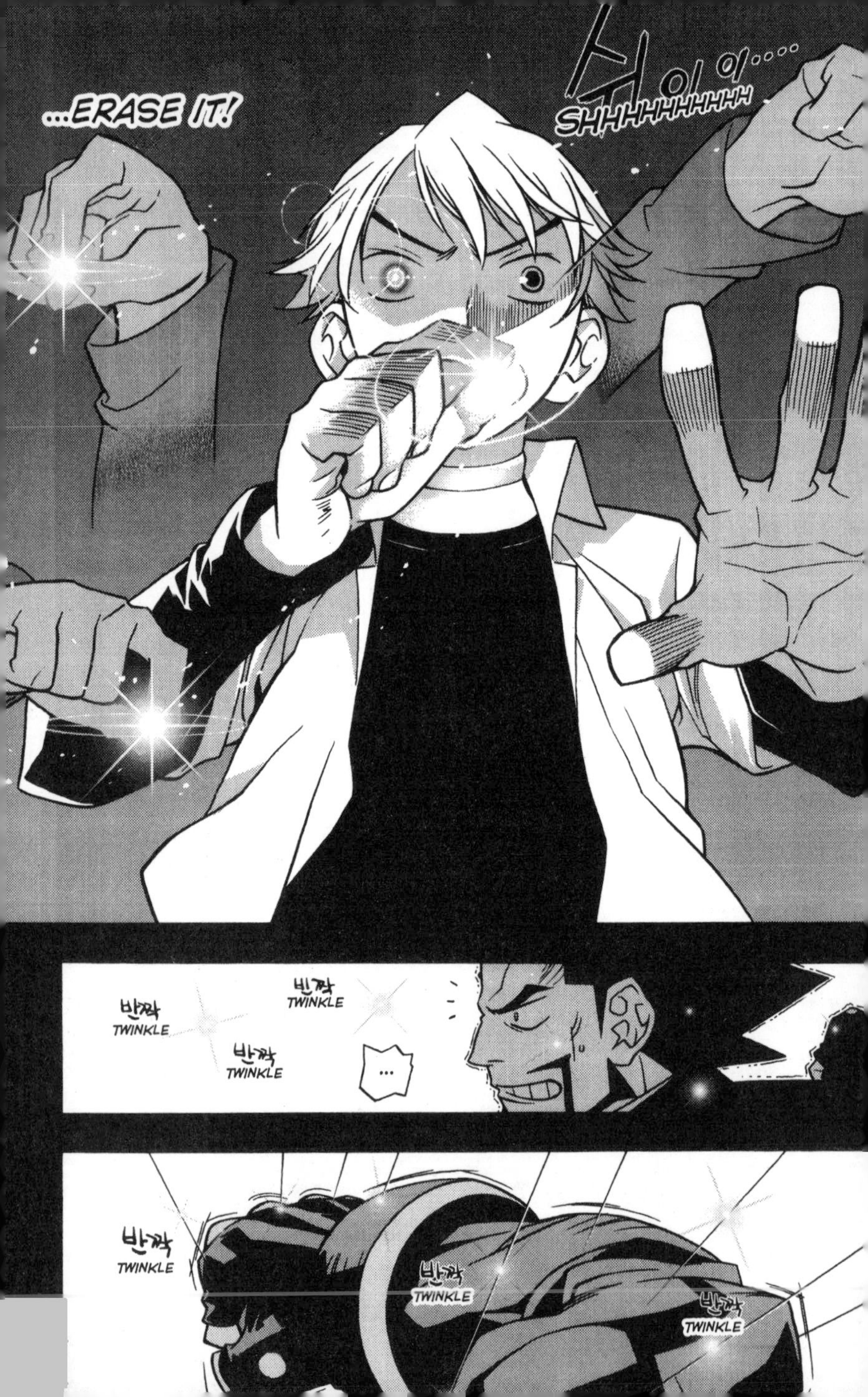
...ERASE IT!
SHHHHHHHHHH
반짝
TWINKLE
반짝
TWINKLE
반짝
TWINKLE
...
반짝
TWINKLE
반짝
TWINKLE
반짝
TWINKLE

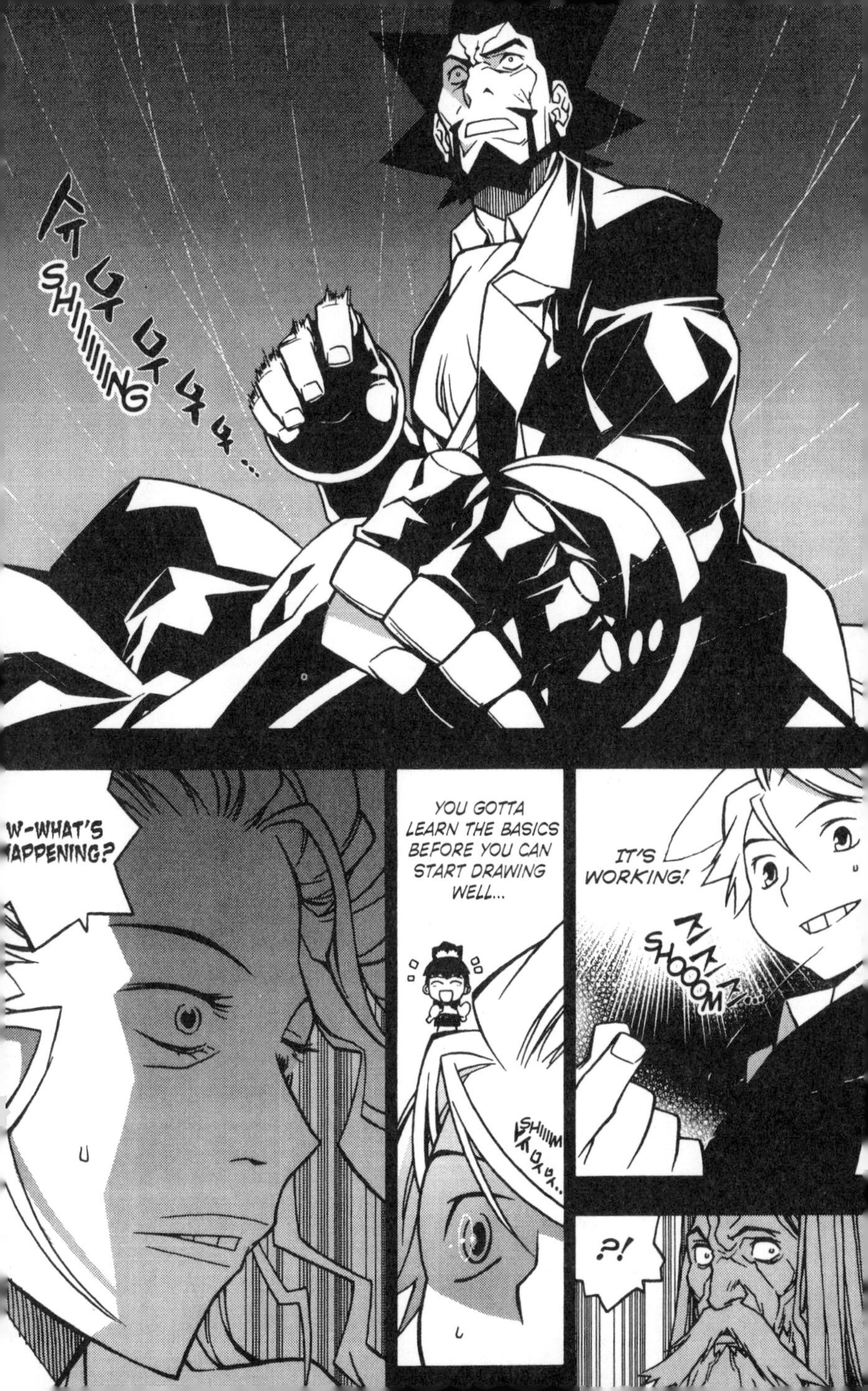
SHIIIIIIING
IT'S WORKING!
SHOOOM...
YOU GOTTA LEARN THE BASICS BEFORE YOU CAN START DRAWING WELL...
SHIIIIM
W-WHAT'S HAPPENING?
?!

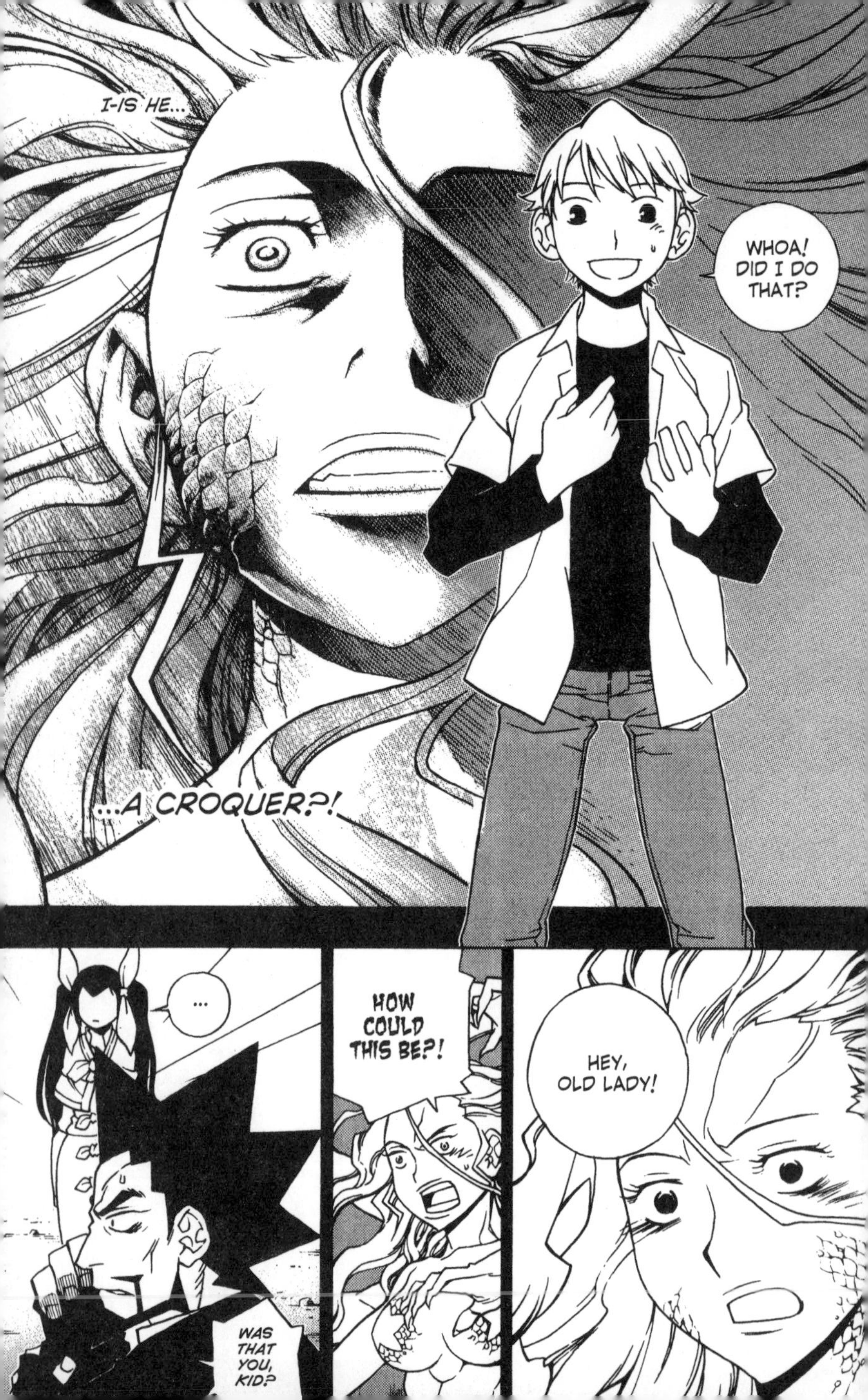
WHOA! DID I DO THAT?
I-IS HE...
...A CROQUER?!
HEY, OLD LADY!
HOW COULD THIS BE?!
...
WAS THAT YOU, KID?

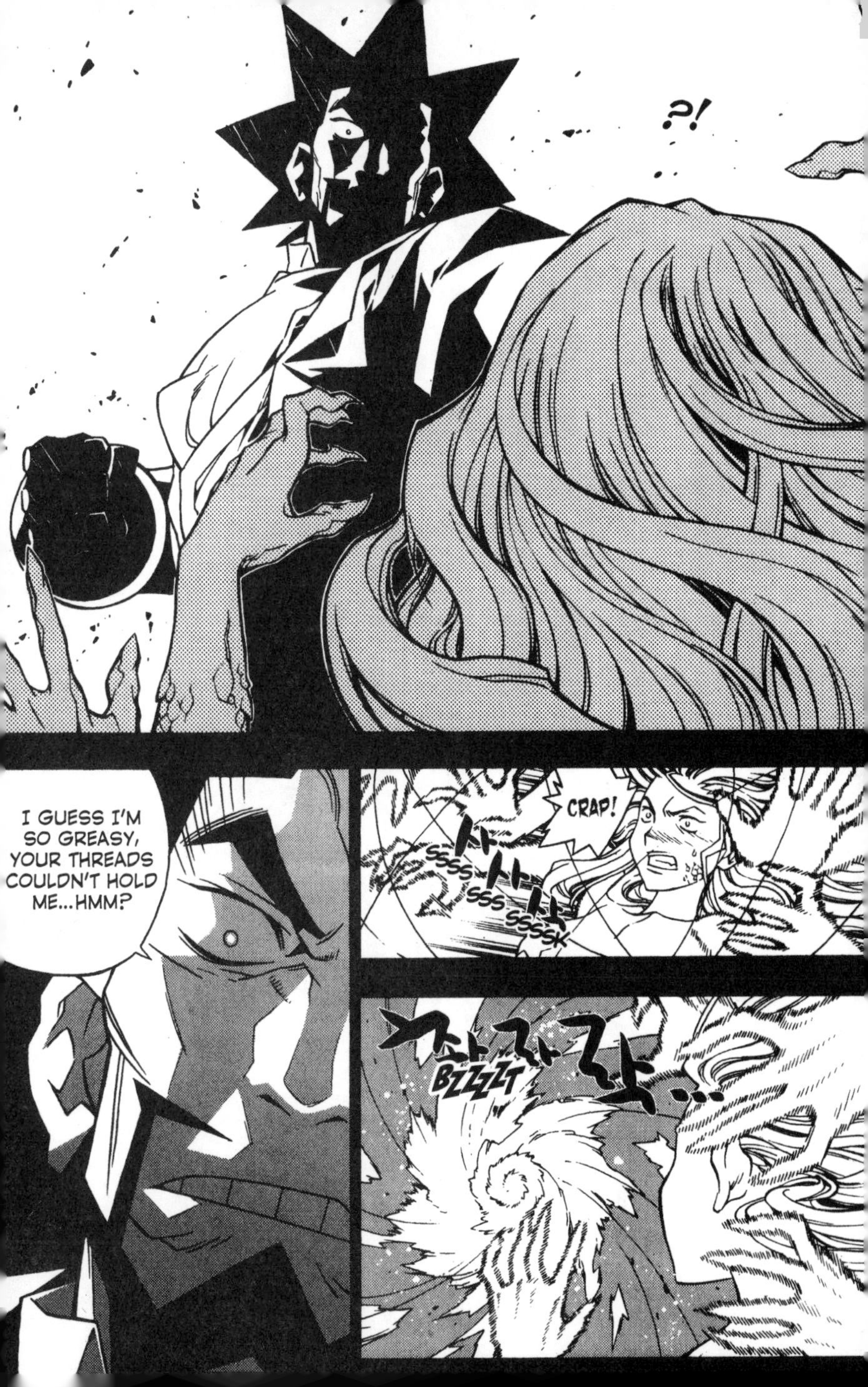
?!
I GUESS I'M SO GREASY, YOUR THREADS COULDN'T HOLD ME...HMM?
CRAP!
SSSSSSSSSSSSK
BZZZZT

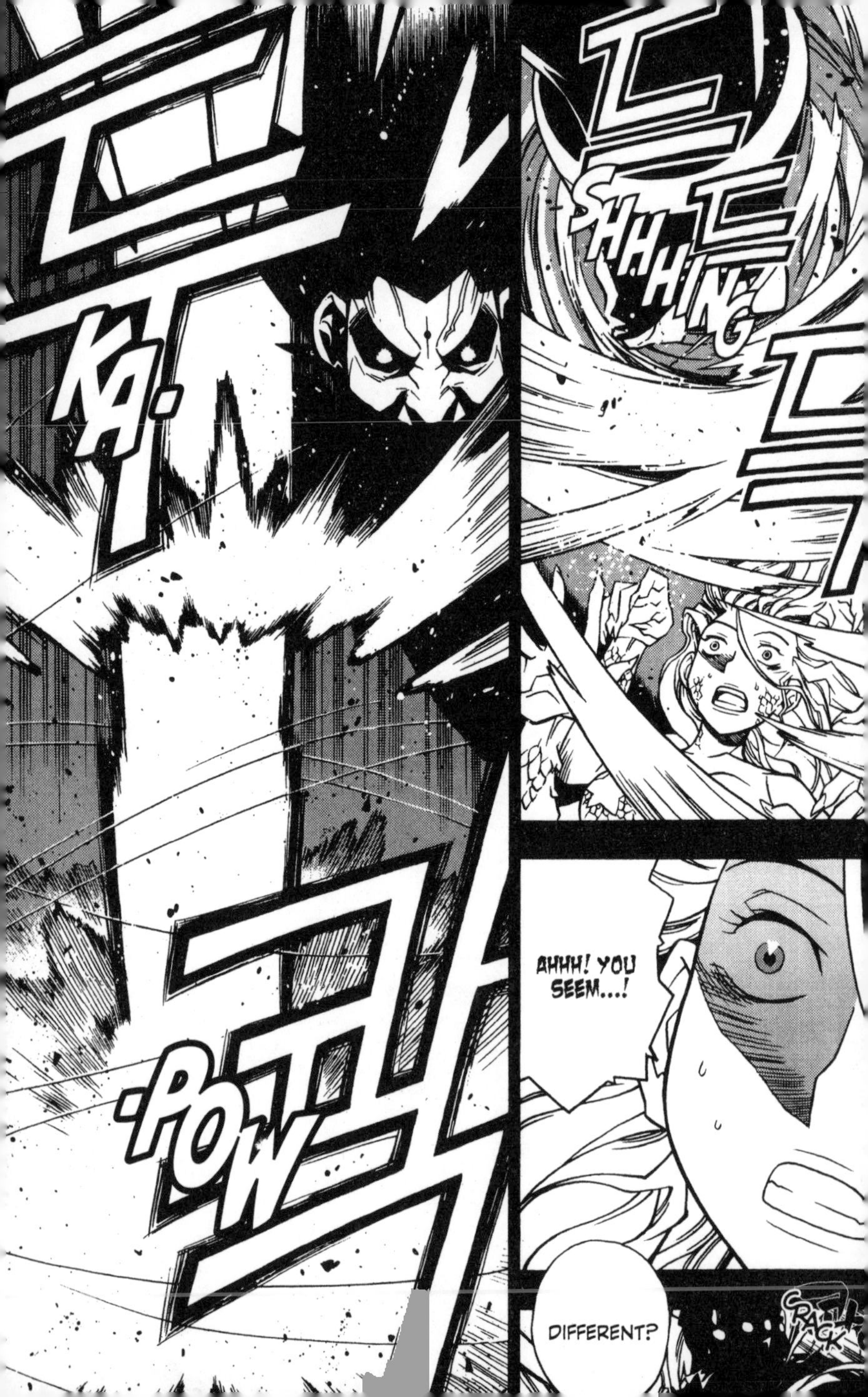
SHHHING!
KA-POW
AHHH! YOU SEEM...!
DIFFERENT?

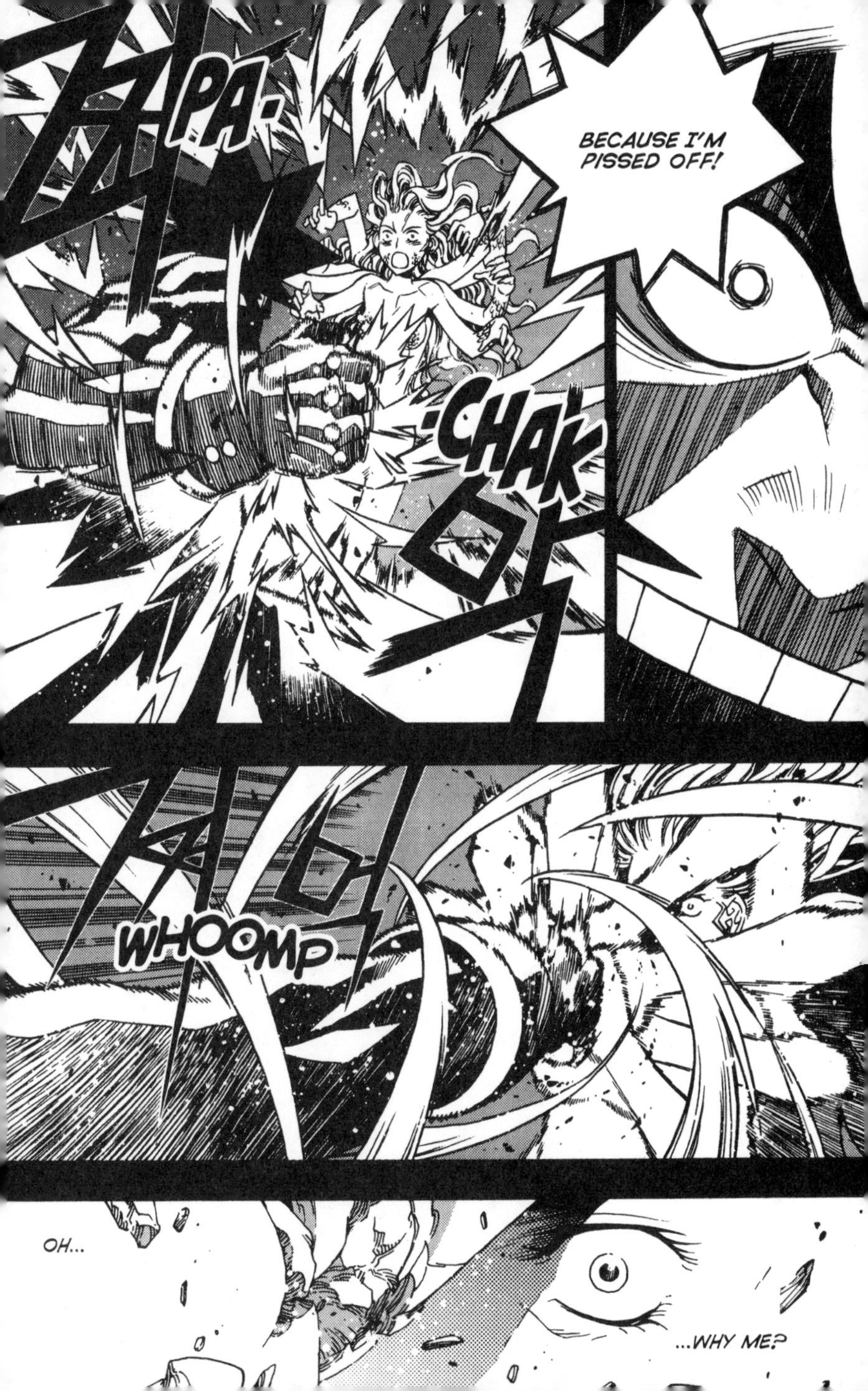
BECAUSE I'M PISSED OFF!
PA-
-CHAK
WHOOMP
...WHY ME?
OH...

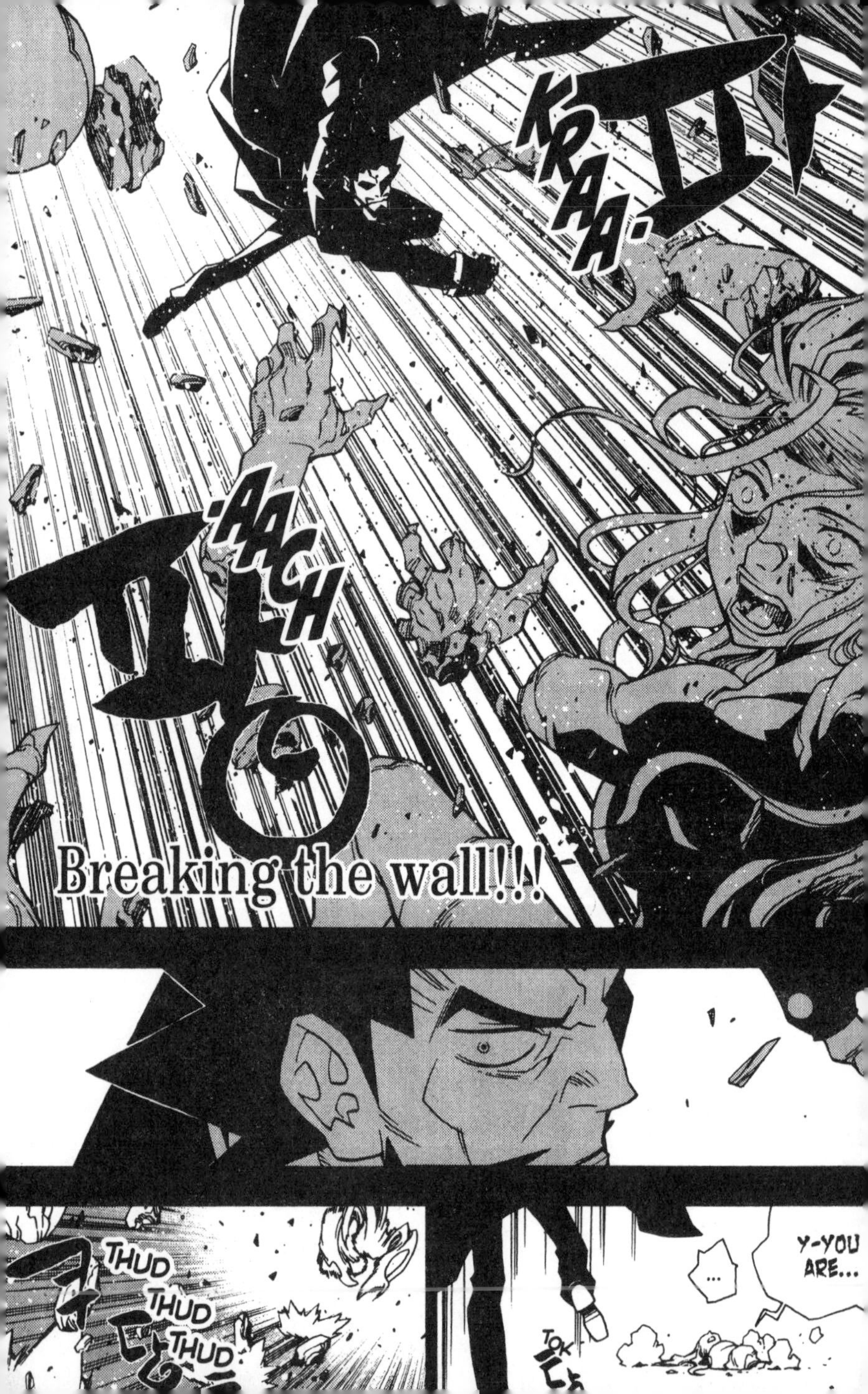
KRAAA-!
-AACH
Breaking the wall!!!
Y-YOU ARE...
...
TOK
THUD
THUD
THUD

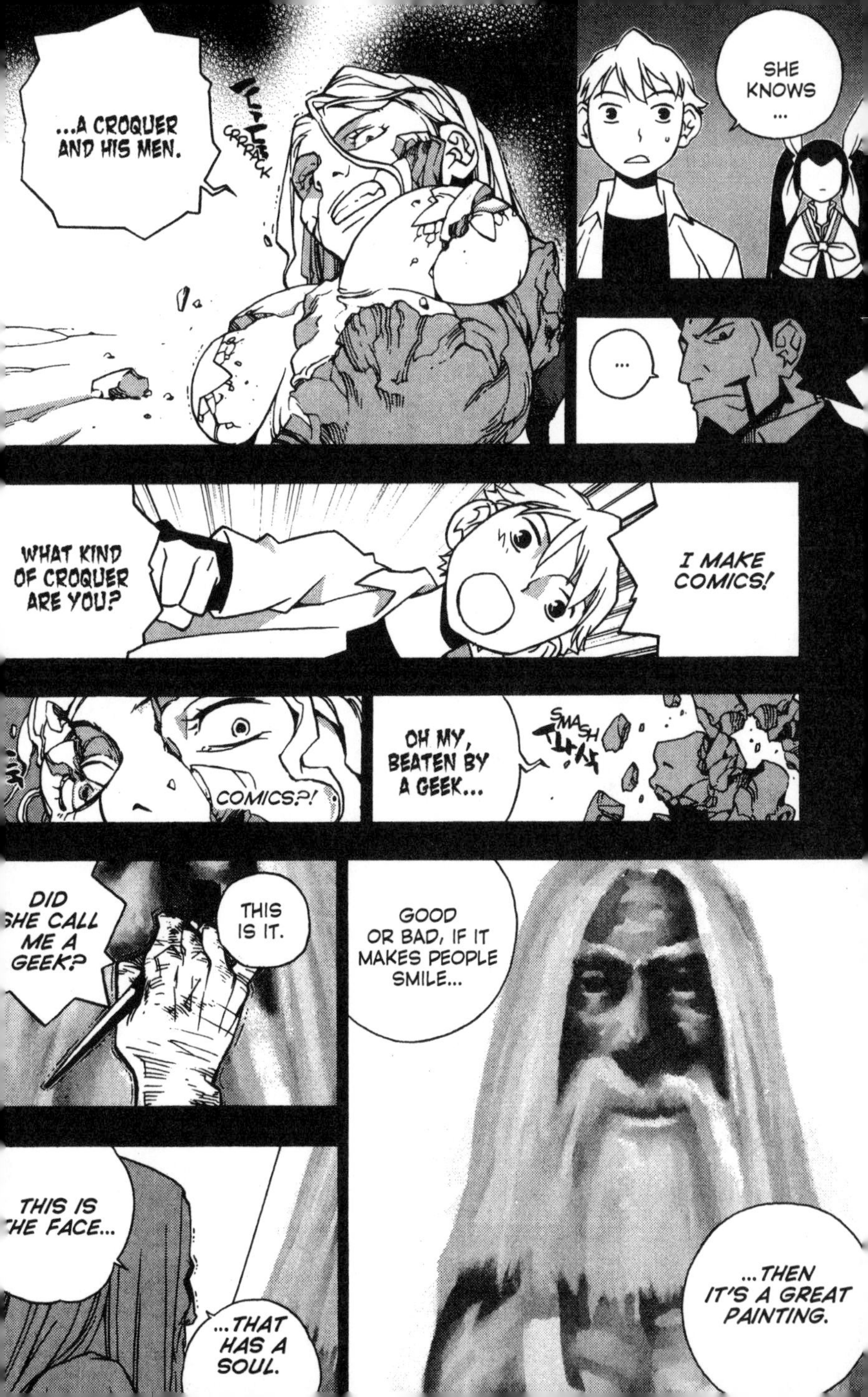
...A CROQUER AND HIS MEN.
CRRRACK
SHE KNOWS ...
...
WHAT KIND OF CROQUER ARE YOU?
I MAKE COMICS!
COMICS?!
OH MY, BEATEN BY A GEEK...
SMASH
DID SHE CALL ME A GEEK?
THIS IS IT.
GOOD OR BAD, IF IT MAKES PEOPLE SMILE...
THIS IS THE FACE...
...THAT HAS A SOUL.
...THEN IT'S A GREAT PAINTING.

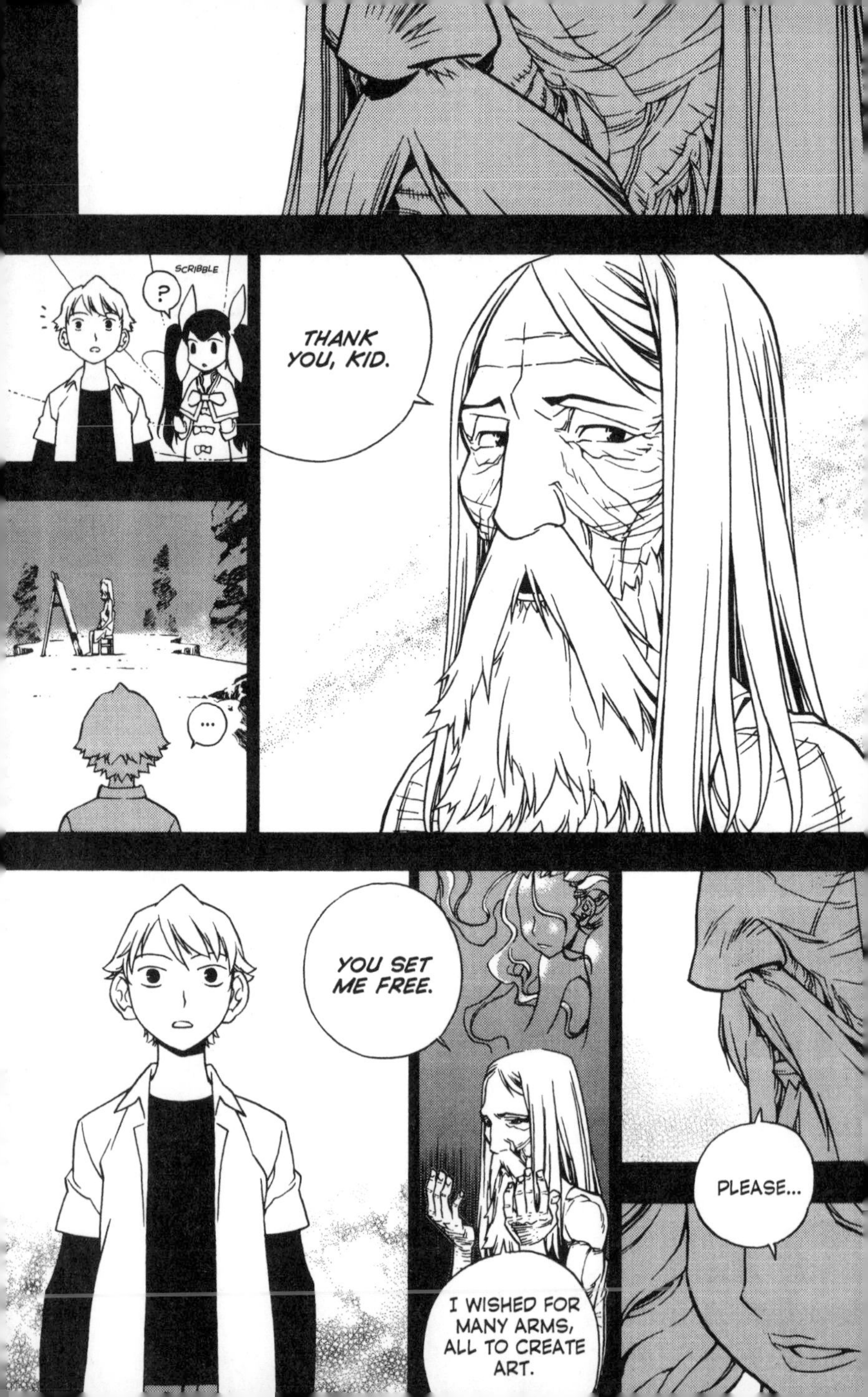
THANK YOU, KID.
SCRIBBLE
?
...
PLEASE...
YOU SET ME FREE.
I WISHED FOR MANY ARMS, ALL TO CREATE ART.

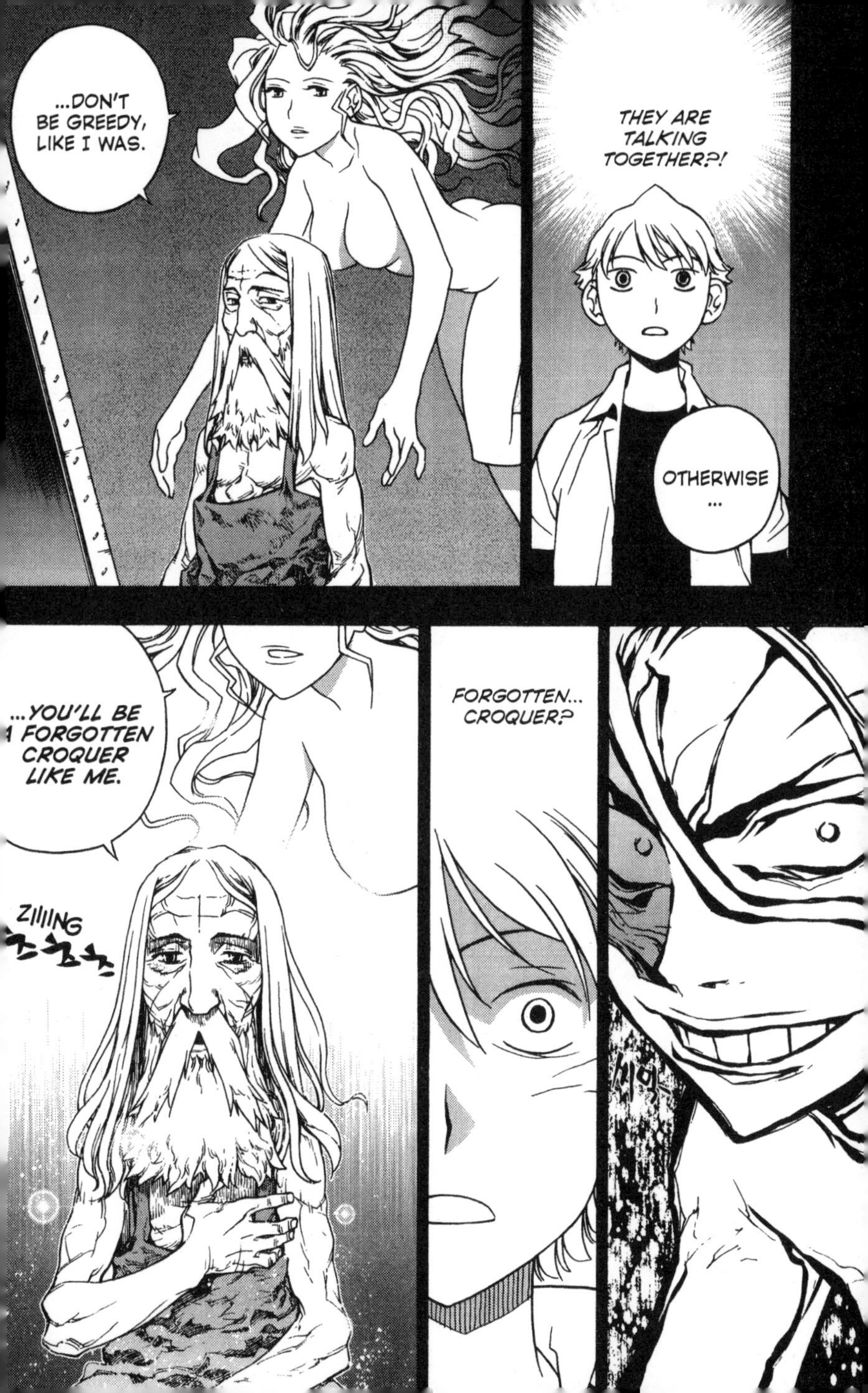
...DON'T BE GREEDY, LIKE I WAS.
THEY ARE TALKING TOGETHER?!
OTHERWISE ...
...YOU'LL BE A FORGOTTEN CROQUER LIKE ME.
ZIIIING
FORGOTTEN... CROQUER?

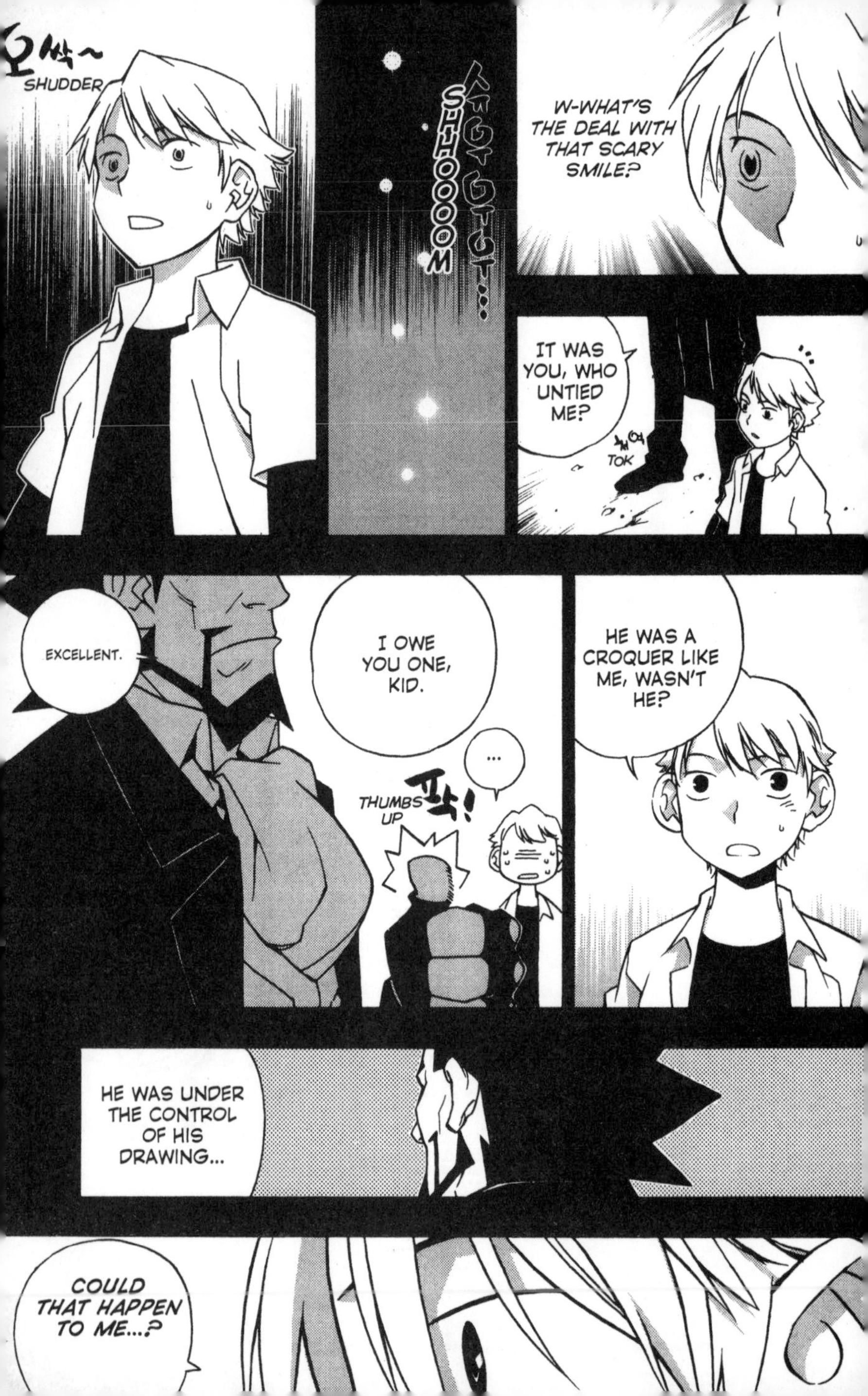
오싹~
SHUDDER
스으으으...
SHHOOOOOM
W-WHAT'S THE DEAL WITH THAT SCARY SMILE?
IT WAS YOU, WHO UNTIED ME?
TOK
...
EXCELLENT.
I OWE YOU ONE, KID.
THUMBS UP
...
HE WAS A CROQUER LIKE ME, WASN'T HE?
HE WAS UNDER THE CONTROL OF HIS DRAWING...
COULD THAT HAPPEN TO ME...?

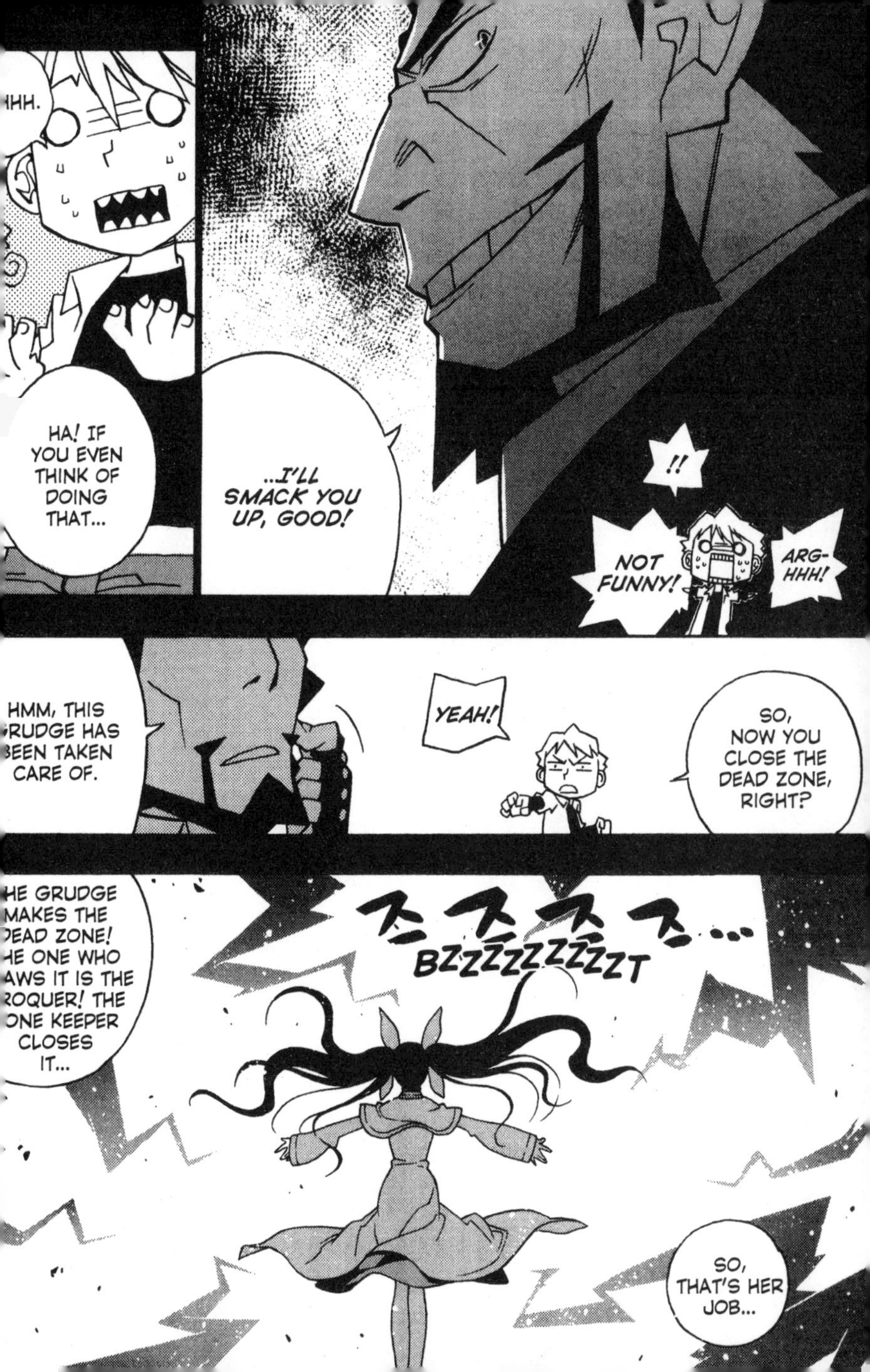
HHH.
HA! IF YOU EVEN THINK OF DOING THAT...
...I'LL SMACK YOU UP, GOOD!
!!
NOT FUNNY!
ARG-HHH!
HMM, THIS RUDGE HAS BEEN TAKEN CARE OF.
YEAH!
SO, NOW YOU CLOSE THE DEAD ZONE, RIGHT?
HE GRUDGE MAKES THE DEAD ZONE! HE ONE WHO AWS IT IS THE ROQUER! THE ONE KEEPER CLOSES IT...
BZZZZZZZZZT
SO, THAT'S HER JOB...

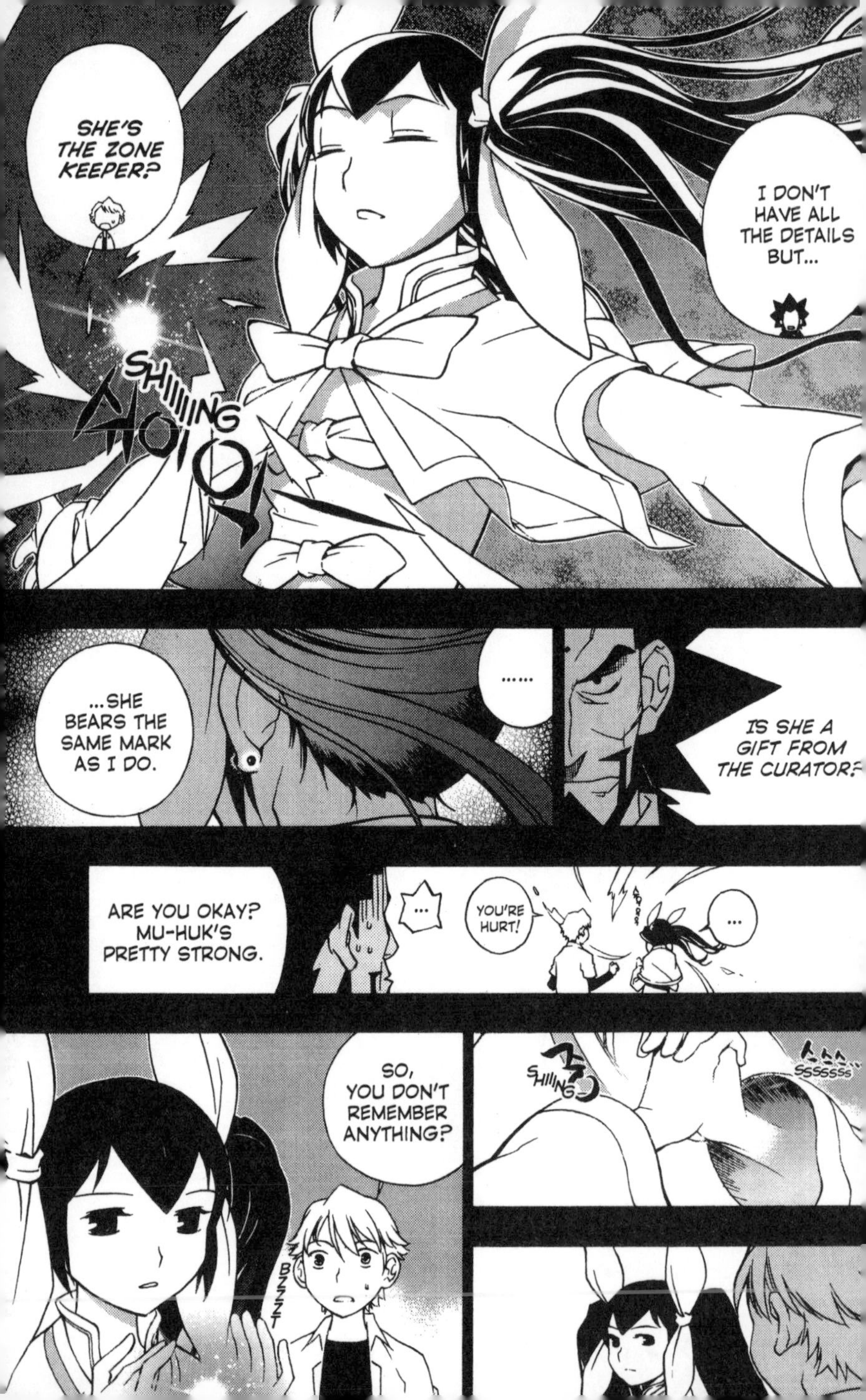
SHE'S THE ZONE KEEPER?
I DON'T HAVE ALL THE DETAILS BUT...
SHIIIING
...SHE BEARS THE SAME MARK AS I DO.
......
IS SHE A GIFT FROM THE CURATOR?
ARE YOU OKAY? MU-HUK'S PRETTY STRONG.
...
YOU'RE HURT!
...
SO, YOU DON'T REMEMBER ANYTHING?
BZZZT
SHIIING
SSSSSSS

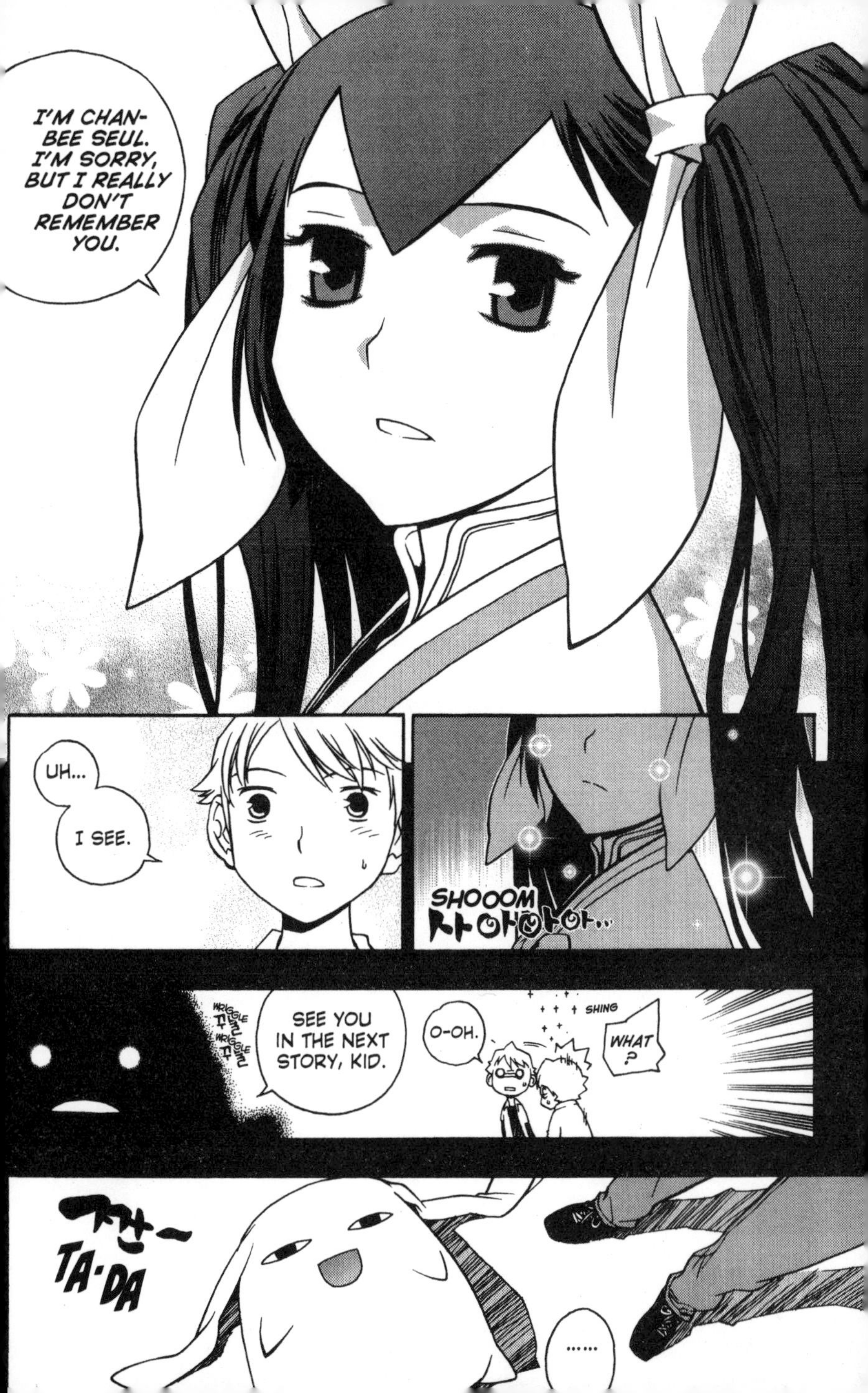
I'M CHAN-BEE SEUL. I'M SORRY, BUT I REALLY DON'T REMEMBER YOU.
UH...
I SEE.
SHOOOM
자아아아아..
WRIGGLE 꾸물
WRIGGLE 꾸물
SEE YOU IN THE NEXT STORY, KID.
O-OH.
SHING
WHAT?
짜잔~
TA-DA
......

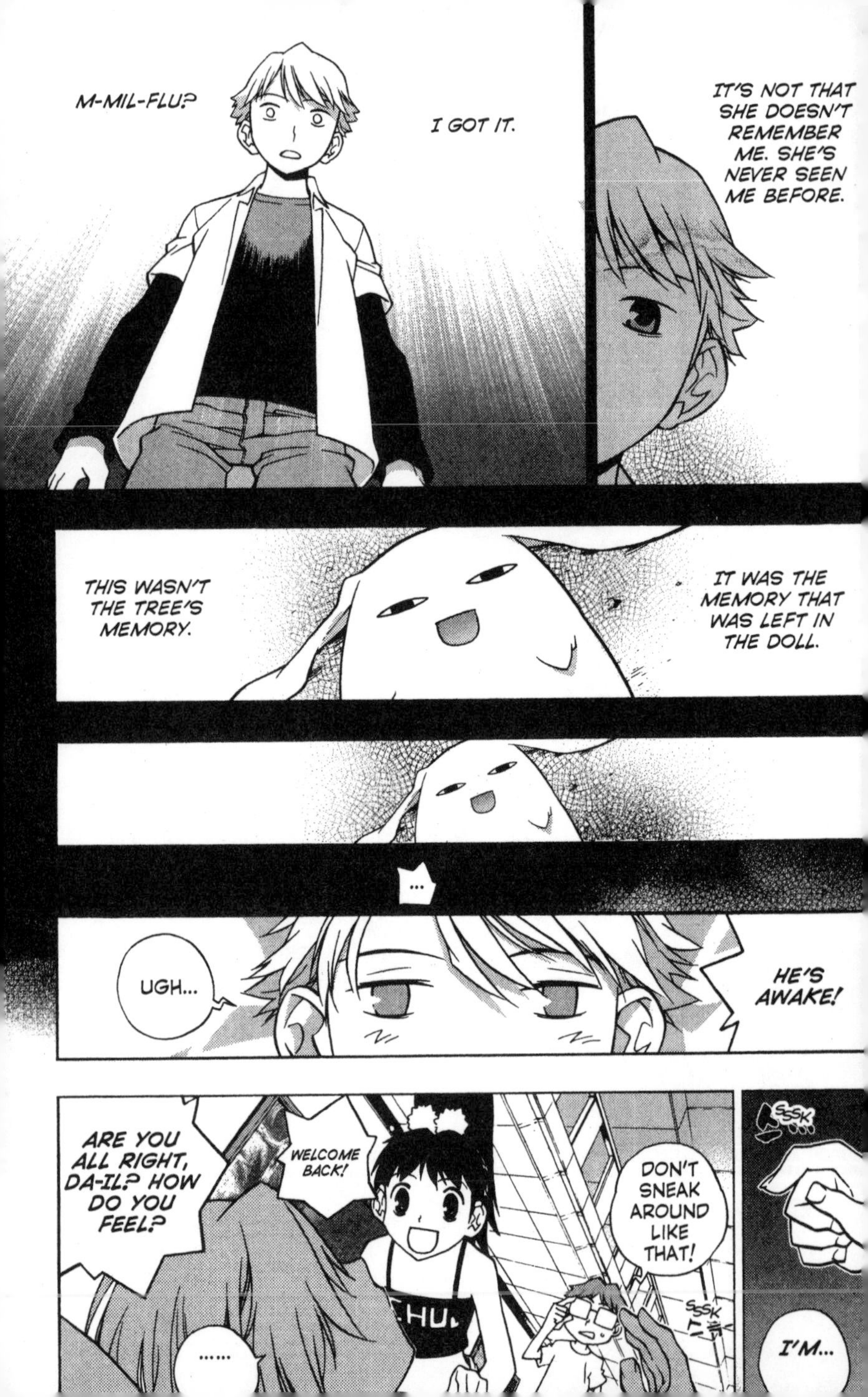

IT'S NOT THAT SHE DOESN'T REMEMBER ME. SHE'S NEVER SEEN ME BEFORE.
I GOT IT.
M-MIL-FLU?
THIS WASN'T THE TREE'S MEMORY.
IT WAS THE MEMORY THAT WAS LEFT IN THE DOLL.
...
HE'S AWAKE!
UGH...
SSSK
I'M...
DON'T SNEAK AROUND LIKE THAT!
SSSK
WELCOME BACK!
ARE YOU ALL RIGHT, DA-IL? HOW DO YOU FEEL?
......

...DA-IL.

YES, YOU'RE DA-IL HAN!

...

WE ALREADY KNOW YOUR NAME! GEEZ!

THE PAINTING...

...HAS BEEN CHANGED!

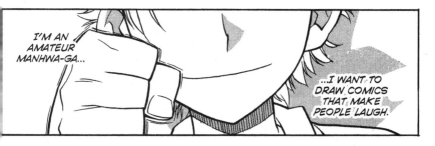

I'M AN AMATEUR MANHWA-GA...

...I WANT TO DRAW COMICS THAT MAKE PEOPLE LAUGH.

HE IS...

WHAT'S HIS PROBLEM?

HE WAS ONLY OUT FOR TEN SEC.

I DUNNO...

HA-HA-HA

...QUITE THE CROQUER.

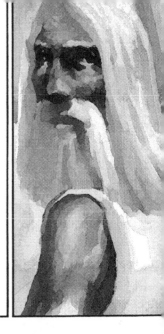

RRRING

......

SO, MIL-FLU AND I SAVED DA-IL.

......

LUCKY.

SO, SHE OWNS THE GALLERY?

MY PRECIOUS GIFT FOR HER-- RUINED!

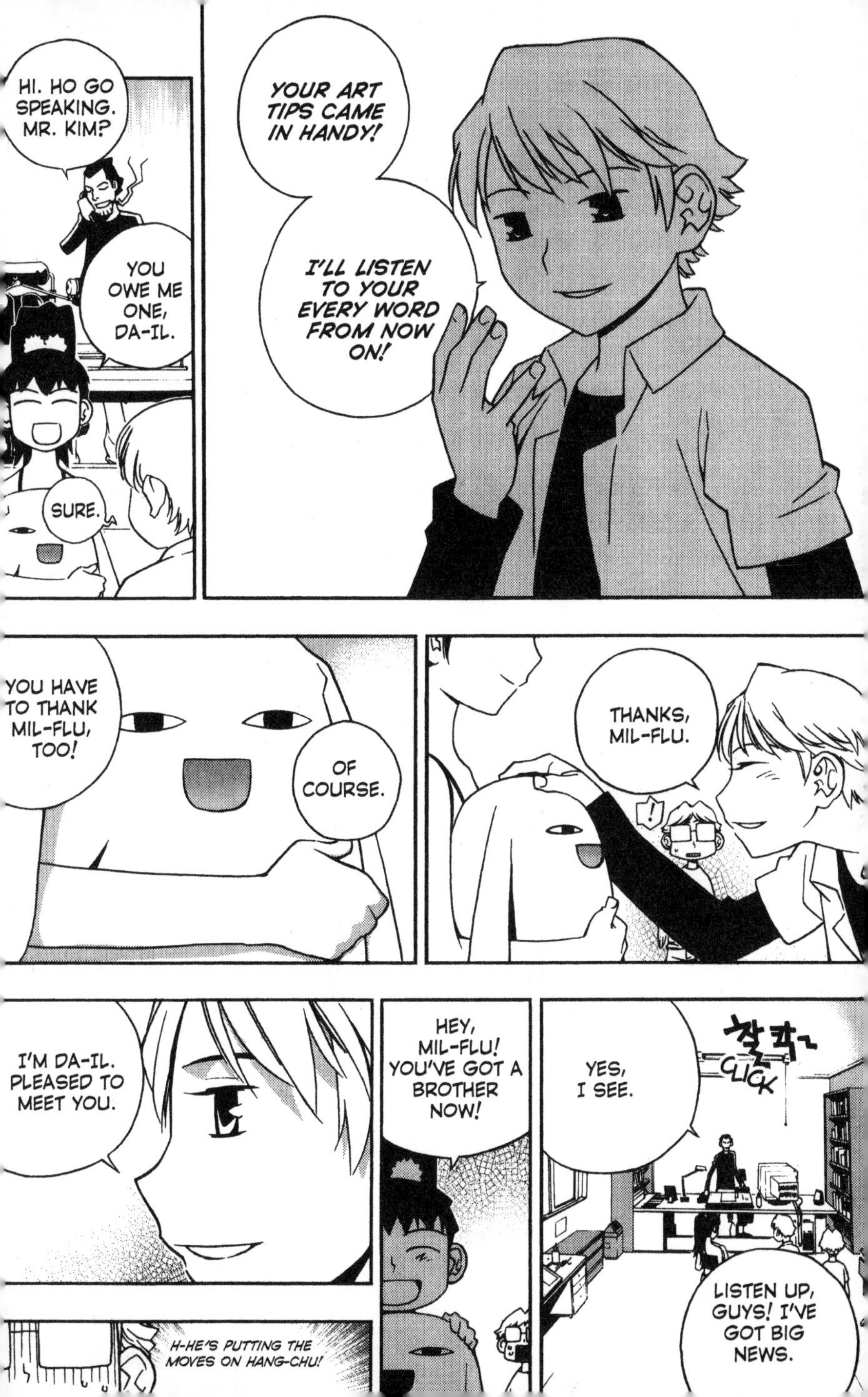
HI. HO GO SPEAKING. MR. KIM?
YOU OWE ME ONE, DA-IL.
SURE.
YOUR ART TIPS CAME IN HANDY!
I'LL LISTEN TO YOUR EVERY WORD FROM NOW ON!
YOU HAVE TO THANK MIL-FLU, TOO!
OF COURSE.
THANKS, MIL-FLU.
!
I'M DA-IL. PLEASED TO MEET YOU.
H-HE'S PUTTING THE MOVES ON HANG-CHU!
HEY, MIL-FLU! YOU'VE GOT A BROTHER NOW!
YES, I SEE.
CLICK
LISTEN UP, GUYS! I'VE GOT BIG NEWS.

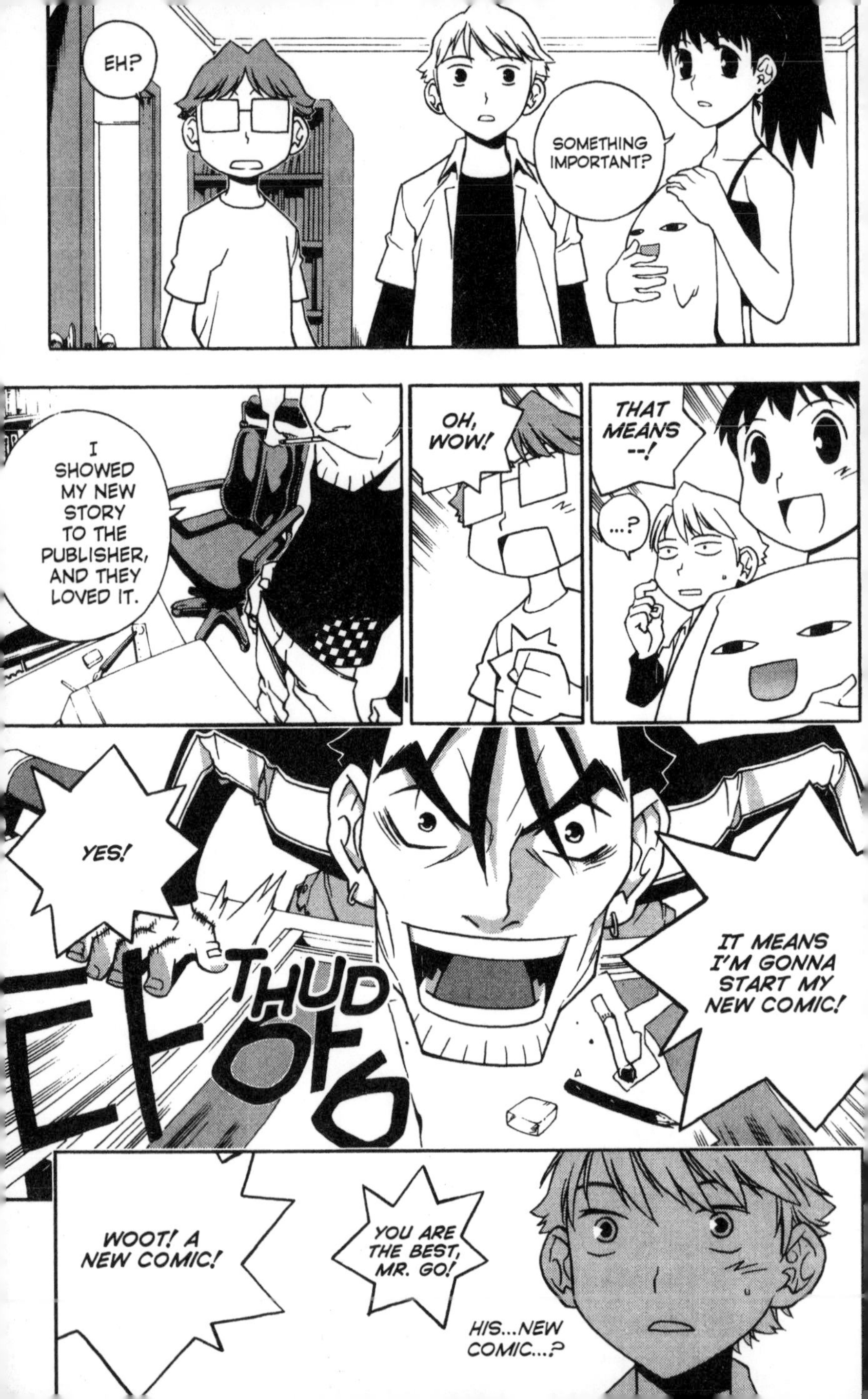
EH?
SOMETHING IMPORTANT?
I SHOWED MY NEW STORY TO THE PUBLISHER, AND THEY LOVED IT.
OH, WOW!
THAT MEANS --!
...?
YES!
THUD
IT MEANS I'M GONNA START MY NEW COMIC!
WOOT! A NEW COMIC!
YOU ARE THE BEST, MR. GO!
HIS...NEW COMIC...?

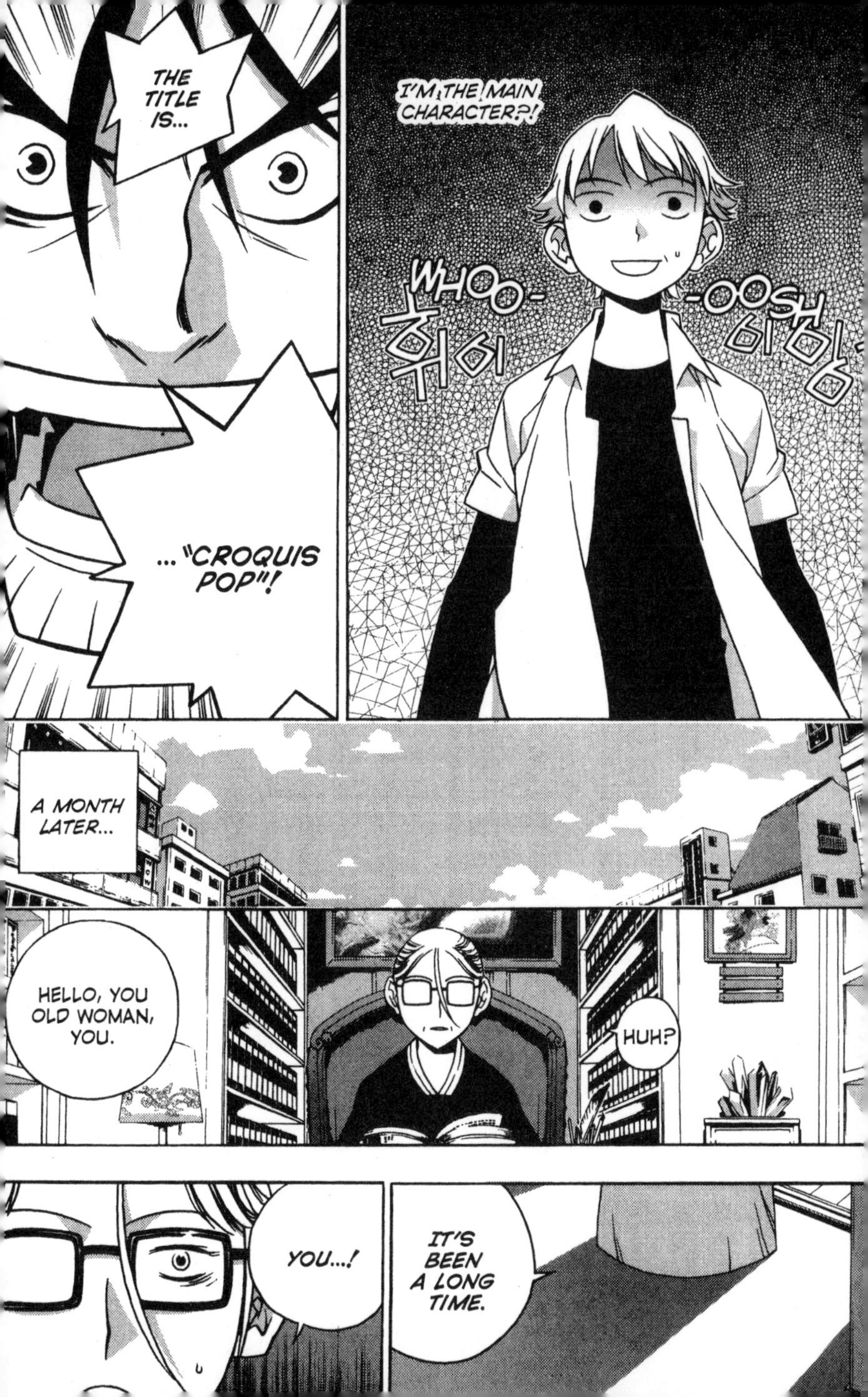
THE TITLE IS...
..."CROQUIS POP"!
I'M THE MAIN CHARACTER?!
WHOO-
-OOSH-
A MONTH LATER...
HELLO, YOU OLD WOMAN, YOU.
HUH?
YOU...!
IT'S BEEN A LONG TIME.

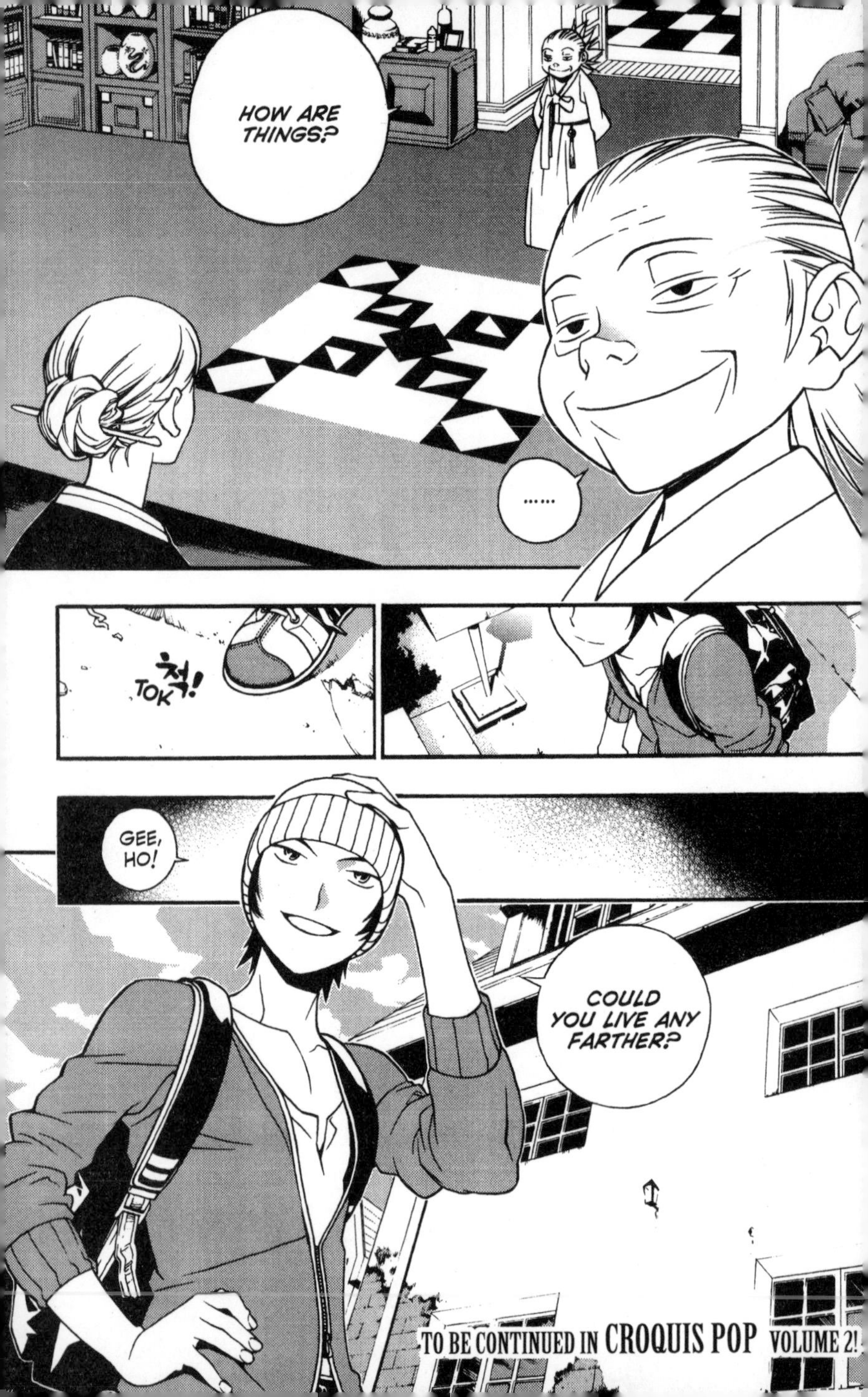
HOW ARE THINGS?
......
척
TOK!
GEE, HO!
COULD YOU LIVE ANY FARTHER?
TO BE CONTINUED IN CROQUIS POP VOLUME 2!

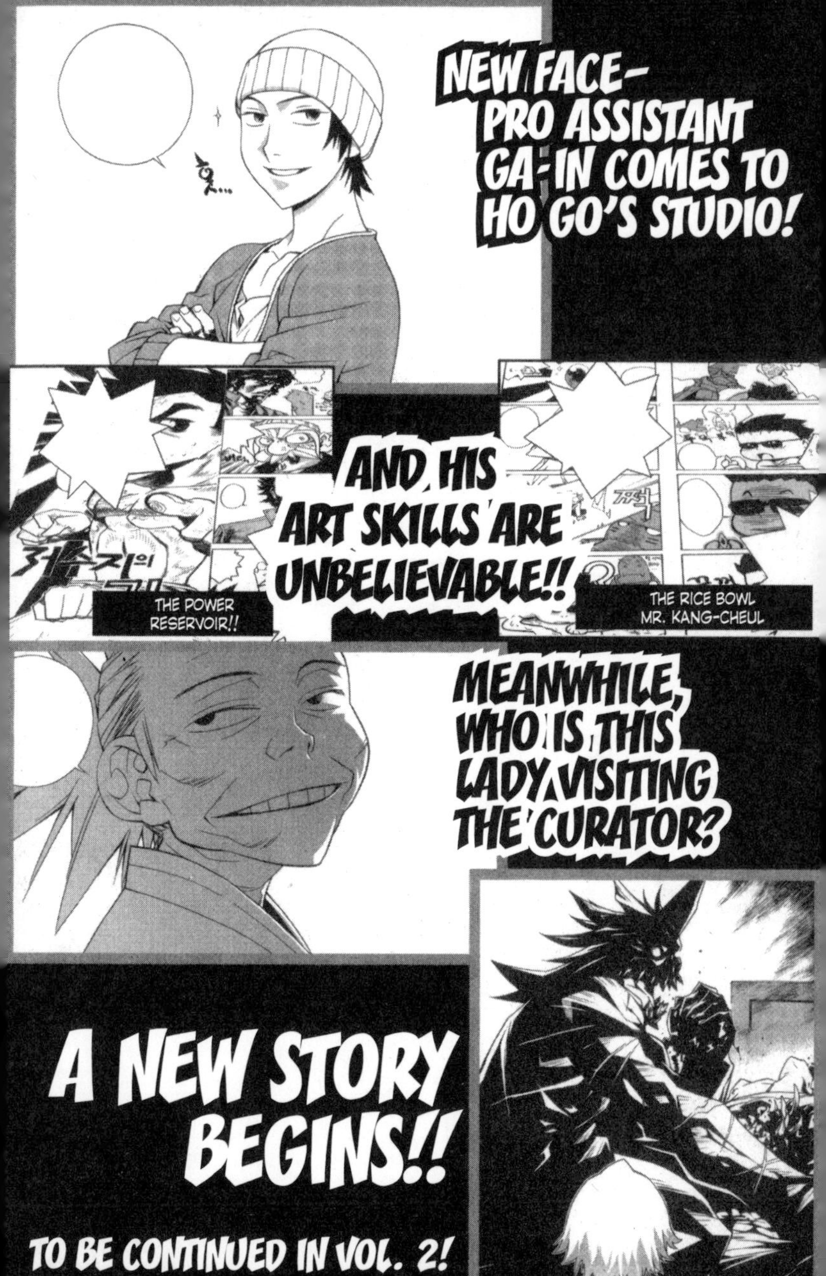
NEW FACE–
PRO ASSISTANT
GA-IN COMES TO
HO GO'S STUDIO!
AND HIS
ART SKILLS ARE
UNBELIEVABLE!!
THE POWER
RESERVOIR!!
THE RICE BOWL
MR. KANG-CHEUL
MEANWHILE,
WHO IS THIS
LADY VISITING
THE CURATOR?
A NEW STORY
BEGINS!!
TO BE CONTINUED IN VOL. 2!

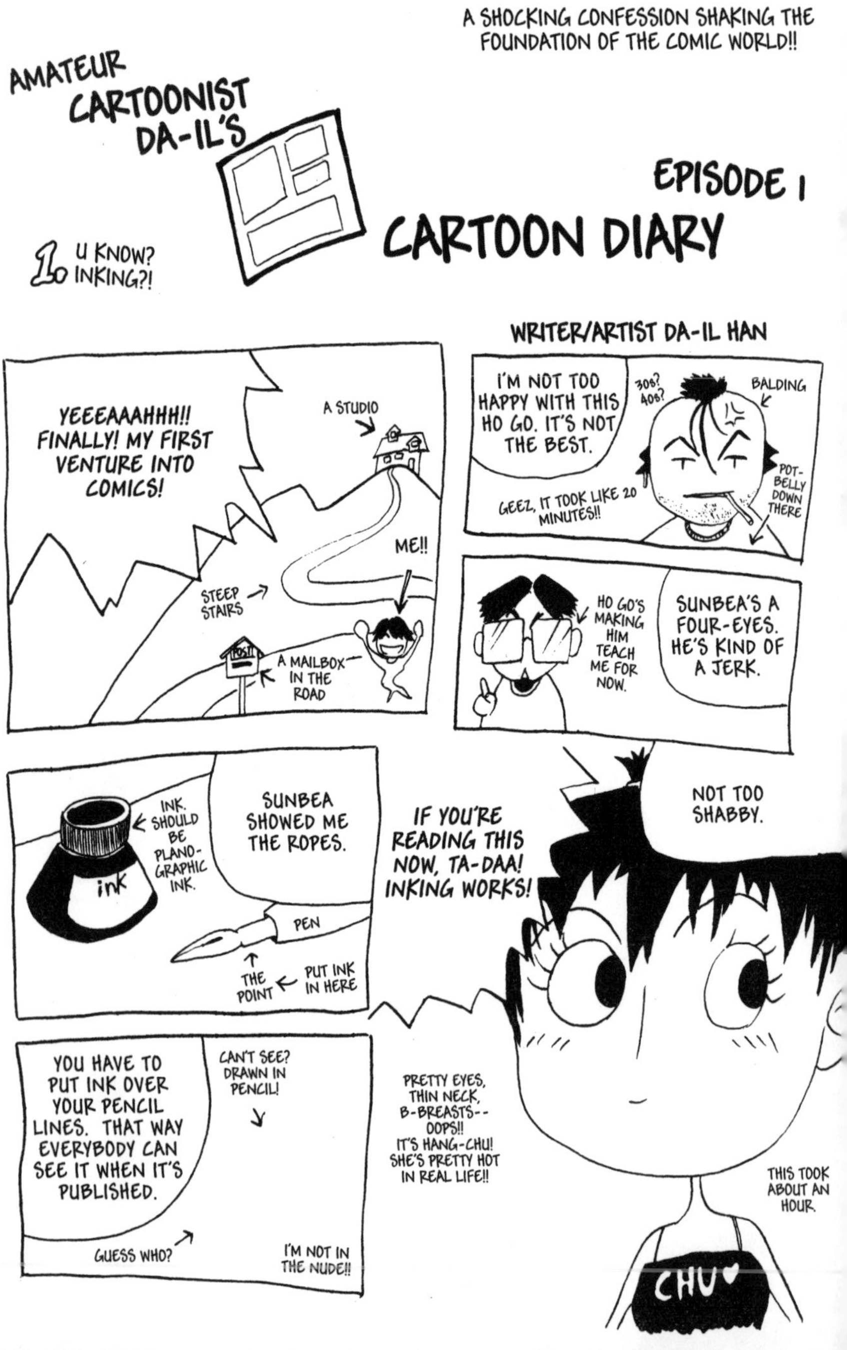
A SHOCKING CONFESSION SHAKING THE FOUNDATION OF THE COMIC WORLD!!
AMATEUR CARTOONIST DA-IL'S
EPISODE 1
CARTOON DIARY
1. U KNOW? INKING?!
WRITER/ARTIST DA-IL HAN
YEEEAAAHHH!! FINALLY! MY FIRST VENTURE INTO COMICS!
A STUDIO
ME!!
STEEP STAIRS
A MAILBOX IN THE ROAD
POST
I'M NOT TOO HAPPY WITH THIS HO GO. IT'S NOT THE BEST.
30s? 40s?
BALDING
POT-BELLY DOWN THERE
GEEZ, IT TOOK LIKE 20 MINUTES!!
HO GO'S MAKING HIM TEACH ME FOR NOW.
SUNBEA'S A FOUR-EYES. HE'S KIND OF A JERK.
SUNBEA SHOWED ME THE ROPES.
INK. SHOULD BE PLANO-GRAPHIC INK.
ink
PEN
THE POINT
PUT INK IN HERE
IF YOU'RE READING THIS NOW, TA-DAA! INKING WORKS!
NOT TOO SHABBY.
PRETTY EYES, THIN NECK, B-BREASTS--OOPS!! IT'S HANG-CHU! SHE'S PRETTY HOT IN REAL LIFE!!
THIS TOOK ABOUT AN HOUR.
CHU
YOU HAVE TO PUT INK OVER YOUR PENCIL LINES. THAT WAY EVERYBODY CAN SEE IT WHEN IT'S PUBLISHED.
CAN'T SEE? DRAWN IN PENCIL!
GUESS WHO?
I'M NOT IN THE NUDE!!

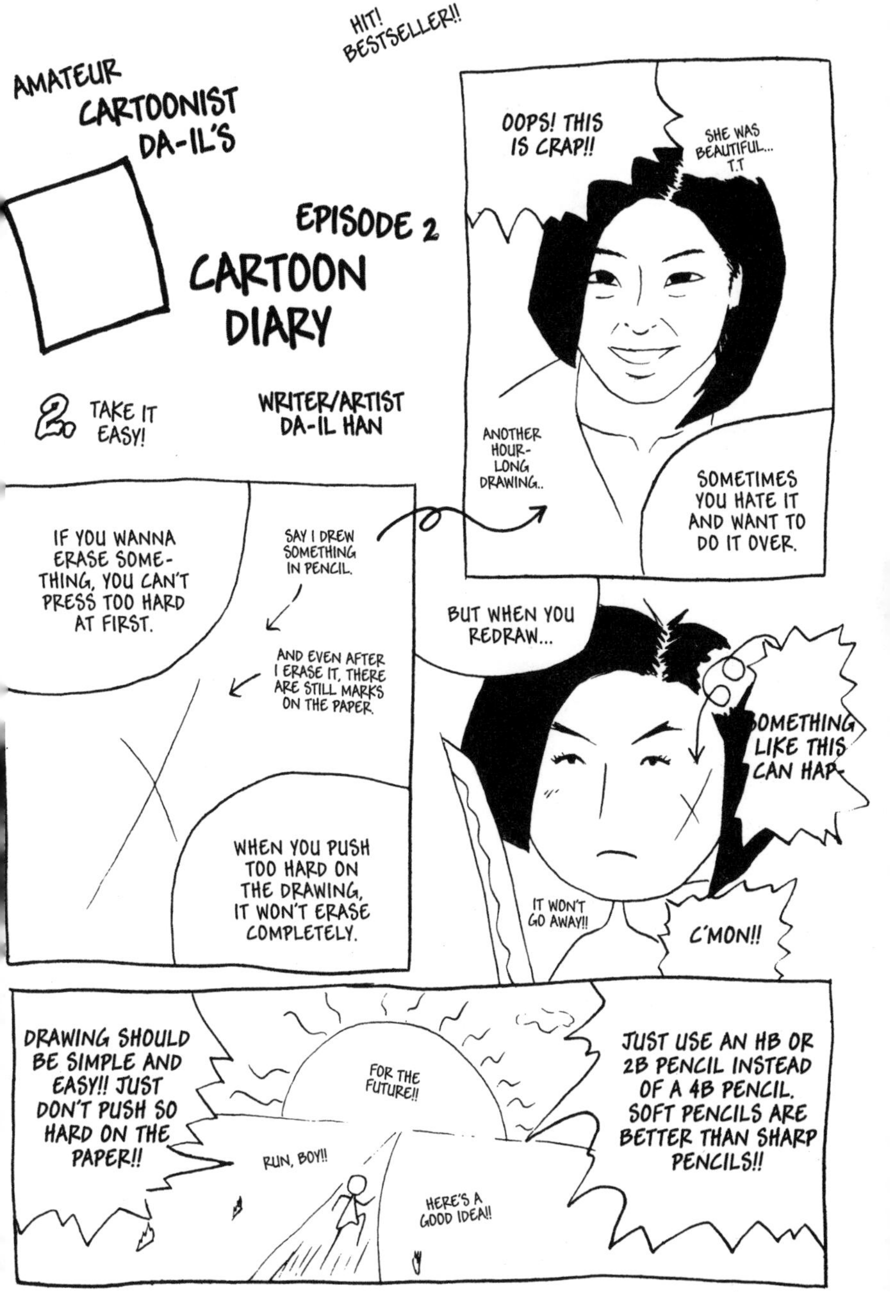

HIT! BESTSELLER!!
AMATEUR CARTOONIST DA-IL'S
EPISODE 2
CARTOON DIARY
2. TAKE IT EASY!
WRITER/ARTIST DA-IL HAN
OOPS! THIS IS CRAP!!
SHE WAS BEAUTIFUL... T.T
ANOTHER HOUR-LONG DRAWING..
SOMETIMES YOU HATE IT AND WANT TO DO IT OVER.
IF YOU WANNA ERASE SOME-THING, YOU CAN'T PRESS TOO HARD AT FIRST.
SAY I DREW SOMETHING IN PENCIL.
AND EVEN AFTER I ERASE IT, THERE ARE STILL MARKS ON THE PAPER.
WHEN YOU PUSH TOO HARD ON THE DRAWING, IT WON'T ERASE COMPLETELY.
BUT WHEN YOU REDRAW...
SOMETHING LIKE THIS CAN HAP-
IT WON'T GO AWAY!!
C'MON!!
DRAWING SHOULD BE SIMPLE AND EASY!! JUST DON'T PUSH SO HARD ON THE PAPER!!
FOR THE FUTURE!!
RUN, BOY!!
HERE'S A GOOD IDEA!!
JUST USE AN HB OR 2B PENCIL INSTEAD OF A 4B PENCIL. SOFT PENCILS ARE BETTER THAN SHARP PENCILS!!

CROQUIS POP ① {#croquis-pop}

KWANGHYUN SEO
JINHO KO

Translation: JiEun Park
English Adaptation: Arthur Dela Cruz

Lettering: Marshall Dillon and Terri Delgado

CROQUIS POP, Vol. 1 © 2005
Croquispop Vol. 1 © 2005 Ko Jin Ho & Seo Kwang Hyun. All rights reserved. First published in Korea in 2005 by Haksan Publishing Co.,Ltd. English translation rights in U.S.A. Canada, UK, and Republic of Ireland arranged with Haksan Publishing Co.,Ltd.

English edition © 2008 Hachette Book Group USA, Inc.

Yen Press
Hachette Book Group USA
237 Park Avenue, New York, NY 10017

Visit our Web sites at www.HachetteBookGroupUSA.com and www.YenPress.com.

Yen Press is an imprint of Hachette Book Group USA, Inc. The Yen Press name and logo are trademarks of Hachette Book Group USA, Inc.

First Yen Press Edition: June 2008

ISBN-10: 0-7595-2905-1
ISBN-13: 978-0-7595-2905-2

10 9 8 7 6 5 4 3 2 1

BVG

Printed in the United States of America